What Every Economics Student Needs to Know and Doesn't Get in the Usual Principles Text

D0886479

What Every Economics Student Needs to Know and Doesn't Get in the Usual Principles Text

John Komlos

UNIVERSITY OF MUNICH, PROFESSOR EMERITUS

Routledge
Taylor & Francis Group

LONDON AND NEW YORK

Many thanks to Michael Ghiselin for insightful comments on an earlier draft of the manuscript and to Scott Eddie, Alex Field, and Peter Salamon for comments on some of its parts. The manuscript was started while the author was a fellow of the National Humanities Center, Research Triangle Park, NC. Many thanks to the colleagues there who contributed substantially by providing innumerable ideas and moral support.

First published 2014 by M.E. Sharpe

Published 2015 by Routledge
2 Park Square, Milton Park, Abingdon, Oxon OX14 4RN
711 Third Avenue, New York, NY 10017, USA

Routledge is an imprint of the Taylor & Francis Group, an informa business

Library of Congress Cataloging-in-Publication Data

Komlos, John, 1944–
  What every economics student needs to know and doesn't get in the usual principles text / by John Komlos.
    pages cm
  Includes index.
  ISBN 978-0-7656-3923-3 (pbk. : alk. paper)
  1. Economics. I. Title.

HB171.K645 2014   2013028453
330—dc23

ISBN 13: 9780765639233 (pbk)

Printed and bound in the United States of America by Edwards Brothers Malloy on sustainably sourced paper.

CONTENTS

Part I. Economic Models vs. Reality

1. **Introduction** 3
    My Credo 4
    Humanistic Economics 6
    Welcome to Blackboard Economics 7
    Toward a Paradigm Shift in Economics 8
    Real-World Economics 9
    Simple Is for Simple Minded 10
    "It's Only a Model!" 11
    Questions for Discussion 13
    Notes 14

2. **Markets Are Neither Omniscient nor Omnipotent** 18
    Markets Are Not Created by Divine Power 18
    The Downside of Free Markets 18
    Government Is Essential 21
    Markets Have Limitations 23
    The "Achilles Heel" of Markets 24
    Morality Should Take Precedence over Markets 26
    Economics Is a Social Science 26
    Ideology 27
    Questions for Discussion 27
    Notes 28

Part II. Consumption On and Off the Blackboard

3. **The Nature of Demand** 33
    What Is Scarce? 33
    Consumer Sovereignty and Endogenous Tastes 33
    Wants and Basic Needs 35
    Budget Constraint 37
    Indifference Curves 37
    Chapter Summary 39
    Questions for Discussion 39
    Notes 39

4. **Is There a Rational Economic Decision Maker?** 41
    Utility Maximization 41
    Utility Maximization Is Impossible for Finite Minds 42
    Our Brain 42
    Neuroeconomics 44
    Bounded Rationality 44
    Satisficing 45
    Biases and Wonders of Intuition 47
    Heuristics 48
    Framing, Accessibility, Anchoring 48
    Prospect Theory 50
    Behavioral Economics 55
    Cognitive Dissonance 55
    Cognitive Endowment 56
    Genetic Endowment 56
    Chapter Summary 58
    Questions for Discussion 58
    Notes 59

5. **Taste Makers and Consumption** 63
    The Influence of Corporate Power 63
    Interdependence 66
    Society 68
    Culture 69
    Fairness 71
    Efficiency vs. Equity 71
    Self-Interest and Altruism 74
    Positive and Normative Economics 75
    Expected vs. Realized Utility 76
    Imperfect Information 76
    Signaling 79
    Time Inconsistency 80
    Patience and Impatience 81
    The Metaphor of the Invisible Hand 81
    The Magic of Competition 82
    Consumerism 83
    Chapter Summary 85
    Questions for Discussion 85
    Notes 86

Part III. Production On and Off the Blackboard

6. **Firms and Competition** 95
    Firms 95
    The Illusion of Perfect Competition 96
    Production Possibilities Frontier 99
    Prices 100

Equilibrium and Disequilibrium 102
Adverse Selection... 104
Technological Change... 104
Chapter Summary 106
Questions for Discussion 107
Notes 107

7. **Returns to the Factors of Production** 110
Factors of Production... 110
Natural Resources 112
Marginal Theory 113
Wages 114
The Cost of Capital 121
Profits 122
Income Distribution 122
Chapter Summary 129
Questions for Discussion 130
Notes 131

8. **The Case for Regulation of Markets** 134
Principal and Agent.. 134
Moral Hazard 135
Opportunistic Behavior.. 136
Regulation in the Public Interest.. 138
Regulatory Capture 139
Moral Constraints... 141
Property Rights 141
Market Failures 141
Exploitation.. 143
Transaction Costs 143
Time and Space 144
Path Dependence.. 145
Nonexistent Markets 148
Limits and Standards.. 148
Chapter Summary 148
Questions for Discussion 149
Notes 149

9. **Microeconomic Applications On and Off the Blackboard** 153
Minimum Wage... 153
Price Controls... 154
Unions 155
Discrimination.. 159
Redistribution... 160
Living Standards 162
Happiness and Growth 166
Poverty 168

Indebtedness and the Obesity Epidemic 169
Chapter Summary 170
Questions for Discussion 170
Notes 171

Part IV: Real-World Macroeconomics

10. **What Is Macroeconomics?** 177
Keynes the Savior 177
Neoclassical Synthesis 180
The Monetarist Counterrevolution... 181
A Macroeconomic Policy Void 182
Chapter Summary 183
Questions for Discussion 185
Notes 185

11. **Macroeconomic Aggregates and Variables** 187
Gross National Product.. 187
Unemployment and Underemployment... 188
The Natural Rate of Unemployment... 192
Economic Growth 193
Chapter Summary 194
Questions for Discussion 194
Notes 195

12. **Aspects of Macroeconomic Performance** 197
The Role of Government... 197
The Impracticality of Keynesian Fiscal Policy 198
Monetary Policy.. 198
Crowding Out... 201
Inflation 201
Nominal vs. Real Wages 201
Savings.. 202
Taxes 203
Cause and Effect: Fiscal Policy at the Beginning of the Obama Administration 207
Chapter Summary 208
Questions for Discussion 209
Notes 209

13. **Open Economy Macroeconomics** 211
International Trade 211
Tariffs and Welfare.. 212
Trade and Growth 214
Infant Industries 214
Unbalanced Trade 215
Import Certificates 215
New Trade Theory 217

Chapter Summary 218
Questions for Discussion 218
Notes 219

14. **Macroeconomic Externalities** 220
Environment.. 220
Sustainability.. 221
Green National Accounting... 222
Chapter Summary 222
Questions for Discussion 223
Notes 223

15. **The Financial Sector and the Great Recession** 225
Business Cycles 225
Expectations.. 227
Minsky's Model and the Meltdown of 2008 227
Deleveraging 230
The Bailout and the Great Recession...................................... 231
Chapter Summary 236
Questions for Discussion 236
Notes 237

Conclusion: Economics Beyond the Basics • 241

Index 247
About the Author... 258

PART I

ECONOMIC MODELS VS. REALITY

INTRODUCTION

We must give to the markets what belongs to the markets
—and retain for the people what belongs to the people.

The recent financial crisis has illustrated vividly how markets can and often do go haywire, yet textbooks remain unchanged, failing to convey the fundamental and systematic weaknesses of the free-market system.[1] They continue to sing its praises as if it had descended straight from Heaven while maintaining a conspiracy of silence about the fact that without government help countless giant corporations would have become a testimony to Schumpeter's creative destruction.[2] When the chips were down, only central banks could print the millions of millions of dollars, euros, pounds, or yen to prop up the markets and save the big banks, auto manufacturers, and an insurance company from immediate bankruptcy.

The doctrinaire approach to the teaching of economics is illustrated by the oft repeated but rather arrogant assertion "We know that markets work." Instead, teachers of economics should admit freely that while markets do work quite well in some circumstances they only do so within an appropriate institutional framework and they not only work inefficiently in others but often tip the stream of benefits toward a few insiders. Hence, our job is also to explore and delineate as clearly as humanly possible the circumstances that prevent real markets from working as well as their theoretical counterparts and suggest remedies for their failings. The ideological commitment to "market fundamentalism," which led to the excessive reliance on markets in the making of public policy, has brought us, in turn, to our current, precarious situation. I hope the present volume can help rectify this misconception and improve the teaching of economics by presenting a more complete perspective.

Surely no other event demonstrates the miscalculations of the fundamentalist approach to economics more vividly than Alan Greenspan's post-meltdown confession that he made a ghastly error in believing in—and aggressively preaching—market deregulation. When asked by Congressman Henry Waxman, "You have been a staunch advocate of letting markets regulate themselves . . . Were you wrong?" Greenspan responded, "I made a mistake in presuming that the self-interest of organizations, specifically banks . . . , were such that they were best capable of protecting their own shareholders and equity in the firms. . . . The problem here is [that] something which looked to be a very solid edifice and indeed a critical pillar to market competition and free markets did break down and . . . that . . . shocked me. I still do not fully understand why it happened." History is, of course, replete with people wearing similar ideological blinders.

Waxman continued, "You had an ideology . . . and this is your statement: 'I do have an ideology, my judgment is that free competitive markets are by far the unrivaled way to organize economies.'" Greenspan answered by offering the congressman a philosophical lesson: "Remember . . . what an ideology is . . . [it] is a conceptual framework with the way people deal with reality. Everyone has one. . . . Yes, I found a flaw . . . in the model that I perceived . . . how the world works. . . ." Waxman: "In other words, you found that your view of the world, your ideology was not right." Greenspan: "Precisely. That's precisely the reason I was shocked."[3]

Greenspan was, in fact, right for a change: ideology is unavoidable in economics because one approaches it with some values and an organizing system of thought, that is, some preconceived notions of how the world works.[4]

What is shocking, though, is that he was so shocked. After all, there had been plenty of Cassandras: Brooksley Born, Edward Gramlich, Paul Krugman, Raghuram Rajan, Nouriel Roubini, Peter Schiff, Robert Shiller, Joseph Stiglitz, Nassim Taleb, and John Taylor, to name but a few eminent proponents of opposing views. They were no strangers to Greenspan or to the establishment. They were not outsiders. They are mostly scholars who have held professorships at major universities or have distinguished themselves in other ways. All one had to do was to listen with care to their well-reasoned warnings with an open mind. Instead, Greenspan dismissed their ideas out of hand and cold-bloodedly thwarted Brooksley Born's valiant efforts to regulate derivatives a decade before the meltdown.[5]

As early as 2002, Dean Baker identified the housing bubble in the making and warned that "the collapse of the housing bubble will lead to a loss of between $1.3 trillion and $2.6 trillion of housing wealth."[6] Similarly, the cover story of the June 2005 issue of *The Economist* referred to the worldwide rise in housing prices as "the biggest bubble in history," and in March 2006, *Forbes* published an article in which the developments were termed "ominous."[7] One did not need a PhD to recognize that housing prices were off the charts.[8]

The notion that ideology plays a major role in the social sciences has a long history. Observers of human societies cannot possibly be free of their preconceived notions "because the understanding of a 'social' experience itself is always fashioned by ideas that are in the researchers themselves."[9] One of the many limitations of mainstream economists is their reluctance to address the problem of ideology adequately and to acknowledge the need to understand its role in economic policy. Textbooks simply ignore the issue. Yet, as Greenspan suggested in the exchange cited earlier, we cannot help but begin to organize our thoughts without making some fundamental assumptions, and these assumptions are necessarily a function of our own mindset, worldview, and intellectual and emotional commitments and therefore influence greatly the rest of the ideas developed in the discipline.

Hence, economics cannot be purged of ideology; our political, moral, and philosophical likes and dislikes—conscious and unconscious—are reflected in our assumptions and thus in how we structure our economic thinking and our understanding of the world around us. Much of that ideology is colored by our political philosophy. In other words, contrary to received wisdom, economics—in spite of the extensive use of mathematics—will not be a rigorous discipline until it is based essentially on verifiable empirical evidence. Our long-range goal should be to provide such an empirical foundation. Our more immediate goal is to present evidence to support the notion that the mainstream view is incomplete and therefore misleading. Our aim is to introduce the student to alternative perspectives on economics thereby providing a complement to standard presentations of the subject and widening the student's understanding.

MY CREDO

Given Greenspan's confession, perhaps I should start by discussing my own credo—the assumptions that underlie my own worldview of the economy. I consider it to be progressive, democratic, and humanitarian:[10] these values imply that I believe that we can do a lot better to improve our lives than we have done so far by focusing on increasing our life satisfaction instead of income growth.[11] I am also convinced that we should begin our economic analysis with empirical evidence rather than on ivory-tower theorizing.[12] Experiential evidence should be at the core of the discipline rather than assumptions. In the words of Deirdre N. McCloskey, an American economics professor and a prolific author, "economics is supposed to be an inquiry into the world, not pure thinking."[13]

In other words, I believe that economics should reduce its reliance on deductive logic and mathematics and become more of an inductive discipline.[14] Human beings are not inanimate objects whose trajectory can be described accurately by a function of a handful of variables. Unlike planets, they can and do change direction. Economics should not attempt to be an axiomatic discipline like Euclidean geometry, in which one can start with the assumption that the shortest distance between two points is a straight line. This is intuitively plausible, of course, but only until one starts to think beyond the Euclidean plane.

To understand the world around us we need an economic theory based on empirical evidence, one that can hold its own when transferred from the blackboard[15] to, say, even the slums of our big cities with a concentration of poverty. The pieces of the economic puzzle do not fit together as smoothly in Harlem's 10035 zip code area with a household median income of $17,700 as they do in Fairfax County, Virginia, with a household median income of $107,000—twice the national average.[16] Moreover, we need a theory of economics that is not isolated from other social sciences but incorporates insights derived from sociology, psychology, political science, and philosophy. Economists who focus on mathematics at the expense of these disciplines tend to neglect those economic problems that are not amenable to such techniques.[17]

In addition to being progressive, my economic principles are humanistic, in that they focus on values that enhance human experience. I prefer to focus on human beings and how they live and feel, rather than inanimate objects such as money or abstract concepts such as output or gross national product, which economists often substitute for the human dimension. I do not believe that the level of money income translates automatically into utility. Hence, it seems to me that consumption, money, efficiency, or gross domestic product (GDP) growth should not be the primary focus of economics. Rather, I believe that the aim of economics should be to improve the quality of life of the population. As constituted, the current economic system has so many problems and contradictions that it will probably never be able to improve. As E.F. Schumacher put it, "The most striking thing about modern industry is that it requires so much and accomplishes so little. Modern industry seems to be inefficient to a degree that surpasses one's ordinary powers of imagination."[18] By "accomplishing so little," he meant that the economy provides so little life satisfaction in spite of high incomes. In other words, we should not set ourselves the goal of producing as much as possible but to improve our sensibilities so that we can obtain the most gratification out of modest production: "the aim should be to obtain the maximum of well-being with the minimum of consumption." Schumacher also insisted that work itself would yield much more satisfaction if the scale of enterprise were smaller so that workers would retain more of their autonomy. Thus, the politicians' admonition to "grow the economy" will get us nowhere.

Furthermore, I believe that we need to start not with Adam Smith's *Wealth of Nations,* but with his *Theory of Moral Sentiments* (1759), in which he asserted quite forcefully that we possess an innate empathy toward our fellow human beings.[19] Morality and ethical principles of fairness are part of our nature. We ought not expunge these ideas from economics. Hence, I begin with the notion that economics ought to aspire to a just society and one in which compassion is more important than efficiency. Admittedly, the meaning of justice is unavoidably ambiguous, but that does not give us the license to disregard it. I think that an important aspect of it has to be that the economy should minimize pain and suffering, enhance human dignity and self-worth. The implication of such a humanistic approach to economics will be teased out in the remainder of this volume.

HUMANISTIC ECONOMICS

Humanistic economics need not be an oxymoron. It implies the vision that a kinder and more just capitalism is possible, one that is imbedded in a truly democratic society that not only empowers people but enables them to live their daily lives with less uncertainty, and less fear that their lives could collapse like a house of cards. This capitalism with a human face encompasses an economy with zero unemployment, zero inflation, zero trade deficits, and zero government debt over the business cycle.[20] You might call it capitalism of the four zeros.

The concept accentuates that a meaningful life goes well beyond the consumption and production upon which textbooks focus. Since human beings are not simply, or even primarily, "economic agents"—the values promulgated by the mainstream—the emphasis on the "bottom line" often conflicts with human values. Instead of advocating growth at any price, capitalism with a human face would enable more people to live fulfilled, less harried, and ultimately more satisfied lives. John Maynard Keynes had a similar opinion: "I think that capitalism, wisely managed, can probably be made more efficient for attaining economic ends than any alternative system yet in sight, but that in itself it is in many ways extremely objectionable. Our problem is to work out a social organization which shall be as efficient as possible without offending our notions of a satisfactory way of life."[21]

I agree with Erich Fromm's assertion that human rights should include "sufficient material basis to live a dignified human life. . . . A man has the same right as a dog has to live and not to starve."[22] Economists should make clear that the purpose of any economic system is not "growth" for its own sake; it is not efficient allocation of resources, but the provision of a decent life in which total output is distributed equitably and people do not need to struggle to meet their basic needs and can realize, insofar as possible, their human potential—and that means having sufficient leisure time to participate in the community's social and political life.

People mistakenly equate economic growth with rising living standards. They harmonize with the politicians' pro-growth chorus. However, polls and surveys contradict this perspective. In spite of all the growth in our lifetime, satisfaction eludes us. Moreover, the growth-at-any-price perspective does not take into account the crucial problem of distribution: economic growth will not help the destitute, the homeless, the uneducated underclass, or the majority of those who are underemployed. There is much discontent with the economy as well as with the political system.[23] The problem is that most of the discontented have yet to understand how the "free marketeers"—extremists who advocate free markets at any price—have led us astray.

De jure equal opportunity is insufficient for a just economy without de facto equal opportunity. Wealth is a privilege. It provides opportunities. Babies born into poor families have much less chance of living a fulfilled life than those born into wealthy ones. Their future development will be on divergent paths determined by their initial endowments. Such random initial allocation cannot possibly be the basis of a just society. Our goal ought to be to create an environment in which babies have more equal opportunities, and those who are born at a disadvantage can be compensated by society for their initial bad luck.[24]

My aim in writing this book is to provide a critical framework that can serve as a complement to conventional textbooks, which claim to be above morality but disregard the inequality it helped to create.[25] As we have seen hundreds of times since the Industrial Revolution, and most vividly in 2008, free markets, being a human invention, are often dysfunctional; they do not deserve our blind faith. Furthermore, there has to be a better way to measure progress than in terms of money.

One need not be a naive utopian to be appalled by a society in which one bumps—sometimes literally—into scenes of gross inequity around every corner. Thus, this book is dedicated to a capitalism with a human face.

WELCOME TO BLACKBOARD ECONOMICS

"What do George Akerlof, Kenneth Arrow, Daniel Kahneman, Paul Krugman, Thomas Schelling, Herbert Simon, Joseph Stiglitz, and Oliver Williamson have in common?" would make a great Econ 101 question except for the fact that the contributions of these Nobel Prize–winning economists to the Dismal Science are usually excluded from mainstream textbooks or relegated to obscure footnotes. Instead of including their critical ideas, introductory textbooks hype a free-market utopia, which does not extend much beyond the edges of the blackboard. Hence, most textbooks are not really suitable for understanding the essentials of the *real existing* capitalism in the globalized world of the twenty-first century. Rather, they present a caricature of the economy at a level of abstraction that distorts the student's vision: how inefficient! They perpetuate a stereotype that markets are efficient, thereby automatically leading to a blissful life, and they continue to sing the praises of the immense achievements of the free-market system, keeping any demurrals muted.

Super rationality reigns in this utopian kingdom inhabited by consumers with sufficient brain power to know every detail of the economy and therefore not satisfied with anything less than doing the very best they can. They possess perfect understanding of all the nuances in small print and perfect foresight from the beginning to the end of their lives and are not inhibited by the challenges of information overload insofar as information is free, available instantaneously, and a cinch to understand. They enter the economy as adults with tastes fully formed, so businesses do not influence their likes and dislikes in their childhood. There are no brands and goods have no quality dimension, so product choice is a no-brainer: two boxes of generic cereal, or three? There is no small print in contracts, no false promises, so buyers need not be on their guard. There are no regrets in this idyllic economy, no need for human judgment or intuition, no emotion, no real uncertainty hence no mistakes, and no need to worry about lawyers' fees or other enforcement or transaction costs.[26] Indeed, there is no society at all, no children, no gender, no glass ceilings, no class and hence no underclass, no power imbalances, and neither space, nor race, and hardly any time dimension. Consumers are not influenced by advertisement or by other people's consumption.

Producers also inhabit this imaginary economy; they also know everything there is to know about consumers' wants as well as their own firms so they can maximize their profits with perfect ease. Actually, there are no firms at all in this economy, in the sense of a modern corporation, just simple entities that act in unison, like a person. There are no shareholders or boards of directors, no CEO who might maximize her own income rather than that of the firm. This pseudo-firm does not need to advertise to persuade consumers to buy its products, much less collude with others, deceive, or game the system.[27] Lobbyists are an extinct species so there is no political process that can tilt the playing field in favor of the wealthy and influential.[28] Problems are posed in terms of a single decision without antecedents and without further implications in subsequent periods. In fact, time does not play much of a role in this static world: the past is passé and the future is obvious. So there is only the right now.

Laws are in place so we do not need to discuss how they came to be or what advantages they provide to the powerful and the extent to which they disregard the dispossessed. If laws go unmentioned it is because they go unbroken, that is, people do not take advantage of each other's lack of information and hence there are no enforcement costs. So oversight would be a waste of effort and of brainpower. Everything runs smoothly—there are no conflicts, let alone wars. Basic needs have given way to benign wants. Free markets are efficient, hence above morality, so questioning their laissez-faire premise would be a waste of ethical scruples. (However, this is also a value judgment implying that efficiency is valuable rather than, say, sufficiency, or sustainability, or fairness, or minimizing risk, poverty, or suffering.) Hence, it is alleged that laissez-faire does not need a moral basis and ethics and aesthetics are superfluous. (Of course, this is also a value judgment.) Well-being is measured by income in monetary terms, but there are no rich or poor so there is neither power nor hunger, therefore the system is democratic: one dollar, one vote. The fact that some hold more dollars than others is their birthright, so there is no need to discuss that; de facto, they do have more votes. These are the basic elements of what is called positive economics at least on the blackboard—that is to say scientific economics, at least at the undergraduate and especially at the introductory level.

However, an increasing number of economists believe that the above "ivory tower" economy, rooted in simplistic assumptions, is a completely idealized one,[29] inhabited by implausible super-rational individuals, a race of *Übermenschen,* or supermen, devoid of emotion, living alone hence without any sense of community, whose only identity is that of being consumers, or producers with hardly any interaction with others.[30]

Furthermore, the conventional wisdom invariably emphasizes the perfectly competitive model, although a negligible segment of the economy can still be conceptualized as such in an economy full of too-big-to-fail banks and super-corporations with global vision who operate above political oversight. The psychological world of the ultra-rational consumer is essentially pre-Freudian and pre-Pavlovian, that is to say, it lacks a sound psychological basis. It is rooted in the much simpler Smithian world of the eighteenth century without the moral fiber of that world. That is like trying to understand molecular motion using Newton's laws instead of those of quantum mechanics; hence, the current state of the economics discipline is essentially inadequate for the post-meltdown world of the twenty-first century.[31]

TOWARD A PARADIGM SHIFT IN ECONOMICS

In other words, we are experiencing not just a financial crisis but a crisis in economic thought so intense that it calls for a paradigm shift. Instead of chasing the elusive "American Dream" in a "rat-race" economy with a few winners and many losers,[32] we should focus on providing ourselves with a decent, sustainable, dignified, creative, secure, peaceful, satisfactory, and enjoyable life, one that is not based on excessive consumption—one that is less materialistic.[33] For the first time in the history of humanity we have the possibility to achieve a standard of living that eluded our predecessors. However, in order to live comfortably, we do not need an ever-increasing quantity of gadgets. Rather, we need to rein in our appetite, our greed, and have a mindset that is less concerned with success measured by money and more concerned about spiritual and social aspects of life.[34] Instead of growing the economy, we need to learn to grow ourselves psychologically, spiritually, and morally. The Canadian Institute of Wellbeing defines well-being thus: "The presence of the highest possible quality of life in its full breadth of expression, focused on but not necessarily exclusive to: good living standards, robust health, a sustainable environment, vital communities, an educated populace, balanced time use, high levels of civic participation, and access to and participation in dynamic arts, culture and recreation."[35]

In short, well-being is by no means identical with GDP or output or income.[36] A satisfactory life in a capitalism with a human face should include the reduction of poverty, inequality, unemployment, stress, anxiety, and insecurity, and an increase in health, leisure time, social relationships, love, respect, ethical considerations, intellectual satisfaction, and a moral life. President Jimmy Carter understood this quite clearly when he said in 1979, "In a nation that was proud of hard work, strong families, close-knit communities, and our faith in God, too many of us now tend to worship self-indulgence and consumption. Human identity is no longer defined by what one does, but by what one owns. But we have discovered that owning things and consuming things does not satisfy our longing for meaning.... It is the truth and it is a warning."[37] However, his warning was not heeded.

The reader should not misunderstand: I am not advocating abolishing markets or creating a leviathan of immense proportions, and I am resolute about protecting freedoms enunciated in the Universal Declaration of Human Rights. I agree that the defense of liberty is non-negotiable. However, I have a wider conception of liberty than Milton Friedman or Ronald Reagan did.[38] My conception is closer to Amartya Sen's notion of capability. It includes the freedom to walk the streets at night without fear,[39] the freedom from anxiety that our pensions will disappear, being entitled to study in decent schools, as well as the freedom from seeing the suffering of the underclass, the unemployed, and homeless.[40] My conception of liberty includes the freedom to live without the hard-press sales pitches of intrusive advertisements,[41] or being free from the feeling of relative deprivation from seeing the lifestyles of the profligate rich and famous. One should also be free to develop one's personality from within rather than having it imposed through the media. Developing one's character autonomously without the interference of the profit motive of big business is an essential aspect of a truly free person who is not inculcated with the fundamental elements of consumerism.

Furthermore, I also believe that many markets work well some of the time and a few markets work well most of the time, but no market works as well as we'd like them to all of the time. We need to think about improving their functioning so that we ourselves can function better in them. While I do believe that we will never improve markets unless we acknowledge and discuss their defects, by no means do I call for their elimination. In fact, I am truly an enthusiastic supporter of markets that enable people to exercise their creativity and individuality of their own free will without interference from trend setters and predatory lenders, but my support is contingent on empirical evidence. I refuse to disregard or rationalize away evidence that does not fit into the orthodox canon. If markets obviously do some of us harm or threaten us, then we, the people, must retain the ultimate right to make alternative arrangements and take collective action to stop the pain. This is the humanistic approach to economics: we should minimize suffering, mental and physical. We should remain the masters of markets, and not vice versa.[42] Furthermore, the benefits of markets should not accrue to a few members of the society, because that would be unfair and because that brings about relative deprivation. This was also at the root of the "Occupy Wall Street" movement.

Actually, there is a continuum of socioeconomic systems, ranging from market fundamentalism to socialism. I advocate finding that constellation of institutional arrangements at the golden mean between the two polar extremes that can provide most of us, as well as future generations, with a reasonably fulfilled life. I do not believe that we need to "grow the economy" at any cost, as politicians have been repeating in the wake of the economic crisis. Rather, we need to create a fairer economy that can sustain future generations and that produces less discontent and less insecurity than does the current version.

REAL-WORLD ECONOMICS

Although many economists have rejected the simple mainstream models, their views have not been adequately represented in mainstream textbooks at the undergraduate level.[43] For instance, W. Brian Arthur, a noted authority in the field of complexity theory, calls for "a more realistic economics." "As recent events show," he cautions, "we badly need to reformulate how we understand the economy."[44] Moreover, under the heading "Aims and Scope," the editors of the journal

Capitalism and Society are explicit in their criticism of the mainstream: "Today's established economics—the economics dominant in classrooms, banks, and governments—misconceives the modern economy. This disconnect has consequences for how we understand history, how we make policy, and how we view capitalism. Its explanations fail and mislead at important junctures in modern history. Until economics is grounded on the basic character of modern economies— the ignorance, the uncertainty, and the new ideas for speculation and innovation—it limits and distorts our view."[45] In short, we need to take a fresh look at the realities around us instead of accepting at face value dubious illusory notions conceived by the ivory tower's self-important inhabitants, no matter how brilliant the theorems and how impressively sophisticated the mathematics employed.

No less an authority than Nobel Prize–winning economist Joseph Stiglitz has declared that "neoliberalism is a doctrine; market fundamentalism is dead,"[46] but you would not know it by reading the most popular textbooks in the field, which influence a million students every single year. This is not a benign oversight. It has immense consequences insofar as it influences the media, political discourse, and the mindset of the voting public. No wonder, then, that many ask "why economics is on the wrong track."[47] This is quite unfortunate as economics is actually a much richer discipline than that, and has been so for a long time. There is no need to omit important developments of the last half-century such as the crucial role of information, strategic behavior, and transaction costs in economic decision making.[48]

SIMPLE IS FOR SIMPLE MINDED

The argument that a simple overview of the discipline suffices in Econ 101, because one has to lay the foundations before students can learn more sophisticated aspects of the discipline, is utterly misguided.[49] It sells the students far too short. The foundations ought not be such a caricature that they distort reality beyond recognition. I dare say that if the straight-talking Nobel Prize–winning physicist Richard Feynman (1918–88) were still with us, he would concur with that view; in his famous 1974 commencement address at the California Institute of Technology, he beseeched the graduating class to practice "scientific integrity," "utter honesty," and "leaning over backwards" so as not to "fool ourselves" (and of course others).[50] I believe that the same is true for us—teachers of economics. From the very beginning of learning the discipline, students must be made keenly aware of the real limitations of real markets as opposed to theoretical ones for at least four crucial reasons:

1. Half-truths hardly belong in scholarship at any time, not any more in the beginning of one's studies than at the end, and omitting important new developments in the field such as Herbert Simon's theory of satisficing or Kahneman and Tversky's prospect theory is not what I think of as being "utterly honest."[51]
2. It is much more efficient to learn a discipline correctly the first time than have to unlearn it and correct it subsequently. It is extremely difficult to unlearn something once one is socialized into accepting the main tenets of the discipline without learning the qualifications. The human mind is not that flexible: once the neural networks are in place, they are extremely challenging to rewire.[52]
3. The more "sophisticated" ideas turn out to be not so complicated after all and can be explained easily at the 101 level. Neglecting them distorts economic theory to such a degree that students leave the course with a fundamentally misleading caricature of the real existing economy.
4. Most students of Econ 101 do not continue to study economics so they are never even

exposed to the more nuanced version of the discipline and are therefore indoctrinated for the rest of their lives.[53] This indoctrination played a substantial role in the political developments of the last half-century in forming an intellectual climate tilted heavily toward the free-market-above-all view of the world that came to prevail. Thus, every statement one makes in the classroom ought to be true and the distinction between theoretical and actual markets clarified and stressed.[54] This is the case although the instructor is expected to cover a lot of material in the introductory course. Nonetheless, unless the various perspectives on economics are presented in a balanced framework, the student can only gain a biased perspective on reliability of market processes.

As *New York Times* columnist (and Nobel Prize–winning economist) Paul Krugman puts it, "the economy is a complex system of interacting individuals—and these individuals themselves are complex systems. Neoclassical economics radically oversimplifies both the individuals and the system—and gets a lot of mileage by doing that. . . . But the temptation is always to keep on applying these extreme simplifications, even where the evidence clearly shows that they're wrong. What economists have to do is learn to resist that temptation."[55]

Many principles texts make the argument that one must simplify in order to begin to understand this complex system. However, finding the right balance between simplification and realism is crucial: oversimplification leads to distortion and to fundamental misunderstanding of the discipline. A simple map of the United States is a wonderful means to understand, say, the relative distances between New York, Chicago, and Los Angeles, but it will not help you at all if you want to find directions to the nearest hospital. For that you need a map with a different resolution. So the simplest is not necessarily always the most effective.

Other economists argue that the models can be unrealistic as long as their predictions are correct. But mainstream economics comes up especially short on this account. On the basis of mainstream models one would predict that our life satisfaction or happiness would have increased substantially in the course of twentieth century. After all, per capita gross national product (GNP) in real terms increased in the United States since World War II by a factor of 3.5. But that prediction is falsified by the fact that the share of people who report that they are either happy or very happy has not changed at all in the intervening half-century. Hence, obviously, the importance of money is overvalued by the economic discipline. In the following pages we will discuss this phenomenon more fully.

Another example in which predictions were completely false is that economists did not foresee the coming of the Great Recession any more than they did the coming of the Great Depression three-quarters of a century earlier. The Federal Reserve predicted that the subprime mortgages would not destabilize the financial system. Fed chairman Ben Bernanke predicted that housing prices would not decline. I'd say that geologists are somewhat better at predicting earthquakes than Ben Bernanke was in predicting the effect of this financial crisis. In addition, economists do not have a solution to our current economic quandary. In other words, when it comes to the major challenges of our time, economic theory has not been useful at all. So the argument that economists can predict accurately even with unrealistic models has been falsified by the evidence.

"IT'S ONLY A MODEL!"

Economists think in terms of theoretical models expressed in forms of equations or geometric diagrams. Blackboard economics is based on assumptions and on conceptualizations of how the variables of the model interact. Although these appear rigorous, given the obvious limitations of the human mind, the number of variables has to be restricted to a handful in order for us to be able to comprehend their mutual influence and interaction. While these simple logical constructs can be—and often are—quite useful, they cannot possibly capture the true nature of an economy with thousands of variables and literally millions of interacting components, which themselves are embedded in an even larger global framework. The enormous complexity soon becomes unfathomable, overwhelming, and computationally intractable. So simplification is surely practical and has a legitimate role to play in analysis and can provide useful insights. However, oversimplification can render models destructive, as we saw during the 2008 financial crisis. Unfortunately, much too often the distinction between the world of the model and reality is not stressed sufficiently so that students and practitioners confuse the two. Teachers are doing their students a disservice if they allow them to leave their classrooms with the differences between the two worlds blurred in their minds.

The reason is that all too frequently, oversimplified blackboard models are applied to real-world situations erroneously so that instead of enhancing our understanding, they obscure, lead us far astray, and become a powerful destructive force. Alan Greenspan and Ben Bernanke's overlooking the power of systemic risk—externalities—in the financial sector prior to the run-up to the Great Meltdown is a recent vivid example of the damaging forces of models that are inappropriate to the actual circumstances that exist at street level. Another example is the recurrent misguided application of models of perfect competition (to unions and to the minimum wage most prominently, see Chapter 9) to markets that are far from perfectly competitive; after all, in today's economy an insignificant share of economic activity takes place in a perfectly competitive environment. Thus, an enormous intellectual problem arises in popular culture to the extent that the theoretical models are misused every day and especially so in political discourse.

This is hardly a minor phenomenon. Instead, it is at the root of the current economic, social, and political malaise—a watershed in U.S. history. For instance, perfectly competitive models have been applied mechanically and inappropriately in situations that were characterized by sticky information flows. Hence, it is, in the main, the economics profession's responsibility that the public, the media, and politicians are so ill informed. It has not followed strictly enough the spirit of Feynman's admonition, and did not bend over backwards to explain with sufficient clarity and ample emphasis the qualifications that accompany the blackboard models. It is absolutely insufficient to mention the assumptions at the beginning of the semester and assume that the students will remember them at its end. We have to be much more careful to delineate the circumstances under which it is appropriate to apply the perfectly competitive model to the real world. Without such clarification and incessant qualification, most textbooks fundamentally mislead and do more harm than good, insofar as they fail to provide a nuanced understanding of flesh-and-blood economic processes.

The failure to emphasize real-world economics has immense implications for the body politic and civil society, insofar as the fact that millions of students go on with their lives and years later choose among political candidates based partly on their economic policies, or become newspaper editors, radio commentators, small-town mayors, congressional aides, or political activists—in other words, their careers take them to responsible positions within the society—mistakenly thinking that they have understood the basics of economic theory, that markets work efficiently when left alone. Thus, the deficiencies of the standard Econ 101 become a powerful damaging force. Because they then become vulnerable to, or perpetrators of, simplistic slogans particularly vitriolic in the current political climate: "Competition will lead to growth"; "the free market is efficient;" "lowering taxes will create jobs"; "government is not the solution to our problem, government is the problem;"[56] "no consumer protection is needed as we all know what we are doing." To avoid such stereotypical pitfalls, it is incumbent upon us teachers to "lean over backwards" in the first course in economics to avoid half-truths at all costs before the students are socialized into thinking that competitive markets have the magic formula to provide the answer to all or even most of our actual economic problems.

Examples abound. As a matter of fact, the overwhelming majority of economic models are applied inappropriately. For instance, one finds such gobbledygook in a leading textbook as: "Health care is an economic commodity like shoes and gasoline."[57] This invidious contention disregards the essential differences between these markets. It has been known at least since a seminal article on the subject in 1963 that the standard models do not apply to health markets, because of the crucial role of imperfect and asymmetric information between doctor and patient, because of the conflict of interest between the various counterparties, in which very complicated decisions have to be made with uncertainty, and because there is no price competition to speak of. These factors make the health market completely different from the shoe market.[58] One does not usually purchase insurance for one's shoes, and health is not considered a luxury item, while shoes often are.[59] "If a designer shoe goes up from $800 to $860, who notices?"[60] Clearly, the quality of a shoe is much easier to ascertain than the quality of a health insurance contract. Moreover, doctors know much more biology than we do and there is no practical way for us to ascertain the most prudent treatment. I have not heard of anyone wanting to get an MRI when it was unnecessary but I have heard of doctors wanting to prescribe one to increase their profits. Gasoline is also entirely different from the other two products. It is produced from an exhaustible resource, pollutes, and therefore has a major environmental effect. Thus, the essence of the three markets could not be more different. To conflate them is to willfully defy common sense and confuse the student.

Another example from the current political discourse is the oft-cited allegation that "taxing the rich is bad for economic growth," which overlooks the inconvenient evidence that economic growth was quite robust in the 1950s and 1960s, when the tax rates were notably higher on top income earners than they have been recently. The proponents of the view also overlook empirical evidence that other countries—such as Germany, Switzerland, and Japan, to name just a few of the many—manage to invest just fine without having a U.S.-like abyss between rich and poor. Lowering tax rates on the rich is supposed to increase investments, again overlooking the obvious fact that a goodly share of their income is spent on conspicuous consumption.[61] I do not know of studies that calculate how much the rich invest into actual businesses—as opposed to treasuries—and how much they spend on conspicuous consumption, but the question surely arises whether John Travolta really needs two jet airplanes sitting in his back yard for us to have a growing economy. Does Mitt Romney really need an elevator for his car at his La Jolla beach house in order to put people back to work?[62] If the wealthy had to pay higher taxes, they may not be able to afford such frivolous expenditures, and perhaps there would be more money available for mental health facilities so that the number of mass shootings might be reduced.

In sum, the mainstream has been utterly insensitive to evidence contradicting Econ 101. The 2008 financial meltdown was more than an inconvenient truth to be disregarded lest it disturb the eloquence of their mathematical theories. Rather, it was just one of many examples of markets going awry—think of the savings and loan crisis of the 1980s, the peso crisis of 1994, the Asian crisis of 1997—yet textbooks remain unchanged, failing to convey the fundamental and systematic weaknesses of the free-market system.[63] My goal in the remainder of this volume is to redress this imbalance by expanding conventional theory into the realm of capitalism with a human face.

QUESTIONS FOR DISCUSSION

1. Do you agree with Alan Greenspan that everyone has an ideology?
2. What is your ideology and how does it compare to the ideology of a typical American?
3. Do you think that the assumptions made in economics textbooks about the behavior of individuals and firms are sufficiently realistic to be appropriate and useful, or do you think that they are oversimplifications?

4. Do you think that a values-free economics is possible?

5. Do you think it is useful to distinguish between basic needs and wants?

6. Do advertisements or fashion trends influence your consumption habits?

7. Do you think that ethical considerations are as important as efficiency?

8. Do you think that consumerism should be the dominant culture?

9. Do markets always function perfectly?

10. Can you think of instances when you were disappointed by a salesperson, or deceived, or defrauded, or someone took advantage of your lack of knowledge or experience?

11. Does society have the right to control market activity?

12. Do you expect professors to follow Feynman's admonition to be "utterly honest"?

13. Are you more satisfied with your life than were your parents or grandparents?

14. Do you think that reducing the conspicuous consumption of the rich through higher taxes would improve the supply of public goods such as schools and infrastructure in the United States?

NOTES

1. Bradford DeLong, "Economics in Crisis," *The Economists' Voice,* 8 (2011) 2: 1–2.

2. Joseph Stiglitz observed that there is not much variation in the perspectives conveyed in introductory textbooks. See Stiglitz, "On the Market for Principles of Economics Textbooks: Innovation and Product Differentiation," *Journal of Economic Education* 19 (1988) 2: 171–182; here, p. 172. David Colander, *Economics,* 8th ed. (New York: McGraw-Hill Irwin, 2010), is the most open to heterodox, that is, other than mainstream, perspectives. See also Jane Lopus and Lynn Paringer, "The Principles of Economics Textbook: Content Coverage and Usage," in *International Handbook on Teaching and Learning Economics,* ed. Gail Hoyt and Kim Marie McGoldrick (Cheltenham, UK: Edward Elgar, 2012).

3. "Waxman to Greenspan: Were You Wrong?" YouTube video, 5:05, posted by "NancyPelosi," October 23, 2008.

4. An ideology is a belief system without empirical foundation that justifies social, economic, or political aspirations and policy. As a consequence, it is not open to empirical refutation.

5. On Brooksley Born, see the excellent PBS documentary, "Frontline: The Warning."

6. Dean Baker, "The Run-up in Home Prices: A Bubble," *Challenge* 45 (2002) 6: 93–119.

7. Edward M. Gramlich, *Subprime Mortgages: America's Latest Boom and Bust* (Washington, DC: Urban Institute Press, 2007).

8. The Market Oracle, "Financial Regulators and Insiders Had Foreknowledge of the U.S. Housing Bubble," April 17, 2010.

9. Wikipedia contributors, "Frankfurt School," *Wikipedia: The Free Encyclopedia.*

10. Mark A. Lutz and Kenneth Lux, *Humanistic Economics: The New Challenge* (New York: Bootstrap Press, 1988); George P. Brockway, *The End of Economic Man: An Introduction to Humanistic Economics* (New York: W.W. Norton, 1991).

11. See, for example, the blogs on the Web site of the Center for American Progress.

12. Piero Sraffa, *Production of Commodities by Means of Commodities* (Cambridge, UK: Cambridge University Press, 1960).

13. Deirdre McCloskey, *The Secret Sins of Economics* (Chicago: Prickly Paradigm Press, 2002).

14. Donald N. McCloskey, "The Rhetoric of Economics," *Journal of Economic Literature* 31 (1983) 2: 482–504.

15. I refer to the a priori conceptual analysis—after the famous economist Ronald Coase—known somewhat tongue-in-cheek as "blackboard economics."

16. See http://homes.point2.com/Neighborhood/US/New-York/New-York-City/Manhattan/Harlem-Demographics.aspx; Francesca Levy, "America's 25 Richest Counties," Forbes.com, March 4, 2010. Six of the richest counties lie on the outskirts of Washington, D.C.

17. McCloskey, "Rhetoric of Economics."

18. Ernst F. Schumacher, *Small Is Beautiful: Economics As If People Mattered* (New York: Harper Torchbook, 1973).

19. "How selfish . . . man may be supposed, there are evidently some principles in his nature, which interest him in the fortune of others, and render their happiness necessary to him, though he derives nothing from it except the pleasure of seeing it. Of this kind is . . . compassion, the emotion which we feel for the misery of others. . . . That we often derive sorrow from the sorrow of others, is a matter of fact too obvious to require any instances to prove it; for this sentiment, like all the other original passions of human nature, is by no means confined to the virtuous and humane. . . . The greatest ruffian, the most hardened violator of the laws of society, is not altogether without it." Adam Smith, *The Theory of Moral Sentiments* I.I.1 (London: A. Millar, 1790) [first published in 1759], available at Library of Economics and Liberty).

20. To be sure, nations may want to borrow from one another from time to time but it ought not be a permanent feature of policy in my judgment. I also see the logic of wanting to avoid deflation, but I do not think that a targeted 2% rate of inflation is the closest one can get to zero.

21. John Maynard Keynes, *The End of Laissez-Faire: The Economic Consequences of the Peace* (London: Hogarth Press, 1926).

22. According to Erich Fromm, it is the "right of each man to unfold as an individual and as a human being." From "Erich Fromm pt. 1," YouTube video, 10:04, posted by "Oisin29," November 14, 2008.

23. Thomas E. Mann and Norman J. Ornstein, *It's Even Worse Than It Looks: How the American Constitutional System Collided with the New Politics of Extremism* (New York: Basic Books, 2012).

24. For example, one Anthony Pritzker has a house roughly 20 times the size of an average house, simply because he was luckier than the rest in who happened to be his parents. Mark Holtzman, "Big Is Back," *The Wall Street Journal,* February 10, 2012.

25. A fetish is an irrational reverence or obsessive devotion—a fixation—an almost superstitious trust in something like a totem pole, or in this case, the free market.

26. Oliver E. Williamson, "The Economics of Organization: The Transaction Cost Approach," *American Journal of Sociology* 87 (1981) 3: 548–577.

27. David Cay Johnston, *Free Lunch: How the Wealthiest Americans Enrich Themselves at Government Expense and Stick You with the Bill* (New York: Portfolio Books, 2007); David Cay Johnston. *The Fine Print: How Big Companies Use 'Plain English' to Rob You Blind* (New York: Portfolio Books, 2012).

28. David Cay Johnston, *Perfectly Legal: The Covert Campaign to Rig Our Tax System to Benefit the Super-Rich—and Cheat Everybody Else* (New York: Portfolio Books, 2003).

29. See, for example, the newly created Institute for New Economic Thinking, an important initiative in this direction, as well as the journal *Real-World Economics Review.*

30. Stephen A. Marglin, *The Dismal Science: How Thinking Like an Economist Undermines Community* (Cambridge, MA: Harvard University Press, 2010).

31. "We are the hollow men / We are the stuffed men / Leaning together / Headpiece filled with straw. Alas! / Our dried voices, when / We whisper together / Are quiet and meaningless . . ." T.S. Eliot, "The Hollow Men," 1925.

32. Robert H. Frank and Philip J. Cook, *Winner-Take-All Society* (New York: Free Press, 1995).

33. B.F. Skinner's answer to "What is the Good Life?" in his *Walden Two* was: It is "a life of friendship, health, art, a healthy balance between work and leisure, a minimum of unpleasantness, and a feeling that one has made worthwhile contributions to one's society." Wikipedia contributors, "B.F. Skinner," *Wikipedia: The Free Encyclopedia.*

34. See Pope John Paul II's socioeconomic encyclical *Centesimus annus* (1991) in which both private property and the organization of labor unions are included among a variety of fundamental human rights.

35. "What Is Wellbeing?" Canadian Index of Wellbeing, available at https://uwaterloo.ca/canadian-index-wellbeing/wellbeing-canada/what-wellbeing.

36. An overview of the many shortcomings of GNP accounting can be found in Joseph E. Stiglitz, Amartya Sen, and Jean-Paul Fitoussi, *Mismeasuring Our Lives. Why the GDP Doesn't Add Up* (New York: New Books, 2010).

37. David Shi asserts that "[Carter] totally ignored the fact that the country's dominant institutions—corporations, advertising, popular culture—were instrumental in promoting and sustaining the hedonistic ethic. . . ." See David Shi, *The Simple Life: Plain Living and High Thinking in American Culture* (Athens: University of Georgia Press, 2007), 272.

38. Milton Friedman, *Capitalism and Freedom* (Chicago: University of Chicago Press, 1962).

39. Lydia Saad, "Nearly 4 in 10 Americans Still Fear Walking Alone at Night," Gallup, November 5, 2010.

40. "Men are qualified for civil liberty in exact proportion to their disposition to put moral chains upon their own appetites,—in proportion as their love to justice is above their rapacity,—in proportion as their soundness and sobriety of understanding is above their vanity and presumption,—in proportion as they are more disposed to listen to the counsels of the wise and good, in preference to the flattery of knaves. Society cannot exist, unless a controlling power upon will and appetite be placed somewhere; and the less of it there is within, the more there must be without. It is ordained in the eternal constitution of things, that men of intemperate minds cannot be free. Their passions forge their fetters." Edmund Burke, *Letter to a Member of the National Assembly* (London: J. Dodsley, Pall-Mall, 1791), 68–69.

41. There is an incipient effort to counteract the overarching power of advertisements called *Adbusters*.

42. Writing about the period immediately prior to the Great Meltdown, Benjamin M. Friedman states that "the economy was doing pretty well, but most of the people in it were not. The chief reason is widening inequality." Benjamin M. Friedman, "Widening Inequality Combined with Modest Growth," *Challenge* 52 (2009) 3: 76–91.

43. Drucilla K. Barker and Susan F. Feiner, *Liberating Economics: Feminist Perspectives on Families, Work, and Globalization* (Ann Arbor: University of Michigan Press, 2004), 5.

44. W. Brian Arthur, external professor, Santa Fe Institute, "Interests," available at http://tuvalu.santafe.edu/~wbarthur.

45. "Aims and Scope," *Capitalism and Society*, A Journal of the Center on Capitalism and Society.

46. In a speech documented on YouTube in November 2008, Stiglitz declared, "This September has been to market fundamentalism what the fall of the Berlin Wall was to communism. We all knew that those ideas were flawed, that free market ideology didn't work; we all knew that communism didn't work, but these were defining moments that made it clear that it didn't work. . . . America really has a system . . . a kind of corporatism corporate welfarism . . . under the guise of free market economics. And it is that mixture that was fundamentally flawed, incoherent, was intellectually bankrupt from the beginning, that has been shown not to work." Joseph Stiglitz—"Market Fundamentalism Is Dead," YouTube video, posted by "ForaTV," November 10, 2008.

47. McCloskey accuses the mainstream of "cultural barbarism," and "historical ignorance." See McCloskey, *Secret Sins*.

48. Amartya Sen, "Rational Fools: A Critique of the Behavioral Foundations of Economic Theory," *Philosophy and Public Affairs* 6 (1977) 4: 317–344.

49. Bernard Guerrien, "Is There Anything Worth Keeping in Standard Microeconomics?" *Post-Autistic Economics Review* 12 (2002).

50. Richard Feynman, "Cargo Cult Science," *Engineering and Science* 37 (1974) 7: 10–13.

51. Herbert Simon, "Rationality in Psychology and Economics," in *Rational Choice: The Contrast Between Economics and Psychology,* ed. Robin M. Hogarth and Melvin W. Reder (Chicago: University of Chicago Press, 1986); Amos Tversky and Daniel Kahneman, "Judgment Under Uncertainty: Heuristics and Biases," *Science,* New Series 185 (1974) 4157: 1124–1131.

52. B.F. Skinner has shown that it takes much more time to unlearn something than to learn it in the first place. See his *Science and Human Behavior* (New York: Free Press, 1965), 62–71.

53. Bruno S. Frey and S. Meier, "Are Political Economists Selfish or Indoctrinated? Evidence from a Natural Experiment," *Economic Inquiry* 41 (2003): 448–462. The full version is taught at least in some departments at the graduate level, but not sufficiently. See The Cambridge 27, "Opening Up Economics: A Proposal by Cambridge Students," *Post-Autistic Economics Network* 7 (2001): article 1.

54. We should also stress the difference between facts and beliefs.

55. Paul Krugman, "A Few Notes on My Magazine Article," The Conscience of a Liberal, *New York Times* blog, September 5, 2009.

56. Ronald Reagan's first inaugural address, January 20, 1981, Ronald Reagan Presidential Library.

57. Paul Samuelson and William Nordhaus, *Economics,* 19th ed. (New York: McGraw-Hill/Irwin, 2009), 221.

58. Kenneth Arrow, "Uncertainty and the Welfare Economics of Medical Care," *American Economic Review* 53 (1963) 5: 141–149.

59. One of Nike Air's athletic sneakers was selling for $300 the day it was released. Jacques Slade, "Release Reminder: Nike Air Foamposite One 'Metallic Red,'" KicksOnFire.com, February 3, 2012.

60. Stephanie Clifford, "Even Marked Up, Luxury Goods Fly Off Shelves," *The New York Times,* August 3, 2011.

61. According to the International Society of Aesthetic Plastic Surgeons, the United States has the most plastic surgeries in the world—about 1 million. See "ISAPS International Survey on Aesthetic/Cosmetic Procedures Performed in 2011," available at www.isaps.org/files/html-contents/Downloads/ISAPS%20 Results%20-%20Procedures%20in%202011.pdf.

62. Reid J. Epstein, "Mitt Romney's 4-Car Fantasy Home," *Politico,* March 27, 2012.

63. David Harvey, *The Enigma of Capital: And the Crisis of Capitalism* (Oxford: Oxford University Press, 2010).

2

MARKETS ARE NEITHER OMNISCIENT NOR OMNIPOTENT

MARKETS ARE NOT CREATED BY DIVINE POWER

According to conventional wisdom, free markets are practically flawless, acquiring an almost divine aura. Arguably, we have replaced the divine rights of kings with the divine laws of the market. We ought to keep in mind, however, that markets are created by human beings and not by a deity. They are by no means natural.[1] Rather, they are man-made institutions and hence can be formed and reformed to suit our purposes; they are not above criticism; and they cannot possibly be flawless. They are not infallible and should not be idolized.[2] They are a means to an end and not an end in themselves. Thus, we should remain the masters of markets, and not vice versa.

To be sure, with the advent of the Industrial Revolution, we used markets to unleash Prometheus and thereby increase incomes, make a super-abundance of material goods, raise life expectancy, and create miracles in medicine, in communication, and in information technology. These advancements obviously represent a phenomenal array of achievements. Yet, that is by no means the whole truth. There are some inconvenient facts to consider: for instance, immense poverty and deprivation, both relative and absolute, remain and continue to haunt our society and others around the world.

THE DOWNSIDE OF FREE MARKETS

The common wisdom is that—in the words of Larry Summers, Treasury secretary under President Bill Clinton—market capitalism "has been an enormous success."[3] However, this is only so if one deliberately overlooks the myriad of negative concomitants of free markets. Summers conveniently disregards the fact that we are faced with an enormous set of social problems that stem directly from the current organization of the economy. Markets have been incapable of ameliorating these problems.[4] To be sure, market aficionados argue that we should keep the social and the economic separate in our minds, but that admonition itself is a value judgment without scientific basis. The two are intricately intertwined: whatever happens in the economy will have social consequences and vice versa.

Unemployment, for example, is a huge burden and not only for the individuals involved but also for their children, families, and the community. It brings about changes in behavior and social relations. Moreover, it is not distributed evenly either spatially or across the labor force. Rather, whole neighborhoods and towns are affected. In October 2011, three years after the beginning of the Great Recession, there were 14 million Americans (9 percent of the labor force) out of work and half of the unemployed had been without work for more than five months. Among teenagers the rate was 25 percent and among blacks 16 percent. What's more, the *under*employment rate is much larger, for there are 9 million additional men and women forced to work part time, and another million who stopped looking for work because they were discouraged about finding a job.[5] So the underemployment rate was closer to 15 percent—some 23 million adults—and the numbers did not change significantly by 2013.[6] The underemployed no doubt have dependents, so it would not be an exaggeration to suppose that perhaps close to 50 million people (one out of six) are leading precarious lives, from hand to mouth so to speak, not to mention the working poor, who are hanging on by the skin of their teeth. In other words, by itself, without government guidance, the labor market has not distributed the given amount of available work—constrained by aggregate demand—equitably across the labor force.[7] The acceptance of such levels of involuntary unemployment is in itself a cultural norm.

As a consequence, rampant and endemic social and economic challenges face us. Members of the anxiety-ridden underclass, who see no way out of their desperate situation, far too often turn on each other out of frustration. That is one reason why the homicide rate in the United States is 5 to 7 times that of the welfare states of Western and Northern Europe, where the state-provided safety net reduces desperation to bearable levels.[8] Crime increases our level of anxiety, thereby diminishing our well-being substantially, and at the same time is indicative of socioeconomic disparities.[9] There are no fewer than 5 million people on probation or on parole in the United States and an additional 2.3 million in prisons.[10] This is the highest rate of incarceration anywhere in the world: with 5 percent of the world's population, the United States has 24 percent of its convicts.[11] The toleration of such levels of imprisonment shows the cruelty of the economic system toward those people who fail to find their niche in the legal labor market and fall into the nebulous underclass that few economists are willing to acknowledge.

Furthermore, there were 1 million personal bankruptcies in 2008—up from 0.3 million in 1980—which challenges the notion of unmitigated progress in the course of the twentieth century.[12] Should we mention that 2.9 million U.S. properties received foreclosure filings in 2010?[13] In 2009, 44 million people lived in poverty in the United States; that is one in seven individuals, the highest rate in 15 years and as high as in the early 1980s.[14] At the end of 2010, 47 percent of the population considered themselves to be struggling financially.[15] That adds up to some 140 million people. In June 2011, many people in the richest country on earth were unable to satisfy their basic needs: 18 percent of adults were without health insurance and 18 percent did not have enough money to buy sufficient food at least sometime during the course of the last year.[16] All this anxiety has had an effect on mental health. The number of people seeking outpatient care for depression in the United States increased from 0.7 percent of the population in 1987 to 2.3 percent in 1997 and then to 2.9 percent by 2007.[17] The use of medication among these patients increased from 37 percent to 75 percent in the same time span.

Does this society sound like a free-market nirvana? The answer is obvious, but there is more to consider: 600,000 people were counted as homeless (in shelters and in the open) on one day in 2009, a large number of them families with children.[18] The number of children who were homeless at some time in 2011 reached 1.6 million.[19] All of this is tolerated as normal in the United States at a time when there are 400 billionaires[20] and 237,000 millionaires (who earn on average $3 million per annum)[21] whose checks could go a long way to alleviate such misery. That is to say, there is more inequality in the United States than in any other advanced industrialized country in the world[22] (Figure 2.1).

The rate of poverty among U.S. children—20 percent—is twice that of Switzerland and higher than in any Western European country.[23] One reason for the high rate of poverty among children is that the divorce rate has about doubled,[24] and the number of female-headed households has tripled

Figure 2.1 **Percent of Population Living Below 50% of Median Income**

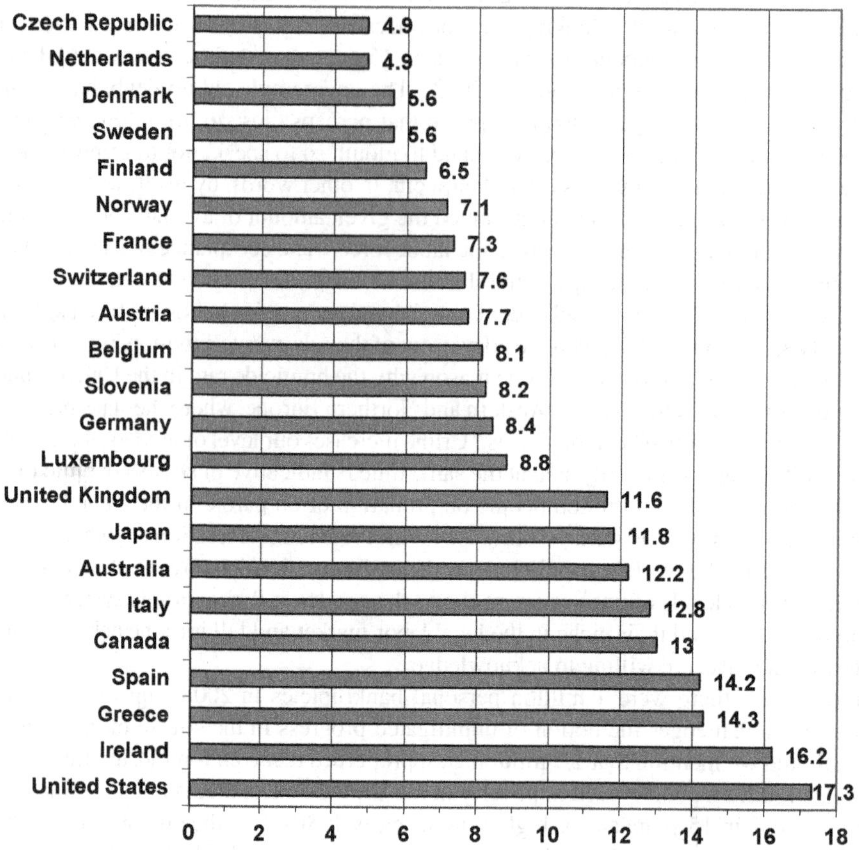

Czech Republic	4.9
Netherlands	4.9
Denmark	5.6
Sweden	5.6
Finland	6.5
Norway	7.1
France	7.3
Switzerland	7.6
Austria	7.7
Belgium	8.1
Slovenia	8.2
Germany	8.4
Luxembourg	8.8
United Kingdom	11.6
Japan	11.8
Australia	12.2
Italy	12.8
Canada	13
Spain	14.2
Greece	14.3
Ireland	16.2
United States	17.3

Source: Human Development Report, 2009. http://hdrstats.undp.org/en/indicators.

since the 1960s,[25] which also means that it is more challenging for these 20 million children (28 percent of all American children) to obtain a reasonable education with a path to the middle class. In addition, many children live in slums—concentrated areas of poverty—that do not provide them an adequate start in life, particularly in the realms of education and socialization that are so important for their future development.[26] In other words, the free market does not provide a level playing field for those children who find themselves trapped in a culture of poverty.[27] Is it not uncomfortable that the welfare of children living in a country that considers itself the best in the world was rated by UNICEF at the very bottom of the 21 OECD countries considered?[28] Six million children are reported to U.S. agencies annually for maltreatment, and five children die daily due to abuse and neglect.[29] U.S. pre-term birth rates are closer to those prevailing in Africa than in Europe.[30] A teenager in Mississippi is 15 times more likely to give birth than her counterpart in Switzerland.[31] These social problems are based in the economic system and the distribution of wealth and opportunity it affords the population.

Furthermore, because of underfunded school systems, U.S. children are lagging well behind high achievers around the globe: 15-year-olds placed 17th in reading, 23rd in science, and 31st in mathematics.[32] The United States ranked an embarrassing 48th out of 133 developed and developing nations in quality of math and science instruction available to students.[33] This depressing performance does not bode well for our ability to compete in the IT sector in the years to come.[34]

Ultimately, the low-quality of the U.S. education system is a result of the public's antigovernment disposition and its refusal to provide the government with sufficient funding. Depriving government of revenue is a conservative strategy called "starving the beast."[35] As a consequence of this strategy, public goods such as adequate schools are in especially short supply, and the government is unable to provide quality education to its citizens. In this vein, John Kenneth Galbraith contrasted "private affluence" with "public squalor"—a comparison that is as valid today as it was a couple of generations ago.[36]

There are many other problems with the current state of the economy: In a list of the best places to be a mother, the United States was ranked in 25th place in 2012.[37] General consumer complaints are endemic. There are even scammers who offer "bogus" help to save homes from foreclosure.[38] Infrastructure (i.e., dams) in the United States has not been adequately maintained, as evinced by the collapse of a bridge in Minneapolis in 2007 that killed 13 people and injured 145.[39] We have mortgaged the welfare of our children by taking on excessive debt. We are continuing to degrade the environment to such a degree that global warming threatens our very survival in an extreme and uncanny resurrection of a Malthusian menace.

It should be clear even from this limited list that we have an overwhelming set of problems and that Summers's "enormous success" basically ignores the "elephant in the room." Actually, all rankings pertinent to measuring quality of life indicate that the United States is far from being a frontrunner in those aspects of life that really matter: health, peace of mind, security, safety, education, social mobility, children's welfare, and human development. The culprit is not the mean income in the country but its skewed distribution, and economists have been silent for far too long on the chasm between the mean income and the quality of life it provides the population. In short, progress has been much more tentative than most mainstream economists are willing to concede and, moreover, it has been limited to a small segment of society. As a matter of fact, we could have done a much better job of improving the quality of life for society at large, given our immense wealth. Progress ought not be measured by growth in average income alone. Distribution also matters—it matters a lot; well-being is much more multifaceted than the conventional viewpoint allows.

GOVERNMENT IS ESSENTIAL

Government does many things well, including building the interstate network of roads, providing health care to senior citizens, veterans, and members of Congress, as well as the Social Security program, which has taken care of citizens effectively for decades. Government should not be constantly disparaged. Instead, we should emphasize that markets would not function at all without sufficient laws and appropriate institutions that are created for the most part by government. There were crucial moments in our history when markets would have imploded without sufficient government aid and when GM and Chrysler desperately needed to be resuscitated by the help of the state. The government built dams and bridges, educated our children, stabilized the banking system, and spurred innovation in hundreds of ways by supporting basic research in medicine, IT, the Internet, and biotechnology. In short, there are very good reasons not to sing hymns to free markets unconditionally.[40] Markets did not achieve our current level of wealth by themselves and could not have done so. It was a partnership of individual and community effort.

Markets are institutions just like governments, and like governments they should also be under our control. Markets are not sovereign; we are. We, the people, retain the ultimate right in a democratic society to determine what our goals are and how we will accomplish them. Some of those goals should be left to markets while others should be retained for us to determine through our elected representatives or other nonmarket institutions. No matter how much we vilify it, the government is we. Government should represent our collective will—our collective interest—which we cannot adequately enforce as individuals. Admittedly, this has not been the case of late. Powerful interests have co-opted government institutions.[41] Otherwise it is difficult to comprehend the transfer of trillions of dollars from 99 percent of the population to the top 1 percent.[42] The economic system as currently constituted has led to such concentration of wealth that our democracy (1 person, 1 vote) is being turned into a plutocracy (1 dollar, 1 vote).[43] For example, the carbon industry has successfully generated a misguided effort to deny the existence of global warming, the National Rifle Association has prevented a ban on assault rifles, and Wall Street has been able to resist stringent financial reform legislations.[44]

Without government regulation, a functioning legal system, and effective enforcement mechanisms most markets would implode rather quickly. Governments can do many things better than markets, such as providing public goods and guaranteeing our bank deposits. Markets are not good at providing protection of, for instance, consumers, children, the environment, the weak, the poor, minority rights, or the interests of future generations. Markets would sell cigarettes and alcohol to children. It was not until government regulation that cigarette smoking was cut by half in the United States.

One of the roles of government is to maintain the balance of power within the economy. An unregulated market does not mean a free market if monopoly power exists, or where parties have markedly different access to information, or where one party can bear the transaction costs more easily than other parties because of wealth differences. Such markets would not be "free" for those who do not enjoy those advantages. So the lack of government intervention does not lead to free markets. Just the opposite happens. Without government, power accumulates in the hands of the few and it is government's role to prevent such imbalances.

In addition, governments must establish and continuously adjust the institutions within which the economy functions. Governments define property rights and the procedures by which such rights can be exercised and enforced. Should we forget that the government, not markets, abolished slavery? Without government I should think that slavery would be reinstituted.[45] Governments also need to provide safety nets; otherwise the political structure would be unstable, as Marie Antoinette found out, as did many other rulers who failed to make provisions in that regard. Hunger is a mighty political force. Furthermore, we need government to be the lender of last resort in order to maintain the stability of the financial system. The laws enacted by Franklin Roosevelt served us well until they were abolished under the Reagan, Bush, Clinton, and Bush administrations. And, of course, we need government's help for people in dire need. This includes those who need aid in an emergency such as Hurricane Katrina in 2005, which killed 1,836 people and caused $90 billion in damages. I did not see companies rushing out and rescuing people. Instead, some 50,000 members of the National Guard were assigned to the affected areas. The government must also help those who are left behind in the competition for jobs. There are simply not enough jobs for everyone looking for work. It is the collective responsibility of the society to help those who are unable to meet their basic needs through no fault of their own. Helping them is not only charitable but also ensures social stability. Seeing them starve in the open would be a messy business. Besides, they just might not go quietly to the other world.

MARKETS HAVE LIMITATIONS

Markets are not endowed with supernatural powers. They are not efficient at providing for all of our needs, such as our need for infrastructure and for basic research (such as in biotechnology or science) nor even for health care, because preventive care is a bone of contention, and because individuals have biased predictions of their future health needs. Moreover, in the case of health care there is "adverse selection": those with the most health needs have a higher probability of insuring themselves than those who believe that they are healthy. As a consequence, the price of health insurance increases so that fewer people are able to afford it (around 16–18 percent of the population in the United States before Obamacare). Besides, insurers can entrap customers with fine print that enables them to deny coverage just when it is needed most. As a consequence, the U.S. population has less confidence in its health-care system in general than people in other advanced industrialized countries in spite of the fact that it is much more dependent on free-market principles than all other wealthy countries.[46] People are healthier and live longer in countries where the government plays an important role in health care (and 100 percent of the population is fully insured, as in Western and Northern Europe). Life expectancy at birth in the United States is three years below that of Canada and Cuba, 3.3 years below that of Australia, and well below Western European levels in spite of the fact that expenditure on health care is twice as much in the United States as in other developed countries[47] (see Figures 2.2 and 2.3). Life expectancy among black males in the United States is at the level of Slovakia and Algeria, and below that of Tunisia, Libya, and China.[48] Something must be awry with market principles if a service that is so expensive delivers such inferior outcomes. Competition is simply not transparent enough for the free market to offer adequate health care at affordable prices.

Markets are also extremely impatient institutions and hence are not good at planning far into the future. So markets will not produce an education policy that provides broad-based, quality education. They were not designed to do so and the incentive structure is biased toward the present. That is why our primary and secondary educational system lags well behind those of other developed nations. Where would the education system be if the government had not provided one for the population from the very beginning? Today, homeless teenagers need government help just to finish high school.[49]

Markets are also ineffective at providing safe products for consumers inasmuch as it is a difficult-to-ascertain, intangible attribute and because there is a psychological bias toward the present on the part of both producers and consumers. Hence, safety does not pay in the short run, and insofar as providing safe products in the long run is costly, price competition gets in the way of provisioning safety. For example, seat belts in automobiles were hardly used until they were mandated in 1968.[50] Now, of course, we are so used to them that most of us don't even have to think about buckling up. Or take the example of baby cribs, which certainly do not need rocket scientists to design. Yet, it was not until dozens of babies accidentally suffocated in cribs that the Consumer Product Safety Commission Agency, after years of wrangling with industry groups, finally mandated the safe design of cribs in 2011. Producers had had decades to design and sell safe cribs but were incapable of doing so because it required action that the market was incapable of coordinating.[51] The incompetence of businesses at providing safety is indicated by such disasters as Union Carbide's deadly gas leak in Bhopal, India, the grounding of the Exxon Valdez in Alaska, and the explosion aboard the Deepwater Horizon in the Gulf of Mexico. Such disasters caused immense suffering and environmental degradation. Markets are also incapable of providing vital basic research. Thus, markets are good at exploring for

Figure 2.2   **Life Expectancy at Birth, 2008**

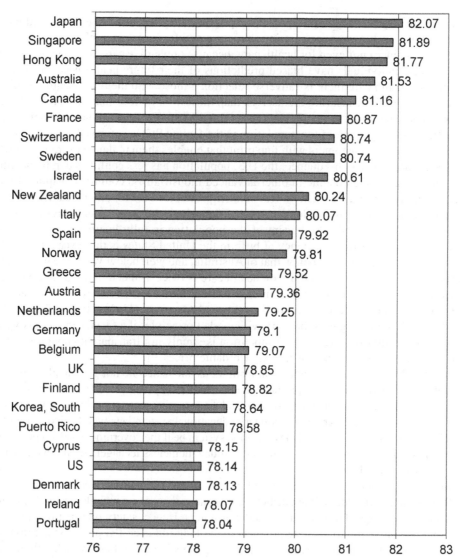

Source: Human Development Report, 2009. http://hdrstats.undp.org/en/indicators/69206.html.

energy sources using fracking technology but not reliable at all at researching the environmental effects of such exploration.

THE "ACHILLES HEEL" OF MARKETS

Actually, there are reasons why we are confronted with so many socioeconomic and political problems. We have not recognized that markets are incapable of achieving everything entrusted to them. Markets have an "Achilles heel" that interferes with their smooth functioning and detracts from

Figure 2.3 **Annual Expenditures on Health Care per Capita, 2008**

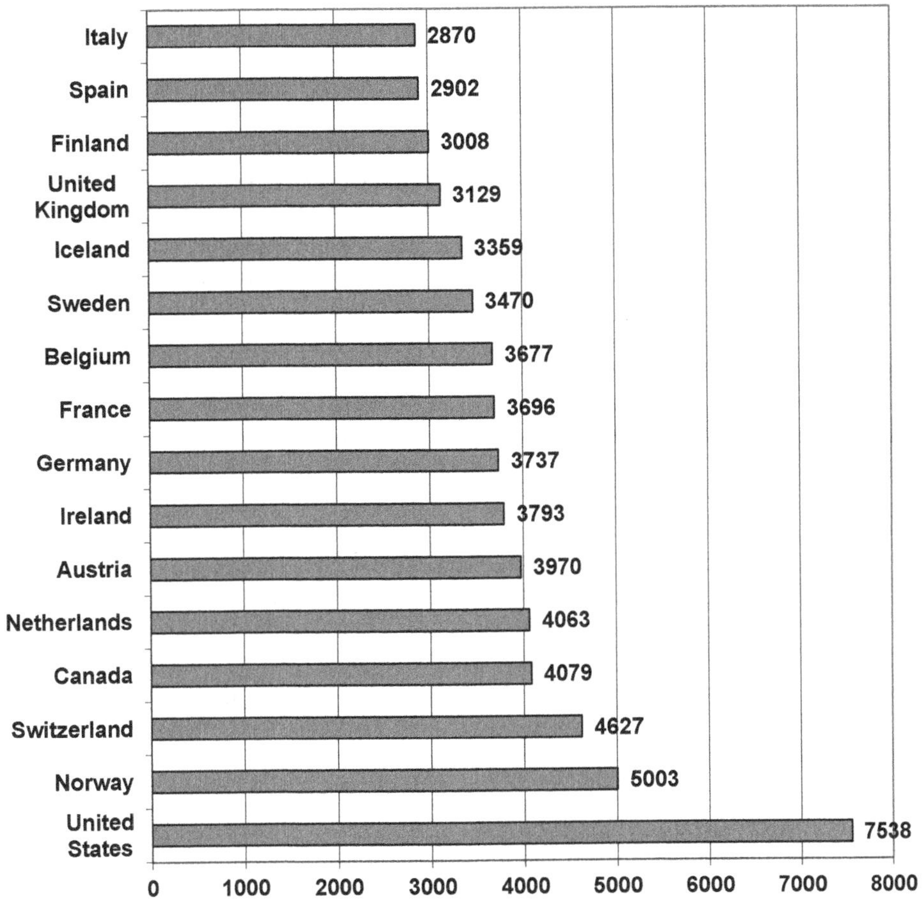

Italy	2870
Spain	2902
Finland	3008
United Kingdom	3129
Iceland	3359
Sweden	3470
Belgium	3677
France	3696
Germany	3737
Ireland	3793
Austria	3970
Netherlands	4063
Canada	4079
Switzerland	4627
Norway	5003
United States	7538

Source: OECD Health Data 1010–Version: June 2010

their ability to efficiently improve the quality of life. I call these inconvenient truths the "curses" of markets. There are intrinsic problems—such as pollution, imperfect and asymmetric information, transaction costs, bounded rationality, monopolies, power imbalances, social interaction, conspicuous consumption—that are associated with the workings of *real* free markets as opposed to imaginary ones, preventing them from working efficiently as they do on the blackboard. These problems are usually omitted from conventional textbooks at least at the undergraduate level even though many an economist received the Nobel Prize for illuminating these issues decades ago. To be sure, volumes have been written on these curses at the advanced level, but excluding them from introductory textbooks implies that millions of students leave their basic economics course without having seriously reflected on the nuances of the models discussed.

Of course, there are many practicing economists who disagree with the main thrust of the mainstream view and chide their colleagues for not questioning their own assumptions more seriously.[52] To be sure, conclusions reached by the process of deduction from assumptions as practiced by the mainstream are logically valid in theory, but could well turn out to be toxic at street level.[53]

MORALITY SHOULD TAKE PRECEDENCE OVER MARKETS

Being human inventions, markets ought not take precedence over our moral values. Markets are part of our cultural and ethical system, and we should arrange them in such a way that they do not exploit or hurt people, and distribute the fruits of the economy in an equitable fashion. If markets obviously do us harm or threaten us, then we, the people, ought to retain, must retain, the right to make alternative arrangements and take collective action to stop the pain caused by market processes. Market outcomes ought by no means be above ethical considerations. When they do not lead to a satisfactory outcome or when they malfunction, they should be modified.

The market system is with us, for better or for worse; a world without it is unimaginable—like a world without fire. Both undoubtedly improve our lives, but uncontrolled, both are dangerous and can have devastating consequences. Left to burn itself out, as it were—without the intervention of firefighters to contain the conflagration—the system would have culminated in 2008 in an even greater depression than the famous one of the 1930s. In short, free markets can be as devastating as forest fires if we do not learn to control them and to make sure that they serve our purposes and not the other way around. We should be vigilant that we do not become subservient to markets.

Moreover, there are many valuable socioeconomic and moral goals that markets are incapable of achieving, such as providing for an equitable distribution of rewards, insofar as even a small early advantage can bring about substantial subsequent benefits. For instance, markets were not particularly helpful in enabling African American citizens to purchase coffee at a lunch counter of their choice or to sit where they liked on buses and trains. People had to sacrifice their lives before the rights of a desegregated market were granted.[54] Also, selling babies might well be efficient from an economic point of view, but we decided against doing that out of moral considerations. So in principle we ought not to rely on markets to create a moral socioeconomic framework for us.

ECONOMICS IS A SOCIAL SCIENCE

Economics is not at all like a hard science. It is too insensitive to evidence contradicting its basic assumptions. Alternative theories as well as facts from other disciplines are disregarded, which is not accepted scientific practice. Would chemists be allowed to overlook results from physics? Certainly not! Yet economists regularly disregard results from psychology, sociology, political science, and other sister disciplines. Social psychology, for example, frames the problem of human action in terms of group dynamics. However, such group interactions are generally overlooked by economists, although economic activity obviously does take place in a society and within a political system and not between isolated individuals.[55] The use of mathematics for model building does not make economics into a rigorous science.[56]

Another reason why economics is not like a natural science is that it is not based on controlled experiments in the same way as psychology, for example. Essentially, economics is built on assumptions about people's behavior and motivation from which principles can be derived using deductive logic. This is similar to the methodology medieval philosophers used to argue about "how many angels can dance on the head of a pin." St. Thomas Aquinas, for example, assumed that God was perfect, infinite, and immutable.[57] If one were to imagine the nature of God in the abstract, this is the way God would be, according to Aquinas. Economists imagine perfect markets in which there is an authority figure called the auctioneer who calls out prices in a similar fashion. Just as Aquinas supposed that there is a perfect God and his theology followed from that, economists suppose that there is a perfect market with perfect competition without considering all its frictional components, distortions, and shortcomings.

Such a methodology is actually quite risky because intuitively plausible assumptions are not necessarily borne out by experiment. It seemed obvious and logical for a couple of thousand years after Aristotle that heavier objects fall faster than lighter ones until it was disproved by Galileo. Hence, experiments and experience are a more reliable guide to economics than theorems based on logical deductions from basic premises, which themselves are a matter of controversy.

Moreover, the results of experimental economics—particularly the anomalous ones—are not integrated into mainstream thought and are treated as epiphenomena. Their inconvenient results, such as those that contradict the rationality assumption, are mainly disregarded; by doing so, economists deviate from the scientific approach. Furthermore, the lack of precision of economic predictions implies that the models are rudimentary. Former Federal Reserve chairman Alan Greenspan's version of economic theory implied that markets won't crash, but that prediction was falsified. Yet there is no rush to scrap old theories so that such mistakes will be avoided in the future.

When the results of laboratory experiments contradict the fundamental assumptions of the economics discipline, these are ignored, in the main, or rationalized away as being insufficiently realistic. For example, in an experiment called the "ultimatum game" it was demonstrated without a shadow of a doubt that people have an innate sense of fairness that blatantly contradicts the common assumption that *Homo economicus* is selfish, guided by reason, and a utility maximizer. Instead, these experiments revealed the importance of emotion, empathy for others, and the feeling of revulsion if we believe that we were treated unfairly. Decisions are also mediated by hormonal levels that trigger emotional responses, rather than pure reason. In other words, our feelings of justice and honor enter into our interaction with others and our willingness to cooperate.

IDEOLOGY

Hence, as the discussion on Greenspan in the previous chapter implies, ideology is an integral part of economics and will continue to be so until it has a more substantial empirical foundation. Ideology stems from the judgments made about the appropriateness of initial assumptions. We are unable to organize our thoughts without making some initial assumptions, and these assumptions are necessarily a function of our own mindset, world view, and intellectual and emotional commitments, and therefore influence greatly the ideas deduced from them. Ideology is similar to a heuristic that enables us to get along in a complex world when we have to make decisions on limited information and are unable to understand fully the intricate network of interconnectedness among an infinite number of variables. It is our rule of thumb for action.

Hence, economics cannot be purged of ideology and perhaps never will be; our political, moral, and philosophical sympathies are reflected in our fundamental assumptions and, thus, in how we structure our thinking and our understanding of the world around us. Its conclusions are largely derived from assumptions, intuition, introspection, opinion, and yes, ideology.[58] That is one of the reasons there are so many different schools of economics—Neo-Keynesian, post-Keynesian, neoclassical, monetarist, heterodox, feminist, Austrian,[59] behavioral, institutional, evolutionary, socialist, Marxist, radical—and that is why economists do not have coherent advice on some of the most important issues of the day.[60]

QUESTIONS FOR DISCUSSION

1. Do you think that the "starving the beast" strategy has been successful? Is it moral?
2. Do you think that the social ills of the United States such as poverty and crime are rooted in the way the economic system distributes wealth?
3. How is it possible that so many people are struggling in the United States, one of the richest countries in the world?

4. Why is it that health care is so incredibly costly in the United States, yet the free market is unable to provide better health for the population than in the welfare states of Western Europe?
5. Why is the poverty rate so high in the United States?
6. Would you favor increasing taxes or decreasing military spending in order to lessen the poverty rate, improve the infrastructure, or invest in education and innovation?
7. Discuss: The quality of life in the United States is very good; people just do not appreciate what they have.
8. What are the differences between quality of life, living standards, income, and gross domestic product (GDP)?
9. Discuss: Market outcomes based on competition ought not to be questioned. They are above moral considerations.
10. Do you think people act rationally all the time, most of the time, some of the time, or none of the time?
11. What is the difference between the unemployed and the underemployed?
12. What kind of a labor market would you devise if you were deciding behind a "veil of ignorance," that is, not knowing where in the labor market you'd end up?
13. If children are not responsible for choosing their parents, then why should they inherit the living standards of their parents?
14. Is it fair to have such a high level of inequality as in the U.S.?
15. Should market outcomes be questioned from an ethical viewpoint?
16. What do governments do well?
17. Have you been tricked or entrapped into buying something you regretted?
18. Have you or someone you personally know been defrauded?
19. What essential services are markets not particularly good at providing?
20. What products are not provided by markets?
21. What does the "Achilles heel" of markets refer to?
22. Should we set ourselves the goal of catching up with Canada in life expectancy and with Finland in educational attainment?

NOTES

1. "[F]or the past quarter century we have worshiped the 'free' market as an ideology rather than for what it is—a natural product of human social evolution and a set of economic tools with which to construct a just and equitable society. Under the spell of this ideology and the false promise of instant riches the America's [sic] immigrant values of thrift, prudence and community concern—traditionally the foundation of the Dream—have been hijacked by an all-consuming self-interest." See Peter C. Whybrow, "Dangerously Addictive: Why We Are Biologically Ill-Suited to the Riches of Modern America," *The Chronicle of Higher Education*, March 13, 2009.

2. "We must not make an idol . . . out of the market," says Robert P. George, about 32 minutes into a 62-minute videotaped dialogue titled "The Scandal of the Cross," with Cornel West. See Bloggingheads: Greed Is Bad, *The New York Times*, 8:15, December 16, 2010.

3. Lawrence Summers, "Why Isn't Capitalism Working?" *Reuters*, January 9, 2012.

4. Arianna Huffington, *Third World America: How Our Politicians Are Abandoning the Middle Class and Betraying the American Dream* (New York: Crown, 2010); Robert Reich, *Aftershock: The Next Economy and America's Future* (New York: Knopf, 2010).

5. U.S. Department of Labor, Bureau of Labor Statistics, "The Employment Situation—July 2012."

6. U.S. Department of Labor, Bureau of Labor Statistics, "Table A-15. Alternative Measures of Labor Underutilization."

7. Of course, the amount of labor available is flexible, but given the wage rate, the institutional structure of the economy, and the amount of output demanded there was available work in the United States for only about 140 million people, of which 25 million were part-time workers.

8. United Nations Office on Drugs and Crime, *Global Study on Homicide* (Vienna: 2011), Table 8.1.

9. The U.S. murder rate of 42 per million per annum is in contrast to Canada's rate of 15 per million. "Murders (per capita) by Country," available at www.NationMaster.com.

10. Office of Justice Programs, Bureau of Justice Statistics, *Key Facts at a Glance: Correctional Populations*.

11. Cecil Adams, "Does the United States Lead the World in Prison Population?" *Straight Dope,* February 6, 2004. In many states, these people will be denied the right to vote after their release.

12. "Business and Non-Business Filings," BankruptcyAction.com. See also Teresa A. Sullivan, Elizabeth Warren, and Jay Lawrence Westbrook, *The Fragile Middle Class: Americans in Debt* (New Haven, CT: Yale University Press, 2001). Warren, formerly a professor at Harvard Law School and now senior U.S. senator from Massachusetts, has been working on the difficulties and challenges of contemporary middle-class American life. See, for example, her 2007 lecture "The Coming Collapse of the Middle Class: Higher Risks, Lower Rewards, and a Shrinking Safety Net." See also Juliet B. Schor, *The Overspent American: Why We Want What We Don't Need* (New York: HarperPerennial, 1999).

13. This number refers to those who experienced default notices, bank repossessions, and scheduled auctions. "Record 2.9 Million U.S. Properties Receive Foreclosure Filings in 2010 Despite 30-Month Low in December," RealtyTrac, January 12, 2011.

14. Erik Eckholm, "Recession Raises Poverty Rate to a 15-Year High," *The New York Times,* September 16, 2010.

15. "Gallup Daily: U.S. Life Evaluation," available at www.gallup.com/poll/110125/gallup-daily-life-evaluation.aspx.

16. Dan Witters, "Recession Persists in Terms of Americans' Access to Basic Needs," Gallup, July 15, 2011.

17. Mark Olfson, Steven C. Marcus, Benjamin Druss, Lynn Elinson, Terri Tanielian, and Harold A. Pincus, "National Trends in the Outpatient Treatment of Depression," *Journal of the American Medical Association* 287 (2002): 203–209; Steven C. Marcus and Mark Olfson, "National Trends in the Treatment for Depression from 1998 to 2007," *Archives of General Psychiatry* 67 (2010): 1265–1273.

18. Some 1.6 million people use shelters per annum. See U.S. Department of Housing and Urban Development, Press release for 2009 Annual Homeless Assessment Report to Congress; "About Homelessness," The National Alliance to End Homelessness. The number of homeless families (parent[s] with child) living in shelters increased from 130,000 to 170,000 in 2010. See Michael Luo, "Number of Families in Shelters Rises," *The New York Times,* September 11, 2010.

19. Not all of them were living full-time on the street though. Some were living in shelters, motels, or with other families. Marisol Bello, "Child Homelessness Up 33% in 3 Years," *USA Today,* December 13, 2011.

20. "The Forbes 400: The Richest People in America," *Forbes,* September 21, 2011.

21. U.S. Internal Revenue Service, S*OI Tax Stats—Individual Statistical Tables by Size of Adjusted Gross Income.*

22. Writing about the period prior to the Great Meltdown, Benjamin M. Friedman states, "the economy was doing pretty well, but most of the people in it were not. The chief reason is widening inequality." See Friedman, "Widening Inequality Combined with Modest Growth," *Challenge* (May–June 2009): 76–91.

23. Organization for Economic Cooperation and Development (OECD), *Growing Unequal? Income Distribution and Poverty in OECD Countries* (Paris: OECD, 2008); OECD, *Divided We Stand: Why Inequality Keeps Rising* (Paris: OECD, 2011).

24. National Center for Health Statistics, "Advance Report of Final Divorce Statistics, 1988," *Monthly Vital Statistics Report* 39 (1991) 12, suppl. 2.

25. Terry A. Lugaila, "Marital Status and Living Arrangements: March 1998 (Update)," *Current Population Reports* P20–514 (1998).

26. In a dozen metropolitan areas such as New York, Chicago, and Cleveland, the average poor black child lives in neighborhoods in which one-third of the children are poor. See Nancy McArdle, Theresa Osypuk, and Dolores Acevedo-Garcia, "Disparities in Neighborhood Poverty of Poor Black and White Children," *Diversity Data Briefs* 1 (2007).

27. About one-half of black youth graduate from high school. Half of the dropouts end up in prison by the time they are in their mid thirties. "Why Are 1 in 9 Black Men in Prison?" NAACP of Otero County, New Mexico, March 27, 2008.

28. UNICEF Innocenti Research Centre, *Child Poverty in Perspective: An Overview of Child Well-Being in Rich Countries* (Italy: The United Nations Children's Fund, 2007), Report Card 7.

29. "National Child Abuse Statistics," Childhelp; Centers for Disease Control and Prevention, "Nonfatal Maltreatment of Infants—United States, October, 2005–September 2006," *Morbidity and Mortality Weekly Report* 57 (2008) 13: 336–339.

30. Christopher P. Howson, Mary V. Kinney, and Joy E. Lawn, eds., *Born Too Soon: The Global Action Report on Preterm Birth* (Geneva: WHO, 2012).

31. "Our view is that teen childbearing is so high in the United States because of underlying social and economic problems. It reflects a decision among a set of girls to 'drop-out' of the economic mainstream; they choose nonmarital motherhood at a young age instead of investing in their own economic progress because they feel they have little chance of advancement." Melissa S. Kearney and Phillip B. Levine, "Why Is the Teen Birth Rate in the United States So High and Why Does It Matter?" *Journal of Economic Perspectives* 26 (2012) 2: 141–166.

32. "An International Education Test," *The New York Times,* December 7, 2010.

33. Editorial, "48th Is Not a Good Place," *The New York Times,* October 26, 2010.

34. Secretary of Education Arne Duncan said that this should be seen as a "wake-up call." Sam Dillon, "Top Test Scores from Shanghai Stun Educators," *The New York Times,* December 7, 2010.

35. "Beast" in this phrase refers to the government. The "starving the beast" strategy, based on the idea that if taxes are reduced then the increasing deficits will put downward pressure on expenditures as well, was first articulated by Alan Greenspan in a congressional testimony. The strategy was pernicious, because it fails to consider the government's ability to finance the deficit by borrowing. Bruce Bartlett, "Tax Cuts and 'Starving the Beast': The Most Pernicious Fiscal Doctrine in History," *Forbes,* May 7, 2012.

36. John Kenneth Galbraith, *The Affluent Society* (New York: Houghton Mifflin, 1958); Lester C. Thurow, "Galbraith, John Kenneth (1908–2006)," in *The New Palgrave Dictionary of Economics,* 2nd ed., ed. Steven N. Durlauf and Lawrence E. Blume (Basingstoke, UK: Palgrave Macmillan, 2008).

37. It was up from 31st in the previous year. "The Best and Worst Places to Be a Mom," PBS NewsHour video, May 8, 2012.

38. Jennifer Saranow Schultz, "Top Consumer Complaints in 2009," *The New York Times,* July 27, 2010.

39. Wikipedia contributors, "I-35W Mississippi River Bridge," *Wikipedia: The Free Encyclopedia;* Paul Krugman, "America Goes Dark," *The New York Times,* August 8, 2010; Bob Herbert, "The Corrosion of America," *The New York Times,* October 26, 2010; Walter Euken, *The Foundations of Economics: History and Theory in the Analysis of Economic Reality* (Berlin: Springer, 1950).

40. Joseph Stiglitz, *Freefall: America, Free Markets, and the Sinking of the World Economy* (New York: W.W. Norton, 2010).

41. The financial sector spent $2.7 billion on lobbying from 1999 to 2008, while individuals and committees affiliated with the industry made more than $1 billion in campaign contributions. Sewell Chan, "Financial Crisis Was Avoidable, Inquiry Finds," *The New York Times,* January 25, 2011.

42. Simon Johnson, "The Quiet Coup," *Atlantic,* May 2009.

43. The Supreme Court has exacerbated this development by an incomprehensible twist of the English language conceptualizing money as speech in its 2010 *Citizens United* decision, in which it interpreted the First Amendment so as to imply that corporations can spend an unlimited amount of funds on political campaigns. The decision has allowed big money to play an even larger role in the electoral process.

44. Chris Mooney, *The Republican War on Science* (New York: Basic Books, 2005); Andrew C. Revkin, "Climate Expert Says NASA Tried to Silence Him," *The New York Times,* January 29, 2006.

45. Nicholas Kristof, "A Woman. A Prostitute. A Slave," *The New York Times,* November 28, 2010.

46. Angus Deaton, "Income, Health, and Well-Being Around the World: Evidence from the Gallup World Poll," *Journal of Economic Perspectives* 22 (2008) 2: 53–72, p. 68.

47. Maggie Mahar, *Money-Driven Medicine: The Real Reason Health Care Costs So Much* (New York: Harper/Collins, 2006). People in Israel live 2.5 years longer but spend one-fourth of what U.S. citizens do on health care.

48. U.S. Census Bureau, *The 2012 Statistical Abstract: 107—Expectation of Life and Expected Deaths by Race, Sex, and Age:* 2008; Wikipedia contributor, "List of Countries by Life Expectancy," *Wikipedia: The Free Encyclopedia.*

49. Kevin Sieff, "The Plight of the High School Homeless," *Washington Post,* December 27, 2010.

50. Ralph Nader, *Unsafe at Any Speed. The Designed-In Dangers of the American Automobile* (New York: Grossman, 1965).

51. "Crib Information Center," U.S. Consumer Product Safety Commission.

52. See, for example, Heterodox Economics Newsletter. McCloskey declares that "the progress of economic science has been seriously damaged" by ivory-tower economics; Deirdre McCloskey, *Secret Sins.*

53. "Our criticism of the accepted classical theory of economics has consisted not so much in finding logical flaws in its analysis as in pointing out that its tacit assumptions are seldom or never satisfied, with the result that it cannot solve the economic problems of the actual world." John Maynard Keynes, *The General Theory of Employment, Interest and Money* (London: Macmillan, 1936), Chapter 24.

54. For instance, the civil rights activists Andrew Goodman, James Chaney, and Michael Schwerner were murdered in 1964.

55. Karl Polanyi, *The Great Transformation: The Political and Economic Origins of Our Time* (New York: Rinehart, 1944).

56. Ariel Rubinstein, "A Sceptic's Comment on the Study of Economics," *The Economic Journal* 116 (2006): C1–C9.

57. Wikipedia contributors, "Thomas Aquinas," *Wikipedia: The Free Encyclopedia.*

58. Steven Rappaport, "Abstraction and Unrealistic Assumptions in Economics," *Journal of Economic Methodology* 3 (1996) 2: 215–236.

59. The reference here is not to the nation, but to a school of economic thought.

60. Nick Wilkinson, *An Introduction to Behavioral Economics: A Guide for Students* (London: Palgrave/Macmillan, 2007); Binyamin Appelbaum, "Politicians Can't Agree on Debt? Well, Neither Can Economists," *The New York Times,* July 17, 2011.

PART II

CONSUMPTION ON AND OFF
THE BLACKBOARD

3

THE NATURE OF DEMAND

In this chapter we emphasize a few issues in the microeconomics of consumption that are generally either not discussed in introductory economics courses or are taught without proper balance. These issues are, however, necessary to understand the actual workings of real markets. Chapter 2 provided some criticisms of the mainstream approach. In this chapter we argue that mainstream economics is incomplete and hence misleading and that this has dire consequences for economic theory and policy. We emphasize the need to understand the psychology of consumption, an issue that is not taught sufficiently in standard treatments of the subject. This is of utmost importance, because by disregarding this aspect of the topic most introductory economics textbooks become anachronistic and will be overtaken by the newer budding field of behavioral economics. This chapter will provide an introduction to viewing demand from a behavioral perspective.

WHAT IS SCARCE?

Usually one of the first conventional assumptions is that we live in a world of scarcity, which implies that our desires are basically infinite. Yet our desires are not innately endless and depend fundamentally on external influences. In fact, most of our desires, except the obvious basic ones, are primarily culturally constructed. They are not fixed at birth. In other words, we are not born with a desire for iPhones. Thus, the demand for most of what we desire is by no means self-generated (exogenously given) except for such basic needs as food, clothing, and shelter.

To associate the overdeveloped part of the world, overflowing with goods, with a pervasive level of scarcity is a misapplication of the concept.[1] On the contrary, our societies in the developed world are best characterized as examples of abundance. Our closets and garages are cluttered with things we do not use and never needed. Actually scarce today are things such as stress-free leisure time with our family and friends, decent jobs, trust, respect for one another, and public goods such as good schools and safety. In contrast to the common wisdom, Mahatma Gandhi taught us that "Earth provides enough to satisfy every man's need, but not every man's greed."[2] If our desires are man-made and not natural, we should consider where they come from.

CONSUMER SOVEREIGNTY AND ENDOGENOUS TASTES

Consumer sovereignty is the doctrine that consumers dictate what businesses produce insofar as they "vote" with their dollars to channel production in such a way as to satisfy their desires (Figure 3.1). Tastes are supposedly determined outside of economics; that is to say, they are exogenous to the economic system. Insofar as they are predetermined, consumers' tastes, expressed through their wants, supposedly induce corporations to produce the right amount and quality of goods in order to satisfy those wants. In the end, the consumer is king as he/she determines what is being

Figure 3.1   **Consumer Sovereignty**

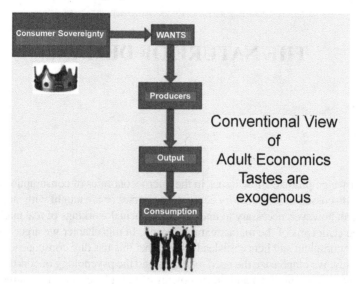

produced. If we would not demand stuff, firms would not produce stuff. So our wants are satisfied and everyone is happy, or at least it is claimed by conventional textbooks.

However, this model makes the crucial but unfounded assumption that tastes are exogenous, that is to say, that wants are completely determined even before the individual enters the economy. This presupposes that corporations do not affect our desires, that is, that consumers' likes and dislikes are immutable by the time they make decisions in the marketplace and are guided by their innate desire for products, such as iPhones, and act accordingly. This is a convenient but completely erroneous assumption as it is all too obvious that the corporate world influences our culture and desires in pro-found ways. Therefore our tastes are endogenous to the economic system. In other words, our wants are determined within the economic system in which corporations do influence our wants. Hence, the theory of consumer sovereignty is essentially pre-Freudian and pre-Pavlovian.[3] Sigmund Freud, the father of psychoanalysis, emphasized at the turn of the twentieth century that much of what we do is not under the control of the rational mind. We are often directed not by our prefrontal cortex but by emotions and desires of which we are unaware—which originate in the unconscious mind and are not subject to the laws of logic. These thought processes influence our actions in profound ways, motivate us, and induce feelings in us without our explicit awareness. Freud suggested that "Not only does the unconscious mind contain buried memories, but it is also the source of instinctive drives, particularly sexual and aggressive ones. Although the conscious mind has no direct access to the content of the unconscious mind, it is strongly affected by that content."[4] Though not all of Freud's ideas have withstood the test of time, the importance of the unconscious mind has remained a standard concept in cognitive psychology.[5] The important point is that the unconscious is not open to introspection. For example, the manipulation of children's unconscious by the media lays the foundation for a culture of consumerism and cannot be undone by rational processes once the child reaches adulthood.[6] Hence, it would be important to create an environment in which the development of children's unconscious mind is largely protected from business influence.

The other important psychological principle prominent in marketing,[7] though overlooked in economics, is Pavlovian conditioning, named after Ivan Pavlov, the Nobel Prize–winning Russian physiologist who discovered the phenomenon that dogs learned to respond involuntarily to stimulus. The dogs in Pavlov's experiment salivated in response to food; Pavlov found that if he added a stimulus by ringing a bell at the same time that he fed the dogs, they soon learned to associate the bell with the food. The dogs then began to salivate reflexively at the ringing of the bell, even without the food. Advertisers can take advantage of this kind of response by depicting young good-looking people with wide smiles in fashionable attire having a good time drinking a particular brand of soft drink. After a while we will involuntarily associate that soft drink with having a good time and purchase the product. This is called classical conditioning. We may choose to buy coke instead of milk without thinking about it and yet to an outside observer it may well appear as a rational decision.[8]

Another kind of conditioning is reinforcing behavior by rewarding it. That is the reason why we have many such programs as frequent-flyer miles, bonus points with credit cards, free gifts, and premiums. The conditioning starts at an early age: fast-food chains give away toys to toddlers as a way of conditioning them to want to frequent those eateries even when they no longer receive the toys[9] and "the firearms industry has poured millions of dollars into a broad campaign to ensure its future by getting guns into the hands of more, and younger, children."[10] Parents have not been successful in shielding their children from this multibillion-dollar effort at conditioning.

The discoveries of Freud and Pavlov pose a substantial challenge to conventional economics. The reason many economics texts ignore these major thinkers of the twentieth century is that their discoveries undermine the assumption upon which all of neoclassical economics rests, namely the rational agent model, which says that *Homo economicus,* who is objective about her wants, is super rational, and is in perfect control of her taste, emotions, and desires. This pre-Freudian and pre-Pavlovian perspective overlooks the fact that we do not enter the economy as adults with fully developed tastes. Instead, we enter the economy at birth, and develop mentally within that economy and therefore interact with it in critical ways from the very beginning of our lives. This is a critical oversight in most conventional economics textbooks.

WANTS AND BASIC NEEDS

Although the convention is to consider demand exclusively in terms of "wants," it is essential to distinguish between three sources of demand depending on the type of goods demanded (necessities, comforts and social necessities, and luxuries):

(A) Necessities are goods that fulfill basic survival needs, such as food sufficient to avoid hunger, safe drinking water to relieve thirst, shelter that includes sanitation facilities, clothing appropriate to the weather conditions, and medical care; we could not continue to live without these goods and services for long. Natural needs derived from the instincts of reproduction would also be in this category.[11]

(B) Comfort goods or products are considered socially necessary to live a dignified life in a particular society, such as an automobile in most areas in the United States, for example, because of the shortage of public transportation and the large distances that need to be traveled on a daily basis and the need for mobility for daily needs. Access to education, computer, and telephone are also in this category, as we cannot function effectively without these things in the society in which we live.

(C) Luxuries are goods that are not necessary for life either biologically or socially but (i) are consumed on account of an acquired taste; or (ii) are consumed because we are manipulated into wanting them; or (iii) are consumed in order to obtain social status by virtue of their being trendy or because of their exclusiveness due to their price. These are also called luxury goods, Veblen goods, or positional goods. These goods differ from the goods in the two previous categories in that they confer social status and thereby create a negative externality on others: envy. The share of these types of goods in total expenditures has increased over time from 20 percent in 1901 to 32 percent in 1950 to 50 percent by 2003.[12]

These distinctions should not be considered a complete typology but suffice to get us started thinking about the underlying source of demand and the key distinction between basic needs and wants. Even if this is a fuzzy distinction in some ways, it is crucial to understanding the fundamental differences between the consumption of bread, a used car, and a new BMW.[13] To conflate these goods under the general rubric of consumption misses a number of crucial attributes of these products. The above typology is based on two characteristics of demand: the source of the need for the good, and the consequences of being without it. The need for the goods in group A, above, stems from natural sources and is inherent to existing as a human biological organism. These goods enable us to survive and their lack is associated with pain, suffering, and even death, if they are not supplied in the right proportions. The need for goods in group B stems from the structure of a particular socioeconomic system, and these goods enhance one's capability to function with self-respect within that society.[14] Thus, access to the Internet and telephone facilitates communication necessary to work effectively in today's developed world, while being capable of driving to work or dressing in a manner required by the job description is a precondition of holding a job. In 2010, a single person earning less than $11,000 was considered poor by the U.S. government, while for a family of four the poverty line was at $22,000.[15] These amounts were deemed sufficient to meet basic needs (A) as well as minimum social needs in category (B).

In contrast to the first two types of goods, the need for luxury and status goods in group C stems from external sources influencing us to "keep up with the Joneses" or wanting to attain a higher position in society, or to avoid the shame of being seen as inferior or as an outsider. The satisfaction obtained from these goods is due to their exclusive nature, or habit, or having our subconscious manipulated in such a way that we associate a particular good with something desirable. People flaunt their wealth in order to attain social status, so these goods are highly visible. It is difficult to exhibit one's saving deposit unless one carries the bank statement around, and that is not considered socially appropriate behavior. Flaunting has its cultural norms as well.

In the affluent post-industrial societies the basic necessities of life make up a small share of total expenditures. Hence, the conventional assumption that "wants" are "unlimited" is by no means warranted for goods in groups A and B, especially since storage of goods is costly. Our priority as a society ought to be to meet the basic social and physical needs for all first before we indulge in luxuries. In other words, goods in groups A and B ought to take precedence over goods in group C. As the humanistic psychologist Erich Fromm put it: human rights should include "sufficient material basis to live a dignified human life. . . . A man has the same right as a dog has to live and not to starve."[16] Basic needs are finite, as the size of the stomach is limited.

The great problem with free-market economics is that Madison Avenue has the power to influence us in such a way that we feel a psychological dependence on consumption per se. Consequently, leaving consumption entirely up to free-market processes will never lead to a good life inasmuch as the market is not content with producing goods to satisfy the needs in groups A and B and devotes considerable effort and resources to induce people to covet goods in a capricious manner, subject to whim and impulse. It supports an excessive and insatiable desire for goods recommended by the rich, famous, beautiful, and powerful. In this fashion, we are made to feel that goods in group C actually belong in group A or B. In other words, we develop a Pavlovian conditioned response to advertisements to such a degree that we are not even conscious of our dependence. Corporations have gained the upper hand by creating fads and inducing us to buy their products. They succeed in imposing upon us their worldview through their full-court-press marketing campaigns.[17] We would be much more frugal and our wants would be much more modest otherwise. Our wants have become so extravagant through the influence of nearly $300 billion per annum expenditure tempting us to buy and consume today and not wait until tomorrow.[18] That amount of money is a persuasion bombshell and just a little less than the value of the output of the automobile sector in 2010.[19] In contrast, practically no one is telling us to be circumspect, frugal, or less impulsive shoppers.[20]

We should consider the hierarchy of needs as outlined by the humanistic psychologist Abraham Maslow. For instance, 3 of the 8 Millennium Development Goals of the United Nations pertain to health: child health, maternal health, and combating diseases. Furthermore, Articles 23 and 25 of the UN's Universal Declaration of Human Rights state that "Everyone . . . has the right to social security" and "to a standard of living adequate for the health and well-being of himself and of his family, including food, clothing, housing and medical care and necessary social services, and the right to security in the event of unemployment, sickness, disability, widowhood, old age or other lack of livelihood in circumstances beyond his control." Mothers and children are singled out for being "entitled to special care and assistance."

However, the mainstream is oblivious to the distinction between basic needs and wants, thereby adopting a misleading framework. This omission is by no means benign. It has major consequences on account of the fact that it enables economists to tolerate deprivation and ill health among the poor while the elites are spending obscene amounts of dollars on birthday parties with impunity.[21] If there is no distinction between needs and wants, then it is unnecessary to be concerned with such lopsided consumption: the health of a baby does not take priority over a quarter-million dollars spent on children's playhouses.[22] Yet basic needs in the estimation of most of mankind have a different place in the scheme of consumption than Andrey Melnichenko's $300 million yacht,[23] or the 300,000 breast augmentation procedures performed in the United States in 2011 at a cost of about $10,000 each.[24] (That adds up to about 10 of Melnichenko's yachts.) Instead of being sovereigns, we have become willing executioners of business interests as we are socialized into the established mode of consumption and accepting the degree of income inequality.

BUDGET CONSTRAINT

The income of the consumer is her budget constraint. In Figure 3.2, given prices of x and y one could buy a maximum of Qmax(x) if one spent all of one's money on buying x or a maximum of Qmax(y) if one spent all of one's money on buying y. The straight line connecting these two points indicates the combination of x and y that are feasible to purchase given one's income. Then one is supposed to choose that combination of x and y where the constraint reaches the highest level of indifference curve. That is the optimum combination that maximizes utility. The problem with this theory is that the constraint is not as firm as suggested, given the availability of credit. So most people face a "soft" or a "fuzzy" budget constraint. Purchasing on credit has increased considerably in recent decades, so income is no longer a constraint on current consumption as it used to be. In 1970, the amount of revolving consumer credit outstanding in the United States (in 2010 prices) was $220 per adult, whereas in 2010 it was $3,500, an increase by a factor of 16.[25] The hard budget constraint is not a very useful concept for today's consumer.

INDIFFERENCE CURVES

Indifference curves indicate the combination of goods (x and y in Figure 3.2) that yields the same amount of utility. Hence, the amount of utility along one of the lines is a constant. One problem with the highly stylized indifference curve analysis is that we are not buying x and y—say, food and clothing—at either the same time or the same place. This is challenging because at the time I am buying food I have only a vague notion of what clothing costs and I am not sure when I will get

Figure 3.2   **Conventional Depiction of Indifference Curves**

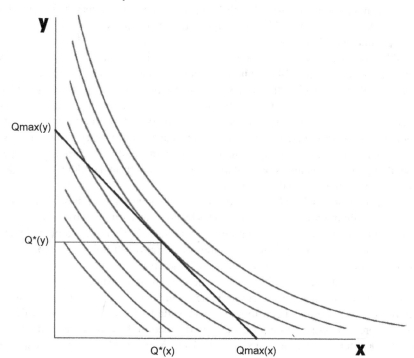

around to buying clothing. So I have to balance buying food now for a price I am able to ascertain, with buying clothing in the future at a price that is fuzzy. Hence, the decision needs to be framed in terms of fuzzy logic, which has not yet been well integrated into economics.[26]

Psychologist Daniel Kahneman, who received the Nobel Prize in economics, points out another problem, namely that the standard indifference curve diagram fails to indicate the current level of consumption. It is as though we've never consumed food and clothing before, so we come to the problem in a pristine state, without indicating the amounts of food and clothing we are adapted to. This is important not only because the level of consumption we are accustomed to is important, but also because of the endowment effect. This effect implies that people are willing to give up an object only at a higher price than the price at which it was acquired, that is, it is psychologically more difficult to give up an object than to acquire it.[27]

This, however, implies that there is a kink in the indifference curves at the current level of consumption: lowering consumption of x below the current level requires a larger amount of a compensating good y to maintain the same level of utility than if there were an increase in x. An increase in x would require less y to maintain the same level of utility. In other words, decreasing one's consumption from the current level is more painful than increasing consumption from the current level is beneficial. "[The standard indifference curve] depends on the implicit assumption that indifference curves are reversible. That is, if an individual owns x and is indifferent between keeping it and trading it for y, then when owning y the individual should be indifferent about trading it for x. If loss aversion is present, however, this reversibility will no longer hold."[28] Experimental evidence contradicts the standard assumption that indifference curves are smooth and that they do not cross. It does make a difference what one's initial endowment is. This is the endowment effect: there is some discomfort associated with giving something up: there is a "status quo" bias.

CHAPTER SUMMARY

In this chapter we discussed different kinds of goods and distinguished between necessities and luxuries. We argued that our unconscious is open to being manipulated by the media. Advertisers make profit by convincing or conditioning us to think that we need stuff that powerful corporations want to sell.[29] However, this does not lead to a good life because we are never allowed to remain satisfied. We are continually made to feel like we do not have enough if we do not have the latest gadgets. Hence, rather than being sovereign, we lose our control over our consumption. We have to replace adult economics with an economics that begins at birth and acknowledges that tastes are endogenous. Most importantly, we need to protect the individuality of our children from the conditioning of the corporate world. That can only be accomplished if we can limit the power of Madison Avenue from depicting an unrealistic view of the American Dream.

QUESTIONS FOR DISCUSSION

1. Do we live in an age of scarcity?
2. Can you give examples of firms trying to condition you to buy their product?
3. Can you give examples of firms trying to influence your unconscious so you'll buy their product?
4. Do you think it is worthwhile to seek status?
5. Have you bought something in order to impress your friends?
6. Are your purchases influenced by Madison Avenue or by Hollywood?
7. Do you know anyone who copies what celebrities wear?
8. Does keeping up with the Joneses lead to a satisfactory life?
9. Do you think that conspicuous consumption is socially acceptable?
10. Can you name some Veblen goods?
11. Do you think that a BMW is a basic need?
12. Is there a difference between fixing a toothache and buying a luxury yacht?
13. Do you think that basic needs including health care should be available to everybody in society?
14. What do you think of a tax on frivolous products such as plastic surgery undertaken for reasons of vanity?
15. Do you know people who are maxed out on their credit cards?
16. Do you know people who charge products frivolously on their credit cards?
17. Do you think people spend similarly when paying cash or paying with a credit card?
18. Do you think that mothers and babies should be entitled to health care?
19. How much credit card debt do your parents have? What did they spend it on?
20. Have you ever regretted purchasing something or signing a contract?

NOTES

1. According to James Crotty, *The Wall Street Journal* observed that "from cashmere to blue jeans, silver jewelry to aluminum cans, the world is in oversupply." See also James Crotty, "Why There Is Chronic Excess Capacity—The Market Failures Issue," *Challenge* 6 (2002): 21–44.

2. Ernst F. Schumacher also argued a generation ago that less is more: "A Buddhist economist would consider . . . [the conventional] approach excessively irrational: since . . . the aim should be to obtain the maximum of well-being with the minimum of consumption. . . ." and the "essence of civilisation [is] not in a multiplication of wants but in the purification of human character." See Ernst F. Schumacher, *Small Is Beautiful: Economics As If People Mattered* (New York: Harper Torchbook, 1973). By "accomplishing so little," he means that it provides so little satisfaction.

3. Actually, it is adult economics insofar as it disregards the crucial first 18 or so years of life.

4. Peter Gray, *Psychology,* 4th ed. (New York: Worth, 2002), 17.

5. Louis M. Augusto, "Unconscious Knowledge: A Survey," *Advances in Cognitive Psychology* 6 (2010): 116–141.

6. Juliet Schor, *Born to Buy: The Commercialized Child and the New Consumer Culture* (New York: Scribner, 2005).

7. Philip Kotler and Gary Armstrong, *Principles of Marketing,* 14th ed. (New York: Prentice Hall, 2011).

8. Similarly, ads for Marlboro cigarettes target men by associating the smoking of Marlboros with a macho image, while other brands are marketed to women using images of sophisticated or liberated females.

9. Center for Science in the Public Interest, "CSPI to Sue McDonald's If It Continues Using Toys to Market Junk Food to Children," June 22, 2010.

10. Mike McIntire, "Selling a New Generation on Guns," *The New York Times,* January 26, 2013.

11. The UN Universal Declaration of Human Rights states, "Everyone has the right to a standard of living adequate for the health and well-being of himself and of his family, including food, clothing, housing and medical care and necessary social services, and the right to security in the event of unemployment, sickness, disability, widowhood, old age or other lack of livelihood in circumstances beyond his control."

12. U.S. Department of Labor, Bureau of Labor Statistics, *100 Years of U.S. Consumer Spending: Data for the Nation, New York City, and Boston: 1950.* Last modified August 3, 2006.

13. Lotfi A. Zadeh, "Fuzzy Logic and Approximate Reasoning," *Synthese* 30 (1975): 407–428.

14. Amartya Sen, *Commodities and Capabilities* (Amsterdam: North-Holland, 1985).

15. "How the Census Bureau Measures Poverty," U.S. Census Bureau, last modified June 25, 2012.

16. "The right of each man to unfold as an individual and as a human being" should be our goal, according to Erich Fromm. "Erich Fromm pt. 1," YouTube video, 10:04, posted by "Oisin29," November 14, 2008.

17. Nick Wingfield, "All the World's a Game, and Business Is a Player," *The New York Times,* December 23, 2012.

18. Douglas Galbi, "U.S. Advertising Expenditure Data," *Purple Motes,* September 14, 2008.

19. U.S. Department of Commerce, Bureau of Economic Analysis, *Income and Product Accounts Tables: Table 1.2.5. Gross Domestic Product by Major Type of Product,* last revised August 29, 2012.

20. Exceptions are anticonsumerist organizations such as Adbusters, founded by Kalle Lasn, and people like Naomi Klein, who advocate against addictive consumerism.

21. Former CEO of Tyco International Dennis Kozlowski spent $2 million on his wife's birthday party but ended up in jail for unscrupulous business practices. See Wikipedia contributors, "Dennis Kozlowski," *Wikipedia: The Free Encyclopedia.*

22. "Childhood is a precious and finite thing," said one of the builders of these houses. "And a special playhouse is not the sort of thing you can put off until the economy gets better." See Kate Murphy, "Child's Play, Grown-Up Cash," *The New York Times,* July 20, 2011.

23. Robert Frank, "Baccarat Meets Bomb-Proof Glass on the High Seas," *The Wall Street Journal,* April 23, 2010.

24. Leeann Morrissey, "Plastic Surgery Statistics: Breast Augmentation Increases in Volume," available at www.plasticsurgery.com/breast-augmentation/plastic-surgery-statistics-breast-augmentation-increases-in-volume-a1173.aspx. There were also 20,600 chin implants performed for about $5,000 each in 2011. Lauren Keiper, "Best Face Forward: Chin Implants Surge in Popularity," *Reuters,* May 3, 2012.

25. Nonrevolving credit, that is, for cars and education, amounted to $5,600 per adult in 1970 and $7,000 in 2010, so that increased moderately. See U.S. Census Bureau, *The 2012 Statistical Abstract: 1190—Consumer Credit Outstanding and Finance Rates;* U.S. Department of Labor, Bureau of Labor Statistics, *Consumer Price Index.*

26. Zadeh, "Fuzzy Logic."

27. This psychological principle invalidates the Coase theorem according to which an efficient allocation will obtain in case of an externality regardless of the initial allocation of a property right as long as there are no transaction costs. The reason why the endowment effect invalidates this theorem is that the person who has the initial allocation of the property right might well demand a higher price to give it up than the other person is willing to pay for it. So the initial allocation of rights can determine the final outcome, which may not be efficient. See Daniel Kahneman, Jack L. Knetsch, and Richard H. Thaler, "Experimental Tests of the Endowment Effect and the Coase Theorem," *Journal of Political Economy* 98 (1990) 6: 1325–1348.

28. With an endowment effect, indifference curves can also cross. See Daniel Kahneman, Jack Knetsch, and Richard Thaler, "Anomalies: The Endowment Effect, Loss Aversion, and Status Quo Bias," in *Choices, Values, and Frames,* ed. Daniel Kahneman and Amos Tversky (Cambridge, UK: Cambridge University Press, 2000), 159–170.

29. Advertisement creates a feeling of scarcity in us so that we feel deprived unless we own the latest gadget. This is difficult to resist because the mind is so focused on the deprivation that it has a difficult time overcoming the temptation. See Sendhil Mullainathan and Eldar Shafir, *Scarcity: Why Having Too Little Means So Much* (New York: Times Books, 2013).

4

IS THERE A RATIONAL ECONOMIC DECISION MAKER?

The biggest mistake in economic theory is its clinging to the fiction that markets are inhabited by rational agents although all psychologists agree that this is dead wrong. Psychologists should know since they study the mind on an experimental basis. In this chapter we stress the importance of abandoning the rational-agent utility-maximizing model and explore the importance of intuition, emotion, power, and status seeking in economic behavior.

UTILITY MAXIMIZATION

The conventional assumption in economics is that people are rational, they know what they want; they need no help from anyone else. Consequently, they can maximize their own welfare, referred to as utility. Rationality is the use of reasoning in order to achieve optimal ends in an objective manner logically, without emotion, reflex, intuition, or instinct.[1] One consumes in such a way as to obtain the most satisfaction out of the money and time spent. In order to be able to accomplish this: (a) the consumer needs to have perfect knowledge of all goods (she should not be confused about quality and should read the fine print carefully); (b) she needs to know her own preferences (utility function) so that she can arrange the goods in order of her preferences; (c) she should not choose randomly or capriciously: her preferences should be stable; and (d) transitivity has to hold in her preferences, that is to say, if she likes hamburgers better than hot dogs and hot dogs better than grilled cheese, then if she is rational, she must like hamburgers better than grilled cheese sandwiches. The reasons behind these conditions are understandable: if the consumer does not know all the attributes of all the goods available to her, as well as their prices and their qualities, then she would not be able to make a rational choice among them. If she does not know herself sufficiently to know what she likes or dislikes, how could she possibly satisfy her desires? And if transitivity did not hold, she would not be able to order the goods according to her preferences. She would be incoherent.

The above set of assumptions has been used extensively, because they are eloquent and simple and because a lot of interesting models and theorems can be derived from them. When consumers maximize their utility and producers produce under perfectly competitive conditions, the economy will be efficient provided there are no externalities. And that is a desirable result. So economists are quite fond of this assumption, which implies that people choose consistently with reason, thinking through their needs and wants, with full knowledge of prices and the quantities they want. Their actions are governed by logic rather than habit or intuition.

However, textbook examples are always straightforward: they provide examples in which the choice is between a very simple set of alternatives. It is a single decision among well-known generic goods and no time dimension is involved. Surely one knows whether one likes hot dogs better than grilled cheese at this moment and under such circumstances a self-interested consumer should be able to choose satisfactorily without much trouble. This simple choice is essentially a "no brainer" requiring no judgment.

However, such examples are fundamentally misleading because they make it appear as though the procedure for such a simple decision can be generalized and applied to all economic choices, including much more complex ones, or ones that require a sequence of decisions and for which quality is extremely difficult to ascertain and which include lots of fine print and attention to detail. Decisions pertaining to mortgages, insurance, cell phone contracts, apartment leases, investments, or buying any complex product that one does not purchase frequently are qualitatively different from buying cereal.[2] Hence, the simple examples and the generalizations derived from them to complex products is a major mistake of standard economics with unfortunate consequences for consumers' welfare. Rationality is an insidious assumption because it implies that consumer protection is superfluous, thereby making it difficult for many consumers to navigate smoothly through our complex economic system. Without consumer protection there are too many gullible people who fall prey to unscrupulous marketing techniques.

UTILITY MAXIMIZATION IS IMPOSSIBLE FOR FINITE MINDS

Every single psychologist, including Daniel Kahneman, knows perfectly well that humans are incapable of being rational and of maximizing utility in a coherent manner.[3] Understandably, we do not like to admit it, insofar as much of what we do appears obviously right to us on the surface, but our brain is incapable of living up to such expectations. "The purely economic man is indeed close to being a social moron."[4] With this memorable assertion, Noble Prize–winning Harvard economist Amartya Sen refuted the concept of *Homo economicus* for a litany of reasons. We are often unaware of why we desire something, as the reasons are hidden from our conscious thought processes or are embedded in evolutionary physiology, as is our craving for sweets. Our attention span is limited, we experience information overload, we do not have the time to pay attention to the contract we are signing, we lose our patience, we act impulsively, and we have great difficulty assessing probabilities. Moreover, usually there is not enough time to think about decisions carefully, and insufficient time to sort out the relevant information from background noise; we also have difficulty assessing the quality of information. All these issues play a role in our inability to reach an optimum decision, and explain why we frequently make mistakes and come to regret the decisions we made.

Most decisions call for human judgment under conditions of uncertainty about outcomes whose probability is known only vaguely. Hence, very few of our decisions, from the most trivial to the most momentous, can be considered rational. They are informed, in the main, by our unconscious, by wishful thinking, faith, intuition, and emotion, and are based on partial knowledge or are merely random. We also make vague guesses about probabilities. We discuss below the evidence supporting this perspective.[5]

OUR BRAIN

We are unable to doggedly pursue our self-interest to maximize our utility because our brain is imperfect. It is a product of evolution, as are all our other organs, and that implies that we do not have the brain of a Superman; we do not all have an IQ score of 130, as academic economists seem to believe. Our brain is much more complex than economists think it is. It is made up of many specialized modules, which sometimes work together well, but at other times hold contradictory beliefs, vacillate between polar opposites, and violate strongly held moral beliefs.[6]

According to Peter Whybrow, professor of psychiatry at UCLA and award-winning author, "The human brain is a hybrid: an evolved hierarchy of three-brains-in-one." We have a reptilian "lizard" brain, which controls our bodily functions such as our breathing and heart muscles. Around this primitive core developed, during the course of millennia, "the limbic cortex . . . the early mammalian brain, which is the root of kinship behavior and nurturance."[7] The expansion of this part of the brain culminated in the development of our species' unique prefrontal lobes, which is where reasoning takes place. While this enables us to reason, that does not imply that every choice we make is made through rational thinking using perfect information. If the process of making choices in our self-interest came to us so easily, our society would not be so frustrated. There would not be so many of us discontented with our lives, struggling, unhappy, depressed, taking Prozac, wantonly killing people, or behind bars. If this is the best we can do maximizing utility, our brains must not be such reliable guides to action.

Our brain, our hormones, our genetic make-up, our nervous system all stand in the way of making rational decisions. Whybrow continues: "we remain driven by our ancient desires. Desire is as vital as breathing . . . [but] when the brain's reward circuits are overloaded or unconstrained, then desire can turn to craving and to an addictive greed that co-opts executive analysis and commonsense."[8] In other words, the rational part of our brain is not always in control of our actions. Our craving for sweets, for instance, provided an evolutionary advantage millennia ago when nourishment was scarce. But evolution did not give us hormones to switch off this desire, nor the will power to resist it. Thus, when combined with the ability of companies to profit from selling sugary drinks, our uncontrollable cravings make us sick by inducing a diabetic epidemic. So roughly two-thirds of the U.S. population has became either overweight or obese. In sum, our hormonal system and our cravings, which came into being through evolutionary time, help explain why the rational utility-maximizing model is unrealistic.

Evolution did not favor only rationality. In the course of evolution it would not have been optimal to rely entirely on reasoning in making decisions as hunters and gatherers, because many significant problems could not be solved logically given the uncertainties and incomplete information normally associated with them. In such complex circumstances, rationality could have led us to become catatonic. Instead, we were selected for being able to make quick decisions on little information. Sometimes we could reason through a problem, but more frequently our actions were guided by intuition, emotion, instinct, judgment, reflex, stereotypes, conditioning, as well as by our unconscious. After millions of years of evolution we continue to make decisions in such a manner, often using contradictory and inconclusive information. In other words, human beings have not become optimal decision makers through evolution.

Nonetheless, our brain is as wonderful an instrument as our eyes, but note that evolution did not eliminate either the "blind spot" or color blindness. In short, none of our organs is perfect. They nonetheless have sufficed to ensure our reproduction. Similarly with consumption: our mental abilities are good enough to ensure our survival and reproduction, but optimality is not within our reach in our extremely complex world. It is not useful to consider rationality as a binary characteristic. "Human behavior . . . requires a fluid interaction between controlled and automatic processes. . . . However, many behaviors that emerge from this interplay are routinely and falsely interpreted as being the product of cognitive deliberation alone. . . . [W]e naturally tend to exaggerate the importance of control."[9]

NEUROECONOMICS

The brain is made up of 100 billion neurons. Neurons communicate with each other using chemical signals. Economists have recently begun exploring how our neural networks affect economic behavior and thus the field of neuroeconomics was born. Experiments were conducted using functional magnetic resonance imaging, which registers blood flow in the capillaries of the brain and thereby identifies neurons firing electrochemical signals. These experiments revealed weaknesses in the standard theory of utility maximization. Brain activity showed that the hardwired circuits postulated by standard decision theory are not always activated. The brain can use other processes as well. For instance, if the choice is to be made between an alternative involving certainty and one involving choice, the processing takes place in a different part of the brain than when both alternatives are risky.[10] Amazingly, parallel processors are used for different tasks, and the hardwired circuits of reason are not always in control. This can also explain why emotions can override rational considerations. "[B]rain mechanisms combine controlled and automatic processes, operating using cognition and affect [emotion]. . . . [R]eason has its hands full with headstrong passions and appetites."[11]

BOUNDED RATIONALITY

More than half a century ago, Herbert Simon argued convincingly that rationality has its limits: people are unable to maximize a utility function in the real world insofar as it is beyond their capacity to do so. Simon received a Nobel Prize in economics for his research, yet many textbooks continue to ignore his insights even though it is widely recognized that "psychology and economics provide wide-ranging *evidence* that bounded rationality is important."[12] Actually, it is so important that I believe it should be the default model in economics instead of the more convenient optimizing-rational-agent one.

The utility function is an abstraction; it does not exist in reality as our ability to feel temperature or see light does. Not being able to optimize an imaginary utility function does not mean that we are altogether silly, but we need to recognize that in actual decision-making optimization is beyond our capacity. It would be too burdensome even if we had the cognitive ability to do so. Off the blackboard we have too many serious limitations that constrain us from attaining an optimum consumption bundle. These limitations might be lack of information of price or quality, limitations of our own intelligence to ascertain the conditions specified in a contract, inability to assign probabilities to future events, inability to pay attention to a salesperson's presentation, forgetting to ask all relevant questions, or misunderstanding the terms of a contract. The limitation might also be information overload by which one has too much information for the brain's working memory capacity and it leads to confusion, misinterpretation, or misjudgment, or it might be time pressure—not having enough time to think about a problem.[13] If we are harried or under stress we may not be able to concentrate on understanding all the properties of the product we are buying. The causes of bounded rationality are innumerable.

An additional issue is that with most important decisions, we are not immediately aware of the alternatives offered. It takes time, effort, and money—transactions costs—to find out what kinds of health insurance are being offered. Generating these alternatives and then understanding them is a lengthy undertaking requiring patience and perseverance, and a major hindrance to achieving an optimum in a world that has become extremely complex. We are able to solve the kind of trivial and transparent problems presented in textbooks. However, the problem becomes intractable when deciding among multifaceted products such as health insurance, employers, or a career, especially if the counterparty attempts to hide conditions and obfuscates the terms relevant to the choice. Only a Superman or Superwoman could separate fact from fiction and find the optimum under such adverse circumstances, but with our limited cognitive capacity the ordinary human mind has no chance at all to ascertain the optimum in finite time.

Thus, the concept of bounded rationality implies that even when we do as well as we can, we are far from achieving the perfect solution. Choice involves much more than picking between two simple alternatives; it is a problem-solving process requiring a great deal of intelligence, patience, experience, and ultimately human judgment more often than not associated with probabilities. This complex and difficult process of searching for alternatives and examining their consequences in real time prior to making the choice is completely left out of consideration in conventional textbooks.

I had to buy health insurance recently and it became quite obvious to me that the insurance companies are pursuing a strategy to avoid transparency as much as possible by offering plans that are very complicated and structured differently from other plans so that comparison with other offers becomes impossible in practice. Their strategy works in the sense that it softens competition. They do their utmost to hide the essence of the plans from the consumer. In such a case, we have little chance of making an informed rational decision. I used several rules of thumb as I purchased the plan and kept my fingers crossed, but was far from making a rational decision. The companies can devote considerable energy to outsmarting me. For instance, I had a couple of hours to devote to solving this complex problem and no one to turn to for credible advice, whereas the insurance companies can hire an army of math wizards to devote themselves full time to outsmarting people like me. Guess who will win that contest? Corporations have their tricks to outmaneuver the consumer most of the time as they have many more resources to tilt the playing field to their advantage. When I did receive the booklet describing the terms of the contract, it was some 80-pages long. I did not have time to read it.

Consider the drug plans offered for Medicare Part D (Figure 4.1). I do not think there is a mortal on earth who could ascertain what the best plan for her is in a reasonable time. Under such circumstances one resorts to simplification by using a rule of thumb.[14] Insurance corporations obviously make the offer in this opaque way in order to make it difficult to understand the details of the policy so that competition would not eliminate their profit. To be sure, there are organizations that sometimes help consumers make reasoned decisions, such as the AARP and Consumers Union, but these affect but a tiny fraction of our consumption decisions.

SATISFICING

A person constrained by bounded rationality will not be able to maximize her utility and will choose a simpler way to satisfy her desires using a rule of thumb. She will search until she finds a satisfactory solution, given her level of aspirations. This way of deciding is called satisficing. In the mid-1950s, Herbert Simon demonstrated that people seek to find a satisfactory solution to the problem at hand and do not seek the best possible outcome—because that is much too difficult and therefore unattainable.[15] Given the limitations of our brain to process information, the constraints of time and of finances, the harried lives we live, the incredible amount of information we need to process, and the complexity of the problems to be solved, we are content with satisficing, that is, finding a good-enough solution. Trying to maximize would be much too difficult; it would get us bogged down in everyday life, would be frustrating, and ultimately would lead to paralysis. Satisficing is much more realistic than the maximization approach.

One of the critical consequences of the satisficing model is that the sequence in which choices are presented makes a difference to the ultimate outcome, whereas in the maximizing model with

Figure 4.1 **Medicare Part D**

AARP MedicareRx Preferred (PDP) (S5820-007-0)

	Estimated Annual Drug Costs:[?]	Monthly Premium: [?]	Deductibles:[?] and Drug Copay/ Coinsurance: [?]	Drug Restrictions: [?]	Drug Coverage: [?]	Estimated Annual Health and Drug Costs:[?]	Overall Plan Rating:[?]	
☐	$1,670	$33.40 Drug: $33.40 Health:N/A	Annual Drug Deductible: $0.00 Health Plan Deductible: N/A Drug Copay/ Coinsurance: $7 - $81, 33%	N/A	All Your Drugs on Formulary: N/A No Gap Coverage	$4,800 Includes $3,138 for Original Medicare	★★★✦ 3.5 out of 5 stars	Enroll

First Health Part D Premier (PDP) (S5768-039-0)

	Estimated Annual Drug Costs:[?]	Monthly Premium: [?]	Deductibles:[?] and Drug Copay/ Coinsurance: [?]	Drug Restrictions: [?]	Drug Coverage: [?]	Estimated Annual Health and Drug Costs:[?]	Overall Plan Rating:[?]	
☐	$1,752	$37.00 Drug: $37.00 Health:N/A	Annual Drug Deductible: $150.00 Health Plan Deductible: N/A Drug Copay/ Coinsurance: $10, 15% - 32%	N/A	All Your Drugs on Formulary: N/A No Gap Coverage	$4,900 Includes $3,138 for Original Medicare	★★★✦ 3.5 out of 5 stars	Enroll

Humana Enhanced (PDP) (S5884-066-0)

	Estimated Annual Drug Costs:[?]	Monthly Premium: [?]	Deductibles:[?] and Drug Copay/ Coinsurance: [?]	Drug Restrictions: [?]	Drug Coverage: [?]	Estimated Annual Health and Drug Costs:[?]	Overall Plan Rating:[?]	
☐	$1,807	$46.00 Drug: $46.00 Health:N/A	Annual Drug Deductible: $0.00 Health Plan Deductible: N/A Drug Copay/ Coinsurance: $7 - $74, 33%	N/A	All Your Drugs on Formulary: N/A Call plan for details	$4,950 Includes $3,138 for Original Medicare	★★★ 3 out of 5 stars	Enroll

perfect information it does not. In the food example, it makes no difference in which sequence a hamburger is presented: I still know that I prefer it over a hot dog or a grilled cheese sandwich. This choice is presented in such a way that considerations of time and space do not play a role.

Now, let's try out the two models in an imaginary supermarket. The choice at a supermarket is not between two items, as in the textbooks, but among 25,000 items, and my cognitive capacity is unable to handle that amount of information. Hence, as I enter the market I know neither all the goods being offered for sale nor their prices, thereby violating a basic precondition of optimization. Under such circumstances, maximization is out of the question and I resort to shortcuts to accomplish my goals: I satisfice, meaning, I seek an acceptable solution to the problem at hand.

I choose an aisle and the products come into view sequentially. My choices early on influence my subsequent decisions. I see some chicken fingers in the deli department and they look good enough for dinner. I buy some. Yet, if I see another option later on, such as frozen pizza on sale in another aisle, I will not buy it, because it would take too much effort to return the chicken fingers to the deli section. Social norms prevent me from merely leaving the chicken fingers in the pizza section and taking the pizza instead. However, if I had gone down the frozen food section first and I had noticed the pizza on sale, I would have bought it instead of the chicken fingers. In other words, I was not confronted with a fixed set of alternatives as I entered the store. I had to search in real time and space in a purposeful manner: my goal was to buy something for dinner.

The goal was satisfied but my choice was influenced by the happenstance of my walking down one aisle of the supermarket first instead of another, and it was not realistically reversible once I made the initial choice as I would have been embarrassed to return the package to the counter personnel.[16] Moreover, it would have been too time consuming to first find all the available alternatives in the store. In sum, with the limited time and information at my disposal, I satisficed by finding an acceptable solution to relieving my hunger. In the presence of transaction costs, I could not choose the best possible dinner for myself but I did find a good-enough dinner.

And my choices may not be consistent. If I had to do it over again, I might choose to go down a different aisle first and my choices would no doubt be different. Hence, choice in the satisficing model depends on the order in which the alternatives are presented.[17] The optimum can be reached on the blackboard but not by human beings in real situations. The key difference between this example and those presented in textbooks is that the above problem entailed a sequence of decisions under uncertainty with limited information and included transaction costs, with a time constraint. Such choices are not found in the typical textbook because such models are anathema to mainstream economics insofar as it contradicts most—if not all—of the eloquent theorems of neoclassical economics. Satisficing does not conform easily to models of optimality.

BIASES AND WONDERS OF INTUITION

Many researchers, including Daniel Kahneman and Amos Tversky, have gone beyond bounded rationality by demonstrating decades ago that intuition plays a major role in our thinking, and that the rational part of our brain is not always in charge, nor does it generally supervise the decisions we make intuitively.[18] They refer to these two ways of thinking as System 1 (intuition) and System 2 (reasoning). Intuitive thoughts come to mind spontaneously. The operations of System 1 are fast, automatic, effortless, associative, impulsive, and difficult to control or modify. They are not voluntary, whereas those of System 2 are slower, deliberate, and take effort.[19]

As a survival strategy in a complex and uncertain environment, human brains developed ways to make decisions spontaneously and intuitively using rules of thumb. Faced with many unknowns through the millions of years of evolution, we developed skills to make crucial decisions in the blink of an eye, often with little information, which is to say, automatically and mostly without deliberate thinking.[20] We often have to make judgments quickly in order to reduce the heavy load of trying to solve a problem with incomplete information and uncertain outcomes without becoming catatonic. However, the other side of the coin is that the intuition and rule of thumb we use have many biases and consequently we make systematic mistakes; many of our decisions are outright irrational.[21] We make biased assessments of uncertainty and easily become confused, have limited self-control, and have a preference toward the present as opposed to the future. What 20-year old thinks that she'll need a retirement income someday? Our genetic disposition, including our instinct for survival as well as our potent sex drive, also overrides our rational self. In sum, Kahneman and Tversky's experiments suggest that human beings are incapable of being coherent. Yet while far from perfect, our minds have served us well for survival and reproduction up to now.

Most of us are incapable of analyzing complex problems, particularly under time pressure. (Real-life problems differ from those we are given at exam time because for the latter it is at least clear that a solution does exist whereas that is not necessarily so in the case of the former.) People are not used to thinking hard in day-to-day life and in such cases, System 2 gets stuck and System 1 at least provides a tolerable solution even if it is often erroneous. Thus, choice is not always an outcome of reasoning; rather, intuition almost always plays an essential role, unless the choice is of trivial complexity. We tend to trust a plausible judgment that System 1 provides quickly, but it is prone to all sorts of systematic biases and System 2 is incapable of monitoring it properly or overriding its judgments. System 2 supervises System 1 only lightly. Although intuitive judgment is ignored by mainstream economics textbooks, real human beings are not robots; they are prone to a large number of systematic biases, such as severe errors in judgment especially in assessing probabilities.[22]

HEURISTICS

We use heuristics, or attribute substitution, when a demanding decision is made by substituting an easier judgment, perhaps unconsciously. A daunting challenge in many economic situations is to make a decision when the problem is computationally so complex and the available information so meager and uncertain that we are unable to make a reasoned decision. Should I quit my current job? Should I accept this job offer or wait? Kahneman and Tversky have shown that in circumstances in which a problem is too difficult to solve or would take excessive effort, we rely on heuristics—rules of thumb—to make a decision. We substitute a related, but easier, problem for the inaccessible one we are facing. In a sense, the mind makes an information-processing shortcut—an intuitive judgment: "[P]eople are not accustomed to thinking hard, and are often content to trust a plausible judgment that comes to mind."[23]

The problem we use as a substitute is easily accessible to us, perhaps because of our prior experiences or those of others. (I personally used my father's experience with a problem in forming my own decision about a similar problem whose solution was otherwise inaccessible to me.) One solves a problem one can. It is better than being stuck. The substitution is done intuitively, so we are unaware of it and is not under the control of System 2. The use of heuristics is one of the many sources of our cognitive biases. In other words, rationality is beyond the ability of mortal souls.[24]

FRAMING, ACCESSIBILITY, ANCHORING

We do not always react to the same facts identically. Our choices depend on how these facts are presented or "framed." Such framing effects are important in how our unconscious reacts to a problem. It makes a difference if we say that out of 100 people 90 will survive, or if we say that 10 out of 100 will die. The information is the same but our emotional response is not, because it depends on whether we focus our attention on survival or dying. This is not rational. Hence, framing effects can also lead to preference reversals. You might choose chemotherapy if the decision is presented in terms of survival, but decide not to do so if it is presented in terms of dying. In other words, it is not the facts that matter but our perception, and this is important in consumer behavior because it implies that our decisions depend on how choices are framed. The implication is that we are incapable of being rational or coherent insofar as preference reversals contradict the consistency requirement of rational decision making. Of course, marketers know this and frame their advertisements in such a way as to bypass System 2. Watching three hours of TV per day gives Madison Avenue plenty of opportunity to interfere with our ability to use System 2 to make decisions as it affects our subconscious substantially. Neuromarketers are studying ways to reach our subconscious most effectively.[25]

One of the reasons we are prone to many logical fallacies is that intuition overrides the rules of logic and of probability. Behavioral economists have accumulated many examples through years of experimentation. For instance, people are willing to pay more for a life insurance policy that pays in case of terrorist attack while traveling than for one that pays in case of death from any cause, although it is clear upon reflection that the probability of the second scenario is greater than that of the first: after all, it pays in case of death from terrorist attack as well as from other causes. However, focusing on terrorism triggers basic intuitive fears that lead to

Figure 4.2   **An Attribute of These Lines (Average Length) Is Easily Accessible; Others Are Difficult**

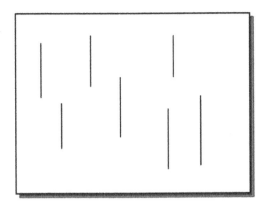

Figure 4.3   **The Perception of the Middle Object Depends on the Surrounding Objects**

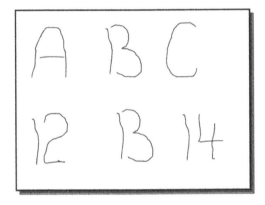

ignoring basic principles of probability.[26] Thus, some very low-probability events, such as being subject to a terrorist attack, are magnified in our brain whereas some high-probability events are attenuated.

In addition, some attributes of objects are more accessible to us than others. In Figure 4.2, the approximate average of the lines is easily and instantaneously accessible to us, but their sum is not. We would need to compute it with some effort. Furthermore, context affects accessibility. What do you see in the top and bottom panels of Figure 4.3 if you cover up one half of it? The middle object is either the letter B or the number 13, depending on the context. That is how the mind works: its interpretation of an ambiguous signal depends on the surroundings. This psychological principle is important in ascertaining the quality of products and is generally exploited by the advertising industry.

For instance, when we look at a car we can immediately see its outside condition—if it has scratches and so forth. But the attributes of its engine and performance are not easily ascertainable. It takes deliberate thinking to try to assess them. Knowing that appearances and context matter, car advertisements often try to influence our mood and emotions using power, sex, or celebrities to focus our attention on attributes that are easily accessible. These are registered automatically in our perceptual system without our consciously thinking about it, that is, without intent or effort.

Preferences are affected by irrelevant features of the advertisement, such as an attractive model standing next to it wearing a revealing dress. Such strategies are frequently used in advertisements because the enticing image is easily accessible and will be unconsciously associated with the car without our even being aware of it.[27] In other words, Madison Avenue tries to turn the decision from a rational one to an emotional one. This also contradicts the rational-agent model, because rational people would not be affected by irrelevant features such as the looks of the woman standing next to the car.

Anchoring occurs when we focus and rely on some information more than we should in making decisions and consequently do not pay sufficient attention to other even more important ones. These anchors are then accentuated in our subsequent decision making. For instance, by stressing and repeating the low initial mortgage rate, thereby turning the customer's attention away from its variable nature, mortgage bankers used it extensively as an anchor in the predatory lending schemes that gave rise to the subprime mortgage crisis.

PROSPECT THEORY

What is more accessible to our brain: changes or levels? According to conventional theory, it is the amount of consumption that yields utility. A given amount of cereal will yield a given amount of satisfaction, regardless of our accustomed level of cereal consumption. Kahneman and Tversky, however, showed a generation ago that this is contrary to human nature. According to their experiments, our judgment of how much we value a bowl of cereal or an iPhone is not a constant but depends on some reference value. They have thereby overturned the utility principle advocated by neoclassical economists. They emphasize that the value of the absolute magnitude of wealth, health, prestige, welfare, or consumption is much more difficult for us to ascertain than changes in these variables. Our brain can evaluate changes much easier than it can gauge the levels themselves because we become accustomed (adapted) to the current levels. In short, perception is reference dependent. So we use a reference level of consumption to be the measuring scale: what others are having or what we had the day before or what we anticipated.

The conventional view of the expected utility analysis of a risk-averse individual is presented in Figure 4.4. There are two possible outcomes, A and B; they have equal probability. Suppose $A = \$0$, $B = \$100$. The expected outcome is $C = 0.5(B + A) = \$50$ and the expected level of utility is $0.5(U(B) + U(A))$ as shown on the y-axis. Now let us compare this with obtaining C with certainty. Notice that the utility of C with certainty is greater than the expected utility if C is uncertain: $U(C) > 0.5(U(B) + U(A))$ even though $C = 0.5(B + A)$. This is the logic behind insurance markets. People are willing to pay a premium in order to avoid uncertain outcomes. The point of the diagram is that $50 with certainty has greater utility than a gamble of $0 or $100.

In contrast, the utility function of a risk-seeking person is convex (Figure 4.5). The gamble in this case is the same as the one depicted in Figure 4.4 except that now the utility function is convex. As a consequence, the utility of the gamble is greater than that of C with certainty: $U(C) < 0.5(U(B) + U(A))$. In contrast to the risk-averse example (Figure 4.4), now a gain of $50 with certainty is less attractive than a gamble whose expected return is $50. This person is risk seeking.

The importance of the distinction between levels and changes is demonstrated by the following example: Suppose Cathy receives a letter from her stockbroker that her portfolio, initially valued at $4 million, has declined in value to $3 million. In contrast, Susan receives a similar letter but her net wealth increased from $1 million to $1.1 million. Who will be happier? According to conventional analysis (Figure 4.6), Cathy should feel happier, because she is still much wealthier, and

Figure 4.4 **Conventional View of a Risk-Averse Gamble**

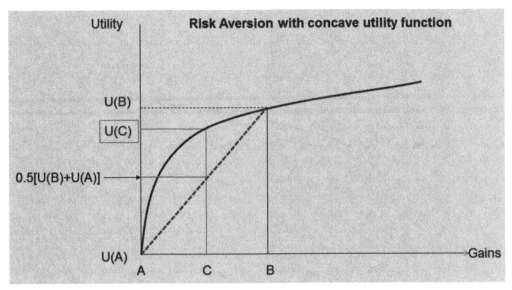

Figure 4.5 **Conventional View of a Risk-Seeking Gamble in Losses**

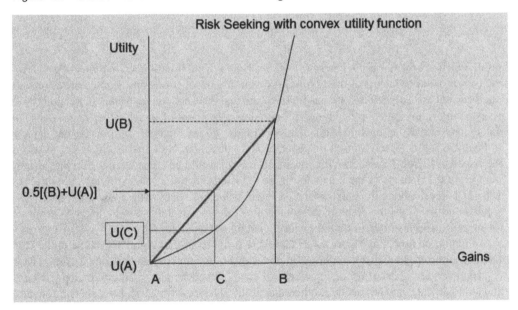

has a higher level of utility, than Susan but that does not adequately reflect the emotional intensity of having transitioned from one state of wealth to another.[28]

Kahneman and Tversky point out that the conventional analysis depicted in Figure 4.6 is incorrect insofar as it disregards the importance of the starting point (reference point). Therefore they reformulated the problem in terms of gains and losses, the foundations of their "prospect theory" (Figure 4.7).[29] Their "value function" consists of two quadrants instead of one (counting clockwise, quadrants 1 and 3 are not being considered). Quadrant 2 is similar to the conventional

Figure 4.6   **Utility at Various Levels of Wealth**

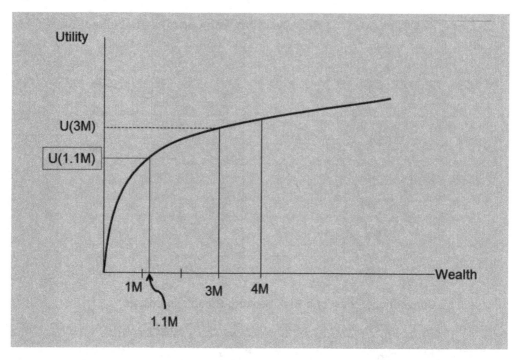

utility function except it is *not* in terms of levels of wealth but is calibrated in terms of gains from the current value, which is at the origin. Zero gain implies that one has become accustomed to one's current level of wealth (or consumption) and that does not convey value. In quadrant 4, the risk-seeking utility function of Figure 4.5 is redrawn in terms of losses rather than in absolute values. Notice that the function in quadrant 4 of Figure 4.7 is exactly the same as the one depicted in Figure 4.5; it is merely shifted in a southeasterly direction. Note that starting, say, at–$1M$ on the x-axis of Figure 4.7 and moving toward the origin would be considered a gain just as moving toward the right along the x-axis in Figure 4.5 is considered a gain. Similarly, moving from $U(-1M)$ upward along the y-axis is increasing in value, just as moving upward in Figure 4.5 is a gain in utility. Thus, the graph in this quadrant is the same as the one in Figure 4.5 except that the origin has been shifted in a southeasterly direction of quadrant 4.

An important aspect of Figure 4.7 is that there is a kink at the origin. The slope of the value function at the origin in quadrant 4 is about twice that of the function in quadrant 2. This is based on experimental evidence that losses decrease our welfare much more than gains increase it. Gains and losses do not compensate one another, that is, they are not symmetric. Loss aversion suggests that people have a stronger preference for avoiding losses than they do for acquiring gains.[30] Losses are about twice as powerful as gains; it takes about twice as much gain to compensate a loss. Note that this diagram can explain why Susan with a gain of $0.1M$ is happier than Cathy with a loss of $1M$ regardless of the level of their wealth: $U(+0.1M) > U(-1M)$. The value of a gain obviously exceeds that of a loss.

In a sense, Kahneman and Tversky did for economics what Einstein's theory of relativity did for physics. Before Einstein, people thought that time was a constant. Einstein showed that it was relative. Similarly, Kahneman and Tversky showed that utility is not a constant. States (levels)

Figure 4.7   **Prospect Theory Is Calibrated in Terms of Gains and Losses, Not in Levels**

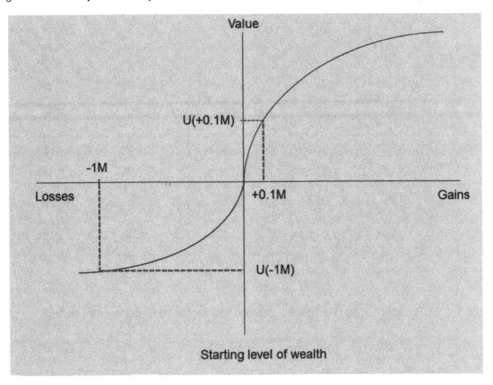

of income or of wealth are not the conveyors of utility; rather, changes in those levels are.[31] As a consequence, when we first purchase an iPod our level of utility spikes, but after we've had it in our pocket for a while we get used to it and it no longer provides as much satisfaction. We have adapted to its use. In short, what we are accustomed to plays a big role in determining the amount of utility we receive from an object.

Consider the following two choices: Option 1: –$100 with certainty; or option 2: a gamble with 50 percent chance of –$200 or 50 percent chance of +$50. The expected value of the second option is –$75 inasmuch as $(0.5 * – 200) + (0.5 * 50) = –100 = 25 = –75$. If you choose option 1 you would lose $100 with certainty, while if you choose option 2 you would have a 50/50 chance of either losing $200 or gaining $50. Which choice would you prefer? Most people are said to be risk averse, implying that they are usually willing to pay to avoid risk, as shown in Figure 4.4. Hence, standard utility theory predicts that faced with these two choices, most people should choose option 1, the certain option since its level of utility exceeds the utility obtained from option 2 (Figure 4.8). However, experiments contradict this inference. Most people actually choose option 2, the gamble, which implies that they are risk seeking since they might lose twice as much as the $100 loss of option 1. This outcome is inconsistent with risk aversion.[32] The probable reason for the anomaly is that people's perception is biased on account of the possible gain of $50, or put another way, the gain is magnified out of proportion, while the loss is mitigated out of proportion. People focus excessively on the gain and discount the probability of a much greater loss.

However, the choice of option 2 can be easily justified in the framework of prospect theory (Figure 4.9). While $U(–200) < U(–100)$, it is only slightly less, so that the value gained

Figure 4.8 **Comparison of Two Gambles Contradicts Standard Expected Utility Theory**

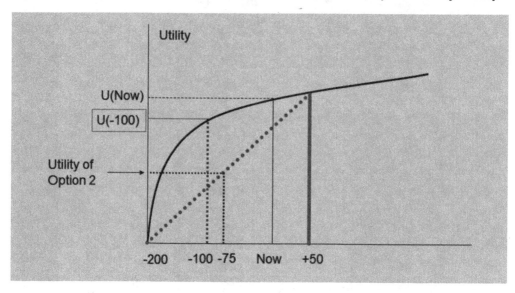

Figure 4.9 **Prospect Theory's Value Function Conforms to Experimental Data**

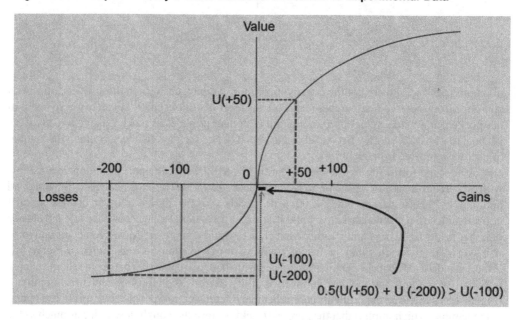

from the possibility of gaining $50 overcompensates for this small difference. Consequently, $0.5 [U(-200) + U(+50)] > U(-100)$. No wonder that most people choose option 2: prospect theory predicts that people will accept the gamble rather than the $100 loss with certainty. Thus, a basic prediction of prospect theory is that people are risk averse in gains but risk seeking in losses. Such a bias was surely part of the reason for the excessive risk taking during the financial crisis of 2008. Understanding prospect theory is an important aspect of the regulation of the financial sector.

Kahneman and Tversky's experiments led to the new field of behavioral economics, which replaces rational actor models with a more psychologically informed view of human decision making.

BEHAVIORAL ECONOMICS

The field of behavioral economics was born in order to overcome the limitations of naïve psychological assumption about our utility function. Thus, it encompasses the role of heuristics, psychological biases, framing effects, anchoring, and emotion in order to understand nonrational decision making. The mispricing of risk, of housing, and of stocks in the run-up to the recent financial crisis is just one example of its concern. Even the stock market, which is supposedly one of the few remaining perfectly competitive markets, overreacts to news and is subject to bubbles and crashes. In behavioral finance, such inefficiencies are due to overconfidence, inattention to price movements, and herding behavior. These can create positive feedback loops. If stock prices begin to rise by chance, then investors can form exaggerated expectations that they will continue to increase, thereby creating a positive feedback effect that contributes to further price increases. Such errors create large inefficiencies as well as negative externalities.

COGNITIVE DISSONANCE

Cognitive dissonance is an important aspect of decision theory insofar as many choices involve irreconcilable conflicting ideas, goals, or values, which in turn induce a feeling of tension in us. In order to reduce this discomfort, individuals modify their beliefs or suppress the importance of one of the conflicting perceptions in order to create a seemingly consistent belief system. This subconscious self-deception leads to biased thinking, as during the run-up to the financial crisis, and is also present in our thinking about environmental hazards, global warming, or the obesity epidemic. The roots of the problem are the same: "dissonance reduction," or "adaptive preference formation."[33] No smoker says to herself, "I am going to increase my chances of lung cancer" by smoking another cigarette. Rather, the person will suppress this notion by making excuses, which is easier to do than quitting, by saying to herself something like, "I'll reduce my smoking starting tomorrow." In that way, she can reduce the discomfort within her of conflicting beliefs.

Another example is Alan Greenspan's belief that financial markets were efficient and did not need government supervision. It was contradicted by many economists who were warning of a bubble in the housing market well before the bubble burst. For example, John Cassidy said as much in an article ominously titled "Blowing Bubbles" on the pages of the *New Yorker* in July 2004: "Given Greenspan's role in promoting and prolonging the stock-market bubble that burst in 2000, the deference that surrounds him seems a little overdone . . . even some of Greenspan's colleagues are concerned that one bubble has given way to another . . . [Yet] Greenspan refuses to contemplate such a catastrophe. On Capitol Hill recently, he insisted that the economy 'seems to be on track.'"[34] Greenspan also failed to listen to one of his own colleagues on the board of governors of the Federal Reserve, Edward Gramlich, who repeatedly admonished him to do something about subprime mortgages.[35]

In other words, faced with new information inconsistent with their prior beliefs, most people will—with high probability—continue to think that their decisions were correct. This is biased thinking: in order to reduce the tension between two views, one is motivated to disregard contrary evidence or deny its validity and justify one's own actions by rationalizing the problem in some way. One has the tendency to defend one's ideas by creating further justification for the policy, such as saying to oneself: "Bankers are sophisticated and therefore must be good at pricing risk. Why should I interfere with that?"

Cognitive dissonance is also well illustrated by Dick Fuld's congressional testimony. He was the CEO of Lehman Brothers at the time of its bankruptcy. He was in denial about his mistakes. He did not admit that he did anything wrong. Such a demeanor can be best understood in terms of cognitive dissonance.[36]

COGNITIVE ENDOWMENT

The cognitive endowment of people participating in the marketplace is quite heterogeneous. This poses an independent challenge for orthodox economics as textbooks tacitly assume that people who participate in the marketplace are homogeneous as far as intelligence is concerned, that is, they are all equally capable of solving the complex economic problems posed by today's global system. However, they are obviously not: both cognitive ability and economic literacy vary enormously in the population.[37] The normal distribution of cognitive ability implies that about 16 percent of the adult population has an IQ below 85 while about the same proportion has an IQ above 115. That means that the latter group can think faster, has a larger working memory, and can solve problems more accurately than the former group. This opens up a myriad of opportunities for deception when the former interacts with the latter in the marketplace. Cognitive ability is an important predictor of lifetime income. Although this issue is neglected in economics, it is an important one especially because businesses can afford to hire the very smartest to entrap those with lower cognitive ability. In such a case, the seller can take advantage of the inability of the buyer to understand detailed aspects of the transaction. That is one important reason for consumer protection. Caveat emptor—let the buyer beware—is not a reliable principle when the two sides to a transaction are not on equal footing.

The smart entrapped and exploited the weaknesses of their clients frequently during the subprime-mortgage debacle as well as with the chronic runaway credit-card debt for which the various complex stipulations were hidden and impossible to understand by many people. The counterparties were not equally informed about the transaction and were not equally capable of understanding the terms and risks involved. And most of the important things we purchase in a modern economy involve agreements that are extremely complicated and difficult to understand. That is why the U.S. Congress created the Consumer Financial Protection Bureau.[38] As Elizabeth Warren, who was in charge of getting the agency off the ground, warned, "The time for hiding tricks and traps in fine print is over."[39]

GENETIC ENDOWMENT

Genetic endowment influences a large number of personal traits that in turn influence an individual's participation in economic activity. Such attributes include cognitive ability, even as the social environment also plays a crucial role. Twin studies indicate that education and earnings are influenced by our genes as well as by our social environment.[40] The emergent field of "genoeconomics" hypothesizes that economic outcomes such as income and wealth may be "about as heritable as many medical conditions."[41] Our genetic codes are an essential aspect of human nature and are therefore an important determinant of economic outcomes.[42] A burgeoning literature argues persuasively that many of the choices we make are actually not the outcome of conscious cognitive processes alone but are influenced in important ways by our genetic endowment and its interaction with the environment.[43] "Variation in a surprisingly wide range of behaviors is substantially influenced by genetic differences."[44] For instance, one study estimated the heritability of the degree of risk aversion to be about 45 percent.[45] The role played by genetics in such attributes as our IQ, education, earnings, sense of empathy, and aspects of our personality such as our impatience, will power, attention span, or risk taking may be as great or greater than the role played by cultural norms and expectations.[46] Future research may well discover the genetic (or hormonal) basis of other personality traits that are important in economics, such as ambition, myopia, the rate of time preference, trust, selfishness, and other latent variables used in economic theory to explain such outcomes as credit card debt, even if these are also influenced by culture. Hence, rational choice is not a rational assumption if the effect of genes is so powerful: "in much of what we think, feel and do we march to ancient drummers."[47] This implies that the salaries we earn are actually to a considerable extent a return to our genetic endowment.

Our sex drive, for example, is a critical aspect of our reproductive mechanism and it is frequently conflated with the drive for power or a disposition to seek the esteem of our peers. Businesses all too often take advantage of these instincts by advertising their products to both sexes with erotic messages that play on our fantasies. Such marketing strategies are both demeaning and exploitative inasmuch as they appeal to our difficult-to-control primordial desires and illusions.[48]

Seeking esteem, cooperating with others, and respecting authority also had evolutionary advantages as they enhanced survival chances in our ancestral environment. Through esteem of our peers we gain security, support, and power, and therefore it must have had a positive effect on our reproductive chances in evolutionary time. Conspicuous consumption is actually a way to seek the esteem of our peers. "Because humans are mostly adapted to Pleistocene environments, psychological mechanisms often exhibit 'mismatches' to the modern environment."[49] Junk food is a good example: in prehistoric times, the craving for scarce goods such as sugar, fats, and salt had a life-enhancing function whereas in today's society of abundance this evolutionary adaptation is misplaced and has become an Achilles heel that businesses exploit to their advantage.[50]

Historically, our survival chances were also enhanced by our willingness to obey authority. The mid-level bureaucrats who participated in the subprime mortgage crisis obeyed the authority of their superiors and abandoned their own ethical judgment: "the essence of obedience consists in the fact that a person comes to view himself as the instrument for carrying out another person's wishes, and he therefore no longer sees himself as responsible for his actions. Once this critical shift of viewpoint has occurred in the person, all of the essential features of obedience follow."[51] The universality of idolizing authority figures and celebrities implies that it must be deeply embedded in our chromosomes. In the primeval forest, those who were not willing to yield to authority were presumably killed or ostracized and were therefore less likely to procreate. So our esteem of contemporary authority figures, the rich and famous, can be used by businesses to sell products, thereby exploiting our genetic disposition.

Furthermore, we have not evolved to be able to handle today's affluence gracefully. According to psychiatrist and author Peter Whybrow, "Human beings grew up under frugal circumstances. They don't know how to manage affluence."[52] In his book *American Mania: When More Is Not Enough,* Whybrow explores the way in which "our ancestral biology [leads to] the dangerous misfit emerging between our consumer-driven culture and the brain systems that evolved to deal with privation 200,000 years ago. In the absence of any controls—any cultural or economic constraints—we are easily hooked on our acquisitive pleasure seeking behaviors. . . . [H]uman biology is ill equipped to cope with the demands of the 24/7, global, information-saturated, rapid-fire culture . . . that we have come to crave."[53] In sum, in many respects our prefrontal cortex does not control us. Rather, our actions are guided by our genetic code and their interaction with the environment. In short, biology influences human behavior significantly. According to Edward O. Wilson, "in order to understand the human condition, it is necessary to accept that we do have instincts."[54]

CHAPTER SUMMARY

Psychology plays a crucial role in economics. Economics makes simplifying but misleading assumptions about the way we make decisions. To be sure, we can make a reasonable choice when it comes to knowing which cereal we want to eat in the morning. However, we are unable to maximize utility in case of complex decisions like on a mortgage or a cell phone contract—when all relevant information—such as the quality of the product or the reliability of the seller—is unavailable to us. In circumstances of imperfect information we would seek an optimum solution in vain, because the human mind is finite. It is not the super-computer of a Superman or Superwoman. Our thinking is biased in many ways. We have considerable problem assessing uncertainty and especially so if the outcome is complex, far into the future or under a time constraint. As a consequence of all these challenges, we use intuition, a rule of thumb, or copy the actions of others in order to avoid becoming catatonic and to make a decision, often unbeknownst to us, guided by our unconscious beyond the control of our prefrontal cortex. We do seek a satisfactory solution, a solution that is often good enough, but we also frequently make mistakes. In addition, a wrong choice may snowball and lead to several other bad decisions.

The limitations of our mind have manifold implications for economic theory and policy. If the consumer is not a Superman or Superwoman, he/she might well need the help of neutral institutions to navigate through the extremely complex and confusing labyrinths of the economy.[55] "Let the buyer beware" is not an ethical approach to creating an economy in which individuals can blossom, retain their individuality, expand their self-esteem, and become respected, self-actualizing members of society who do not aspire to a Hollywood-imposed lifestyle. Businesses have gained too much power. Only if we devise institutions to defend consumers from being taken advantage of and retain their dignity will we be able to create a kind of capitalism with a human face that can enhance both living standards and the quality of life and keep the planet safe for future generations to enjoy. In order to accomplish that economics first has to abandon the rational-agent utility-maximizing framework as its theoretical foundation.

QUESTIONS FOR DISCUSSION

1. Is it moral to take advantage of or profit from the ignorance of others?
2. Would you describe your shopping as satisficing or optimizing?
3. What is the difference between optimizing and satisficing?
4. Were you conditioned to want some products?
5. How much of what you do is rational?
6. Were you ever influenced by advertisement to buy a product? Were you satisfied with that product thereafter or did you find that it was different than what you supposed?
7. Do you agree that you might be very happy to receive a new product but that after a while you get used to it and you begin to take it for granted?
8. Are you influenced by what celebrities are wearing?
9. Do you sometimes choose randomly when the choice is too difficult?
10. Have you ever bought something just because your friend had it?
11. Do you think consumer protection is necessary?
12. Why do you think so many people are depressed?
13. Do you crave sweets? Or are there other things you buy that you know are not good for you?
14. Why do you suppose so many people are unable to control their weight?

15. Do you think that people rationally choose to be obese?

16. Do you order some things in a restaurant while in company just not to be different?

17. Do search costs sometime inhibit you from buying a product?

18. Can you give an example when you were not certain of the need for or quality of a product? How did you make your decision?

19. Are you making plans for your retirement income?

20. Have you ever made a decision that was right for you but which led to other choices that were less palatable? Hint: see, path dependence or sequential choices on page 145.

21. Is buying a shoe the same kind of decision as going to the doctor for chest pain?

22. Can you give an example when you made a decision based on intuition or on emotion?

23. Are some of your tastes similar to that of your parents?

24. Why should one get paid for being born smart?

25. Do you think that predatory loans should be prohibited?

NOTES

1. This definition comes from psychology. Many Econ 101 textbooks do not define what they mean by rationality but assume it as an axiom.

2. Much to my surprise, my monthly ADT alarm bill was raised without my knowledge by $2 from one week to the next. Perhaps it was part of the fine print in the contract I signed without knowing it. My rule of thumb is that whenever I sign such a contract the chances are that I will be deceived in some way.

3. The assumption of rationality is a "nonstarter," according to Kahneman. Links to his extremely informative lectures are available on his home page, www.princeton.edu/~kahneman/.

4. Amartya Sen, "Rational Fools: A Critique of the Behavioural Foundations of Economic Theory," *Philosophy and Public Affairs* 6 (1977): 336.

5. Joan Robinson commented that "utility maximization is a metaphysical concept of impregnable circularity." See Christopher D. Carroll, "Punter of Last Resort," March 13, 2009.

6. Robert Kurzban, *Why Everyone (Else) Is a Hypocrite: Evolution and the Modular Mind* (Princeton, NJ: Princeton University Press, 2011).

7. Peter C. Whybrow, "Dangerously Addictive: Why We Are Biologically Ill-Suited to the Riches of Modern America," *The Chronicle of Higher Education,* March 13, 2009.

8. See ibid., and Peter C. Whybrow, *American Mania: When More Is Not Enough* (New York: W.W. Norton, 2005).

9. Colin Camerer, George Loewenstein, and Drazen Prelec, "Neuroeconomics: How Neuroscience Can Inform Economics," *Journal of Economic Literature* 43 (2005): 9–64.

10. John Dickhaut, Kevin McCabe, Jennifer C. Nagode, Aldo Rustichini, Kip Smith, and Jose Pardo, "The Impact of the Certainty Context on the Process of Choice," *Proceedings of the National Academy of Sciences of the United States of America* 100 (2003): 3536–3541.

11. Camerer, Loewenstein, and Prelec, "Neuroeconomics."

12. John Conlisk, "Why Bounded Rationality?" *Journal of Economic Literature* 34 (1996) 2: 669–700.

13. Herbert A. Simon, *Models of Bounded Rationality* (Cambridge, MA: MIT Press, 1982); Herbert A. Simon, *Models of Man* (New York: Wiley, 1957); Herbert A. Simon, "Designing Organizations for an Information-Rich World," in *Computers, Communication, and the Public Interest,* ed. Martin Greenberger (Baltimore: The Johns Hopkins University Press, 1971), 40–41.

14. A rule of thumb is a procedure derived from experience or word-of-mouth that enables one to find a satisfactory approach to a particular problem (perhaps using analogy) when (1) too little information is available to do so optimally; (2) when there is insufficient time to consider all important aspects of the problem that could influence the decision; or (3) when it is impractical, impossible, or too costly to find the optimal solution. The procedure is similar to an educated guess or common-sense reasoning, but can often be deceiving, far from optimal, and can also lead to stereotyping and prejudice.

15. Herbert A. Simon, "Rational Choice and the Structure of the Environment," *Psychological Review* 63 (1956): 129–138; Herbert A. Simon, "A Behavioral Model of Rational Choice," *Quarterly Journal of Economics* 69 (1955): 99–118.

16. With the Internet, some planning and comparison shopping is likely to improve.

17. Herbert A. Simon, *Reason in Human Affairs* (Oxford: Blackwell, 1983), 23.

18. Mark J. Machina, "Non-Expected Utility Theory," in *The New Palgrave Dictionary of Economics,* 2nd ed., ed. Steven N. Durlauf and Lawrence E. Blume (Basingstoke, UK: Palgrave Macmillan, 2008).

19. Daniel Kahneman, *Thinking, Fast and Slow* (New York: Farrar, Straus and Giroux, 2011).

20. Malcolm Gladwell, *Blink: The Power of Thinking Without Thinking* (New York: Little, Brown, 2005).

21. Dan Ariely, *Predictably Irrational: The Hidden Forces That Shape Our Decisions* (New York: HarperCollins, 2008); Dan Ariely, *The Upside of Irrationality* (New York: HarperCollins, 2010). You can view and hear several of Ariely's great lectures on the Internet: "Dan Ariely: The Upside of Irrationality," ForaTV video, 1:08:58, June 7, 2010; "Dan Ariely Asks, Are We in Control of Our Own Decisions?" TED video, 17:22, filmed December 2008, posted May 2009; "Authors@Google: Dan Ariely," YouTube video, 56:02, posted by "AtGoogleTalks," July 1, 2008.

22. Wikipedia lists more than a hundred cognitive biases. Wikipedia contributors, "List of Cognitive Biases," *Wikipedia: The Free Encyclopedia.*

23. Daniel Kahneman, "Maps of Bounded Rationality: Psychology for Behavioral Economics," *American Economic Review* 93 (2003) 5: 1449–1475, at p. 1450.

24. See Kahneman's Nobel Prize Lecture: "Prize Lecture by Daniel Kahneman," 37:25, filmed December 8, 2002.

25. "If pitches are to succeed, they need to reach the subconscious level of the brain, the place where consumers develop initial interest in products, inclinations to buy them and brand loyalty," says A.K. Pradeep, the founder and chief executive of a neuromarketing firm NeuroFocus. See Natasha Singer, "Making Ads That Whisper to the Brain," *The New York Times,* November 13, 2010.

26. The "conjunction rule" in probability theory states that the probability that a person belongs to both categories A and B cannot be greater than the probability that she belongs to category B alone. Kahneman and Tversky showed that this axiom is violated using the following description of a person: "Linda is 31 years old, single, outspoken, and very bright. She majored in philosophy. As a student, she was deeply concerned with issues of discrimination and social justice, and also participated in anti-nuclear demonstrations." Almost everyone rated the probability that "Linda is a bank teller and is active in the feminist movement" higher than the probability that "Linda is a bank teller." This fallacy occurs because we tend to anchor our thoughts on the description of Linda's feminist nature and intuitively assume that she is representative of feminism. The focus on this representative attribute draws our attention away from the obvious fact that if she is a feminist bank teller, she must be a bank teller as well.

27. Jaedene Hudson, "New Models in the Flesh," *Sydney Morning Herald,* November 3, 2006.

28. One might argue that it is not advisable to compare the utility of two different persons. But then one can also think of this example as Cathy in two different moments in time. Besides, why do we have so many representative agent models in economics if one should not assume that people are the same? The whole literature on microfoundations of macroeconomics is based on the idea that there is a typical person. We also aggregate incomes of different people in order to assess the national income of a country at a moment in time or across time. Macromodels use representative firms. It appears that when it is convenient to do so, economists do assume that there is an average person who can represent the whole society and therefore they do compare utility functions across individuals, but when it would be inconvenient to do so they refuse.

29. Daniel Kahneman and Amos Tversky, "Prospect Theory: An Analysis of Decision Under Risk," *Econometrica* 47 (1979): 263–291.

30. Loss aversion explains the endowment effect.

31. See "NBR Interview with Daniel Kahneman: Your Mind and Your Money," YouTube video, 5:58, from an interview televised by PBS on October 19, 2009, posted by "PBS," November 6, 2009.

32. The experiment has been repeated with a large number of different combinations of numbers. As long as negative prospects are involved, people are risk seeking. For example, "the majority of subjects were willing to accept a risk of 0.8 to lose 4,000, in preference to a sure loss of 3,000, although the gamble has a lower expected value." Daniel Kahneman and Amos Tversky, "Prospect Theory: An Analysis of Decisions Under Risk," *Econometrica* 47 (1979): 263–291, p. 268.

33. Leon Festinger, Henry Riecken, and Stanley Schachter, *When Prophecy Fails: A Social and Psychological Study of a Modern Group That Predicted the Destruction of the World* (New York: Harper-Torchbooks, 1956); Jon Elster, *Sour Grapes: Studies in the Subversion of Rationality* (Cambridge, UK: Cambridge University Press, 1983).

34. John Cassidy, "Blowing Bubbles," *The New Yorker,* July 12, 2004.

35. Micheline Maynard, "Being Right Is Bittersweet for a Critic of Lenders," *The New York Times,* August 18, 2007.

36. The amazing testimony is well worth seeing. Fuld said, "I believed these decisions and actions were both prudent and appropriate," and he never admitted to having made any mistakes. "Lehman Brothers CEO Testifies on Capitol Hill," YouTube video, 2:23, posted by "AssociatedPress," October 6, 2008.

37. William T. Dickens, "Cognitive Ability," in *The New Palgrave Dictionary of Economics,* 2nd ed., ed. Steven N. Durlauf and Lawrence E. Blume (Basingstoke, UK: Palgrave Macmillan, 2008).

38. A fine of $210 million has already been levied on Capitol One for deceptive banking practices. See Ben Prootess and Jessica Silver-Greenberg, "Consumer Watchdog Fines Capital One for Deceptive Credit Card Practices," *The New York Times,* July 18, 2012.

39. Elizabeth Warren, "Fighting to Protect Consumers," The White House Blog, September 17, 2010.

40. Paul Taubman, "The Determinants of Earnings: Genetics, Family, and Other Environments: A Study of White Male Twins," *American Economic Review* 66 (1976) 5: 858–870.

41. Daniel J. Benjamin, David Cesarini, Christopher F. Chabris, Edward L. Glaeser, David I. Laibson, Vilmundur Guðnason, Tamara B. Harris, Leonore J. Launer, Shaun Purcell, Albert Vernon Smith, Magnus Johannesson, Patrik K.E. Magnusson, Jonathan P. Beauchamp, Nicholas A. Christakis, Craig S. Atwood, Benjamin Hebert, Jeremy Freese, Robert M. Hauser, Taissa S. Hauser, Alexander Grankvist, Christina M. Hultman, and Paul Lichtenstein, "The Promises and Pitfalls of Genoeconomics," *Annual Review of Economics* 4 (July 2012): 627–662.

42. Michael J. Zyphur, Jayanth Narayanan, Richard D. Arvey, and Gordon J. Alexander, "The Genetics of Economic Risk Preferences," *Journal of Behavioral Decision Making* 22 (2009): 367–377. Sociological attributes are also associated with genetic propensities. See Guang Guo, Michael E. Roettger, and Tianji Cai, "The Integration of Genetic Propensities into Social-Control Models of Delinquency and Violence Among Male Youths," *American Sociological Review* 73 (2008): 543–568; Arthur J. Robson, "The Biological Basis of Economic Behavior," *Journal of Economic Literature* 29 (2001): 11–33; Arthur J. Robson and Larry Samuelson, "The Evolutionary Foundations of Preferences," in *Handbook of Social Economics,* ed. Jess Benhabib, Alberto Bisin, and Matthew O. Jackson (Amsterdam: North Holland Press, 2010).

43. Deirdre Barrett, *Supernormal Stimuli: How Primal Urges Overran Their Evolutionary Purpose* (New York: W.W. Norton, 2010); A. Knafo, S. Israel, A. Darvasi, R. Bachner-Melman, F. Uzefovsky, L. Cohen, E. Feldman, E. Lerer, E. Laiba, Y. Raz, L. Nemanov, I. Gritsenko, C. Dina, G. Agam, B. Dean, G. Bornstein, and R.P. Ebstein, "Individual Differences in Allocation of Funds in the Dictator Game Associated with Length of the Arginine Vasopressin 1a Receptor RS3 Promoter Region and Correlation Between RS3 Length and Hippocampal mRNA," *Genes, Brain and Behavior* 7 (2008) 3: 266–275. Hormone levels also have a role in our economic behavior. See Terence C. Burnham, "High-Testosterone Men Reject Low Ultimatum Game Offers," *Proceedings of the Royal Society B* 274 (2007) 1623: 2327–2330.

44. William T. Dickens, "Behavioural Genetics," in *The New Palgrave Dictionary of Economics,* 2nd ed., ed. Steven N. Durlauf and Lawrence E. Blume (Basingstoke, UK: Palgrave Macmillan, 2008). This is also the case for social outcomes. See Guo, Roettger, and Cai, "The Integration of Genetic Propensities into Social-Control Models of Delinquency and Violence Among Male Youths."

45. Jonathan P. Beauchamp, David Cesarini, Magnus Johannesson, Matthijs J.H.M. der Loos, Philipp D. Koellinger, Patrick J.F. Groenen, James H. Fowler, Niels Rosenquist, Roy Thurik, and Nicholas A. Christakis, "Molecular Genetics and Economics," *Journal of Economic Perspectives* 25 (2011) 4: 1–27.

46. Jere Richard Behrman and Paul Taubman, "Is Schooling 'Mostly in the Genes'? Nature-Nurture Decomposition Using Data on Relatives," *Journal of Political Economy* 97 (1989) 6: 1425–1446; Björn Wallace, David Cesarini, Paul Lichtenstein, and Magnus Johannesson, "Heritability of Ultimatum Game Responder Behavior," *Proceedings of the National Academy of Sciences* 104 (2007) 40: 15631–15634; David Cesarini, Christopher Dawes, Magnus Johannesson, Paul Lichtenstein, and Björn Wallace, "Genetic Variation in Preferences for Giving and Risk Taking," *The Quarterly Journal of Economics* 124 (2009) 2: 809–842; Anh T. Le, Paul W. Miller, Wendy S. Slutske, and Nicholas G. Martin, "Are Attitudes Towards Economic Risk Heritable? Analyses Using the Australian Twin Study of Gambling," *Twin Research and Human Genetics* 13 (2010) 4: 330–339; Songfa Zhong, Soo Hong Chew, Eric Sct, Junsen Zhang, Hong

Xue, Pak C. Sham, Richard P. Ebstein, and Salomon Israel, "The Heritability of Attitude Toward Economic Risk," *Twin Research and Human Genetics* 12 (2009) 1: 103–107; David Cesarini, Magnus Johannesson, Paul Lichtenstein, Örjan Sandewall, and Björn Wallace, "Genetic Variation in Financial Decision Making," *Journal of Finance* 65 (2009) 5: 1725–1754; Anna Dreber, Coren L. Apicella, Dan T.A. Eisenberg, Justin R. Garcia, Richard S. Zamore, J. Koji Lum, and Benjamin Campbell, "The 7R Polymorphism in the Dopamine Receptor D4 Gene (*DRD4*) Is Associated with Financial Risk Taking in Men," *Evolution and Human Behavior* 30 (2008) 2: 85–92.

47. Peter Whybrow, "Ideas to Challenge and Inspire," available at the Web site of Peter C. Whybrow.

48. Andrea Dworkin and Catharine A. MacKinnon, *Pornography and Civil Rights: A New Day for Women's Equality* (Minneapolis: Organizing Against Pornography, 1988); Matthew Hutson, "Lust Now, Pay Later: Keeping Up with Your Joneses," *Psychology Today,* May 1, 2008.

49. Wikipedia contributors, "Evolutionary Psychology," *Wikipedia: The Free Encyclopedia.*

50. Barrett, *Supernormal Stimuli.*

51. Stanley Milgram, *Obedience to Authority: An Experimental View* (New York: HarperCollins, 1974), xii–xiii.

52. Peter Whybrow, "A Conversation with Doctor Peter Whybrow," *Charlie Rose,* March 18, 2005.

53. "American Mania: About the Book," available at the Web site of Peter C. Whybrow.

54. See Edward O. Wilson, "Evolution and Our Inner Conflict," *The New York Times,* June 24, 2012; Edward O. Wilson, *The Social Conquest of Earth* (New York: W.W. Norton, 2012).

55. I recently wanted to make a call from the airport to my home. The instructions on the phone were ambiguous but implied that it would cost me $1 to make a call. However, the opening to insert the change was closed so I decided to use my credit card. The operator asked me if I wanted to know the price of the call. Thinking that I already knew the price, I replied in the negative and proceeded to give the operator my card information. Learning that it was a MasterCard, he replied that he had to tell me the price, which turned out to be (much to my amazement) $33. At this point I declined to continue, but this is an excellent example of how an intermediary—in this case a credit card company—can protect the consumer from deceptive practices. "Caveat emptor" is insufficient and inefficient.

5

TASTE MAKERS AND CONSUMPTION

We have argued up to now that the standard microeconomic canon of consumption is not objective. It begins with arbitrary assumptions that contradict findings in other disciplines and disregards important aspects of the real economy such as the distribution of power. The standard narrative accentuates a free-market ideology by disregarding theories not in support of the canon such as the concept of satisficing that fits the facts better than the optimizing model favored by the mainstream. Standard textbooks treat major shortcomings of neo-classical theories as epiphenomenon such as imperfect information and are replete with hidden value judgments by disregarding sustainability and the welfare of future generations.

We continue to point to the flaws in the standard treatment of the subject by arguing that we should not idolize markets for their efficiency, because they are not efficient in the first place except in a few irrelevant circumstances and because efficiency itself is a norm adopted on the basis of a value judgment, and its measurement is controversial.

THE INFLUENCE OF CORPORATE POWER

Power is the ability to control either one's own action or thought or those of others. Thus, wealth translates directly into power. This is not new: Adam Smith knew it, as did the founding fathers.[1] Wealth can provide irresistible incentives for politicians to act on behalf of people with money. Power does not exist in perfectly competitive markets insofar as there are many sellers and many buyers and it would not be useful to advertise; in such a market, power is diffused until it becomes negligible and strategic behavior does not pay. While this is the default model used in most introductory analysis, it is obviously misleading because one of the basic principles of free-market economics is the tendency of power to concentrate. This was the case with the "robber barons," of the late nineteenth century: with the expansion of railroads, finance, petroleum, and steel, a new wealthy class gained prominence using questionable business practices to make their fortune.

An early warning came from President Dwight Eisenhower, who spoke unabashedly in his farewell address to the nation of the "unwarranted influence" of the "military-industrial complex," and the "potential for the disastrous rise of misplaced power."[2] Liberal Harvard economist John Kenneth Galbraith forecast that the future economy would be managed by big business, big labor, and big government.[3] He was two-thirds right. How prescient were they both, even if Galbraith could not have foreseen the demise of big labor and Eisenhower could not have foreseen the rise of the lords of finance.[4]

In the half-century since this prognosis, corporations have extended their control over society beyond the military-industrial complex to encompass the financial sector and capture government to a greater extent than ever before. This advance was made so slowly that it was hardly noticed in our day-to-day activities. However, the cumulative effect was to transfer both political and economic power from individuals to mega-corporations. The problem starts with the fact that according to our legal tradition, corporations are legal persons. This makes perfect sense from the point of view of conducting business. However, it makes absolutely no sense to consider a business incorporated for the purposes of conducting production, trade, or finance as a person allowed to exert an influence in the realm of politics or of culture. There are harmful elements in this legal fiction, namely that the political rights of individuals are extended to a fictitious entity.

The First (1791) and the Fourteenth (1868) amendments of the U.S. Constitution were originally intended, respectively, to guarantee the basic rights of free speech to flesh-and-blood human beings and to protect the rights of freed slaves. They had nothing to do with business. However, the extension of these rights to inanimate entities actually demeans our humanity. The rights of corporations ought to be confined strictly to economic activity and ought not to be allowed to extend to the political or cultural sphere. Insofar as inanimate entities cannot speak, they ought not be protected by the First Amendment. That would enable us to limit their advertisements and regain our control over our political processes. To be sure, corporations can have employees speak for them, but that implies that flesh-and-blood individuals have multiple voices in society: both as their real selves and as spokespeople for an inanimate entity. This in itself brings about an uneven distribution of power that is exacerbated, of course, by the imbalance in distribution of financial resources. In this way, profits are translated into political and social power with tremendous feedback effects to the economic structure and its institutions. It is also ridiculous to equate money with free speech, which allows corporations to wield undue influence in elections.

Thus, oligopolies such as Goldman Sachs and JPMorgan Chase do have lots of clout to set prices and to manipulate the market to their benefit. Barclays and UBS were caught manipulating interest rates and fined $450 million and $1,500 million respectively.[5] Power enables vested interests to develop and further skew economic advantages in their favor by rewriting the rules of the market in such a way that their initial advantages lead to further political power imbalances which, in turn, increase their privileges.[6]

This is precisely what is happening to Congress with substantial feedback effects to the economy.[7] The financial sector spent $2,700 million on lobbying from 1999 to 2008, while individuals and committees affiliated with the industry made more than $1 billion in campaign contributions in order to gain further economic advantage.[8] It is incredibly unjust and dangerous that corporations are allowed to give unlimited funds to influence political campaigns without disclosing their contributions even to their shareholders. Thus, CEOs can waste the shareholder's money and lobby even against the interests of their shareholders without them even knowing it.[9] In the meanwhile, the underemployed have no lobbyists and can make no campaign contributions whatsoever. Under such unbalanced circumstances, the market's playing field cannot possibly be level.[10] No wonder corporations have received many benefits from government: "Nationwide state and local subsidies for corporations totaled more than $70 billion in 2010."[11] And trillions of dollars have been pumped into the financial sector by the Federal Reserve since the Meltdown of 2008.

Yet the dispersion of power is the very essence of our democratic political system inasmuch as a democracy turns quickly into a plutocracy if economic power is concentrated among an elite oligarchy. Thus, the concentration of wealth is a major threat to our democratic institutions,[12] and therefore we desperately need to foster countervailing sources of power to check the innate desire of CEOs to further tilt the laws and institutions of government in their favor. Power frequently leads to abuses. Sixty people have pleaded guilty or were found guilty recently by mid-2012 of insider trading crimes, including a former Goldman Sachs board member.[13]

In addition, designing the market system to their benefit, powerful oligopolies squelch competition and thereby reap near-monopolistic profits. The invisible hand could lead to efficient outcomes only to the extent that power is decentralized. Concentration of power works in the opposite direction by infringing on our rights so that we have to compete on the oligarchists' terms rather than on ours. Aldous Huxley, best known for his prophetic nightmare-vision novel *Brave New World,* which warned of the dehumanizing forces of totalitarianism, was of the same opinion: "obviously the passion for power is one of the most moving passions that exists in man; and after all, all democracies are based on the proposition that power is very dangerous and that it is extremely important not to let any one man or any one small group have too much power for too long a time."[14] We have made the big mistake of allowing these power imbalances to expand to such an extent that regaining our individuality will not be an easy matter. Franklin Roosevelt understood this well. He warned us about the "industrial dictatorship" imposing wages on working people, about "economic royalty" expropriating other people's money.[15] Joseph Stiglitz has described this power imbalance as socialism for the rich and capitalism for the rest of us.

Thus, there are different kinds of power: market power; power to influence institutions and legislation in order to further economic gain; power to influence cultural norms; power to influence our buying habits; large buyers can exert power on suppliers to extract discounts and obtain part of their profits. Corporations exert an inordinate amount of power on our culture and our mindset, which form the basis of our utility function. A major oversight of neoclassical economics is that it begins the analysis with adults, because this enables the discipline to ignore the crucial and pernicious influence of powerful mega-corporations on the formation of our taste during our formative years. Desires beyond the basic needs are learned gradually and do not come into being spontaneously from within ourselves. Through this process of socialization we learn the terms under which we can become respected members of the society. Those are the years when the most important aspects of our values are learned, setting in motion Pavlovian conditioning that accompanies our Freudian unconscious for the rest of our lives. That is when we internalize the social norms and become culturally American, or French, or Korean, or whatever.

Hence, by the time we reach adulthood we have gone through a rigorous process of inculcation inasmuch as Madison Avenue inundates us with symbols of sex, power, and cultural icons in order to sell its clients' products. Through this socialization we assimilate a culture in which we learn to mimic the tastes, values, and consumption habits of superstars and assorted other idols projected across the media. Under such intense pressure, children are groomed to grow up to become reliable consumers and choice becomes a "pretense of individualism."[16] As a consequence, it is self-deceptive to think that we are in control of our tastes and values. Nearly three hours of TV watching daily would affect anyone's thinking patterns. Corporations invest extravagantly in order to promote those aspects of the culture on which they can profit, sway our wants, and make us feel like we need their product. They hire trendsetters to admonish us hundreds of thousands of times to forget about the future and buy today before the bargains expire, to indulge in instant gratification, and tempt us with the newest glittering products, to carelessly disregard the future, putting caveats into the fine print.[17]

In stark contrast, there are hardly any advertisements to teach us to save for a rainy day, to practice frugality and moderation, to be circumspect, to appreciate the free things in life, to read the classics in the public library, to be patient and humble, to relax with friends, not to be envious, not to imitate the rich and famous, to show self-restraint, and to appreciate that we are healthy and not hungry. To grow up in such an asymmetric social environment means that we are free to choose our cola drink but we are deprived of a basic right to develop our own taste—utility function—without such overbearing corporate manipulation. However, we are unaware of the fact that we are actually deprived of our right to individuality and autonomy. This is a major hindrance to our ability to develop healthy mental attitudes and to live fulfilled lives, because new desires are implanted in us as soon as the old ones are satisfied. Contentment is unprofitable. No wonder that the average American is overweight, indebted, and fundamentally discontented. We did not choose to be so. It was imposed upon us by powerful profit-seeking corporations that conditioned us to become compulsive shoppers through their advertisements.

> [a] 'yawning void, an insatiable hunger, an emptiness waiting to be filled,' that [Christopher] Lasch identified as animating the typical narcissist of the 1970s has grown only deeper with the passage of time. The Great Recession was supposed to portend a scaling back, a recalibration of our lifestyle, and usher in a new era of making more of less. But the pressures that drive the dysregulated American haven't abated any since the fall of 2008. Wall Street is resurgent, and unemployment is still high. For too many people, the cycle of craving and debt that drives our treadmill existence simply can't be broken.[18]

We have gradually internalized this commercial culture to such an extent that we are no longer aware of this interference with our psyche, this major infringement on our basic right to develop without undue corporate influence.[19] Unfortunately, we are not cognizant of how our tastes were formed and the extent to which our will power, unconscious mind, and all our attitudes have been influenced by those who profit from the choices we make. In sum, consumer sovereignty is merely a mirage in the real existing economy[20] (Figure 5.1). By beginning the analysis after the process of socialization has been completed, economic theory disregards all the feedback effects from the corporate world to consumption and the extent to which the slow accumulation of economic power by the business community leads to an increasingly materialistic culture that values consumption above all and trivializes aspects of life upon which profits are not to be had.[21]

Thus, we should reject "adult economics": economic analysis ought to begin at birth. In order to regain our natural freedoms to develop our personality and reestablish consumer sovereignty we need to begin by protecting ourselves from the massive influence of business interests. Only then can we hope to emancipate ourselves from our current serfdom and become self-actualizing human beings according to Abraham Maslow's hierarchy of needs: people who are able to enjoy some autonomy in personal development, who are rich in spirit, creative and wise enough not to have to depend on Hollywood stars to tell them how to arrange their lives.[22] Until consumer sovereignty is restored de facto, free-market economics will not lead to a fulfilled life for the overwhelming majority of the population, because businesses profit from teaching us to be greedy, but as greed has no satiation we end up on a vicious circle of chasing the desires incessantly implanted in us.[23] Fixation on material needs cannot lead to gratification, because we are blocked from further development. We are hindered from seeking meaning in life in intangibles rather than in material goods, although there is an unlimited supply of good feelings that can be generated from the beauty of nature, from friendships with mutual respect, dignified relationships, love, spiritual connectedness, and other intangibles.[24] The banks and big business are already wielding immense impact on our psyche and we need to regain our fundamental independence from them.

INTERDEPENDENCE

Traditional economic theory assumes that individual consumer preferences are independent of each other. Under this (unrealistic but convenient) assumption, a person's demand for goods will vary only to the extent his own income changes or the prices of goods vary, but not if his neighbor's consumption varies. Thus, in neoclassical theory there is no place either for interaction effects among consumers or for a positive feedback mechanism from consumption leading

Figure 5.1

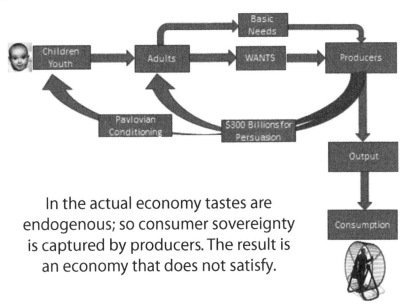

In the actual economy tastes are endogenous; so consumer sovereignty is captured by producers. The result is an economy that does not satisfy.

to further consumption. This is another reason why the official axiom of utility maximization of an isolated individual is far off the mark. In fact, there are many strong interdependent effects in consumption.

More than a century ago, Thorstein Veblen argued forcefully that consumption was governed mainly by social norms, habit, customs, and such irrational motives as status seeking, or snobbism, and by the bandwagon effect, or herding behavior.[25] Consumption has a significant social component; in fact, one seldom consumes in isolation. As society has become more affluent, Veblen's interdependent utility functions have been playing a much bigger role in consumption.[26] There are many more consumption externalities now than there were a century ago and a long list of distinguished economists has argued since Veblen that relative consumption and relative incomes do matter a lot.[27] We should acknowledge the interrelatedness in people's consumption: people copy the buying habits of their peers and of opinion leaders in the media and we care a lot about what others think of our consumption. The externality is particularly relevant for luxury or positional goods—ostentatious display of wealth meant to impress others and to seek social status—because they produce negative externalities as they affect others adversely.[28] These externalities are not considered in the gross national product (GNP) accounts. However, the quest for status is futile from the point of view of the society as a whole, insofar as it is essentially a zero-sum game. If one climbs in the hierarchy, someone else descends in relative terms.

James Duesenberry reformulated the theory of consumption by emphasizing that the independence assumption is contradicted by reality.[29] He suggested that our utility depends on our past consumption as well as that of those around us. Robert Frank suggests that this is similar to an arms race: positional goods are goods that produce externalities; they signal social position and thereby affect the way others feel and what others purchase. If we are concerned with the effect of our consumption on others we will spend more on positional goods than on those goods that are not visible to others. This is a distortion and decreases social welfare. The decline in the savings rate in spite of increases in income can be understood in terms of increased competition for positional goods inasmuch as savings is a nonpositional good—it is not common knowledge in the way a new outfit is. In standard theory, one would expect savings, as a normal good,[30] to increase with income or at least remain constant and not to decline to zero as it did right before the Meltdown of 2008. That was quite an anomaly in conventional economics but can be understood easily in terms of the relative income hypothesis as the middle class was trying to keep up with the consumption habits of the elite, whose incomes were increasing exponentially while those of the middle class were not.

The fashion industry is a good example of the way our taste for clothing is manipulated for profit. With the help of Madison Avenue, fashion outlets create a bandwagon effect that makes us feel uncomfortable if we do not conform to the current dress code.[31] We feel left out and are anxious about being ostracized.[32] Status seeking most probably has an evolutionary basis as people with high status had a higher probability of surviving and reproducing.[33]

Status seeking is a zero-sum endeavor. The increased competition for status is probably the reason why people have been working more recently. In order to keep up with the consumption of the upper 10 percent of income earners, the rest of the population worked longer hours and the average household had two workers in the labor force whereas a generation ago one worker sufficed to maintain a family of four. Insofar as leisure is a normal good, one would have expected people to enjoy more of it as incomes were increasing, as at least until 1998 median household income was rising. Instead, leisure was declining and working hours were increasing independently of income trends as the income of the average person failed to keep pace with the rise of income in the top 10 percent. They chose to work longer hours in order to keep up with the Joneses. Hence, progressive taxation, which counters the exaggerated competition for status and hence the purchase of positional goods, would increase social welfare, contrary to conventional theory. Laws that foster safety, savings, health, leisure activity such as holidays, and consumption taxes on luxury goods would be welfare enhancing from this perspective. Keeping up with the Joneses—in search of the American dream—leads to an epidemic of stress, overwork, and accumulation of debt without fulfillment.

SOCIETY

Society is another concept absent from standard economics: super-individualistic economic theory assumes that we do not interact with one another in our economic activity. The sole contact in textbooks is the brief encounter between consumers and producers, which is not really an interaction but is thought of as an innocuous split-second exchange of money for goods. Yet we are not Robinson Crusoes: behavior in society is highly structured by cultural expectations, institutions, and social norms. These influence our value system, which calibrates our aspirations, constrains our choices, and channels our actions. These norms contribute greatly to defining our aesthetic sense and the terms under which we can become full-fledged and esteemed members of the society. We do not act in a vacuum: very few of our decisions are autonomous.

The overwhelming majority of us does not want to become outcasts and therefore tends to conform to the basic established attitudes, mores, and accepted behavior of our respective societies.[34] That means that we learn from other people's actions how we should act, what we should consider important in our lives, how to gain power and respect within the social order. We follow fashions and fads in the media in order to find out what outfits are in style. The rules are complex: the color coordination must be right and an inch can make a big difference on the size of a lapel or necktie or a hemline. It just might be a deal breaker when applying for a job.

We want to be accepted by our peers and we need to know the terms under which we are going to be accepted. If what we see around us are people idolizing money, we are more likely to devote our lives to its acquisition as a means to achieve acceptance and position than in a society that holds spirituality in high esteem and considers money degrading. Therefore, the values of the culture in which we live have an overarching influence on our attitudes even if we have internalized them to such a degree that we might not recognize them outright. The value structure is ingrained in our subconscious, or might instead be the explicit outcome of overt peer pressure—such as when we have been criticized for the clothes we wear. We might feel left out, rejected, or even disliked if we do not follow the current trends. The point is that we want to belong. That gives us a sense of security. We copy. If people shop a lot in our society, then we too have a good chance of shopping a lot.[35] It takes energy and determination to defy norms and to overcome social pressure.[36]

Group interaction is a crucial element in economic activity.[37] We order differently in a restaurant when we are alone than when we are with others. Someone may convince you to have an extra drink just as you are about to leave a party. We engage in groupthink in order to avoid conflict and adhere to group norms.[38] In other words, we are impressionable and follow convention and social norms. In fact, we do very little consumption by ourselves in isolation. Instead, we consume as a household unit or among friends and are influenced by what others do or don't consume. That is how the culture of consumption is propagated from one generation to the next.

There is a whole discipline—social psychology, disregarded by economists—that focuses on analyzing the ways in which behavior depends on whether we act alone as an individual or act in a crowd.[39] Stampedes at Walmart stores are examples of herding behavior.[40] One person starts running and it becomes contagious. The result is often injury and shoppers have even been trampled to death. People lose their individuality in a crowd: inhibitions that are valid under normal circumstances melt away and one acts as a "faceless" member of the group rather than as an individual.

Gender roles are also socially constructed. Until the 1960s, married women were expected to be homemakers. With the equal rights movement women's labor force participation increased markedly. In 1950 just 20 percent of married women with children worked, whereas today by the turn of the twenty-first century nearly 70 percent do.[41] Such major changes do not come about through utility maximization but require substantial shifts in social norms, expectations, values, and peer pressure.

Household activity is also left out of consideration in most textbooks. How consumption is divided among members of the household is an open question. Child care, considered "caring work" in which the child is dependent on the care giver, does not fit well into the autonomous individualistic model of decision making. How does work within the household enhance welfare? Household production is excluded from the GNP accounts, which consider only paid market activity. As long as we equate income with welfare, all the important unpaid activity that takes place within the household, from child rearing to meal preparation, is not part of the welfare calculus.

Feminist economists argue that the traditional conceptualization of "economic man" has too much affinity with aspects of economic theory that are culturally associated with masculinity, such as competition, selfishness, and rationality, and does not put sufficient emphasis on traditionally feminine perspectives on life that emphasize cooperation, altruism, and emotional intelligence. Moreover, women are more likely to want to include household work in GNP accounts. Hence, mainstream economics is seen as propagating a masculine bias.

CULTURE

Culture is the software of our mind for interpreting the world; it is a system of symbolic codes, the sum total of our mental constructs about our social and physical environment. Culture is the lens through which we see the world, a distinct set of attitudes, mores, symbols, beliefs, and mental reflexes that gives meaning to our life and at the same time defines us as a member of a group. A shared value system is part of culture, such as the way we define private property and the degree to which we hold it sacred. What do we consider as decent behavior, standards for beauty, and what is desirable are all within the realm of culture. Norms of behavior in society are rules that one should adhere to in order to remain a respected member of the group. Thus, the extent to which we feel obligated to keep our word, or are willing to subvert the intentions of incomplete contracts, is also an integral part of the culture. The extent to which we adhere to religious precepts is part of our culture. The Ninth Commandment, for instance, lowered transaction costs and thereby fostered economic growth. This has important economic implications insofar as the extent to which and under what terms we are willing to trust our counterparty is a major determinant of transaction costs.

The extent to which society tolerates deviations from truth will determine such important factors as the kinds of advertising and packaging that are allowed in the marketplace. How much inequality will be tolerated? How are gender roles defined? How much redistribution is the society willing to accept? How much effort are workers willing to expand? Our work ethic, as Max Weber pointed out, is part of our culture. Our degree of impatience and our respect for laws are all part of culture. It is basically all the reflexive actions we take without deeply thinking about them. In other words, most every economic decision has a cultural component, including our preferences and our expectation formations, and our perception of risk. Hence, it defines many, if not most, of the fundamental concepts of the economic system. Economy and cultural norms are inseparable.[42] They interact. Neither precedes the other; they are inextricably intertwined.

What is universal in economics and what is culture-specific? The organization of a Japanese corporation is quite different than that of its U.S. counterpart insofar as they each grow out of distinct cultures. In Japan, workers have more loyalty to the firm while the firm has a long-run commitment to its workers, whereas the relationship between worker and firm is seen as temporary in the United States.

The market is not designed to create social norms such that it will perpetuate itself. This led Daniel Bell to formulate his concerns for the future of capitalism. He argued that the culture created by capitalism generates a need for instant gratification, and that this harms the work ethic that brought about the success of capitalism in the first place. He asserted that there is a problem "of managing a complex polity when the values of the society stress unrestrained appetite. The contradictions I see in contemporary capitalism derive from the unraveling of the threads which had once held the culture and the economy together, from the influence of the hedonism which has become the prevailing value in our society."[43] A "porno-pop culture," "gaudily dressed" and "foul-mouthed," has a hard time sustaining capitalism as the ethic of hard work erodes. The constant search for pleasure crowds out effortful work, savings, investments, and character that takes the public interest to heart.

Christopher Lasch was another critic of the market-driven culture of post-industrial capitalism that created a personality type he characterized as pathologically narcissistic.[44] He observed that people had a weak sense of identity and self-worth. Corporations would not profit from people with a strong identity, strong will power, and a strong sense of self-respect. However, they can profit from those who are developmentally stymied and whose self-control is limited so that they will be open to the influence of trendsetters, buy the latest gadgets, succumb to new fashion fads, and spend money recklessly. People who are spendthrifts benefit business insofar as they can extract the last cent of their paychecks.[45] They do not want people to grow personally and mentally and have a sense of social responsibility. There is no need to worry, then, about the welfare of generations yet unborn. The yuppies were good for the balance sheet of the corporate world.

These are the messages that advertisements, TV, and media personalities perpetuate. As a consequence, we feel inadequate unless we wear the latest fashion and mimic the stars. We take advantage of others to reach for power and prestige. We entertain unrealistic fantasies of the American Dream and need positive reinforcement through our consumption. "To live for the moment is the prevailing passion—to live for yourself, not for your predecessors or posterity. We are fast losing the sense of historical continuity, the sense of belonging to a succession of generations originating in the past and stretching into the future."[46] Lasch wrote those words more than a generation ago. They are even more relevant today than they were when he wrote them.

In other words, our elites have lost the concept of prudence, of setting reasonable limits, of guiding our appetite, of defending cultural values such as delayed gratification and responsible leadership.[47] Instead of providing guidance, our elites have failed to defend our cultural heritage and surrendered leadership to those vested interests who would profit from it: the mega-corporations that channel humongous amounts of money to affect cultural change in such a way that they accentuate the ideology of consumerism from which they can profit. In a sense, culture has been set free of its moorings and allowed to drift in the direction of market forces. The market participants have used this opportunity to their obvious advantage. The feedback effect was a cultural drift toward money making in which people gain constant external validation through the sense of control gained through shopping.[48] As Bell suggested, this poses a contradiction to free-market economics because overconsumption runs into environmental constraints as well as the barrier of indebtedness. This market-driven culture denigrates frugality and saving and instead does everything in its power to make it appear as though consumption will lead to a good life. Consequently, capitalism contains the seed of its own destruction: the market cannot perpetuate itself in a stable manner cut off from its moral anchors.

FAIRNESS

Humans definitely have a sense of fairness, a belief that some actions are impartial, reasonable, and just. Fairness implies the adherence to certain generally acknowledged social norms such as reciprocity, or an equitable distribution of resources, goods, or outcomes.[49] It is consistent with the ethical rules of a society. Some of this disposition is due to innate human nature and some is socially constructed and learned.[50] In either case, most people agree that it is not fair, for instance, to raise the price of gasoline already in storage at the gas station when the wholesale price of oil rises. In experiments, people reveal their sense of fairness in dividing a windfall. The person in possession usually retains about 60 percent of it for herself. This implies that we are not perfectly selfish but that we do care about our gain in proportion to that of others.

Moreover, people tend to be vengeful toward those who betray their culturally dependent sense of the social contract. In other words, people have social preferences and do not only care for their own well-being. People are also averse to inequality in allocation of resources and are concerned with their public image, that is, what others think of their consumption.[51] Such experimental evidence can explain charitable contributions, wage dispersion within firms, strikes, and many other economic phenomena. It should be the goal of the economics discipline to incorporate such psychologically realistic aspects into its theories and policies.

EFFICIENCY VS. EQUITY

Efficiency is a cornerstone of mainstream thinking, an integral part of its value system. The claim is that the market economy is efficient. Consequently, it cannot be improved upon. Neoclassical economists appear to value this attribute of the free market above all. Production is efficient; meaning that firms produce optimally the optimum amount of goods, thus more could not be produced with the given amount of inputs. Likewise, consumption is also efficient and optimal: people know what they want and how to get it, and no more satisfaction could possibly be squeezed out of the goods they consume. No one can be made better off without making someone else worse off. However, under this definition, the institution of slavery was efficient because the slaves' well-being could not be improved upon without making their captors worse off. So an efficient system may well be unjust, as in this example.

This conceptualization of efficiency is not at all value neutral as claimed: Why not emphasize sustainability or morality or fairness or equality or meeting basic needs, instead? Textbooks naively assume that it is obvious that everyone values efficiency above all, but that is hardly the case: I think that most people would prefer to live in a just society more than in an efficient one. Furthermore, the definition implicitly accepts the current endowment of wealth as an integral part of the efficient outcome. This is also an implicit value judgment and is not based on any moral justification as the current distribution of income and wealth is not just at all, according to political philosopher John Rawls.

Rawls argued that the just society is one that you would choose without knowing what your position in it would be if you were dropped into it at random.[52] One would most likely accept the social contract in a just society designed behind a "veil of ignorance" insofar as one is risk averse and did not want to end up at the bottom of the social pyramid. He suggested that the decisions we make now are biased insofar as we know our current standing in the social order. We already have information on our endowments: how smart we are, the color of our skin, our wealth or our socioeconomic status. This knowledge obviously sways our judgment. If we are smart, talented, and have access to education as Bill Gates did—he had use of a mainframe computer in his high school, which only a handful of students had in those days—we would likely support a meritocracy based on education. The descendants of Sam Walton, Fred Koch, or Frank Mars likely have no problem with inherited wealth. If we were Kobe Bryant or LeBron James, we would no doubt think that we deserved our $20–30 million annual salary. We are not likely to attribute our talents to luck, our father's coaching, or our genes and say that we really don't deserve that much money.

However, our opinions would be different if we designed a society from scratch without knowing in advance where we would end up in the society's distribution of intelligence, talent, looks, inherited wealth, or family background. Without that a priori knowledge, we would no doubt be much more careful in constructing a society that distributed income on the basis of luck of birth and created a legal system that ensured that even those with not much luck and with limited talents be able to satisfy at least their basic needs. It would be too risky for most of us to create a society in which the distribution of income was as extremely skewed as it is today if we did not know where we would end up in it. After all, we might end up at the very bottom tail of the distribution. Choosing behind a veil of ignorance, we would maximize the welfare of the least advantaged to ensure that we would not end up marginalized in the society in utter destitution.

There must be something wrong with a definition according to which it is deemed efficient for Victoria's Secret to produce million-dollar bras for each of the last 10 years,[53] and for children to play in quarter-million-dollar playhouses while at the same time other children in slums lack access to decent education and adequate health care. Moreover, the distribution of resources may affect the quantity of output inasmuch as resources may not be in the most productive hands. Some productive persons may well have insufficient capital but no collateral to gain access to the capital market. According to the common wisdom, banks with excess capital would lend to the person who is more productive, but that does not happen automatically in a world in which collateral plays a decisive role in the credit market.

Consider how much the educational achievement and future productivity of the next generation could be increased by equalizing the educational resources available to the youth of this country. An immense amount of human capital is wasted by depriving children and youth of efficient educational systems. A transfer of funds from the million-dollar bras and 300-million-dollar yachts of the wealthy to underprivileged school systems would raise their educational standards up to par, thereby increasing the educational opportunities of the poor immensely without the wealthy really feeling a great strain in their lifestyle besides reducing conspicuous consumption slightly. This would lead to a marked increase in productivity, and hence efficiency, of the population over time. Thus, redistribution can be approached also from a perspective of efficiency rather than of fairness if one defines efficiency as maximizing welfare with a given amount of inputs.

Admittedly, conventional welfare analysis avoids making interpersonal comparisons when it pertains to redistribution of wealth, but it does not avoid aggregating welfare when it is ideologically convenient to do so. For instance, when we calculate national income per capita as a welfare measure, it implicitly assumes that the utility of income is the same across all individuals, which is a violation of the prohibition on interpersonal comparison of utility.[54]

The conventional definition of efficiency is also not very useful in policy considerations. Practically no action could be undertaken from this perspective insofar as some people are invariably made worse off by every economic policy. As a consequence, a rule requiring that an alternative allocation leave no participant worse off overwhelmingly favors the status quo. Consider the North American Free Trade Agreement (NAFTA). It was argued that the increase in trade would improve welfare and economic efficiency. Yet, many people were surely hurt, lost their jobs, or received lower wages as a result. The pro-trade mindset argues that society gains nonetheless insofar as the gains of the gainers are greater than the losses of those who lose. Well enough, but the losers were not compensated for their losses. So the adoption of NAFTA was not Pareto efficient because some people were made better off at the expense of others.[55] We apparently allow such redistribution when it comes to trade policy, but economists (and politicians) advocate against it when it pertains to improving the schooling opportunities of poor children.

There are many other aspects of the status quo that are inefficient. For example, businesses find it beneficial to confuse consumers. There are many hidden charges associated with credit card debt. That is why the government enacted legislation in 2009 in order to rein in the power of credit card companies to charge hidden, gimmicky penalties.[56] Even after the legislation, some companies are charging an unimaginable 79.9 percent interest rate but in such a way that it is not obvious to consumers.[57] Deceptive practices are not efficient, because they enrich some at the expense of others without their consent.

Thus, it is misleading to think that markets are automatically efficient or even that competitive markets are efficient. Markets have to be perfectly competitive in order to be efficient, and all participants have to have perfect information on the contracts as well as on the quality of the product. Yet only a negligible fraction of today's economy is made up of perfectly competitive firms, and imperfect information dominates. In order for a market to be perfectly competitive it has to be made up of many small firms all charging the same price for a homogeneous product without barriers to entry.[58] Guess how significant such markets are in the real-world economy today? Perhaps 1 or 2 percent of U.S. gross domestic product at most is produced under conditions that come close to perfect competition. Yet, many textbooks argue as though such concepts apply to markets in general: "We have seen that markets have remarkable efficiency properties," write Samuelson and Nordhaus,[59] forgetting the qualifier "perfectly competitive" in their generalization and also neglecting completely the complications of imperfect information. That is the reason why the notion that markets are efficient has crept into common usage among the population at large and reflects the spirit of the times. The missing concepts make the above formulation—and many others like it—a damaging assertion insofar as students take away the idea that all markets are efficient without exception, as long as there is competition. Consequently, it is an extremely misleading, even damaging, assertion. Witness the consensus that built up to deregulate the financial sector. Alan Greenspan and his entourage simply applied the perfectly competitive model with perfect information to a sector that was everything but perfectly competitive and had a lot of asymmetric information. Obviously, they were taught Econ 101 incorrectly.

SELF-INTEREST AND ALTRUISM

Altruism is the attribute of being concerned about the welfare of others and considering "the interests of other persons, without the need of ulterior motives."[60] Hundreds of experiments have verified that we are not 100 percent selfish; being self-interested is not a binary attribute.[61] We are capable of self-sacrifice for the benefit of others or for an intangible cause or idea.[62] Rather, there is a culturally dependent continuum between the two polar extremes of being a Mother Teresa or a Dick Fuld (the CEO of Lehman Brothers who famously declared that he wanted to rip out the hearts of short sellers and eat them).[63] I think human nature is likely to be about two-thirds selfish. Neuroscientists have shown that humans are hardwired for empathy and act altruistically in some situations even if they do not derive pleasure from it.

We could not live in families, groups, or societies if we were completely egoistic. Individuals who entirely disregarded group interests would not have been able to reproduce with the same frequency as those who respected these interests. They would have had a difficult time surviving in the wild if they had not cared for the other members of the family or tribe, as they, too, relied on others to hunt and to defend against outsiders. Hunting in groups required cooperation, and hunting big game implied sharing as the best strategy, because the meat obtained was too much to consume by the hunters alone. In other words, humans survived as members of a group and not as individuals. The discovery of fire meant that others had to maintain the home environment while the hunters worked, leading to a division of labor and cooperative behavior. Thus, those without any empathy for the welfare of others would have been ostracized and expelled from the tribe. They would have been isolated, without friends and family. Except for a handful of psychopaths, then, altruism is hardwired into our genetic make-up so that self-centered utility maximization is not at all in our nature and is therefore not a realistic assumption. There is research on neural activity and energy use in brain cells that suggests as much.[64] So those who cared for the welfare of the group had a higher probability of passing on their genes to the next generation.

As Adam Smith himself noted, we are by nature altruistic to some degree without regard to our own advantage.[65] Smith recognized that we are interested in the fortunes of others and feel pity and compassion, even for strangers.[66] We do not like to see the misery of others and "derive sorrow from the sorrow of others."[67] Social norms play an important role on how altruistic we become.[68] Brain research indicates that we have "mirror neurons" that fire when we see others in distress, as though it were our own experience. According to economist Aldo Rustichini, "Smith (and Hume before him) had identified sympathy as a pervasive feature of human nature by the power of introspection. . . . [T]here is now ample evidence that there is a deep reason for Smith's intuition. . . . [S]ympathy has a basis in the way the brain works. . . ."[69]

By neglecting altruism, Econ 101 textbooks lead us astray: it is wrong to suggest that we maximize a utility function that includes only our own consumption. Altruism toward relatives has been discussed in terms of our propensity to propagate our genes. However, this has been extended by the concept of multilevel selection. Edward O. Wilson explains group selected behavior as follows: "hereditary social behavior improves the competitive ability not of just individuals within groups but among groups as a whole. . . ." He continues, explaining that people have an "intense, obsessive interest . . . in other people, which begins in the first days of life." In addition, human nature includes "the overpowering instinctual urge to belong to groups. . . . To be kept in solitude is to be kept in pain. . . . A person's membership in his group—his tribe—is a large part of his identity. . . . [C]ompetition among groups . . . promoted altruism and cooperation among all the group members. It led to group-wide morality and a sense of conscience and honor. . . . To yield completely to the instinctual urgings born from individual selection would dissolve society."[70]

POSITIVE AND NORMATIVE ECONOMICS

Economists are keen on distinguishing between positive economics, which is supposedly objective and describes and analyzes the economy using scientific methods, and normative economics, which pertains to what ought to be. The former is supposedly value free while the latter involves value judgments. Nonetheless, the distinction is essentially artificial, because it is impossible to undertake economic analysis without making some assumptions that themselves involve value judgments even if they appear intuitively plausible. (I demonstrated this above with reference to the concept of efficiency.) How to ascertain the validity of self-evident assumptions is controversial. What issues one considers to be positive economics is itself dependent on cultural norms and requires the use of a value system. For instance, economists assume that people are rational, although psychologists have proven beyond a reasonable doubt that people are not capable of being rational or coherent. Thus, the deliberate disregard of the results of scientific research is itself a major value judgment. Moreover, accepting the current distribution of wealth in theorizing about efficiency also implies a value judgment. It does not come out of a scientific canon. The description of the distribution itself may be objective, but defining the current distribution as efficient is no longer value free. It requires a value judgment.

Emphasizing efficiency over sustainability is another example of a value judgment; it is not anchored in objectivity. Not distinguishing between basic needs and wants is another arbitrary value judgment. In other words, it is impossible to have a value-neutral economic theory: the mainstream would consider the assumption that wants are unlimited to be positive economics, whereas others consider this idea to be merely a part of a culturally determined value system. There is no empirical evidence that insatiability is the norm of human nature. Rather, such attributes are learned in the process of acculturation. The hostility of textbooks toward the government is another distinctly American cultural attribute. That worldview does not consider the need for consumer protection from powerful business interests, even though government protection of consumers has yielded such successes as halving the number of cigarette smokers; that would never have occurred without government help.

Some argue that theories ought not be judged by the verity of their assumptions but by their ability to make valid predictions. However, that is in itself a value judgment open to question. Economics, in any event, is not known for its accurate forecasting. It failed miserably at predicting the Great Recession even though there were enough warnings that people in authority chose to disregard.[71] Instead, Fed chairman Ben Bernanke proudly declared the age of "The Great Moderation" in 2004 about as accurately as George W. Bush declared victory in Iraq aboard the USS *Abraham Lincoln* the previous year. As late as 2007, Bernanke was giving speeches reassuring everyone that the financial sector was not going to experience any problems: "Importantly, we see no serious broader spillover to banks or thrift institutions from problems in the subprime market; the troubled lenders, for the most part, have not been institutions with federally insured deposits."[72] He was obviously using the wrong models to forecast systemic risk. In addition to failing to forecast the severity of the Great Recession, the economics profession is at a complete loss on how to get the economy out of it. To be sure, there are many solutions offered, but a consensus is elusive. In short, economic models are not particularly useful in predicting and forecasting in real-world situations.

EXPECTED VS. REALIZED UTILITY

There is yet another serious problem with conventional utility maximization theory. It rarely distinguishes between expected and realized utility. It assumes that when I purchased chicken fingers for $4.30 I actually received at least $4.30 worth of utility from them. The reasoning is that, because I paid for them I must have gotten that much value from them. Yet, of course, this inference is incorrect: I paid for them before I consumed them. Hence, at the time of the transaction I did not yet know the utility I would receive from them, even if I did expect to receive at least $4.30 worth of satisfaction. Upon consumption, they could turn out to be different than I had anticipated. As a consequence, we need to distinguish between expected and realized utility. Hence, the amount I spend need not be equal to the amount of utility that I actually receive from an item, and this is yet another reason why consumption and income ought not be equated with welfare.

Actually, we are prone to make systematic mistakes in forecasting utility. Many people fail to distinguish between the initial level of utility obtained from a good and future levels of utility. In other words, consumers generally do not account for adaptation in their decisions and do not anticipate accurately the rate at which utility depreciates over time. People tend to exaggerate the effect of purchases on their long-run level of satisfaction. There are also biases in how much we remember experiences. Economists emphasize the experiencing of consumption, but anticipation and remembering generate utility as well. Yet people usually do not give them sufficient weight in their decisions. Suppose you had an ice cream cone a year ago. It no longer provides you any utility. However, expenditure on vacations, for instance, is remembered longer and the rate of decay in remembering is not given sufficient weight at the time we make our decision. In other words, people make many errors in their consumption decisions, including in forecasting the amount of utility obtained immediately from consumption and the rate of decay of that utility. We also tend to be myopic about making long-run decisions.

Furthermore, we often come to regret our purchases, because advertisers take advantage of our psychological weaknesses and entice us into buying products that we subsequently regret purchasing.[73] We are also often misled into accepting contracts without full information. Often the problem is that we do not even know what questions to ask in order to make an informed decision. The use of the Internet frequently leads to frustrated customers who are dissatisfied with the products purchased.[74] I know that I am often duped, particularly when I purchase something complex for the first time or under time pressure, and I generally do so with imperfect information. This is the case when I sign contracts for credit cards, cell phones, satellite TV reception, and similarly complex products.[75]

IMPERFECT INFORMATION

Textbooks imply that the price of a product is all the information one needs to make a rational choice about its consumption. This is correct only if the choice is a trivial one: inasmuch as imperfect information and imperfect markets are pervasive, this should not be the default model. In most cases, obtaining accurate information about a good is costly, difficult, and takes much effort.

In other words, acquiring accurate and reliable information is a huge problem that is trivialized in most textbooks. There are numerous sources of imperfect information, such as information uncertainty, incomplete information, and asymmetric information. These pose an enormous obstacle to efficient consumption and, in turn, to the efficient functioning of markets.[76] According to Joseph Stiglitz, "even a small amount of information imperfection could have a profound effect on the nature of the equilibrium."[77] This means that efficient outcomes are rarely attainable in practice. Information is costly to acquire and producers do their best to manipulate information so as to make certain attributes more accessible than others. Hence, information is unequally distributed and not everyone has the same information at their fingertips, given the unequal distribution of wealth, education, and cognitive abilities.

Crucial data are generally not within easy reach of most people. Thus, we almost always have to act with incomplete evidence, which is a challenge to our ability to make satisfactory decisions, let alone optimal ones. Trying to do one's best is not a very useful procedure if we do not even know how to go about finding out what information we need in order to attain our desired ends. Alternatively, we may not have the funds necessary to find the information we need to attain our goals.

The invisible hand is used as shorthand for the self-regulating mechanism of the market; it implies that the actions of selfish individuals will benefit society. However, it does not work with imperfect information.[78] Stiglitz has repeatedly warned that the invisible hand metaphor ought not be taken seriously: "the reason the invisible hand often seemed invisible was that it was not there. . . . Markets by themselves do not lead to economic efficiency. If we look at examples of market successes and failures around the world, we see that many are understandable in terms of economic theories based on imperfect markets in which governments must play an important role. . . ."[79]

The situation in which one party to an exchange knows more about the good, service, or contract than the other, and it would not be in his/her interest to disclose it or he cannot do so credibly, is referred to as a problem of asymmetric information.[80] For instance, the bankers knew much more about the riskiness of adjustable rate mortgages than did the borrowers who signed on to them during the run-up to the Meltdown of 2008. The person who packaged exotic securities knew much more about the product than the person who bought them. As a consequence, deception played a big role in the period preceding the crisis. Goldman Sachs had to pay a $650 million fine for just one such transaction.

Insider (private) information is another issue. The originator mortgage broker knew the creditworthiness of the borrower but the investors to whom the mortgage securities were sold knew much less, and knowledge decreased down the financial chain. By the time the securities reached purchasers near the Arctic Circle, the information was quite distorted. Asymmetric information is obviously at the root of the subprime mortgage crisis: insiders acted strategically and took advantage of those who did not have as much knowledge of finance as they did. Millions of substandard contracts were signed by parties with asymmetric information. This is precisely the reason why the Consumer Financial Protection Bureau was created—albeit belatedly—in 2010.[81]

The problem is not confined to consumers but extends to investors as well. Eight tiny municipalities in Norway (most of which are above the Arctic Circle) lost all of their investments—on the order of $75 million—by speculating on highly leveraged, incredibly risky, and complicated bonds issued by Citibank and sold through a Norwegian broker. The municipalities obviously did not understand what they were doing and were not well informed. The broker also withheld some crucial information. That the investors were clueless is suggested by the fact that their potential upside was tiny but their downside was enormous and completely disproportionate to their possible gains. Risk was obviously mispriced.[82] This case is a good example of banks and mortgage brokers taking advantage of information asymmetries and gullible investors.

Principal-agent problems refer to an important subset of information problems in which an employee, say a CEO (the agent), works on behalf of someone else (the principal), such as the shareholders. The principal does not have information on all attributes of the agent that are important for the success of the firm, such as his honesty, the amount of knowledge he possesses about the operation of the firm, or the amount of effort he is willing to expand on behalf of the firm. Insofar as it is impossible to write perfect contracts in order to align the incentives in such a way that they benefit both parties in all circumstances, agents often do work mainly for their own benefit in the first instance. Workers shirk for the same reason, as it is difficult to control their labor input perfectly. This is a subset of the information asymmetry problem inasmuch as the agent (the worker or the CEO) has better information on what she is willing and able to do than the principal (employer or the shareholders). This leads to inefficiencies and misallocation of resources, as evinced by the excessive risks CEOs took during the subprime bubble. Dick Fuld walked away from the bankrupt Lehman brothers with nearly half a billion dollars. His employers—the shareholders—walked away with next to nothing. If the risks pay off, the agent gains; if not, the principal loses and not the agent.

The concept of "moral hazard" is another special case of information asymmetry. It often pertains to markets with a wrong incentives structure. For example, the agent may behave inappropriately if contracts are incomplete or the principal does not have credible information on the performance of the agent. Jamie Dimon and Lloyd Blankfein know now, if they did not know it before, that their firms are way "too big to fail," so they will most likely accept excessive risks, thinking that it is a one-sided bet. If everything goes well, they win; if everything does not go well, the taxpayers lose. That is moral hazard in a nutshell. Goldman Sachs, JPMorgan Chase, Bank of America, and Wells Fargo no longer have as much downside risk as upside gains. The risks are asymmetric. The government really cannot monitor their bets but nonetheless provides a shield for them in case of need. Thus, these CEOs have more information on their actions than does the government.[83]

By bailing out Wall Street, the Treasury and the Federal Reserve have increased moral hazard in our economy to dangerous levels. The implication is that JPMorgan, Citibank, and the other major meltdown players are "too big to fail": this refers to a self-fulfilling prophecy that big will get bigger—a forecast of precarious instability that prompted MIT professor and former chief economist at the International Monetary Fund Simon Johnson to refer to this situation as the doom-loop.[84] Joseph Stiglitz calls this privatizing of profits and socializing of losses "socialism for the rich and capitalism for the poor." He thinks that this economic system has evolved into an "ersatz capitalism," a variant of crony capitalism or corporatism.

In sum, the problem of acquiring and processing information has many facets. Students should not study economics without being made aware of the ubiquitous information problem, as it is a major impediment to the efficient workings of markets. The uneven distribution of information is one of the Achilles heels of markets. Laissez faire and the invisible hand do not lead to efficient outcomes in the presence of imperfect information. As a consequence, consumer protection is not at all superfluous. Very often the producer has much more information about the product than the consumer, and in such cases it is unfair to put all the burden of acquiring adequate information on the buyer in order that he make a knowledgeable decision. Letting the buyer beware (caveat emptor) is not a reasonable rule of thumb in such cases. In the presence of asymmetric information, government-mandated dissemination of information can lower transaction costs and improve the buyer's ability to make an informed choice that will lead to satisfactory consumption. Truthful packaging and truthful advertising could raise consumer satisfaction considerably.

I believe that taking advantage of asymmetric information in the course of an economic exchange is taking self-interest and caveat emptor too far. I therefore define such an exchange as exploitation. If one party knowingly takes advantage of a counterparty in order to gain, at the other's expense, from the other's lack of information or lack of ability to understand the information, then he would be engaging in an exploitative exchange. This is quite similar to the idea of "infliction of pain on others for private advantage."[85]

SIGNALING

Signals generate information. In a market with imperfect information, signals are important in that they are frequently substitutes for information that is difficult to convey in other ways. A diploma is a signal of having achieved some degree of academic excellence. Students go to college not only to learn but also to demonstrate to future employers that they have the attributes to perform well under various circumstances. The acquisition of the diploma is, then, a signal that one can successfully complete a complicated educational maze and that one has the requisite stamina, will power, and intelligence to do so. When employers consider hiring someone, they have some information available about the candidate but also want to know about numerous unobservable attributes: reliability, ability to work under stress, flexibility in new situations, willingness to cooperate, and so forth. In a market with imperfect information, the diploma has a large value beyond the value of the knowledge acquired during the years of study. It signals the possession of intangible attributes. That is why people who complete high school or college earn disproportionately more than those who leave school shortly before receiving the certificate, although the additional knowledge gained during the missing time interval is probably not crucial for performance on the job. In that sense, the additional effort of obtaining the credential is inefficient, because the student could have performed as well on the job without the diploma. However, with imperfect information she is not capable of demonstrating that aspect of her character to her future employer; the diploma thus symbolizes—or signals—a bundle of desirable attitudes or abilities.[86]

Thus, there is a divergence between private and social returns to education. For the student it is worth investing in the diploma, but from the point of view of the society, the additional resources spent on generating the signal is wasted and inefficient insofar as the investment did not lead to an increase in productivity. Nonetheless, it is necessary in case information on true productivity is difficult to disseminate in a credible manner otherwise.

The price of a product transmits information that the seller is willing to trade at that price. However, a loss-leader strategy can turn the price of a product that is sold at or below cost into a signal that the seller is a low-price firm. In that case the price is used as a signal to entice consumers to frequent that establishment and is deceptive and can lead to inefficient outcomes, because the consumer's decision is not based on complete knowledge of all the prices she will encounter. Prices on other products offered by the firm might be higher than average; hence, her total purchases may be more than at other firms. Price can also affect directly the amount of satisfaction we obtain from a product.[87] In that case the utility is obtained not only from the product itself but also from its price, which is contrary to the standard model.

Furthermore, firms are constantly sending signals our way with the aim of derailing our plan and enticing us to spend our money the way they want us to. Their advantage is that they can afford to hire the smartest marketing agencies to figure out how to trap us. Under such circumstances, making economic choices are qualitatively not at all like the trivial choices presented in textbooks.

Signaling social status is another type of inefficiency in consumption. Veblen suggested that through conspicuous consumption we signal our status and social position and thereby create a negative externality insofar as it creates a feeling of envy in others. It is an expensive way to let the world know one's place in society and induces others to try to emulate the consumption habits of the rich even at the cost of becoming indebted.

TIME INCONSISTENCY

Mainstream textbooks assume that people discount the future. The future is a nebulous concept for most people and not as important as the present. Of course, not everyone thinks that way. Some people do not discount the future at all, inasmuch as they look forward to the pleasures of tomorrow. Anticipation provides its own utility, generally overlooked. Nonetheless, the conventional wisdom assumes that people use exponential discounting to assess the value of future utility. That means that a dollar one year from now is valued at, say, just 95 cents today. The difference of 5 cents is in a sense a payment for not having to wait a year for the money.

Exponential discounting has the characteristic that the discount rate is constant regardless of how far into the future one considers. Thus, one dollar 10 years from now is worth just about 60 cents today at the compounded annual discount rate of 5 percent, and the sum continues to lose about 40 percent of its value every subsequent 10 years. So the rate of decay in the value remains a constant. Hence, one dollar 50 years from now should be worth 60 cents 40 years from now.

However, this exponential discounting does not hold up in experiments. Instead, people use "hyperbolic" discounting: their rate of discount varies depending on the time horizon—it is higher near the present and lower far into the future.[88] A comparison of hyperbolic with exponential discounting indicates that the two are similar in the near term. In Figure 5.2, both types of discounting arrive at about the same value of one dollar discounted 10 years from now—about 60 cents. However, note that while the rate of depreciation is a constant for the exponential discounting throughout the period sketched, the hyperbolic discounting loses only 18 percent of its value during the 10-year interval between 30 and 40 years and then a still-lower 15 percent between 40 and 50 years. This implies that waiting 10 years today means a lot to you—you are impatient—but viewed from the perspective of today, waiting 10 years 40 years from now is not so important at all. It is as though you were myopic looking into the future; 40 and 50 years appear quite close together so with hyperbolic discounting you do not discount that difference at the same rate closer to the present as you would with exponential discounting. The fact that waiting 10 years today means a lot to you, but waiting 10 years 40 years from now does not mean a lot to you, is inconsistent with standard models of rational choice, because preferences are time dependent. This is an important cognitive bias because it induces us to save too little for our future safety, sustenance, and retirement, or induces us to borrow too much on our credit cards.

This myopia is an important reason for consumer protections such as government-imposed health and social insurance. Young workers are not generally thinking of their retirement income. On the other hand, the older members of society, who are closer to retirement age, are better informed about the need for retirement security. Thus, government, through its power to tax, can make sure that social insurance will be provided upon retirement. Otherwise, people who lack the foresight to plan for the future can cause problems.

Another cognitive bias that leads to time inconsistency in addition to hyperbolic discounting is assessing probabilities. What is the probability that one will become disabled, contract one of the 200 different kinds of cancers, or will need long-term care insurance 30 years from now? We are generally biased toward the present and therefore tend to discount excessively such improbable events in the future.

Figure 5.2   **Hyperbolic and Exponential Discounting**

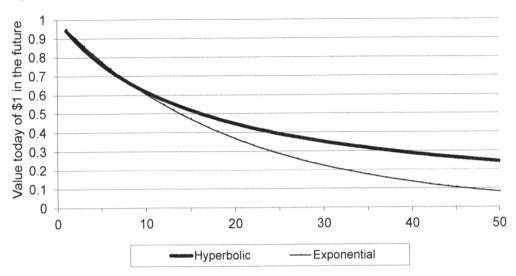

PATIENCE AND IMPATIENCE

Patience is one of the most important parameters of an economy, insofar as it has a major influence on the savings rate and through that the long-run growth rate of the economy. Decisions we make today will have ripple effects for an extended period of time; the inter-temporal choices we make depend on how much we value the future, and how much we disregard or discount the future. Our propensities and inclinations in this regard are learned, in the main, early in life and are part of our cultural attributes. Therefore, we are susceptible to influences from the business community, which has an incentive to broadcast a message that is biased toward impatience. This has been discussed above in reference to Bell's prediction that there is a contradiction between the need for savings in order to have a dynamic economy and the need of the business community to increase its profitability in the present. Therefore, without sufficient government action to counter corporate power, the likelihood that impatience will continue to rise is considerable. That is a main reason that there is so much indebtedness in the U.S. economy today at both the individual and governmental levels.

THE METAPHOR OF THE INVISIBLE HAND

Economists are inclined to cite Adam Smith's famous reference to the invisible hand as a metaphor for the coordinating mechanism of a competitive market in which self-interest of both producers and consumers leads to the right amount of goods being produced, thereby increasing social welfare. However, such a metaphor is anachronistic.[89] Smith was describing an economy in which the quality of the products purchased was not difficult to ascertain; information was not an issue. Moreover, the butcher bought bread from the baker and the baker bought meat from the butcher year in and year out. Under such circumstances, the threat of opportunistic behavior was as good as nonexistent. Obviously, the butcher would not have gained by selling inferior-quality meat nor would the baker have benefited by shortchanging the butcher. They would have been discredited if they tried to deceive, overcharge, or otherwise entrap the customers of their small community.

There was no small print and transactions were based on personal exchange; the products were simple and repeated within the confines of a village with a sense of permanence whose inhabitants knew each other's families throughout their lives and their parents' lives. It is a folly to compare such a market to the market for mortgage-backed securities, for which none of the above conditions holds. Asymmetric information is the essence of the modern economy and makes transacting in the marketplace much more precarious than in Smith's time.

Besides, there was much more social pressure in the eighteenth century to avoid opportunistic behavior: cheaters, deceivers, the greedy, and overreaching people would have been ostracized. The impersonal nature of today's economy implies, in contrast, that Dick Fuld will not be ostracized by Palm Beach society. Moreover, the participants in eighteenth-century markets were much more likely to believe in the Ten Commandments than today's businessmen, and would have been much less likely to want to engage in opportunistic behavior.[90] The Smithian world is far from a reliable guide for today's economy. Peter Whybrow put it this way:

> Although it was well recognized that the human creature left unchecked has a propensity for greed, Smith argued that in a free society overweening self-interest is constrained by the wish to be loved by others . . . and by the "social sentiment" (empathic and common-sense behavior) that is learned by living in community. Therefore, with the adoption of a few rules—such as honesty in competition, respect for private property, and the ability to exchange goods for money—personal desire can be safely liberated to prime the engines of economic growth. Self-love will be simultaneously molded to the common good by the complex personal relationships and the social order in which the "free" market operates; self-interest will ultimately serve the common interest. . . . But Smith lived before the invention of the mega-corporation, before instant global communication, and before the double cheeseburger and hedge funds. Today the tethers that once bound self-interest and social concern into closely knit economic communities, and which gave us Adam Smith's enduring metaphor of an "invisible hand" balancing market behavior, have been weakened by an intrusive mercantilism that never sleeps.[91]

In other words, the incentives are very different in a global marketplace, where anonymous individuals are representing corporations in their dealing with anonymous faces in the crowd. Clearly, people behave differently under such circumstances. Deceiving an unknown entity in a faraway place one may not even have heard of is a very different psychological dilemma than dealing with counterparties in Smith's village economy. Selling Citigroup's mortgage-backed securities in Narvik, northern Norway, the incentives and circumstances are completely different from those of Smith's butchers and bakers.[92] Goldman Sachs paid a $550 million penalty for getting caught deceiving its investors on one of its collateralized debt obligations.[93] A day later, AIG agreed to pay $725 million in a fraud case.[94] The main point is that these firms knew much more about what they were selling than did the buyers, and they took advantage of the latter's ignorance. Thus, invoking Smith's butchers and bakers as stand-ins for twenty-first century turbo-capitalism is anachronistic to the extreme.[95]

THE MAGIC OF COMPETITION

Competition has a positive connotation in our culture. It supposedly provides the solution to economic outcomes that ensures that everything turns out well in the marketplace—that the right quality is produced at the lowest possible price in the right amounts—but reality is different. Competition is not unconditionally good for society: it does not eliminate negligence and the accompanying disasters. A reason why reality does not conform to theory in this case is that markets are not efficient at creating or enforcing safety standards, and there are too many transactions with asymmetric information that carry the possibility of opportunistic behavior and uncertainty about the outcome of a transaction. Competition does not work well when these factors are present.

For instance, suppose a ground beef manufacturer put a label on the product stating "We guarantee that this beef has only 1 million *E. coli* bacteria per pound. In fact, we'll give you a thousand dollars if you get sick." Would people buy such ground beef? I know that I would not, and I doubt that anyone else would, because many of us do not know at all—or do not want to be reminded—that *E. coli* invariably do exist in the ground beef and we do not know what the Food and Drug Administration approved limit is. Moreover, we prefer to suppress the thought from our consciousness even if we have some vague notions about it. All we want to know is that the hamburger made of the ground beef is safe to eat if cooked properly. So labeling cannot be a competitive substitute for government inspection and regulation. Competition cannot solve all problems with complex transactions or when quality is difficult to ascertain.

Competition also does not work well when the fees are in the future and contingent on uncertain conditions that the consumer overlooks or forecasts too optimistically. This is the major problem with the hidden penalties of credit cards. I was subject to a fee by my credit card company as I purchased something from Canada and did not anticipate that there would be a surcharge on foreign purchases.[96] In fact, I am usually surprised by hidden fees when I participate in a complex transaction.

CONSUMERISM

The mainstream argument is that increasing the number of products increases welfare because it increases consumers' choices. However, choice is not good in any quantity. With increased choice comes increased difficulty in choosing and the increased possibility of misperception. So the proposition overlooks the fact that increasing the number of options could decrease welfare on account of the fact that choosing between products takes time and is therefore costly. Choice is good up to a point, after which it becomes a nuisance and leads to confusion. A grocery store in the small town of Charlottesville, VA, carries some 118 varieties of hot pepper sauce, 41 varieties of balsamic vinegar, and 121 different olive oils.[97] Shopping under such circumstances is challenging and confuses the consumer, thereby leading to inefficiencies. I usually choose at random in such cases as I do not have the time or patience to study the many options. Brand differences are usually minor anyhow: tests have revealed, for example, no difference among gasoline brands.[98]

Shopping has become our national pastime and hunting for bargains has become an addictive mania.[99] Consumerism weighs heavily upon society insofar as we sacrifice many of our personal relationships in the process of obtaining material goods and we subject ourselves to longer work hours in order to acquire things we are persuaded to buy.[100] In addition, we mortgage the living standards of future generations in the process. The outcome is a stressed existence. In a *New York Times* article on the thought of Peter Whybrow, Judith Warner writes, "Under normal circumstances, the emotional, reward-seeking, selfish, 'myopic' part of our brain is checked and balanced in its desirous cravings by our powers of cognition—our awareness of the consequences, say, of eating too much or spending too much. But after decades of never-before-seen levels of affluence and endless messages promoting immediate gratification, Whybrow says, this self-regulatory system has been knocked out of whack. The 'orgy of self-indulgence' that spread in our land of no-money-down mortgages . . . has disturbed the 'ancient mechanisms that sustain our physical and mental balance.'"[101]

Our guards are down. Our brain and nervous system have been re-wired by Madison Avenue. Warner continues, "If you put a person in an environment that worships wealth and favors conspicuous consumption, add gross income inequalities that breed envy and competition, mix in stagnant wages for those in the bottom half of the distribution, with an exponentially growing income for the elite and a high cost of keeping up with the Joneses and too-easy credit, you get overspending, high personal debt and a 'treadmill-like existence,' as Whybrow calls it: compulsive getting and spending."[102]

We want to belong; we want to be a part of society, and through shopping we reaffirm our sense of belonging. Hence, the act of shopping itself becomes a habit, an end in itself as a substitute to satisfying basic psychological needs, which, according to Erich Fromm, include wanting others to care about and respect us and to develop loving relationships, to have a feeling of belonging to a social group, to know how we fit into the world, to have goals, to have a sense of accomplishment.[103] However, if consumption is ultimately a poor substitute for gaining the respect of others, then consumerism will lead to an anxious life. The crucial point is that the corporate world has reconstructed culture in such a way that we seek to obtain these psychological rewards through consumption from which corporations can profit rather than from other type of activities that are not monetized—enjoying nature or music, reading, family and friends. Whybrow voices a similar sentiment when he observes that "despite our material riches what eludes many Americans, beyond a good night's sleep, is a genuine sense of fulfillment—a sense of being in harmony with others and oneself."[104]

According to Fromm, one of the symptoms of our collective pathology is the constant urge to consume stuff. In an interview, in 1958 he said "We consume everything with voracity. Behind this consumptive frenzy, lies an inner vacuity, an incapacity of people to be autonomous, to be truly productive citizens and unique selves. The perennial challenge is to imagine an alternative existence for ourselves—one that is ever more intelligent, humane and compassionate." Fromm continued, "There is, in fact, a sense of depression, a sense of loneliness. We find the clinical evidence for this connection in the fact that, very often, overeating and overbuying are the results of states of depression or intense anxiety. . . ."[105] "What we feel as freedom is, to a large extent, the freedom to buy or to consume; that is to say, to choose between many, many different things and to say: 'I want this cigarette. I want this car. I want this thing rather than another.' Precisely because many of the competing brands are not in reality very different, the individual feels the great power of being free to choose."[106] In reality, however, our choices are limited and are manipulated by the market.

Fromm continued: "There is a certain sickness in this drive for ever-increasing consumption and the danger is that, by being filled with a need for consumption, the person does not really solve the problem of inner passivity, of inner vacuity, of anxiety, of being depressed—because life in some way doesn't make sense." Consumption should be a means of satisfying our needs first and then our wants, and not an end in itself to consume. "We are consumption crazy and production crazy,"[107] he observed, while "our emotional life has become impoverished."[108] Fromm urged us to regain "the right to be one self." "We live in . . . [a] Western industrialized society . . . which creates a . . . type of Man whom one could call *homo consumens,* the consumer Man. . . . He devotes his life to producing things and consuming things,"[109] and in the process he is losing his human nature and becoming an object to be manipulated—"not much more than a mechanism."[110]

Similarly, Aldous Huxley saw presciently that the threats to our individualism and freedom can come from institutions other than governments. He noted astutely that Madison Avenue discovered long ago that the shortest way to the parents' bank account is through their offspring: "Today's children walk around singing beer commercials and toothpaste commercials. . . . this whole question of children, I think, is a terribly important one because children are quite clearly much more suggestible than the average grownup; and . . . all the propaganda [is] an extraordinarily powerful force playing on these children, who after all are going to grow up and be adults quite soon. . . . [T]he children of Europe used to be called 'cannon fodder' and here in the United States they are 'television and radio fodder.' . . . after all, you can read in the trade journals the most lyrical accounts of how necessary it is, to get hold of the children because then they will be loyal brand buyers later on."[111]

Huxley's insights were prescient. We were so preoccupied with the threat of big government controlling our lives that we were blind to the threat posed by other institutions, namely Madison Avenue, Wall Street, Hollywood, Silicon Valley, and the mega-corporations that slowly but incrementally, year in and year out, did exactly that which we feared the most: limit much of our freedoms and manipulate much of our individuality.

Having lost control of ourselves, we become depressed in ever greater numbers. We can maintain overconsumption and social stability only with the use of antidepressants, such as Prozac and Valium.[112] The use of such drugs has increased phenomenally, in step with our consumption without gratification. In the United States, a remarkable 213 million prescriptions for such drugs were dispensed in 2010.[113]

CHAPTER SUMMARY

The concentration of power is dangerous in a democracy. Inequality of wealth poses as many problems as the inequality of political power. Those with wealth have a disproportional influence on political outcomes. They spend billions on lobbying and make substantial contributions to political coffers, a legal but unethical way of getting laws passed that provides them additional economic advantages. In the absence of countervailing power, the playing field is thereby tilted increasingly in their favor. In addition, oligopolies have the power to set prices and to manipulate us to want their products. While power is ubiquitous and an extremely important aspect of the real existing economy, there is no mention of it in conventional textbooks, a substantial oversight.

In spite of all their shortcomings, the goal, however, should not be to eliminate markets but to reform them in such a way that they can serve humanity better. We should use inductive methods to replace the current orthodoxy with a methodology based on empirical evidence. We have to replace adult economics with one that begins at birth and acknowledges that tastes are endogenous. Most importantly, we need to protect the individuality of our children from the conditioning of the corporate world. That can only be accomplished if we can limit the power of Madison Avenue from depicting an unrealistic hype of the American Dream.

QUESTIONS FOR DISCUSSION

1. Do you think corporations should be treated like people?
2. Do you think that power corrupts?
3. Do you think we need to spend more money on the military than we do on education?
4. Do you think that teachers should earn as much as CEOs?

5. What do you think Aldous Huxley would think of our society today? And Thomas Jefferson?

6. Explain what Joseph Stiglitz meant when he described our economic system as socialism for the rich and capitalism for the rest.

7. Do you think that you are in charge of your utility function?

8. Does TV or the Internet have the greater influence on our mindset?

9. Do you know anyone who was surprised by the fine print in a contract?

10. To what extent do you think advertisements infringe on our lives?

11. Do you know any compulsive shoppers?

12. Would you be in favor of prohibiting advertisements aimed at children under the age of 12 as they do in Norway?

13. Why do you think Americans save so much less today than they did a generation ago although their income is higher?

14. Why do you think Americans enjoy so much less vacation time than Europeans?

15. To what extent are you influenced by the consumption of others?

16. Do social and cultural norms influence your consumption?

17. How is our culture influenced by the market forces of capitalism?

18. Do you think the American Dream is within reach of most people?

19. To what extent do you think people are altruistic?

20. Do you think that a sense of fairness is innate in human nature or is it learned in the process of growing up?

21. Do you think it is more important to have an efficient society or a fair one?

22. Is the current distribution of wealth efficient or fair?

23. What do you think would be a reasonable definition of efficiency?

24. What kind of a wealth distribution would you advocate?

25. Can you think of waste in the economy?

26. What is more important: efficiency or justice?

27. Is it moral to take advantage of or profit from the ignorance of others?

28. What kind of a society would you create if you were to begin to construct it from scratch?

29. Do you agree that "too big to fail" banks should be too big to exist?

30. Do you agree with Erich Fromm that we are consumption crazy?

NOTES

1. "Wealth, as Mr. Hobbes says, is power." See Adam Smith, "Of the Real and Nominal Price of Commodities, or Their Price in Labour, and Their Price in Money," Book I, Chapter V, in *An Inquiry into the Nature and Causes of the Wealth of Nations*, ed. Edwin Cannan (London: Methuen, 1904), available online at Library of Economics and Liberty.

2. "Eisenhower Warns Us of the Military Industrial Complex," YouTube video, 2:31, posted by "RobUniv," August 4, 2006; James Ledbetter, "What Ike Got Right," *The New York Times*, December 13, 2010.

3. John Kenneth Galbraith, *American Capitalism: The Concept of Countervailing Power* (Boston: Houghton Mifflin, 1952).

4. As noted MIT economist Simon Johnson put it, "Power corrupts, and financial market power has completely corrupted financial markets." See Simon Johnson, "The Market Has Spoken, and It Is Rigged," *The New York Times,* July 12, 2012.

5. Alexandra Alper and Kirstin Ridley, "Barclays Paying $435 Million to Settle Libor Probe," *Reuters,* June 27, 2012.

6. Economists can be also captured by wealth, as is so vividly portrayed in the award-winning film *Inside Job.*

7. Bill Moyers Journal, "Simon Johnson and Marcy Kaptur, interview," October 9, 2009.

8. Sewell Chan, "Financial Crisis Was Avoidable, Inquiry Finds," *The New York Times,* January 25, 2011.

9. Mike McIntire and Nicholas Confessore, "Groups Shield Political Gifts of Businesses," *The New York Times,* July 8, 2012.

10. In a revealing Freudian slip, Representative Spencer Bachus of Alabama, the chairman of the House Financial Services Committee, told *The Birmingham News* that "Washington and the regulators are there to serve the banks." He could not have made it clearer that the banks have captured Washington for all intents and purposes. See Editorial, "How to Derail Financial Reform, *The New York Times,* December 26, 2010.

11. David Cay Johnston, "How Corporate Socialism Destroys," Reuters, June 1, 2012.

12. Charles Wright Mills, *The Power Elite* (Oxford: Oxford University Press, 1956); G. William Domhoff, *Who Rules America?* (Englewood Cliffs, NJ: Prentice-Hall, 1967).

13. Peter Lattman and Azam Ahmed, "Rajat Gupta Convicted of Insider Trading," *The New York Times,* June 15, 2012.

14. Aldous Huxley, interview with Mike Wallace, May 18, 1958.

15. "A small group had concentrated into their own hands an almost complete control over other people's property, other people's money, other people's labor—other people's lives. For too many of us life was no longer free; liberty no longer real; men could no longer follow the pursuit of happiness. Against economic tyranny such as this, the American citizen could appeal only to the organized power of government. The collapse of 1929 showed up the despotism for what it was. The election of 1932 was the people's mandate to end it. Under that mandate it is being ended. The royalists of the economic order have conceded that political freedom was the business of the government, but they have maintained that economic slavery was nobody's business. They granted that the government could protect the citizen in his right to vote, but they denied that the government could do anything to protect the citizen in his right to work and his right to live. . . . If the average citizen is guaranteed equal opportunity in the polling place, he must have equal opportunity in the market place. These economic royalists complain that we seek to overthrow the institutions of America. What they really complain of is that we seek to take away their power. Our allegiance to American institutions requires the overthrow of this kind of power. In vain they seek to hide behind the flag and the Constitution. In their blindness they forget what the flag and the Constitution stand for. Now, as always, they stand for democracy, not tyranny; for freedom, not subjection; and against a dictatorship by mob rule and the over-privileged alike." Franklin D. Roosevelt, "Speech before the 1936 Democratic National Convention" (Philadelphia, PA, June 27, 1936).

16. Wikipedia contributors, "Theodore W. Adorno," *Wikipedia: The Free Encyclopedia.*

17. Marketers know that sex sells. Many advertisements for Pepsi, for instance, use sex as their theme and end with the message "LIVE FOR NOW!" See for instance "Pepsi Max Beyonce 'Mirrors'—Official 2013 video," available at www.youtube.com/watch?v=_qp8WodZg1U. Natalie Zmuda, "Pepsi Tackles Identity Crisis," *Advertising Age,* May 7, 2012. See also "Super Bowl Teleflora Ad 2012 Commercial," www.youtube.com/watch?v=-N0jwGRU00E.

18. Judith Warner, "Dysregulation Nation," *The New York Times,* June 14, 2010.

19. See the 1997 documentary *Affluenza,* which depicts how this ethic became ingrained in the culture after World War II.

20. The Internet is supposed to change this: "Businesses today tend to herd customers as if they were cattle, but a revolution in personal empowerment is under way—and buying will never be the same again." We'll have to wait and see if this prediction turns out to be realistic. See Doc Searls, "The Customer as God," *The Wall Street Journal,* July 20, 2012.

21. Vance Packard, *The Hidden Persuaders* (New York: Pocket Books, 1957).

22. Abraham Maslow, "A Theory of Human Motivation," *Psychological Review* 50 (1943): 370–396.

23. Thorstein Veblen, *The Theory of the Leisure Class: An Economic Study of Institutions* (London: Macmillan, 1899), 110.

24. Stephen A. Marglin, *The Dismal Science: How Thinking Like an Economist Undermines Community* (Cambridge, MA: Harvard University Press, 2010). Mihaly Csikszentmihalyi, *Flow: The Psychology of Optimal Experience* (New York: Harper, 2008). Martin Seligman, *Flourish: A Visionary New Understanding of Happiness and Well-Being* (New York: The Free Press, 2012).

25. Geoffrey M. Hodgson, "Veblen, Thorstein Bunde (1857–1929)," in *The New Palgrave Dictionary of*

Economics, 2nd ed., ed. Steven N. Durlauf and Lawrence E. Blume (Basingstoke, UK: Palgrave Macmillan, 2008).

26. "How many people ruin themselves by laying out money on trinkets of frivolous utility?" Adam Smith, *The Theory of Moral Sentiments* (London: A. Millar, 1759), IV.I.6, available online at Library of Economics and Liberty.

27. Richard Easterlin, "Does Economic Growth Improve the Human Lot? Some Empirical Evidence," in *Nations and Households in Economic Growth: Essays in Honor of Moses Abramovitz*, ed. Paul David and Melvin Reder (Palo Alto: Stanford University Press, 1974), 89–125; Robert Frank, *Choosing the Right Pond: Human Behavior and the Quest for Status* (New York: Oxford University Press, 1985); Robert Frank, "The Demand for Unobservable and Other Nonpositional Goods," *American Economic Review* 75 (1985) 1: 101–116; Richard Easterlin, "The Economics of Happiness," *Daedalus* 133 (2004) 2: 26–33.

28. Veblen, *Theory of the Leisure Class,* 110.

29. James Duesenberry, *Income, Saving, and the Theory of Consumer Behavior* (Cambridge, MA: Harvard University Press, 1949).

30. A normal good is one whose consumption increases with rising income, as long as its relative price remains unchanged.

31. Solomon Asch, "Opinions and Social Pressure," *Scientific American* 193 (1955): 31–35; Harvey Leibenstein, "Bandwagon, Snob, and Veblen Effects in the Theory of Consumers' Demand," *Quarterly Journal of Economics* 64 (1950) 2: 183–207.

32. Robert H. Frank, "Consumption Externalities," in *The New Palgrave Dictionary of Economics*, 2nd ed., ed. Steven N. Durlauf and Lawrence E. Blume (Basingstoke, UK: Palgrave Macmillan, 2008).

33. Arthur J. Robson, "The Biological Basis of Economic Behavior," *Journal of Economic Literature* 29 (2001): 11–33.

34. "Anybody who is not like everybody, who does not think like everybody, runs the risk of being eliminated," wrote Spanish philosopher José Ortega y Gasset in 1929. See *The Revolt of the Masses* (New York: W.W. Norton, 1994).

35. See "Shopaholics Anonymous," a Web site of the Shulman Center for Compulsive Theft, Spending & Hoarding; and the film *The Confessions of a Shopaholic,* directed by P.J. Hogan (2009).

36. Solomon E. Asch, "Opinions and Social Pressure," *Scientific American* 193 (1955): 31–35.

37. Robert H. Frank, "Positional Externalities Cause Large and Preventable Welfare Losses," *American Economic Review* 95 (2005) 2: 137–141.

38. William H. Whyte, Jr., "Groupthink," *Fortune,* March 1952, 114–117. Whyte emphasized that in the corporate ethic our individuality becomes subservient to a group ideology. Groupthink becomes a rationalized conformity in order to maintain our position in the organization or increase our income.

39. "Men, it has been well said, think in herds; it will be seen that they go mad in herds, while they only recover their senses slowly, and one by one." See Charles MacKay, *Extraordinary Popular Delusions and the Madness of Crowds* (London: Office of the National Illustrated Library, 1852).

40. See "Black Friday Stampede," YouTube video, 1:57, posted by "kopret," July 17, 2007.

41. Sharon R. Cohany and Emy Sok, "Married Mothers in the Labor Force," *Monthly Labor Review* 130 (2007) 2: 9–16.

42. Luigi Guiso, Paola Sapienza, and Luigi Zingales, "Does Culture Affect Economic Outcomes?" *Journal of Economic Perspectives* 20 (2006) 2: 23–48.

43. Bell continued: "In the early development of capitalism, the unrestrained economic impulse was held in check by Puritan restraint and the Protestant ethic. One worked because of one's obligation to one's calling, or to fulfill the covenant of the community. But the Protestant ethic was undermined . . . by capitalism itself . . . [by] the invention of the installment plan, or instant credit. Previously one had to save in order to buy. But with credit cards one could indulge in instant gratification. The system was transformed . . . by the creation of new wants and new means of gratifying those wants." The Protestant ethic limited consumerism. "When the Protestant ethic was sundered from bourgeois society, only the hedonism remained and the capitalist system lost its transcendental ethic." "The cultural, if not moral, justification of capitalism has become hedonism, the idea of pleasure as a way of life." "In a modern society the engine of appetite is the increased standard of living. . . . But it is also, in its emphasis on display, a reckless squandering of resources . . . If consumption represents the psychological competition for status, then one can say that bourgeois society is the institutionalization of envy." "[T]he culture . . . is prodigal, promiscuous, dominated by an antirational, anti-intellectual temper." Daniel Bell, *The Cultural Contradictions of Capitalism* (New York: Basic Books, 1976), 21–22.

44. Christopher Lasch, *The Culture of Narcissism: American Life in an Age of Diminishing Expectations* (New York: W.W. Norton, 1979).

45. Robert H. Frank, *Luxury Fever* (Princeton, NJ: Princeton University Press, 1999).

46. Lasch continued, "The determinants of this shift are social, not psychological: the increasingly dangerous and warlike character of the social environment, the fragility of friendship and family ties, the social emphasis on the consumption rather than the production of commodities, the rise of the mass media with their cult of glamor and celebrity, the disruption of the sense of historical continuity." "A society that fears it has no future is not likely to give much attention to the needs of the next generation, and the ever-present sense of historical discontinuity, the blight of our society, falls with particularly devastating effect on the family." Christopher Lasch, "The Narcissist Society," *The New York Review of Books,* September 30, 1976.

47. Christophe Hayes, *Twilight of the Elites* (New York: Crown, 2012).

48. James Galbraith calls this the "corporate republic" in *The Predator State: How Conservatives Abandoned the Free Market and Why Liberals Should Too* (New York: The Free Press, 2008).

49. Golnaz Tabibnia and Matthew D. Lieberman, "Fairness and Cooperation Are Rewarding: Evidence from Social Cognitive Neuroscience," *Annals of the New York Academy of Sciences* 1118 (2007): 90–101.

50. Peter Corning, *The Fair Society: The Science of Human Nature and the Pursuit of Social Justice* (Chicago: University of Chicago Press, 2011).

51. Colin F. Camerer, "Behavioural Game Theory," in *The New Palgrave Dictionary of Economics,* 2nd ed., ed. Steven N. Durlauf and Lawrence E. Blume (Basingstoke, UK: Palgrave Macmillan, 2008).

52. John Rawls, *A Theory of Justice* (Cambridge, MA: Harvard University Press, 1971).

53. "Heidi Klum 11 Million Dollar Bra," YouTube video, 1:21, posted by "Jadesmythcom," June 5, 2007; Mandi Bierly, "Victora's Secret Fashion Show: 10 Years of Fantasy Bras," *Entertainment Weekly,* November 29, 2011.

54. Similarly, when it adopts the Kaldor-Hicks criterion to undertake economic policy, it assumes implicitly that utility levels can be compared across individuals.

55. In such a case, one is allowed to make interpersonal comparisons, but not when it comes to redistribution.

56. "To amend the Truth in Lending Act to establish fair and transparent practices relating to the extension of credit under an open end consumer credit plan, . . ." U.S. Congress, House, *Credit CARD Act of 2009,* HR 627, 111th Congress, 1st session, January 6, 2009.

57. James Kwak, "When a 79.9% APR Is Good?" The Baseline Scenario, January 8, 2010.

58. Other conditions include that market participants have perfect information, are infinite buyers and sellers, have perfect factor mobility, and no transaction costs. Such firms will not have profit in the long run.

59. Paul Samuelson and William Nordhaus, *Economics,* 19th ed. (New York: McGraw-Hill/Irwin, 2009), 164. To be sure, on page 169 they do admit that such firms are "hard to find," and on page 187 they say that they are rare. Nonetheless, the question remains if it is advisable to continue such inconsistency in a textbook's 19th edition.

60. Thomas Nagel, *The Possibility of Altruism* (Oxford: Clarendon Press, 1970), 79.

61. In evolutionary biology, altruism is defined in terms of one organism raising another organism's reproductive success at the expense of its own.

62. James Andreoni, William T. Harbaugh, and Lise Vesterlund, "Altruism in Experiments," in *The New Palgrave Dictionary of Economics,* 2nd ed., ed. Steven N. Durlauf and Lawrence E. Blume (Basingstoke, UK: Palgrave Macmillan, 2008).

63. Stephen G. Post, "It's Good to Be Good: 2011 Fifth Annual Scientific Report on Health, Happiness and Helping Others," unpublished manuscript.

64. Dharol Tankersley, C. Jill Stowe, and Scott A. Huettel, "Altruism Is Associated with an Increased Neural Response to Agency," *Nature Neuroscience* 10 (2007): 150–151; Tabibnia and Lieberman, "Fairness and Cooperation."

65. Smith, *The Theory of Moral Sentiments* (1759).

66. To be sure, there was self-interested reciprocity as well, and we can also derive pleasure from believing that we are altruistic.

67. Smith, *The Theory of Moral Sentiments* I.I.1; also see Alexander J. Field, *Altruistically Inclined? The Behavioral Sciences, Evolutionary Theory, and the Origins of Reciprocity* (Michigan: University of Michigan Press, 2002).

68. Experiments reveal that women are more altruistic than men. See Rachel Croson and Uri Gneezy, "Gender Differences in Preferences," *Journal of Economic Literature* 47 (2009) 2: 1–27.

69. "[T]here is a substantial overlap between the areas [of the brain] that are activated when we experience an emotion and when we observe someone experiencing that same emotion." Aldo Rustichini, "Introduction. Neuroeconomics: Present and Future," *Games and Economic Behavior* 52 (2005): 201–212.

70. Edward O. Wilson, "Evolution and Our Inner Conflict," *The New York Times,* June 24, 2012.

71. "[T]he collapse of the housing bubble will lead to a loss of between $1.3 trillion and $2.6 trillion of housing wealth." Dean Baker, "The Run-up in Home Prices: A Bubble," *Challenge* 45 (2002) 6: 93–119; John Cassidy, "Blowing Bubbles," *The New Yorker,* July 12, 2004.

72. Board of Governors of the Federal Reserve System, Chairman Ben S. Bernanke, Speech, "The Subprime Mortgage Market," May 17, 2007.

73. This is known as buyer's remorse.

74. "Ripoff Report," available at www.ripoffreport.com/reports/specific_search/internet.

75. My mother passed away recently and I was searching for a moving company to move her things into storage until I was ready to pick them up. This does not appear to be such a complicated service, but it was surely more complicated than choosing cornflakes. I called around for several hours and chose Three Sons Movers, who offered to do the job at the lowest cost. They did the job well and my mother's belongings were put into storage. All was fine until I was going to move her belongings out of storage. Much to my surprise, I learned that there was an additional $450 fee to move the items from storage to the loading zone so that another moving company could move them to my house. That was not mentioned and was not in the written contract. The lesson here is that in generating alternatives, I did not even know the right questions to ask as I never imagined the possibility of such fees. The manager did not observe the eighth commandment. So my comparison shopping was incomplete, I made my choice with incomplete information, and was not clever enough to figure out all contingencies. Ultimately, I was outsmarted by someone with inside information who thought full time about how to trick me. The contract just specified moving in and said nothing about moving out. See James Kwak's description of his experience moving his DSL service with Verizon at "More Telecom Hell," *Baseline Scenario,* August 18, 2010.

76. Joseph Stiglitz, *Information and Economic Analysis,* vol. 1 of *Selected Works of Joseph E. Stiglitz* (Oxford: Oxford University Press, 2009).

77. Joseph Stiglitz, "Information and the Change in the Paradigm in Economics," *American Economic Review* 92 (2002) 3: 460–501, at p. 461.

78. Bruce C. Greenwald and Joseph Stiglitz, "Externalities in Economies with Imperfect Information and Incomplete Markets," *Quarterly Journal of Economics* 101 (1986): 229–264.

79. Joseph Stiglitz, "Doctor of Honoris Causa Ceremony Speech," University of the Basque Country, Bilbao, Spain, May 23, 2006. See also his Nobel Prize lecture: Joseph Stiglitz, "Information and the Change in the Paradigm in Economics," Stockholm University, Aula Magna, December 8, 2001. Joseph Stiglitz, *Making Globalization Work* (New York: W.W. Norton, 2006); Joseph Stiglitz, *The Roaring Nineties* (New York: W.W. Norton, 2003).

80. George Akerlof, "The Market for 'Lemons': Quality Uncertainty and the Market Mechanism," *Quarterly Journal of Economics* 84 (1970): 488–450; George Akerlof, "Behavioral Macroeconomics and Macroeconomic Behavior," *American Economic Review* 92 (2002) 3: 411–433.

81. "Bureau of Consumer Financial Protection (CFPB)," U.S. Department of the Treasury, last modified July 23, 2012.

82. The details of this incredible case are worth reading in full. Wikipedia contributors, "Terra Securities Scandal," *Wikipedia: The Free Encyclopedia.*

83. Secretary of the Treasury Timothy Geithner effectively underwrote Jamie Dimon's insurance policy by stating clearly enough in a testimony before Congress that the taxpayer will foot the bill, rationalizing the large financial transfer from the poor to the rich by claiming that: "in a system that's fragile, an economy that is fragile today, it's very important that we act effectively to help stabilize our system and to prevent the kind of broad-based catastrophic damage we have seen when the market or the government is unwilling or unable to prevent that kind of failure." "Geithner Testifies on 14 'Too Big to Fail' Banks," YouTube video, 3:17, posted by "TheySayNothing," February 12, 2009.

84. Simon Johnson and Michael Perino, interview with Bill Moyers, PBS, April 24, 2009; Simon Johnson, interview with Bill Moyers, PBS, February 13, 2009; Simon Johnson and James Kwak, interview with Bill Moyers, April 16, 2010. All of these interviews appeared on Bill Moyers Journal, available at www.pbs.org/moyers/journal/index.html.

85. Avner Offer, "A Warrant for Pain: Caveat Emptor vs. the Duty of Care in American Medicine, c. 1970–2010," *real-world economics review* 61 (2012): 8599–.

86. Michael Spence, "Job Market Signaling," *Quarterly Journal of Economics* 87 (1973) 3: 355–374.

87. Hilke Plassmann, John O'Doherty, Raba Shiv, and Antonio Rangel, "Marketing Actions Can Modulate Neural Representations of Experienced Pleasantness," *Proceedings of the National Academy of Sciences of the United States of America* 105 (2008) 3: 1050–1054.

88. Richard Thaler, "Some Empirical Evidence on Dynamic Inconsistency," *Economic Letters* 8 (1981) 3: 201–207; Shane Frederick, George Loewenstein, and Ted O'Donoghue, "Time Discounting and Time Preference: A Critical Review," *Journal of Economic Literature* 40 (2002) 2: 351–401.

89. It is about as appropriate for today's economy as Newton's principles of motion are to subatomic particles.

90. Kleptocrat refers to a greedy and corrupt government official, but it could also be applied to greedy corporate managers.

91. Peter Whybrow, "Dangerously Addictive. Why We Are Biologically Ill-Suited to the Riches of Modern America," *The Chronicle of Higher Education,* March 13, 2009.

92. Stephen LeRoy, "Is the 'Invisible Hand' Still Relevant?" *FRBSF Economic Letter* no. 14, May 3, 2010.

93. Ibid.

94. Ibid.

95. Ibid.

96. Simon P. Anderson, "Product Differentiation," in *The New Palgrave Dictionary of Economics*, 2nd ed., ed. Steven N. Durlauf and Lawrence E. Blume (Basingstoke, UK: Palgrave Macmillan, 2008).

97. Ibid.

98. Elisabeth Leamy, "Generic vs. Brand-Name Gas: Are They Different?" *ABC News Good Morning America*, March 24, 2007.

99. Tibor Scitovsky, *The Joyless Economy: An Inquiry into Human Satisfaction and Consumer Dissatisfaction* (Oxford: Oxford University Press, 1976); Shirley Lee and Avis Mysyk, "The Medicalization of Compulsive Buying," *Social Science and Medicine* 58 (2004) 9: 1709–1718.

100. Peter Whybrow, *American Mania: When More Is Not Enough* (New York: W.W. Norton, 2005); Peter Whybrow, "Dangerously Addictive."

101. Judith Warner, "Dysregulation Nation."

102. Ibid.

103. Wikipedia contributors, "Erich Fromm," *Wikipedia: The Free Encyclopedia.*

104. Peter Whybrow, "Books: Get Satisfied."

105. "Homo Consumens," YouTube video, posted by "Q&A projects." Theodor Adorno, a major social critic of the mid-twentieth century, was of a similar opinion, writing: "the easy pleasures available through consumption of popular culture made people docile and content, no matter how terrible their economic circumstances" (See Wikipedia contributors, "Theodor W. Adorno," *Wikipedia: The Free Encyclopedia*).

106. Mike Wallace Interview: Erich Fromm, May 25, 1958.

107. Ibid

108. Ibid.

109. Ibid.

110. Ibid.

111. Aldous Huxley, interview with Mike Wallace.

112. Robin Marantz Henig, "Valium's Contribution to Our New Normal," *The New York Times*, September 29, 2012.

113. Wikipedia contributors, "Antidepressant," *Wikipedia: The Free Encyclopedia.* The use of antidepressant drugs increased by a factor of four between 1990 and 2003. Ramin Mojtabai, "Increase in Antidepressant Medication in the U.S. Adult Population Between 1990 and 2003," *Psychotherapy and Psychosomatics* 77 (2008) 2: 83–92.

PART III

PRODUCTION ON AND OFF THE BLACKBOARD

6

FIRMS AND COMPETITION

In this chapter we stress issues in the microeconomic theory of the firm that are usually glossed over in Econ 101. Standard economic theory usually focuses on the perfectly competitive model of firms and markets. These models assume that there are innumerable firms which produce a homogenous product for millions of consumers. In such a case everyone is a price taker and the consumer is "king": firms produce what the consumers want. The price of the product is determined by aggregate supply and demand; no one has power to manipulate the price. Hence, the demand for the product of each firm is given by the exogenously determined price; there is no incentive to try to influence demand by advertising. Consequently, firms are producing efficiently at the minimum unit cost and have just enough revenue to stay in business.

This is fundamentally misleading and hence poor pedagogy, because it puts the emphasis on a market structure that is essentially irrelevant in today's economy. In our time practically all of the important products are produced in markets with imperfect competition. The concentration of production implies a concentration of power to set prices, wages, and to manipulate consumers and influence the political process so that such firms can amass further market power. Competition among oligopolists and monopolists has very different consequences for market outcomes than competition among price takers. Hence, we focus in this chapter on the salient aspects of imperfect competition and delineate how that affects market outcomes particularly pertaining to consumers.

FIRMS

In conventional accounts, a firm is described as an individual decision maker, analogous to the consumer, who is also assumed to be the sole decision maker. The shoe repairman near my house owns his own shop and works by himself for himself. His would be such a textbook firm, but one has to think hard to come up with other such entities. They are actually a negligible part of the economy. Most firms are bureaucratic, hierarchical, and authoritarian organizations within which the visible hand of management replaces the invisible hand of the market.[1] In this sense they resemble other types of bureaucratic institutions such as government agencies.

A corporation, then, is not a person and does not make decisions as a person. Rather, it is a bureaucratic organization with an army of managers employing a labor force of hundreds of thousands: Bank of America employs 288,000 people and IBM employs 436,000 people around the globe.[2] The efficient coordination, monitoring, and commanding within such a mega-corporation are nearly impossible because oversight by the actual owners of the firm is too diffuse to implement effectively and because there are many layers of authority, each with imperfect information between owners, managers, and employees. To be sure, the wasting of resources in large firms is compensated by the gains obtained through economies of scale and lowering of transaction costs.[3]

Such giant firms employ too many people with conflicting goals to be able to optimize. It is not feasible to align the incentive of each employee with that of the firm, especially since they presumably want to do the best for themselves and not for the firm. Monitoring them is unwieldy. Other hindrances to optimization include the fact that firms face too much uncertainty about demand, do not have perfect foresight to know how much to produce, and do not know the elasticity of product price with respect to output so that they cannot possibly determine the profit-maximizing output. The best a responsible manager can do is to satisfice with bounded rationality, as do consumers. As consumers, firms adapt rule-of-thumb approaches to solving their problem, such as the markup rule, which multiplies the cost of a product by a constant factor in order to obtain the selling price.

The firm is not organized internally as a market. This is a seeming contradiction in the theory of those who advocate the beneficial effects of both the free market and corporations. The two are established on very different principles. The former is supposed to be democratic, with power diffused. The latter, in contrast, is authoritarian, with concentration of power and with the incentive for those lower on the command structure to obey, especially given current high levels of unemployment.

THE ILLUSION OF PERFECT COMPETITION

Most students of Econ 101 remember that competition is the mechanism that leads to efficient markets. That is also the formulation that reverberates frequently in the media and has entered public consciousness. Hence, it is important to understand that it is actually wrong, insofar as it is incomplete. Competition by itself is insufficient to bring about economic efficiency. In order for the standard efficiency conditions to hold, the market has to have countless sellers and an unlimited number of buyers of an undifferentiated product. In addition, both sellers and buyers have to be rational, know everything about the product perfectly well, and transaction costs have to be nonexistent. In such a case, both producers and consumers would be price takers, that is, they would have no power to influence price. If anyone knows of a market like that, please do let me know. Certainly none exists of any significance that pertains to consumers on Main Street.

Product differentiation is one form of nonprice competition through which firms attempt to avoid the perfectly competitive solution of zero profits and obtain the advantages of some market power. As long as Louis Vuitton has monopoly rights to manufacture products with its name, and its designs are protected by law, it will be able to earn some profits even though its handbags are close substitutes to those of its competitors Gucci, Dior, Prada, and Chanel.

The few wholesale markets that perhaps come close to being perfectly competitive are raw material markets traded on mercantile exchanges, but even these are subject to irrational bubbles and busts. Hence, the perfectly competitive rational agent model is completely irrelevant as far as consumers are concerned, and the default model should be one with imperfect competition, such as oligopolistic or monopolistic competition.

Imperfect competition exists when either firms or consumers can affect the price of the commodity in question. This happens in case of concentration of market share or product differentiation. Such producers are considered oligopolies or monopolies. Competition among such firms does not lead to an efficient solution in which price equals both marginal and average cost and firms produce at the minimum unit cost. Rather, price invariably exceeds average unit cost and generally profits are generated. In addition, oligopolies and monopolies do not produce at the minimum of average cost. Therefore, they produce inefficiently in spite of competition.

The mainstream argues that in the long run, firms will enter the market until the profits of oligopolies are competed away. However, that contention is essentially misleading, because it does not specify how long the "long run" is, so the length of time needed for the profits to be competed away is indeterminate and therefore may not even be pertinent in the relevant time frame. Moreover, only if there are no barriers to entry and only if the expected future profits are sufficiently high to warrant entry of a new firm will they enter the industry. In any case, such firms do not easily acquiesce to the theoretical long-run solution, and do everything in their power to erect barriers to entry using advertising to guarantee that potential competitors have a large lump sum of investment to make before they can become viable competitors and gain a sufficiently large market share to make it worthwhile for them to enter the industry. Alternatively, they tweak their products sufficiently so as to avoid the long-run outcome. Besides, even if they were not earning a profit, oligopolies and monopolies are still inefficient, because the prices they charge for their products virtually always exceed marginal cost, and because they still produce with excess capacity. The Walgreens around the corner, in other words, is empty most of the time.

Another form of imperfect competition is spatial monopoly, such as Walgreens or gas stations, since they have a monopoly on selling at a certain location. Yet, there is hefty competition, so most of them earn tiny profits. Nonetheless, it is an inefficient form of market organization, insofar as there are too many gas stations and none of them is used at optimal capacity, leading to a misallocation of land, labor, and capital that could be put to other uses. Such a form of industrial organization dominates much of the retail sector: drugstores, restaurants, supermarkets, department stores, and similar brick-and-mortar firms are very competitive, are not great profit makers, and are inefficient. The real monopoly profits are made by the pharmaceutical companies who deliver to the drugstores, the oil companies who deliver to the gas stations, and of course Goldman Sachs is doing well also. In addition, the oil industry receives large subsidies from the government while banks can get loans from the Fed at a near-zero percent interest rate.[4] It is difficult not to make profits that way.

Creating and promoting brands is another response to avoid perfect competition. Although Apple's iPod does compete with other similar music players, it still reaps big profits because it has unique features that are protected by copyright law and cannot be duplicated. Hence, iPods do not have a supply curve. Apple supplies as many iPods as it deems appropriate for demand conditions. The company does not vary price much. Instead of competing with price, it competes with features. In order to stay ahead of competition, it brings out a new generation of the product yearly. The price has been in the $300–$400 range since its introduction in 2001.[5] So competition does not have the effect in the long run as it does in theory because the real world is dynamic, whereas the world of theory is static. The firm does not stand still in response to competition but devises ways to elude the consequences.

Unlike perfectly competitive firms, nearly all oligopolies and monopolies are able to avoid the long-run solution and do earn hefty profits even in the presence of competition, because competition is too meager to eliminate them. These profits are far from temporary. In 2010 the following profits (in billions of dollars) were earned: Exxon, $19; Microsoft, $15; Walmart, $14; Goldman Sachs, $13; JPMorgan Chase, $12; Wells Fargo, $12; Chevron, $10; Bank of America, $6; Apple, $6; Coca Cola, $7; and Conoco, $5.[6] These profits were not competed away and are not likely to be competed away any time soon.[7]

Corporate business profits reached $1.66 trillion in 2010 and 28 percent of them was obtained in the financial sector.[8] In other words, an intermediary has been able to capture a large share of the total profits generated by the economy. The long run seems never to arrive for these firms. Thus, the default model of industrial organization should be one in which all profits are not competed away.

Moreover, government expenditures (federal, state, and local), consisting of consumption plus investments, account for about 20 percent of gross national product (GNP) and much of what it purchases, such as military equipment, is not transacted in perfectly competitive markets. Governments employed 22 million people in 2007 (without the military), some 15 percent of the labor force.[9]

Competition is supposedly the mechanism by which the more productive firms producing a better product survive, but better in what sense? When competition intensifies it may well be that the unscrupulous and the immoral are the ones to survive. Competition can become brutal under such circumstances and there is no guarantee that the outcome will be socially desirable.[10] To be sure, many inefficient firms that took on too much risk, such as IndyMac, Countrywide, Washington Mutual, and Lehman Brothers, did not survive the 2008 meltdown, but many other similarly structured firms did, thanks to the government bailouts and subsidies. Furthermore, their managers survived the Meltdown of 2008 with their hundreds of millions intact.

The meltdown is an example of how individual and group interests often diverge. Competition cannot redress that imbalance; in fact, it intensifies the imbalance. The interest of Angelo Mozilo, CEO of Countrywide Financial, a pioneer and major originator of subprime mortgages, was to extract as much money as possible from his firm without consideration of the millions of people who would be thrown out of work as a consequence of his actions. This implies that Adam Smith's "invisible hand" metaphor does not apply in case of systemic effects, which are practically ubiquitous.

Far from benefiting all concerned, competition is a two-edged sword that all too often degenerates into a race to the bottom of the moral ladder. CEOs abhor the low profit rates when markets are in perfectly competitive equilibrium. This is particularly so in that Wall Street pressures firms to reach for profit margins beyond expectations. Thus, management will do everything in its power to avoid a perfectly competitive outcome, including scrambling information, innovation, product differentiation, advertisement campaigns, or recently—and all too often—engage in unethical or even illegal behavior. This often injures society and forces competitors to follow suit and mimic the unethical behavior. The well-known *New York Times* columnist David Brooks concludes astutely:

> The corruption that has now crept into the world of finance and the other professions is not endemic to meritocracy but to the specific culture of our meritocracy. . . . Today's elite lacks . . . [a] self-conscious leadership ethos. . . . The best of the WASP elites had a stewardship mentality, that they were temporary caretakers of institutions that would span generations. They cruelly ostracized people who did not live up to their codes of gentlemanly conduct and scrupulosity. . . . [in spite of all their shortcomings] they did believe in restraint, reticence and service. . . . The language of meritocracy . . . has eclipsed the language of morality. . . . If you read the e-mails from the Libor scandal you get the same sensation you get from reading the e-mails in so many recent scandals: these people are brats; they have no sense that they are guardians for an institution the world depends on; they have no consciousness of their larger social role.[11]

Such moral imbalances did not exist in Adam Smith's time on a comparable scale.

We should note that while perfectly competitive markets have supply curves, oligopolies and monopolies do not have one, since they have market power and choose that combination of price and quantity that yields satisfactory profits. They are large relative to the market and have a unique product to sell and therefore are not price takers (Figure 6.1).[12] For example, the

Figure 6.1   **Profit of a Monopolist (Without Fixed Costs)**

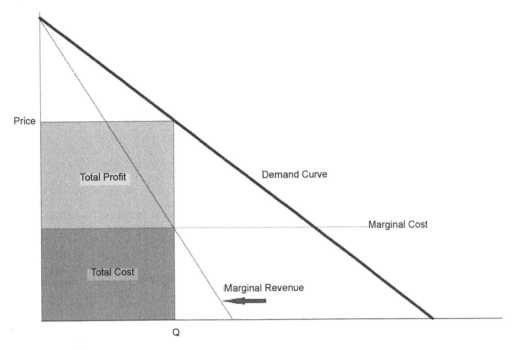

Windows operating system is a monopoly in an oligopolistic market structure competing mainly with Apple computers. Thus, Microsoft has market power and is not willing to supply its products at the socially optimal price. It offers its software at a price that obtains a substantial profit for the firm: $15 billion in 2010.

PRODUCTION POSSIBILITIES FRONTIER

The production possibilities frontier (PPF) describes the maximum quantity of commodities that can be produced efficiently in an economy at a point in time with the given amount of resources, know-how, technology, labor, and capital. However, the concept is ambiguous insofar as the maximum depends on many factors that are flexible and not well specified within the economic framework, including cultural factors. For example, during World War II the mobilization of female labor implied a sudden increase in the amount of goods the economy could produce, although a substantial portion of it went to the military rather than to households. Similarly, the cultural change that induced more women to participate in the labor market beginning with the 1970s increased the PPF substantially inasmuch as home-produced goods are not considered in PPF. The PPF also depends on the prevailing laws and morality. Prohibition on child labor, for instance, shifts the PPF inward in the short run, though it will increase it over time if the children receive an education instead of working. If firms hire illegal immigrants, or provide an unhealthy work environment, the economy can produce outside of the legal (or morally constrained) PPF. In short, the PPF is by no means carved in stone.

The economy is supposedly producing efficiently if it is producing on its PPF. However, that is never obtained except in times of war as there are always unemployed resources in a modern economy. With chronic unemployment of both labor and capital, the concept of PPF loses its

Figure 6.2   **Production Possibilities Frontier with Institutional Constraint**

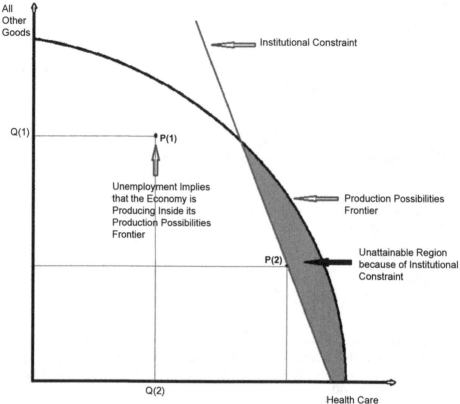

significance. In June 2011 the unemployment and underemployment of labor was around 18 percent of the labor force while factories were producing at 77 percent capacity.[13] That means that 23 percent of the capital stock in the private sector was essentially unemployed, implying that we are very far from producing on the PPF—as at point P(1) in Figure 6.2. In other words, at P(1) production is inefficient as it is well inside the PPF because of unemployment. Institutions and cultural factors can also impede the economy from reaching the PPF. Laws, for instance, can impose inefficient structures on firms, which can imply that a segment of the PPF curve is unattainable because of institutional constraints such as at P(2). At P(1) the institutional constraint is not binding: the constraint does not affect production. However, at point P(2) the institutional constraint is binding and the efficient level of production is unattainable.

PRICES

Prices, determined by markets at the intersection of the supply and demand curves, are sanctified in conventional thinking. Yet their determination is more complicated than that. As mentioned above, oligopolies and monopolies do not have supply curves so the demand curve cannot intersect with anything. Additionally, most firms have only a vague idea of the price elasticity of demand, so they are satisficing with respect to the price they should charge. Furthermore, there is no auctioneer to help in the determination of price; so in order to increase profits, firms devote a lot of effort to scrambling the price-quantity-quality relationship so as to focus consumers' attention on the attractive aspects of the offer.

Firms use multiple strategies to distort perceptions in order to tilt the playing field in their favor, for instance, by increasing the transaction costs of acquiring information on the attributes of the product or making it difficult to do comparison shopping. This is a selection device to separate those seriously interested in the product from those who are not, and once the serious consumers invest in finding out the price, they are less likely to go to a competitor, where they would have to invest again facing an uncertain payoff. In addition, such a strategy keeps the information out of the easy reach of competitors, thereby avoiding the ill effects of price competition.

Thus, it is in the firm's interest to garble prices. They use anchoring and framing strategies to focus on how much is to be saved by purchasing a product rather than on its actual price; they set deadlines on discounts so that the consumers feel like they have limited time to think about the purchase; they offer two for the price of one while stocks last; final day of sale offers; 0 percent financing for the first six months; they conceal the length of the contract, that is, that renews automatically until canceled. Another strategy is to put unsavory information into small print: offering low interest rates to begin with but many penalties along the way if certain conditions are not met. The list of gimmicks, traps, and deceptions is practically infinite. But the main insight is that firms hire the smartest to do their utmost to confuse the consumer and make comparison shopping as demanding as possible. That is why, for example, the weight of cereal boxes is not uniform.

There are practically no price signals of consumer products that can be characterized as being generated by perfectly competitive markets. So applying such a model to the real world is downright archaic. For instance, gasoline prices are determined by Organization of the Petroleum Exporting Countries, or OPEC—a cartel—and not by perfectly competitive markets. While there is still some competition, they consider how much they want to charge given other supplies on the market and then calibrate their supply to that price. In other words, the causation is not from supply to price, but from price to supply.

Quantity demanded is determined not only by current prices but also by the history of prices. Higher prices today do not always lead to a decline in the quantity demanded inasmuch as demand also depends on price expectations. Suppose price of a good has been rising for a while. I might interpret the current increase in price as a signal that prices will continue to rise and therefore buy even more of the good now in order to avoid higher prices in the future. Or suppose that prices fall, I might interpret this development as an indication that quality has declined and buy less of the good. So the relationship between price of a good and the quantity demanded of that good depends also on expectations formation and signaling.

Allowing prices to ration goods has a moral aspect to it as well when the goods pertain to basic needs. It is inhumane to see famine amid plenty. In August of 2011 there was a famine in Somalia with 2 million children at risk,[14] while on the same day supermodel Linda Evangelista was asking the French billionaire Francois Henri-Pinault for $46,000 a month in child support for their four-year-old son.[15] While Louis Vuitton shoes were selling for $1,500 a pair, and some handbags carried price tags in the $3,000 range,[16] people were killing their children because of financial desperation.[17] Every day one learns about such obscenely colossal discrepancies. The only logical inference is that the winner-take-all society has very great difficulty preventing such excesses, such as setting common-sense limits so that such great disparities will not prevail. Rationing basic necessities by price is callous and cruel toward the poor, homeless, desperate, or otherwise disadvantaged.

EQUILIBRIUM AND DISEQUILIBRIUM

The conventional view presented in textbooks is that the law of supply and demand implies that equilibrium—where supply equals demand—exists in all markets at all times. Yet it is unclear what mechanism enables the markets to reach such an equilibrium, and it is never specified how long it will take to reach it. Price depends on two crucial variables often absent from conventional depiction of the supply and demand model: location and time. This omission is one of the many Achilles heels of the standard model. We do not always have the patience to wait for the market to find equilibrium. As Keynes famously said, "in the long run we are all dead"—that is, if you are hungry, you do not have time to wait for the price of bread to come down until you can afford it.

With information and transaction costs it is not easy to match buyers and sellers; and decentralized markets do not have a straightforward mechanism to accomplish the task. Therefore, some models imagine a hypothetical auctioneer who calls out prices and quantities in order to find the equilibrium. But such a fictitious character is not very convincing since the auctioneer would either be an authority figure, a dictator who would not perform such a service free of charge and would have to be compensated, driving an inefficient wedge between prices paid and prices received, or a benevolent dictator, which would not be consistent with the mainstream view that the economy is made up of selfish individuals. The auctioneer would have to come from outside the system. This is quite a conundrum for mainstream theory, especially since the auctioneer must unilaterally prohibit trade from occurring before the equilibrium solution is found. So she would have to have plenary powers to maintain order and not allow sales prior to reaching the equilibrium price. In short, price discovery is a much more complex process than students are led to believe. Such a theoretical auctioneer implies that the coordinating power of the price mechanism is of limited value without an authority figure.[18]

Admittedly, the Internet might well improve price discovery, but note that firms are already learning how to extract extra profits using price discrimination even on the Web. For instance, Staples Inc. has offered different prices on Web sales depending on the buyer's physical location.[19] I personally had a similar experience purchasing a ticket from US Airways. To my amazement, the price depended on the portal from which I accessed the company's Web site.

The process of matching buyers to sellers can even have fatal consequences: when Walmart ran a "doorbuster" sale for the day after Thanksgiving in 2008 in which some products were priced as "loss leaders"—products sold at below cost—a person was trampled to death.[20] Moreover, would GM and Chrysler go bankrupt if matching supply and demand were so easy? The fact is that such matching is by no means trivial because producers and consumers are not in the same place at the same time, middlemen are involved, and there is a considerable time lag between the onset of production and consumers buying a product. Thus, producers have a formidable information problem and have to anticipate market developments well in advance, with plenty of uncertainty. There is consequently a constant volatility of demand and inventory cycles, leading to turmoil in the labor market and generally detracting from the quality of life.

Economists have mostly a static equilibrium in mind. The forces of supply are balanced by the forces of demand. However, there are other models that might be more appropriate than these. Consider the ocean. Is it in equilibrium? Well, it is certainly not flying away, but it is not static either. Although it is in instantaneous equilibrium, it is incessantly in motion. I think that is a more appropriate view of the kind of equilibrium that exists in most markets.

A geological analogy is another useful way of considering the equilibrium of markets and their sudden chaotic movement from one equilibrium to another: tectonic forces can be in equilibrium along fault lines as energy builds up and stresses accumulate until the potential energy overwhelms the resistance of rocks and an earthquake occurs. Geological friction and occasional earthquakes find ready analogy in the catastrophic changes that occur in markets: for example, the financial rating agencies were giving Lehman Brothers and AIG "AAA" ratings until the bitter end. The geological analogy would compare the dissipation of potential energy through earthquakes to the bankruptcy of Lehman Brothers. It was preceded by smaller tremors such as the insolvency of Bear Stearns. The catastrophic collapse of a market is easier to visualize with a geological analogy than with the usual demand and supply framework.

Catastrophe theory was developed in mathematics to analyze dynamic systems since the 1960s but has not found its way into mainstream economics. Such a system might well appear to be in equilibrium for an extended period of time; however, suddenly, for no apparent reason, it can implode; the initial appearance of equilibrium was deceiving. It was temporary and portended a transformation to chaotic behavior. So there are different kinds of equilibrium and the static conceptualization of equilibrium in the usual demand–supply framework seems mostly an ivy-tower abstraction.

There are many other reasons why market equilibrium does not emerge simply, spontaneously, and instantaneously: friction, resistance, uncertainty, search costs, transaction costs, spatial separation between buyer and seller, and imperfect information all contribute to the difficulties buyers and sellers face in the ordinary course of exchange. While equilibrium is conceivable at an auction, where sellers and buyers are in proximity of one another, auctions are extremely rare, and so is equilibrium as conventionally conceived. In the real world, equilibrium is elusive. Instead, prices fluctuate as wavelets on an ocean similar to the price of stocks on an exchange; they can also appear to be steady and solid, as the earth along a geological fault line, only to change dramatically. For example, house prices reached a peak in the second quarter of 2006 and collapsed thereafter precipitously and unexpectedly, falling at an average rate of about 2.4 percent per quarter for a cumulative 30 percent until 2010.[21] It takes an extended period of time to reach a new equilibrium, and economic theory is unable to predict how long the adjustment will take.

Hence, the economy is an evolving system. While prices are changing, demand and supply are changing simultaneously as well. It may well be that a conventional equilibrium is never reached, as conditions in the economy evolve continuously. This is the message of complexity economics.[22] Rather than converging, complex systems are constantly in motion and small changes in the initial conditions of such systems can lead to radically different trajectories.[23] Think of the off ramp of a highway: a few inches' difference in the position of the steering wheel can send you 50 miles in the wrong direction. This is the law of large effects of small initial differences. According to W. Brian Arthur, a more realistic economics should begin with the assumption "that the actors in the economy do not necessarily face well-defined problems or use exaggerated forms of rationality in making their decisions. And they react to the outcomes they together create. Viewed this way, we find that the economy is not in stasis, but always forming, always evolving, and always 'discovering' fresh novelty."[24] The aggregate behavior of the economy as a complex system is not that of a representative agent but includes complicated interaction effects among individuals.[25]

It seems, therefore, that there is a ubiquitous mismatch in most modern markets: sellers almost always want to sell more than buyers are willing to buy. So usually there is excess capacity and unemployment and perpetual disequilibrium should be the default model.[26] There is oversupply in the housing market as well as in the labor market, and our shopping malls are full of unsold merchandise. Markets have too many frictional components to clear easily: the labor market was in equilibrium most recently during World War II—about 68 years ago.

Moreover, there is not a single price even for homogeneous goods within the same market. Firms try to be nimble and avoid a single price at any cost as there is less profit to be had with one price. For instance, groceries do not sell for the same price even within the confines of a single supermarket, as those with a club card get a lower price on many items. (Club membership is just one of the many gimmicks by which businesses increase profits by charging higher prices to unaware customers. It is called price discrimination.) Even the same supermarket chain has different prices for milk of the same brand and same quality in stores only a few miles apart. So the market is highly segmented even for homogeneous products. In sum, with search costs the law of one price need not hold even in the same market.[27]

We have difficulty keeping even a handful of prices in mind, let alone the 25,000 prices in a typical supermarket. Of course, if the quality of the product is more difficult to ascertain than that of milk, which is often the case, or if the product is complex, such as mortgage-backed securities or credit card contracts, it is much more difficult for the consumer to make a satisfactory decision.

ADVERSE SELECTION

If the quality of a product is not easily distinguishable by buyers, there may be multiple equilibriums or markets may implode, that is, disappear like the subprime mortgage market in 2008. Some people may gravitate toward buying the lower-quality product. Others, however, may take the price as a signal of quality.[28] Such problems arise in many markets with asymmetric information about the quality of the product, including credit markets, used car markets, and insurance markets.[29] The insurance company does not know about the applicants' health or driving ability as much as the applicants themselves do. In labor markets, the employer does not know as much about the worker's productivity as the worker does.

Markets with adverse selection are generally inefficient. If insurers set a price for health insurance with a given level of coverage on the basis of the average health of the population, then the less healthy people will find the insurance a better buy and will be more likely to buy it than those who have higher probability of remaining healthy. As a consequence, the average health of those insured will be lower than that of the population at large, implying that the company will incur higher costs and lower profits than expected, inducing it to raise the price of insurance. This, in turn, will induce more of the healthier people not to buy insurance. In markets with such a negative feedback loop, the insurance company will have a "bad selection" of customers, that is, there will be an adverse selection of customers from the company's point of view and this could well lead to a spiral of price increases, prompting a collapse of the insurance market as an increasing number of customers find it unattractive to buy the product. In such cases, government-mandated insurance may be the only way to improve the efficiency of the market.

TECHNOLOGICAL CHANGE

Technological change includes the discovery of new ways of producing goods and services, as well as the discovery and application of new machines and new products. So the invention of chairs was a terrific technological improvement as it facilitated production and made life more pleasant in numerous ways. But not all technological change is benign; there are hidden dangers that we need to weigh against its benefits. Aldous Huxley warned of the unbridled power of technological change, which has substantial hidden social effects and unintended consequences.[30] For instance, the recent wave of innovation with financial technology posed systemic risks as we recently found out (after the fact), to our considerable surprise.

The application of innovation generally involves what Joseph Schumpeter dubbed "creative destruction"—the new brings about the obsolescence of old technologies. The new firm or new product competes with its older counterpart and destroys it. Creativity is at once constructive and destructive: progress is at the expense of the losers in the process of change. In other words, technical progress has winners and losers as some people are invariably hurt by it. Thus, the downside of innovation is that it is never "Pareto efficient"—often leading to much suffering and social dislocation. It is inconsistent that those same economists who resist redistribution of wealth unequivocally on the grounds that it is not Pareto optimal, even if it would increase output, revere technological change unconditionally, although it is also not Pareto efficient. I think this is another blatant inconsistency in mainstream theory. A major deficit of our current economic system is that those who are hurt are not compensated by those who gain, although it is certainly unjust to have people benefit at others' expense.[31] Until we can create institutions that compensate the losers adequately, the economic system will never be able to improve life satisfaction as technical progress is obtained at the cost of inflicting pain.

Creative destruction can be viewed as an externality that detracts from the true value of GNP. If an innovation creates a new product valued at $10, GNP increases by $10. Suppose, however, that the product that it replaced had a value of $5, but now unexpectedly becomes obsolete, so its value declines to zero. The depreciation of the old product is a negative externality that is not subtracted from GNP. Thus, the whole value of the new product is not a net value added to society's well-being. In this example, the innovation created a net gain in actual GNP of $5, yet added $10 to measured GNP.

Furthermore, not all new products are actual improvements. Windows was a great technical achievement but some subsequent versions of it such as Vista were released just to enrich Microsoft and were not a worthy improvement. This strategy is profitable for the firm because the quality of a new product is not immediately obvious. There are hidden qualities that are not apparent until one has some experience with the product.[32]

Thus, there is a built-in process of obsolescence in the economic system that leads to an overestimation of GNP growth, insofar as it does not subtract from it the value of the product that was prematurely destroyed. When we buy an iPhone we are not informed when the next version will be released. A new generation of iPhones makes the previous version unfashionable and thrusts consumers out of their equilibrium. The depreciation it induces in the current value of iPhones is not anticipated and is not subtracted from GNP, that is, it increases with the full value of the new iPhone. The fashion industry has similar properties. By creating and promoting new fashion, our inventory of clothing is devalued. That means that we do not obtain as much utility from the clothing we now have as we anticipated at the time of purchase. The new fashion depreciates the value of the old.

The people hurt by technical change are often displaced workers who are unable to find employment in other sectors of the economy. The economies of the developed world may be at a stage in which technological unemployment is a permanent feature of the system. In a *New York Times* article on the work of authors Erik Brynjolfsson and Andrew McAfee we find the following:

> Since the Great Recession officially ended in June of 2009 G.D.P., equipment investment, and total corporate profits have rebounded. . . . The employment ratio, meanwhile, has only shrunk and is now at its lowest level since the early 1980s when women had not yet entered the workforce in significant numbers. So current labor force woes are not because the economy isn't growing. . . . They're because these trends have become increasingly decoupled from hiring—from needing more human workers. As computers race ahead,

acquiring more and more skills in pattern matching, communication, perception, . . . this decoupling will continue. . . . So it's possible we are facing . . . a fundamental change in the way technology and employment interact with each other. . . . All previous waves of automation affected only a small subset of human skills and abilities. . . . [T]he industrial revolution was about building machines that had (much) more brute strength than we did. For all mental work, the industrial revolution was meaningless—you still needed people. Until recently, the digital revolution also didn't affect that many human skills and abilities. . . . So employers needed to hire humans if they wanted to listen to people speak and respond to them, write a report, pattern-match across a large and diverse body of information, and do all the other things that modern knowledge workers do. Employers also needed people if they wanted lots of physical tasks done. . . . The same with most tasks involving sensory perception . . . All of the above abilities have now been demonstrated by digital technologies. . . . So employers are going to switch from human labor to digital labor to execute tasks like those above. In fact, they're already doing so. I expect this process of *switching* to accelerate in the future . . . because computers get cheaper all the time, are very accurate and reliable once they're programmed properly, and don't demand overtime, benefits, or health care. . . . "There is no economic law that says everyone benefits from technological improvement. . . ." The total number of non-farm jobs in the country is now 5 million less than in January, 2008. The 3.7 million jobs added to the economy have not been enough to make up for the 8.7 million jobs lost in 2008–9.[33]

In short, we need to make contingency plans on how to allocate the benefits of production in a system in which people are becoming increasingly redundant through technological change.[34] We should not assume simply that things will somehow work themselves out. Fair and equitable distribution of available work should not be left up to happenstance.

CHAPTER SUMMARY

According to the common wisdom efficient production is a cinch: firms combine the factors of production in the right proportions to produce the right amount of goods just at the right time and at the right price as long as unions and governments do not interfere. There are no profits in the long run so distribution is a no-brainer: employees and employers receive their just rewards, so there is no conflict and no need to moralize about the distribution of income.

However, we have documented many difficulties when that model is applied to real-world situations. The mainstream lets the perfectly competitive model do most of its heavy lifting although that model is outdated in an economy in which oligopolies and monopolies dominate and information is crucial but costly to attain and in which opportunistic behavior is more important than ever before.

Firms are not individuals and do not act with a single mind or single purpose. Employees have their own mind and supervising them is costly. Today's economy is not made up of perfectly competitive firms. To be sure, there is competition but the competition is among oligopolists or monopolists and such market structures do not lead to efficient outcomes as a rule. Such markets are inefficient and that implies that there is waste in the private sector too. Government waste is emphasized in the media but the private firms waste as much and consumers do as well. It is impossible to consume or to produce or to govern without waste. In addition, oligopolists have the power to set prices and differentiate their products from those of their competitors and as a consequence earn super profits.

QUESTIONS FOR DISCUSSION

1. Can you give some examples of businesses wasting the time of their consumers?
2. Has your boss ever been impolite to you?
3. Do you think that charging $36 for overdrawing a bank account is the marginal cost to the bank of taking care of that account or are they taking advantage of a fine print in the agreement and earning pure profit on that charge?
4. Is the price of pizza the same everywhere in your town?
5. Is there a product whose price is uniform throughout your town?
6. Do you know of any perfectly competitive firms where you live?
7. What do you think about the concentration of power in the hands of large corporations?
8. Do you know how much profit Apple earns on an iPhone?
9. What do you think the difference is between the Apple 4S, Apple 5, and Apple 5S iPhone?
10. Can you tell the difference between an original Louis Vuitton handbag and an imitation?
11. Do you think that Goldman Sachs' $13 billion profit in 2010 (based on taxpayer subsidies) was legitimate?
12. What is the value of the marginal product of a professor? Of a policeman? Of a nurse?
13. Have you ever been deceived by unscrupulous marketing strategies?
14. Do you think there should be laws so that Angelo Mozilo would have to forfeit his wealth for the great damage he did to the American economy?
15. Do you think there should be a right to work?
16. How many prices do you remember?
17. Do you think that innovation is always good for us?
18. Can you give examples of products with built-in obsolescence?
19. Do you think that competition leads to consumer satisfaction?
20. Did you ever see shirking where you worked?
21. Does the "invisible hand" always guarantee perfect solutions to our problems?
22. Will the profits of Apple Inc. be ever competed away?
23. What are some differences between firms in the textbooks and firms in the real economy?
24. Do you ever get confused by all the products you see in a supermarket?
25. Do you know anyone who was deceived by his/her cell-phone contract?
26. Did you make a rational choice in buying your cell phone?
27. Did you ever make a mistake in buying a product?
28. Have you experienced some opportunistic behavior?
29. How much money do you estimate you waste in a year?

NOTES

1. Alfred Chandler, *The Visible Hand: The Managerial Revolution in American Business* (Cambridge, MA: Belknap Press, 1977).

2. The largest employer in the United States is not a private competitive firm at all but a governmental agency, the Department of Defense.

3. I sold my car recently and the private purchaser obtained an auto loan from a local bank. The person handling the loan had great difficulty following the written instructions she received from headquarters. She

had to call for help three times and took about an hour longer than anticipated. She was obviously incompetent in handling such a transaction.

4. David Kocieniewski, "As Oil Industry Fights a Tax, It Reaps Subsidies," *The New York Times*, July 3, 2010.

5. The iPod touch, introduced in 2007 as a successor to the original product, was in the $300–$500 range.

6. "Fortune 500, 2010," CNN Money.

7. "Our merchants and masters complain much of the bad effects of high wages in raising the price and lessening the sale of goods. They say nothing concerning the bad effects of high profits. They are silent with regard to the pernicious effects of their own gains. They complain only of those of other people." Adam Smith, "Of the Wages of Labour," Book I, Chapter VIII, Section 24 in *An Inquiry into the Nature and Causes of the Wealth of Nations*, ed. Edwin Cannan (London: Methuen, 1904), available online at Library of Economics and Liberty.

8. U.S. Department of Commerce, Bureau of Economic Analysis, "Gross Domestic Product: Third Quarter 2010 (Second Estimate). Corporate Profits: Third Quarter 2010 (Preliminary)," News Release, November 23, 2010.

9. See 2007 Census of Governments, "Summary of Public Employment and Payrolls by Type of Government: March 2007," available at www2.census.gov/govs/apes/emp_compendium.pdf.

10. Robert Frank, *The Darwin Economy: Liberty, Competition, and the Common Good* (Princeton, NJ: Princeton University Press, 2011).

11. David Brooks, "Why Our Elites Stink," *The New York Times*, July 12, 2012.

12. Edward Chamberlin, *The Theory of Monopolistic Competition: A Re-Orientation of the Theory of Value* (Cambridge, MA: Harvard University Press, 1933). Joan Robinson, *The Economics of Imperfect Competition* (London: Macmillan, 1933).

13. Textile product mills are at 58 percent of capacity. Board of Governors of the Federal Reserve System, Federal Reserve Statistical Release, G.17 (419) Supplemental Tables, August 15, 2012.

14. "Horn of Africa," UNICEF. See www.unicefusa.org/work/emergencies/horn-of-africa/.

15. Robert Frank, "How Does a Four-Year-Old Spend $46,000 a Month?" *The Wall Street Journal*, August 3, 2011.

16. The handbag is called Saumur. Stephanie Clifford, "Even Marked Up, Luxury Goods Fly Off Shelves," *The New York Times*, August 3, 2011.

17. Being unable to take care of her two children a financially desperate unemployed woman killed them; Robbie Brown, "Mother in South Carolina Killed 2 Children, Police Say," *The New York Times*, August 17, 2010.

18. F.H. Hahn, "Auctioneer," in *The New Palgrave Dictionary of Economics*, 2nd ed., ed. Steven N. Durlauf and Lawrence E. Blume (Basingstoke, UK: Palgrave Macmillan, 2008).

19. Based on the IP address of the computer, the difference was about 10 percent. "A Tale of Two Prices," *The Wall Street Journal*, December 24, 2012.

20. "Store Worker Trampled, Dies," YouTube video, 1:56, posted by "CBS," November 28, 2008. Walmart is appealing the ridiculously low $7,000 fine by OSHA. Megan Woolhouse, "Walmart Still Battling Fine in '08 Trampling," *The Boston Globe*, November 22, 2012.

21. "S&P/Case-Shiller Home Price Indices," MacroMarkets.

22. Wikipedia contributors, "Complexity Economics," *Wikipedia: The Free Encyclopedia.*

23. W. Brian Arthur, Steven N. Durlauf, and D.A. Lane, eds., *The Economy as an Evolving Complex System II* (Reading, MA: Addison-Wesley, 1997).

24. W. Brian Arthur, External Professor, Santa Fe Institute, "Interests." See http://tuvalu.santafe.edu/~wbarthur/

25. Alan Kirman, "Economy as a Complex System," in *The New Palgrave Dictionary of Economics*, 2nd ed., ed. Steven N. Durlauf and Lawrence E. Blume (Basingstoke, UK: Palgrave Macmillan, 2008).

26. *The Wall Street Journal* observed that "from cashmere to blue jeans, silver jewelry to aluminum cans, the world is in oversupply." James Crotty, "Why There Is Chronic Excess Capacity—The Market Failures Issue," *Challenge* 6 (2002): 21–44.

27. Joseph Stiglitz, "Information and the Change in the Paradigm in Economics," *American Economic Review* 92 (2002) 3: 460–501, at p. 477.

28. That is exactly what I did in buying an electric stove, even though both options had looked the same but one was twice as expensive as the other. I was hoping that the more expensive one had better hidden qualities. I will never know if I was tricked, as I am not expecting to buy the other product to compare performance.

29. George Akerlof, "The Market for 'Lemons': Quality Uncertainty and the Market Mechanism," *Quarterly Journal of Economics* 84 (1970): 488–500.

30. Aldous Huxley, interview with Mike Wallace, May 18, 1958. YouTube video.

31. Some argue that hypothetical compensation should suffice for efficiency. According to this theory, compensation does not actually have to take place, but the mere possibility of compensation suffices. Thus, as long as gainers gain more than losers lose, the policy is efficient, but of course the theoretical possibility of compensation does not help the lives of the losers and is therefore not a humanistic approach to economic policy, as losers are never compensated by the winners.

32. For instance, it took some years before the new financial instruments became toxic so they were very profitable until some of the inferior characteristics of the innovation came to light.

33. Erik Brynjolfsson and Andrew McAfee, *Race Against the Machine*, as cited in Thomas Edsall, "The Hollowing Out," *The New York Times*, July 8, 2012.

34. Sean Patrick Farrell, "The Robot Factory Future," *The New York Times*, video, 3:58, August 18, 2012.

7

RETURNS TO THE FACTORS OF PRODUCTION

In perfectly competitive markets firms pay competitive wages, and labor, capital, managers, and capitalists all receive their opportunity cost. There is hardly any role for government in that model as everything is running smoothly. Everyone receives their just rewards and since there are no profits at all to quarrel over, all problems are solved conveniently by the market. The takeaway impression that millions of students retain years after their introductory course ended is that competition solves all the important problems in the economy and hence markets left to their own devices will be efficient. Government guidance is superfluous and mostly inefficient. As we see below, this is not a reasonable description of the real existing economy made up of oligopolies and monopolies rather than perfectly competitive firms. Because of the absence of countervailing power to defend wages and because of the constant threat of unemployment, wages have not kept pace with productivity growth. In turn imperfect competition meant that the profits of corporations have exploded, which has led to an offensive distribution of income. We accentuate the need for thinking creatively about two of these outcomes: the determination of the rewards of labor and of the distribution of income in the real existing economy.

FACTORS OF PRODUCTION

The corporation employs and combines factors of production (conventionally labor, land, and capital) in order to produce goods and services. Infrastructure, social capital, institutions, knowledge, human capital, culture, the legal system, and natural resources are additional important factors of production. The market could not function without infrastructure, most of which is financed from public funds. In an increasingly information-driven knowledge economy, we should accentuate the role of intangible factors such as human capital in the process of production.

Institutional capital constitutes the basic framework within which an economy operates and is also crucial for its functioning. The legal system provides enforcement mechanisms for laws and regulations. These intangible factors of production have the unique characteristic that they are not created by markets but by social, political, and cultural processes. These evolve slowly out of the historical experience and the value system of the population. This is just one example of how markets depend in crucial ways on the institutional and legal frameworks and, in fact, cannot exist without them.[1] Institutional capital is often taken for granted by economists even though it is very cumbersome and costly to devise and takes a very long time to put in place. Just think about the incredible challenges of institution building after the Arab Spring or in Iraq and Afganistan. Yet markets do not create institutions although they interact with them and can affect them over time. This is crucial because free markets are compatible with many different institutions. The variety of institutions in the labor markets around the globe is just one example.

Institutions affect economic performance crucially: they channel behavior and market processes into one of several paths of development. They have an impact on output and therefore on efficiency. Moreover, they can constrain production just as the conventional factors can (Figure 6.2). Consequently, we can think of institutions as an input into the production process. Furthermore, this also means that sociopolitical processes rather than economic ones are important determinants of economic efficiency. An institutionless economics is misleading.

For example, a legal system that allows for nonrecourse mortgage loans has different economic implications than one that does not. With a nonrecourse loan, in case of default the borrower is not personally liable for the whole amount of the loan outstanding. So if you still owe $10,000 on your mortgage but are unable to pay the monthly installments, with a nonrecourse loan you are able to walk away from the loan if you forfeit your right to the property. In most European countries, the borrower would be liable for the remainder of the debt for the rest of his life.

Similarly, cultural attributes such as "trust" and the ability to cooperate without costly bargaining, contracts, and legal costs have an important role in economic performance.[2] "Virtually every commercial transaction has within itself an element of trust."[3] We found it out the hard way in September 2008, when trust suddenly evaporated and banks were unwilling to lend money even to other banks. The lack of trust can lead to bank runs. Markets have great difficulty functioning without adequate trust, because contracts are costly to write as well as to enforce and can seldom be written to specify every eventuality. Just imagine what it would be like if we needed to sign a contract before we were seated in a restaurant. It would be a substantial additional cost of doing business. Would the contract have to specify what happens in case the customer does not like the food? Would we sign a contract releasing the restaurant from liability in case of food poisoning? It is a lot more efficient to instill in everyone the obligation to pay their restaurant bill without thinking much about it so that the restaurant owner can trust the guest to pay for the meal without much ado.

Intangible forms of capital stock—social capital, institutional capital, and knowledge—differ from the common factors of production insofar as they are public goods, that is, they are not the property of any individual or firm, and no one can be excluded from their use. The whole community benefits from having a functioning legal system or a constitution, for instance, and does not have to pay for using and benefiting from it. How much is the legal system worth? Just consider if each generation had to pay for it anew. It would cost enormous sums. While we are unable to repay this valuable gift to those who came before us, we can honor their legacy by passing it on to subsequent generations. This aspect of institutions becomes important in discussing productivity, because it is impossible to measure individual productivity accurately if public goods—including institutions—are used extensively in the process of production.

Another way the intangible forms of capital, such as knowledge, differ from conventional factors is that they do not diminish (depreciate) over time through use the way physical capital does. They are not subject to wear and tear. On the contrary, their productivity most often increases with use, although it can become obsolete through the discovery of new knowledge.[4] Knowledge embodied in people is called human capital. This term also includes health, inasmuch as health increases productivity.

The feeling of community and the network of friends and acquaintances are referred to as social capital. One cannot help but think that those bankers involved in predatory lending who sold mortgages to individuals unable to repay them would not have done so if they had had a greater feeling of responsibility toward their community. If they had had a greater sense of belonging, they would not have been willing to benefit at the expense of their fellow citizens. This is an example of the absence of social capital. In other words, the financial disaster of 2008 could have been avoided if the culture within which the financial sector operated had taken the interests of the community into greater consideration. Social capital based on mutual sympathy, social cohesion, and shared cultural norms and values fosters trust and cooperation within the community and thereby lowers transaction and enforcement costs. In sum, intangibles also have an enormous effect on economic processes.

In addition, human beings are different from the other factors of production in that they are sentient—they have feelings and a sense of fairness. Moreover, they have basic needs without which they are unable to work. A machine can stand idle some time without much attention, but labor cannot. Labor has to be nourished every day. Labor can choose to shirk; a machine cannot. Labor decides the amount of effort to expand; a machine does not. To treat labor and capital symmetrically is a simplification that leads one down a slippery slope. It is important not to treat labor as an object. In order to improve the welfare of society it is crucial to treat workers with appropriate human dignity—independent of the monetary value of their labor—and not dehumanize work by treating it as any other factor of production.

Natural resources differ from the other factors of production in that they are essential for life (i.e., water, air, earth) and also important for production (i.e., minerals), yet many of them are nonrenewable and many are being depleted at an accelerated rate since the Industrial Revolution. Many resources are exhaustible—available in finite amounts. In addition, there are many ominous developments in climate change, water and air quality, biodiversity loss, and loss of ecosystems. This is a considerable problem, as the depletion of natural resources and changes in weather patterns are not accounted for properly in the GNP accounts and, in addition, threaten our economy as we know it. This is a potential time bomb of mass-destruction intensity.[5]

NATURAL RESOURCES

Natural resources are important inputs into the production process. Some are reproducible, such as trees and fisheries, while others are exhaustible, such as minerals. There are a finite amount of minerals on earth and these therefore could be depleted in the future depending on the rate of extraction and discovery of new reserves. While the total amount available is unknown and we can only guesstimate how long they will last, it is clear that the supply is finite. The atmosphere and oceans have not been seen as an exhaustible resource until the recent realization that their capacity to absorb carbon dioxide and carbon monoxide without major changes in the weather system is, indeed, limited. Insofar as many resources, such as the atmosphere or the ocean, are public goods, safeguarding them for future generations is extremely difficult. They do not have a price, and setting a price on pollution at the international level has proven to be impossible. That raises the possibility that the Industrial Revolution might have sowed the seeds of its own destruction, as global warming and pollution threaten us in so many ways.[6]

There are those who argue that technical progress has solved our problems in the past and thus will do so in the future as well, but this is plain wishful thinking without scientific evidence. It might but then again it might not. We simply do not know. Is it reasonable to take a chance on an issue of such importance? Would it not be preferable to have a fail-safe strategy in order to make sure that the earth and the human race will survive these challenges? A fail-safe strategy would entail focusing more on sustainability and less on growth and consumption. Those who advocate a "greed is good" policy fail to comprehend that it leads to disregard of the welfare and natural rights of future generations. Sustainability presupposes the willingness to sacrifice consumption now for the welfare of generations yet unborn, which is not likely in a greed-is-good cultural environment.

MARGINAL THEORY

Marginal utility, marginal cost, marginal product, and marginal revenue—let's just call these abstractions marginal everything (ME)—play a fundamental role in economic thought. If people were rational and if ME could actually be knowable and measurable, then it would make sense that they would hold the key to determining output and consumption. Output would be constrained by marginal cost, wages would equal the value of the marginal product of labor, marginal revenue would be equal to marginal cost, and the thousand other optimal conditions would hold that have been derived on blackboards millions of times. Yet there are myriad problems with this theory.

It assumes that everything is continuously divisible and so that all the functions are differentiable. The calculation of ME would require tiny variation in the amounts produced or consumed so that these values could be calculated. But that is hopelessly difficult, if not outright impossible, to determine in real-world situations. Firms cannot hire managers by the hour in order to ascertain what their contribution is to total product, for instance. Automobiles are not divisible either.

Furthermore, there are many professions whose marginal products—even theoretically—are unknowable even in theory. Teaching, policing, fire fighting, and civil service fall into this ambiguous category. One-fifth of the labor force works for the government in the United States—plus 1.4 million people are in the military—with no measurable marginal product. With so many people working in occupations whose marginal product's value is in principle undefined, the rest of the labor market is distorted anyhow so that even if we could measure marginal product it would not be accurate.

What is the marginal utility of my consuming a piece of cake? I am unable to have a clear sense of it. It is a surge of fleeting pleasure that soon turns into enduring regret. Daniel Kahneman and Amos Tversky have shown how many cognitive errors people make about their own utility; it would be far-fetched to think that they can determine ME accurately or even approximately. Given the impossibility of calculating ME, we generally substitute a rule of thumb, a heuristic, a convention, or follow historical precedent in order to reach a good-enough solution. That is to say, both consumers and producers are satisficing without the use of ME. Otherwise we would become catatonic.

There is an additional problem of aggregation of the factors of production. How do we add up the capital stock? How do we add computers and automobiles and buildings? And how should we aggregate the clean-up crew with the shop foreman or the information technology (IT) department to get the total labor force? If we are unable to compute the aggregates, we are unable to find the output of the marginal worker or that of the marginal capital stock. And what is the contribution of public goods such as the Internet?

Another contentious issue is that often there are fixed proportions in consumption as well as in production. I type on one keyboard. The addition of a second keyboard would not contribute to my output. Take it away, though, and I won't be able to use the computer at all. So how would we ascertain our joint product between the keyboard and me? The marginal principle does not help in such cases.

A firm's output is limited by the quantity demanded of its product. Most firms are best represented by constant returns to scale technology; that is, marginal cost is generally not increasing for most firms because large-scale unemployment and underutilization of capital stock mean that they could expand production without incurring rising costs of their inputs. Hence, constant marginal and average costs should be the default model. Demand constrains output of firms in most cases and not increasing marginal costs. In any case, price is almost always greater than marginal cost, so that the perfectly competitive market should not be the default model.

WAGES

In traditional theory, firms pay wages equal to the value of marginal product. According to this theory, real wages should keep pace with productivity. Yet this conjecture is easy to refute, because wages have not kept pace with productivity at all since 1970 (Figure 7.1). Between 1947 and 1970 there was no difference between productivity growth and the growth in real wages, just as theory predicted; both almost doubled in the intervening quarter-century, growing at an annual compounded rate of 2.7 percent.

This post–World War II golden age of economic growth ended in the early 1970s when the economy was subject to two major oil shocks and inflation. A slowdown ensued subsequently in the rate of increase of both productivity and real wages; however, the first signs of a structural break in the relationship between wages and productivity appeared as wages increased at a slightly slower rate than productivity. After 1982, the productivity–wage gap became much wider: while productivity picked up to 2.2 percent per annum, real wages lagged far behind, increasing at less than half that rate (1.0 percent) (Table 7.1). This meant that productivity increased by 85 percent

Figure 7.1   **Index of the Productivity-Wage Gap in the United States, 1947 = 100**

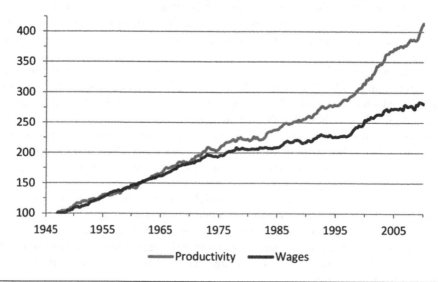

Table 7.1

Growth in Productivity and Real Wages, U.S., 1947–2011

Years		Productivity Growth %		Wages Growth %		Ratio Difference %	
Range	Total	Total	Annual	Total	Annual	Annual	Annual
1947–1970	23	85	2.7	83	2.7	0.98	−0.0
1970–1982	12	19	1.4	14	1.1	0.74	−0.3
1982–2011	29	85	2.2	35	1.0	0.45	−1.2

Source: Susan Fleck, John Glaser, and Shawn Sprague, "The Compensation–Productivity Gap: A Visual Essay," *Monthly Labor Review*, January 2011: 57–69 (accessed July 21, 2012)

Note: "Total" refers to the total percent increase during the period. "Annual" is the annual compounded growth rate. "Ratio" is the ratio of annual growth rates.

during the following three decades while wages increased by just 35 percent. The divergence is an obvious contradiction of the hypothesis that wages are equated to the value of marginal product through competition. There is more: these numbers hide the fact that CEO salaries and bonuses on Wall Street are included in the wage data. Hence, the growth of the income of the median worker on Main Street has fallen even farther behind the growth in productivity.

There is yet another inconvenient truth to consider: the annual earnings of men working full time have not increased at all since 1973 adjusted for inflation (Figures 7.2 and 7.3). Actually, they have decreased by some $300 per annum.[7] That implies that the 35 percent increase in wages has been limited mainly to women and to a small group of men. The annual salaries of women employed full time increased substantially, from $20,000 to $36,000 per annum. Median weekly income data provide a similar pattern (Figure 7.3). Men's income has been stuck at about $375 per week since 1980 while that of women has increased by $50 per week in the interim.[8] It is not at all plausible to suppose that the productivity of men would have declined in this period and that only the productivity of women would have risen. Hence, the productivity hypothesis of wage determination is not convincing at all.

How are wages determined if not by using ME theory? Given the difficulty of ascertaining the marginal product of labor and the uncertainty associated with it, firms satisfice in order to find a viable solution to their problem. They use heuristics and signals to determine the wages of their workers. Of course, education, diploma, work experience, age, gender, ethnicity, and appearance also all play a role. That does not mean that anticipated productivity is not part of the guesstimate, but the above signals are used as proxies or rough gauges of expected productivity. In addition to the above attributes, the history of wages, custom, the degree of unionization, concentration within the industry, the rate of profit of the firm, and the institutional structures in place also matter a lot.

While education does play a role in determining wages, it does not explain as much of the differences in income across various occupations as is often argued. "Even in terms of wage determination, while the variables associated with human capital enter equations with high significance, they are not the dominant factor in variations in wages among individuals: in a typical log-earnings equation, education may explain five per cent of the variation and education and years of experience may explain 15 per cent in total. . . ."[9]

The institutional setting is also crucial. Some 40 percent of wages in the oligopolistic finance sector is actually rent, that is, that much above the wage of comparable employees in other sectors. The extra earnings of those employed in the finance sector were linked to the era of deregulation beginning in the 1980s, that is to say, to the changes in the institutional framework (Figure 7.4).[10] In other words, the employees in those sectors are able to capture a share of the extraordinary profits being earned by these oligopolistic firms.

Custom also has a key role to play, for example in the male–female wage gap. Part-time workers also earn much less than those who work full time even if the two work "side by side," that is, for the same firm in the same occupation and have the same education and other characteristics.[11] The inference is that their productivity should be similar to those of full-time workers. Such wage gaps have historical roots: it has been customary to pay part-time workers as well as women less insofar as their work used to be supplementary to the salary of the head of household. Students and mothers worked part time and were willing to do so at a lower wage than the main breadwinner, their income seen as a bonus to the household's budget. Of course, this is no longer the case; millions of part-time workers are unable to find full-time employment and thus must join the ranks of the working poor.

Figure 7.2   **Median Income of Full-Time, Year-Round Workers by Gender, 2011**

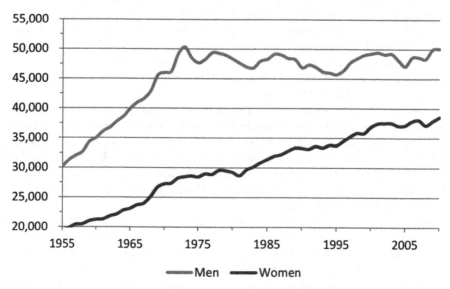

Source: U.S. Department of Commerce, U.S. Census Bureau, www.census.gov/prod/2009pubs/acsbr08-3.pdf

Figure 7.3   **Median Weekly Income of Full-Time Workers by Gender, 1982–1984**

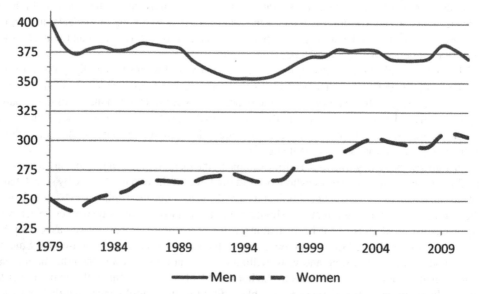

Source: U.S. Department of Labor, Bureau of Labor Statistics, Weekly and Hourly Data from the Current Population Survey, Series ID LEU0252881900, http://data.bls.gov/cgi-bin/surveymost?le (accessed July 21, 2012)

Figure 7.4   **The Extent to Which Wages in the Financial Sector Exceed Those in Other Sectors with Comparable Education**

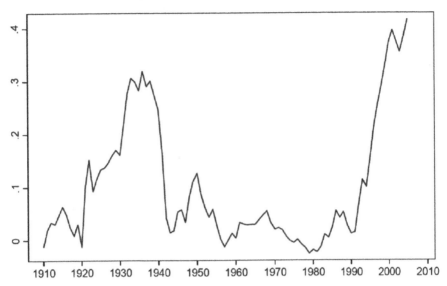

Obviously, the wage is a payment for services rendered. However, what is being paid for is less obvious. The payments are partly for the time spent at work physically, the effort expended during that time (which is more difficult to ascertain and is initially uncertain), and the skill, education, and experience of the employee since these affect productivity (also difficult to determine; that is why the diploma is used as a signaling device). These aspects are not controversial. However, that is not all: part of the wage is a return on other attributes of the employee, such as her natural intelligence, physical features, and inborn talent. While these attributes also generally enhance productivity, the difference between these and the former set of attributes is that the employee did not have to do anything to acquire those characteristics. Instead, it was a matter of luck that she was born with those features. According to John Rawls, workers do not deserve to receive compensation for those traits inasmuch as those payments are pure rent, that is, they did nothing to acquire them. Hence, paying for those attributes is not an incentive to supply more of those attributes (as at this writing genetic engineering is not far enough advanced to create such characteristics).

Another major issue is that employees generally also benefit from public goods such as roads or satellites used for internet communication created at the taxpayers' expense. Insofar as the workers or sports teams did not pay for these or do anything to create them, they should not benefit from them either. The Internet is a good example. The basic research for it was at taxpayers' expense, so the taxpayers should gain a substantial portion of the benefits derived from the innovation rather than its accruing to private individuals. Consider, for instance, that in 1980, major league baseball players earned about 10 times as much as K–12 teachers. This obviously was way out of line, because the contribution of teachers to social welfare is considerably larger than that of ball players, and the only reason that baseball players could earn such humongous salaries is that the market for sports is highly privileged through the exemptions from antitrust laws and public subsidies to sport stadiums and communications networks and technology. However, by the year 2000 the average baseball salary had increased to 45 times that of teachers, because the Internet enabled a much larger audience to view the games.[12] In other words, the value of baseball players—

and this is true for all athletes and other celebrities—is not determined only by their own effort but is also crucially contingent on the contributions of society which, by the way, also owns the airwaves through which the broadcast travels. So the value created by a game is produced jointly by the individual and the society. Therefore, its distribution is not determined by market forces alone but also by institutional structures and the laws of the land.

If sport is to be treated as a privileged industry and be exempt from antitrust legislation, the people who participate in sports should not reap the benefits of that legislation. Without these laws, LeBron James and Kobe Bryant would not be earning $17 and $28 million respectively. Their salaries are not the product of free-market supply-and-demand forces but of the laws that allow the National Basketball Association to effectively be a cartel. The whole structure of mega-sports is built on a foundation of government-sanctioned privilege that protects the teams from competition and allows them to have monopoly power. Of course, they can earn extraordinary salaries from these monopoly rights. Is that privilege for sports fair? Even if this might be a reasonable way to organize sports, there is no reason why the players or the franchise should profit from the legislation. Their salaries are not the outcome of their achievements alone. There is no reason that workers in the sports industry should profit from the Internet more than the average worker. It is merely their good fortune that they have occupations that benefited from the Internet, and in a fair society wages would not be a function of chance.

Similarly, the Lords of Wall Street would not be earning their billions if it were not for the Internet. After all, the Internet helps them communicate globally and enable them to manage distant associates thereby extending their market power. In addition, the Internet helps them move their billions instantaneously around the globe to take advantage of lucrative opportunities. Without the Internet the global reach of Wall Street would be limited. Those who rail against government involvement in markets might consider that their extraordinary profits are possible only because the taxpayers have created an infrastructure and make it available to them free of charge. The incomes earned by the likes of Lloyd Blankfein, Jamie Dimon, Walid Chammah, or John Havens, whose annual compensation (in 2009) was in the $10 million range, and of John Stumpf and Thomas Montag, who earned two to three times as much (all with taxpayers' assistance),[13] would not be as high if the market for CEOs were perfectly competitive. The conclusion is warranted that "financiers are overpaid."[14] They are not paid their opportunity cost. Even those CEOs who ran their companies into the ground received astronomical figures. For instance, John Thain received $83 million before Merrill Lynch became insolvent. This evidence defies the theory that wages equal the value of marginal product.

The laws and institutions created by prior generations also enhance the productivity of the current labor force. We all benefit from the contributions of generations who preceded us. Entrepreneurs cannot achieve by themselves and they do not deserve all that they earn as their output is produced jointly with the social and institutional capital that belongs to society. How that joint product is to be apportioned is essentially a collective political decision. Markets ought not decide that by themselves. People who preceded us often even sacrificed their lives in order to create and defend those institutions that are now public goods. Yet everyone uses and benefits from them. There is no reason people should be paid for the portion of their productivity derived from public goods. These were created by the blood and sweat of prior generations. In short, we are all benefiting from the sacrifices men made at Gettysburg, Guadalcanal, or Gold Beach. How much should Jay-Z and other celebrities pay the descendants of the men who fought in those places for not having had to fight there?

Another example of the extent to which institutional structure affects salaries is the success of the American Medical Association (AMA) in restricting competition in the name of fostering excellence in medical care.[15] By restricting the number of students of medicine, the AMA inflates

Figure 7.5   **Physicians per 1,000 Population**

Source: OECD Health Data 2011. http://stats.oecd.org/Index.aspx?DataSetCode=HEALTH_REAC

doctors' salaries well above competitive levels. Only half of those applying to medical schools are accepted. In spite of the shortage of doctors, the medical profession is opposing foreign medical schools sending their students to the United States for internships.[16] American doctors earn five times as much as Japanese doctors. I doubt seriously that they are five times more productive.

It is rather odd that the United States can produce all other professions in abundance but is unable to produce as many doctors (per capita) as other advanced industrial societies (Figure 7.5).[17] In order to increase the number of physicians per capita to Norway's level, the number of doctors in the United States would have to be increased by some 480,000. Compared to the 750,000 physicians in the United States currently, this would be a 60 percent increase. This market situation is depicted in Figure 7.6. With the AMA constraining the number of doctors to N there are fewer doctors than there would be in competitive equilibrium (N'); consequently the wage of MDs is above the competitive level. The high earnings of U.S. doctors are not brought about by market forces; they are not predicated entirely on their investment in education, but by the fact that the

Figure 7.6   **The Supply and Demand for MDs with Supply Constraint Brought About by the American Medical Association**

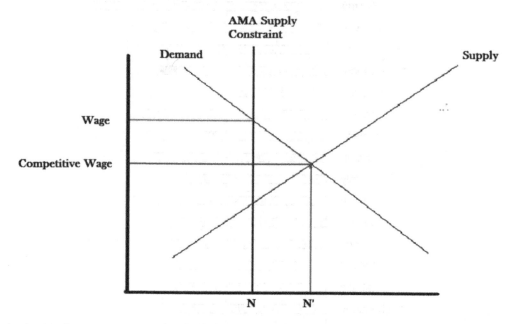

institutional structure protects doctors from market forces. In short, the AMA has been much more effective than other organizations in maintaining the salaries of its members well above competitive levels by restricting supply.[18]

While executive compensation is part of the official statistics on labor income,[19] it differs from the wages of ordinary workers in that there is actually no market for top managers and CEOs. The positions are seldom advertised and there is no transparency on how chief executives are chosen. Once chosen, they can essentially pack the board of directors with their supporters and eventually write their own salaries. "Those close to the soup bowl get served first." Those salaries are determined in boardrooms or in the course of bilateral bargaining. Negotiations over salaries take place under circumstances in which the board has no incentive to strike a hard bargain since it is disposing of the shareholders' money and not its own. It would not retain any of the potential savings for itself. Thus, the principal–agent problem emerges in full view. The power of the shareholders is diluted, whereas the power of the CEO is vested in himself alone.[20] So the power relationship is asymmetric in favor of management.

Moreover, it became a social norm to pay CEOs enormous salaries and deviation from that norm becomes difficult due to expectations and peer pressure. CEOs have lot of inside information, so they can use their power to exert undue influence on the board of directors. In addition, they can appoint their own protégés to the board thereby making sure that their salaries are assured independently of their productivity. If the market were competitive, salaries would decline markedly because the current salaries are way above opportunity costs. Just consider if one could have found someone to run Bank of America for less than $4 million in 2009 (that is almost $2,000/hour) at a time when the bank was propped up in any event by the U.S. taxpayer.[21] There were likely plenty of executives who would have run it as efficiently for under $0.5 million.

The usual argument that capping salaries would be inefficient does not hold in this case, because most of the salaries are rents. So supposed incentives do not bring forth more talent or intelligence. The CEOs would work as hard at 10 percent of their current salaries provided the cap is economy-wide. What else would they do? It would still be the most they could earn. What would happen if salaries were capped? Would all the CEOs emigrate? Where would they go? CEOs in other countries earn substantially less. The marginal tax rate in the top income bracket under the Eisenhower administration was about 88 percent and under Nixon it was still around 70 percent and yet there was no shortage whatsoever of CEOs or celebrities or football players. Note that the U.S. president earns $400,000 a year. In contrast, Angelo Mozilo of Countrywide Financial, a major culprit in the subprime mortgage crisis, earned some $500 million between 2000 and 2008. He was fined $67 million for fraud, a mere 13 percent of his pay.[22]

In sum, the wage is a payment for the education, skill, effort, talent, and intelligence of the employee, all of which are affected by the public goods she is using in the process of production. Labor productivity is not due exclusively to our private exertion and our investment in our human capital. Much of it is due to aspects outside of our control for which we should not receive a reward. Wages are related to productivity, but productivity is difficult to measure because of the heterogeneity of workers. Employers therefore use rules of thumb to guesstimate the wages they pay.[23] In other words, fair wages are far from optimally determined, and will take us some time to consider how best to do it.

THE COST OF CAPITAL

In order to be able to calculate profits we also need to know the cost of capital, which depends on the stock of capital as well as its price. But that requires that we add different kinds of capital, which cannot be done in physical units. This is different from resources such as oil, which can be calculated in barrels, or labor, which can be measured in hours worked. Capital is different in that we have hammers and computers and thus cannot use physical units. The only thing we can do is to add their value using either historical cost or the present value of the future output stream produced by the capital stock.

The historical cost of capital is its price at the time of purchase. However, capital depreciates; it is used up over time. Therefore, its annual cost depends on the rate of depreciation, δ, and the rate of interest, r: cost = $(r + \delta) \times$ price. Given the market rate of interest on corporate bonds, r depends on the funds rate set by the Federal Reserve; thus, the cost of capital is not set by the market alone but is also influenced by a government-sponsored institution. To be sure, the market value of the capital stock would generally be less than the historic cost as the secondary market in most physical capital has more imperfect information than for new products. Just as new cars lose value immediately upon being driven from the dealership's parking lot, if a firm buys a computer with a certain configuration, it will not be possible for it to later sell it for close to what the firm paid for it. The same is true for most specialized machinery. However, real estate might appreciate in value, in which case the market value might be more appropriate to use (except during a bubble).

However, if we calculate the value of the capital stock using the discounted expected future value created by the capital stock—as most mainstream economists would like us to do—we run into the following problems: First, we need the future interest rate in order to discount the future income stream produced by the capital stock, but the market interest rate is supposedly determined by the marginal product of capital. Hence, this method of calculating the capital stock is circular. Second, we do not know how accurate these expectations will be—we can only make rough guesses about what future production and prices will be, which is not very helpful in actually calculating the cost of capital prior to production. We do not know how much of the firm's net revenue should be allocated to profits and how much to the return on capital until we know the value of the capital stock.[24] So estimating the value of the capital stock is quite a conundrum.

Example: Suppose a firm pays $1 wages annually and buys a machine for $1 that lasts only one period. Together, the machine and worker produce goods worth $3.05, leaving $1 profit (calculated as profit = revenue – expenses), as the rate of depreciation is 100 percent and the rate of interest is 5 percent. So the 5 cents pays for the interest on the invested capital. Yet others might argue that the value of the machine was really $2 and profit was actually zero, because the historical cost of capital is immaterial: what counts is the value produced by the machine; the owner of the firm would have been able to sell the machine for $2 so that determines its market value (the rate of return on the $1 invested would then be 100 percent). However, why would someone pay $2 for a machine that could be purchased for $1, especially since the future revenue was unknown at the beginning of the period? So the value of the machine at the beginning of the period was the historic price; it could not be a function of an unknown entity—future sales. There is no reason why the $1 profit should be attributed to capital rather than to labor. The product, after all, was produced jointly. The two factors of production should be treated identically. The issue of how to calculate the value of capital is a major conundrum in economics known as the Cambridge capital controversy.[25]

PROFITS

Profits are the residual from revenues after the costs of labor, raw materials, and capital are subtracted. In perfect competition, there would not be any profits at all, but that is irrelevant to today's economy as most of it is concentrated in oligopolistic firms. Profits have been large, as mentioned above. For instance, Apple had $8.2 billion profits in 2008 on assets of $47.5 billion. As a whole, the U.S. commercial banks earned a 14 percent return on equity between 1994 and 2007.[26] Even during the Great Recession (in 2009), the profits of the financial sector were $242 billion, 17 percent of all corporate profits as a consequence of the fact that the taxpayers paid for their losses.[27] That was very far from zero and also much above the long-term interest rate of 2.8 percent return on Treasury securities. Furthermore, profits have been growing: after-tax profits of the corporate sector more than doubled between 2003 and 2010 from $660 billion to $1.4 trillion,[28] but only because it was bailed out at taxpayers' expense.

After Joseph Schumpeter, profits are due to innovation, which prevents the economy from settling down to a long-run equilibrium in which profits would be zero. Innovation creates monopolies in new products or services and therefore leads to a disequilibrium. Profits are also associated with any development that prevents competition, such as barriers to entry, for instance, due to brand loyalties accumulated through advertisement campaigns. Opening up of new markets through globalization can also increase profits.

INCOME DISTRIBUTION

The conventional theory of income distribution is straightforward: both labor and capital receive the value of their marginal product, and since profits are zero, distributing the rewards is child's play. However, as we have just seen, profits are by no means zero, and have not been since the beginning of industrialization in the early nineteenth century. Thus, the question naturally arises: How are the profits distributed? The residual claimant is a matter of legal and institutional structure and not one of economic theory. In our current system it accrues to the shareholders, with the top managers obtaining an unduly large share of it and not to the workers employed by the firm who produce the products jointly.

It is common knowledge that income distribution has become dizzyingly top heavy in the United States (Figure 7.7). The income received by the lowest fifth of all households makes up

Figure 7.7   **Distribution of Income by Ethnicity, United States, 2009**

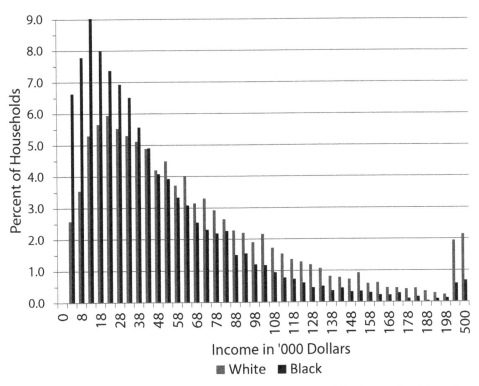

Income in '000 Dollars

■ White ■ Black

Source: U.S. Department of Commerce, U.S. Census Bureau, The 2012 Abstract. 693-Money Income of Households—Number and Distribution by Race. Origin: 2009. www.census.gov/compendia/statab/ (accessed July 25, 2012)
    Note: First and last categories are open ended.

just 3.4 percent of total income, while the top fifth earned 50 percent of total income (Figure 7.8). Similarly, the top 5 percent of income earners earn almost twice as much as the bottom 40 percent combined (Figure 7.9). The bottom 20 percent of households earned less than $20,500 in 2009 while the top 5 percent earned more than $180,000. There is no economic or ethical justification for such a skewed distribution of income.

Moreover, in the United States the growth in incomes has accrued exclusively at the very top of the income distribution: the bottom 20 percent experienced an increase in income of a paltry $1,500 since 1973 (in 2009 dollars) while those in the top 5 percent saw their income increase by some $55,000, or by 37 times as much. Furthermore, the share of the top 1 percent of income earners has increased between 1982 and 2006 from 13 percent to 21 percent of total income, whereas the share of the bottom 40 percent has declined from 12 percent to 9 percent,[29] and the top 1 percent controls not less than 40 percent of the nation's wealth.[30]

Income differences by ethnicity are also substantial: only 16 percent of U.S. white households earned incomes below $20,000 in 2009 while 32 percent of U.S. black households did. In contrast, more than half of white households earned above $50,000 while only one-third of black households did (Table 7.2). The Hispanic distribution was between that of the whites and blacks, whereas the Asian distribution was closer to that of the whites.

Figure 7.8   **The Distribution of Income in the United States, 2009, Percent of Total Income**

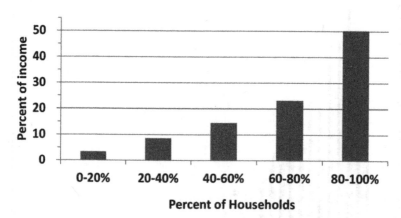

Source: U.S. Department of Commerce, U.S. Census Bureau, The 2012 Abstract. 694-Share of Aggregate Income Received by Each Fifth and Top 5 Percent of Households, www.census.gov/compendia/statab/ (accessed July 25, 2012)

Figure 7.9   **Trend of the Distribution of Income by Households, 1967–2009**

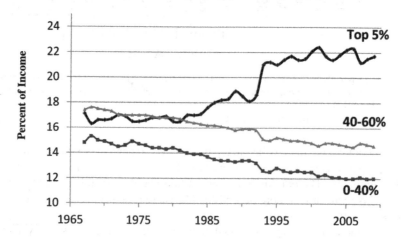

Table 7.2

Household Income by Ethnicity (%)

	White	Black	Hispanic	Asian
Below $20,000	16	32	24	16
$20–50,000	30	35	38	23
Above $50,000	54	33	39	61

Source: U.S. Census Bureau, The 2012 Statistical Abstract

Table 7.3

The Tax Returns of the Super-Rich

All Returns (%)	Number of Returns (000)	Total Income ($ trillions)	Average Income ($000)	% of Total U.S. Income
Top 0.5%	730	1.1	1,507	14
Top 2.8%	3,900	2.0	513	26

Source: Internal Revenue Service, SOI Tax Stats—Individual Statistical Tables by Size of Adjusted Gross Income

Tax returns enable us to examine the income of the super-rich a bit closer. The top 2.8 percent of income recipients earn a total of $2 trillion, or 26 percent of total declared personal income (Table 7.3). This is equal to the amount received by the bottom 64 percent of all taxpayers. Put another way, the total income of the top 3.9 million people equals that of the bottom 90 million. Similarly, the top 730,000 people earn as much as the bottom 65 million. There is no imaginable way that one can consider this a just division of the total output of society. That the income distribution has become even more skewed in the last generation reflects the fact that the salaries of the top earners increased hyper-dramatically while those of the bottom 90 percent of income earners have more or less stagnated since around 1980.

Common sense suggests that such immense income inequality is neither justified nor a healthy development for the future stability of the socioeconomic system. Joseph Stiglitz argues that while those at the top enjoy the best health care, education, and benefits of wealth, they fail to realize that "their fate is bound up with how the other 99 percent live."[31] Even Alan Greenspan, an idol of the ultra-conservative Ayn Rand Republicans and an ardent advocate of the excesses of free markets, sees the fundamental threat to the system: "you cannot have the benefits of capitalist market growth without the support of a significant proportion, and indeed, virtually all of the people; and if you have an increasing sense that the rewards of capitalism are being distributed unjustly the system will not stand."[32]

Zbigniew Brzezinski is also not a socialist by any means, but expresses similar concerns: "I'm deeply worried that . . . what has held our society together is coming unstuck. . . . I think we have allowed a situation to develop in America in which the rich have gotten rich out of *any* legitimate proportion either morally or pragmatically. And I think we may be heading towards a social conflict. It could be very destabilizing. . . . I think the basic division between the very poor and the rich and the loss of opportunity for the middle class is a serious problem. Today a new-born American has less chance of going beyond the level of his parents than a European. . . . I think the problem . . . [has] become so built into . . . our financial system . . . [that] the country [should] really ask itself, what is really the standard by which a decent fair society ought to be defined. It's not rigid equality like the Communist systems but it certainly is some limit on self-advancement financially—by speculation mostly—which is socially not productive and involves some notion of fair standards of opportunity."[33] The founding fathers also knew all too well that democracy turns into oligarchy if the distribution of wealth and power and the privileges that accompany them becomes disproportionate.

In short, there are no legitimate reasons for such hyper-discrepancies in income.[34] The current level of inequality defies common sense: it was not brought about by a simple market mechanism and does not reflect the social value created by the people concerned, even though the myth of the "self-made man" is widespread and embedded in the folklore of the American Dream. However, the success of the elite has been predicated mainly on initial endowments at birth, first-mover advantages, good fortune, and privileges conferred by government in addition to a number of institutional changes and technological developments, many of which were given a major initial boost by government. Other contributions of government included a long-term commitment to deregulation, a general ideological preference for pro-business policies such as indirect job-creation mechanisms instead of pro-labor policies that would have protected workers. In addition, governments unleashed the forces of globalization, thereby creating valuable business opportunities that accrued to the financial elite, who were able to capture those benefits while unions were put under continuous political pressure. Thus, the government failed miserably to defend the living wages of the people on Main Street.[35] Instead, it stepped in and defended vigorously the income, wealth, and political power of the top 1 percent through the Great Bailout of 2008–2009 that was rationalized as defending all Americans. The 99 percent received very little benefit from the trillions of dollars printed by the Fed. In other words, if Schumpeter's creative destruction had been allowed to proceed according to market forces, the great inequality would have been reversed and substantially mitigated.

Malcolm Gladwell argues convincingly that there are few self-made man and women among the elite as their career paths were determined mainly by circumstances outside of their control, such as luck or innate talent.[36] For instance, it appears as though Bill Gates is a self-made man, but the inconvenient truth is that he had a privileged start in life. His parents were wealthy enough to enroll him in an exclusive high school that just happened to have a computer for its students. How many 13-year-olds had unrestricted access to a mainframe computer in 1968? Obviously, Gates was born smart, with considerable aptitude and entrepreneurial savvy, and he also expended lots of effort, but these were by no means proportional to his ultimate wealth. He received the initial impetus from his parents, from his school, and from the IT revolution that was in process, but he also benefited greatly from plain luck insofar as IBM's negotiations with another potential provider of a PC operating system broke down and IBM approached Gates, who ultimately provided them with one, although he did not write most of the program himself.

Gates served more or less as a middleman. Hence, in a Rawlsian just state, he would not have been given his current riches. His wealth is not in proportion to his contribution to society. It was the way in which his life unfolded, the way the legal institutions function, and the winner-take-all economic system that granted him rights that enabled him to become the richest man on the planet. In other words, the market unfairly magnifies the gains of the winners in proportion to their performance.[37] To be sure, he did deserve a small portion of his wealth for his genuine contribution, but the actual financial outcome is not the system we would have devised behind a veil of ignorance if we had started from scratch.

Here is how the billionaire legendary investor Warren Buffett explains his fortune:

> My luck was accentuated by my living in a market system that sometimes produces distorted results, though overall it serves our country well. I've worked in an economy that rewards someone who saves the lives of others on a battlefield with a medal, rewards a great teacher with thank-you notes from parents, but rewards those who can detect the mispricing of securities with sums reaching into the billions. In short, fate's distribution of long straws is wildly capricious.[38]

No one's contribution to society is worth tens of millions of dollars. It is as if the CEOs were writing their own checks to themselves, as though they were the owners of the firms. Buffett, who has been on the board of some 19 companies over the course of 40 years of investing, describes the "boardroom atmosphere" as follows:

Accountability and stewardship withered in the last decade, becoming qualities deemed of little importance by those caught up in the Great Bubble. As stock prices went up, the behavioral norms of managers went down. By the late '90s, as a result, CEOs who traveled the high road did not encounter heavy traffic. . . . Too many of these people, however, have in recent years behaved badly at the office, fudging numbers and drawing obscene pay for mediocre business achievements. . . . If able but greedy managers over-reach and try to dip too deeply into the shareholders' pockets, directors must slap their hands. Over-reaching has become common but few hands have been slapped. Why have intelligent and decent directors failed so miserably? The answer lies . . . in what I'd call "boardroom atmosphere." . . . [W]hen the compensation committee—armed, as always, with support from a high-paid consultant—reports on a mega-grant of options to the CEO, it would be like belching at the dinner table for a director to suggest that the committee reconsider . . . My own behavior, I must ruefully add, frequently fell short as well: Too often I was silent when management made proposals that I judged to be counter to the interests of shareholders. In those cases, collegiality trumped independence . . . In recent years compensation committees too often have been tail-wagging puppy dogs meekly following recommendations by consultants, a breed not known for allegiance to the faceless shareholders who pay their fees . . . This costly charade should cease.[39]

This is not a blackboard economist writing, or an antiglobalization radical, but one of the richest men in the world, who spent his career in the corporate world and is an ardent advocate of free markets. But he has seen first hand the operation of many boardrooms and has sufficient common sense to recognize when a manager is being overpaid.

There is no empirical evidence that higher taxes on the super-rich or capped salaries at the top of the income distribution would bring forth less managerial skill. Lower managerial salaries have not hurt German, Swiss, French, or Japanese firms even though their CEOs make a fraction of their counterparts in the United States. Not counting stock options, average CEO pay in the 15 largest companies was $10.4 million in the United States but "merely" $3.6 million in the Netherlands, $6.8 million in Germany, and $6.0 million in Australia. Including stock options, the average U.S. CEO earned some $24.4 million in 2007. Between 2003 and 2007 CEO compensation increased by 45 percent in the United States while the pay of the average worker increased barely by 3 percent.

Nowhere is the ratio of CEO compensation to average employee pay as high as in the United States. Today a CEO earns more than 350 times the earnings of an average worker. In 1980 the comparable ratio was closer to 50.[40] Could it be that the productivity of CEOs has increased by a factor of seven relative to the rest of the workforce? That is extremely unlikely. It did not do so in other countries. In a perfectly competitive economy there would not be such discrepancies in earnings. In the Netherlands, for example, the ratio is "only" 103.[41] Rather, these distortions are due to "deficiencies of corporate governance." There is no evidence that American CEOs are that much more productive than their foreign counterparts.[42]

American workers have been utterly left behind managers and executives in their pay. The new privileged class are no longer the owners of capital, that is, the shareholders of the corporations, but rather those who are in control of capital and near the checkbook, namely the executives. William F. Buckley, Jr., a prominent conservative, referred to CEO pay as "extortion."[43] So the executives can basically determine their own salaries as though they were the owners of the corporation. According to a 2008 paper on executive compensation:

As shareholders have only imperfect information about action developed by executives the abilities of the former to control the behavior of the latter are limited. This restricts the possibility of the shareholder to enforce the agency contract significantly . . . executive compensation is a product of . . . the discretion and power of executive officers themselves. Apart from information asymmetry, the executive's discretion results from the dispersion of shareholders which weakens their bargaining power and from the entrenchment of the CEO in the board which increase his/her bargaining. . . . In addition, the non-programmatic nature of executives' positions makes it difficult for shareholders to establish straightforward performance criteria and to evaluate the effort made by the executive. . . . Furthermore, managerial power theory contests that the board of directors, which is in charge of determining executive compensation packages, necessarily acts in the interest of shareholders, and that loyalty to shareholders depends on whether their interests are related more closely to the shareholders or to the executives. . . .[44]

The distribution of rewards within today's mega-firms is not uniquely determined but depends on bargaining power in which the CEO has a strong position on account of her information set and because he is bargaining with a board of directors, who have meager incentives to bargain hard; they are agents themselves: working on the shareholders' behalf and not their own. So agents are supposed to oversee other agents. That shields CEOs from the real stakeholders. Furthermore, there are problems with incentive compatibility over time: it is difficult for the shareholders to distinguish between short- and long-run profits. During the years before the Great Meltdown, "bonuses were paid, and CEOs profited from their options. Only much later did shareholders learn that the reported earnings were a sham."[45]

As a consequence of its institutional, legal, and tax structures, the United States is the most unequal society among developed countries (Figure 7.10). The value created by the economy is not distributed justly. There are those who argue that all we need for a just society is equality of opportunity, but then there are others who believe that it is not enough to have legal equality if people are disadvantaged de facto through no fault of their own by having been born on the wrong side of the tracks or through other attributes that are disadvantageous to earning capacity. In other words, people should not be penalized for factors that are not of their own making, such as their endowment of talent, intelligence, or wealth at birth.[46] The distribution of income and wealth should not be influenced by arbitrary factors such as race, gender, or social class at birth.[47] Society has a moral obligation to provide a level playing field so that privileges of birth are not the dominant factors determining social and economic outcomes. The advantages that are due to a matter of birth are in principle not different than the privileges enjoyed by the aristocracy of birth in the feudal age that we consider illegitimate. I suspect that future epochs will look upon our forms of privileges with similar disdain. Capping U.S. executive salaries at European levels would be a reasonable start to turning the tide. Of course, this would not work unless it were applied generally throughout the United States. Individual firms are not likely to succeed at such reforms by themselves.

The theory that factors of production receive the value of their marginal product is not borne out by the evidence. In addition to the factors mentioned above, the distribution of income also depends on the degree to which people are morally constrained to maintain their activity within legal limits. That moral code has been breached all too often and many executives have been jailed and fined even as many culprits eluded prosecution. For instance, Rajat Gupta, former board member of Goldman Sachs, received a 2-year sentence; Raj Rajaratnam, his partner, received 11 years; Fabrice Tourre was convicted but not yet sentenced; and Michael Milken was charged with 98 counts of securities fraud in 1989, spent two years in prison, and paid $600 million in fines and restitution. However, he still retained $2 billion in wealth.[48]

Figure 7.10   **Inequality Compared in Selected Countries**

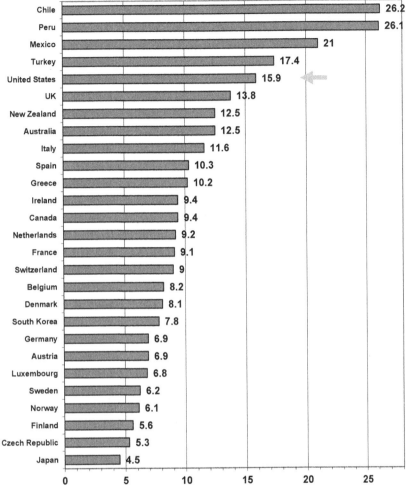

Source: World Bank (2009). "World Development Indicators." Washington DC: World Bank. Data pertain to 1992–2007, as cited in Human Development Report, 2009. http://hdrstats.undp.org/en/indicators/160. html

CHAPTER SUMMARY

"Something is rotten in the state of Denmark." Or in this instance, it is not the state of Denmark that is awful but the way the market rewards the people who toil in it. The new normal is that prosperity is concentrated among the few while the majority are excluded from enjoying the fruits of their labor. This issue is essential, because it weighs heavily on the life satisfaction of the majority of the population. Moreover, this is not the kind of economy we would construct if we were to start from scratch behind a "veil of ignorance," that is, if we did not know in which part of the income distribution we would end up. It would be too risky unless we created an inclusive economy where all had the right to work and in which wages kept pace with productivity and the benefits of growth were not monopolized by a few privileged individuals.

In contrast, in the real existing economy productivity increased much faster than wages. Therefore workers failed to receive their just reward. The gains in productivity did not accrue to them but to owners of capital, to managers, and to CEOs who were running the corporations and could write their own checks because of lack of oversight from board of directors. The immense profits of the financial sector were also aided by deregulation and by the taxpayer bailout. In 2013 there were no less than 13 million millionaires in the United States at a time when there were 50 million people living in poverty.[49]

Oligopolies take advantage of their market power and do not produce the socially efficient amounts at the efficient price. The mainstream principal textbooks overlook the gist of the Greenwald-Stiglitz theorem which proves that in the presence of imperfect information—and that means practically always—markets are inefficient. That implies that in real-world conditions there are plenty of opportunities for governments to improve market outcomes and to achieve a more desired distribution of wealth and income. The focus on the magic of the invisible hand inhibits us from concentrating on the shortcomings of market allocations and is therefore an insidious research program. We need to explore systematically ways to improve our production, consumption, and distribution of resources. That research program should begin at the beginning of the student's career, namely in the first course of economics, and the present chapter takes an initial step in that direction.

QUESTIONS FOR DISCUSSION

1. How much do you think the U.S. Constitution is worth?
2. Do you think trust is increasing in the economy?
3. Explain why trust is important in the economy.
4. Do you think that labor should be treated by firms like they treat other factors of production such as physical capital?
5. How does knowledge capital differ from physical capital?
6. Why is social capital important for the economy?
7. Should we be more careful about how we use natural resources in the process of production?
8. Do you think we do enough to protect the environment?
9. What is the value of the marginal product of a professor? Of a policeman? Of a nurse?
10. Why do you suppose that wages have not kept pace with the productivity of labor?
11. Who benefited from the increased productivity if not workers?
12. Why do you suppose women's wages have increased while those of men have stagnated at best?
13. Do you think CEOs receive competitive wages?
14. How much of the income of superstars such as LeBron James or Beyoncé is due to the Internet?
15. Should celebrities pay a special Internet tax for the benefits they reap through its use?
16. Should we care about the welfare of future generations yet unborn?
17. Should we make sure that people working for Walmart receive health insurance?
18. Should CEO salaries be determined by the owners of the firm, namely the shareholders, rather than the board of directors?
19. Should firms be forced to pay the same salaries for men and women for the same work?

20. Should part-time workers be paid the same hourly wage as their full-time counterparts for the same job?

21. Should luck play a role in determining salaries in a just society?

22. Should people be paid for having been born smart, beautiful, talented, or tall?

23. Do you think football players should earn more than primary school teachers? Which job is more important?

24. Do you think it is warranted to grant monopoly rights to sports teams?

25. Is it just that those who contribute most to social welfare, like scientists who develop new vaccines to fight diseases (or those who fought in Iwo Jima), earn little (or nothing) in comparison to celebrities?

26. "No man is an island." Discuss.

27. Do you accept Rawls' conception of a "just" state? How would you define a "just" society?

28. Are we living in a "just" society? Why or why not?

29. Should we be even concerned with justice in economics?

30. Do you think that the distribution of income in the United States is acceptable?

NOTES

1. Daron Acemoglu of Harvard University suggests that "well-designed institutions and regulation are necessary for the proper functioning of markets." Daron Acemoglu, "Structural Lessons For and From Economics," January 12, 2009; Daron Acemoglu and James Robinson, *Why Nations Fail: The Origins of Power, Prosperity, and Poverty* (New York: Crown, 2012).

2. Robert Putnam, *Making Democracy Work* (Princeton, NJ: Princeton University Press, 1993); Francis Fukuyama, *Trust: The Social Virtues and the Creation of Prosperity* (New York: Free Press, 1995).

3. Kenneth Arrow, "Gifts and Exchanges," *Philosophy and Public Affairs* 1 (1972): 343–362.

4. This generalization may not hold for professional athletes, who can be injured or whose capabilities decline with age.

5. We shall discuss this issue further in Chapter 14 under Green National Accounting.

6. The loss of biodiversity is another problem whose consequences are unclear.

7. U.S. Department of Commerce, U.S. Census Bureau, 2012 Statistical Abstract. Income, Expenditures, Poverty, & Wealth: Income for Persons.

8. The difference between the two data sets is that for weekly wages one does not have to be working the whole year to be included in the sample.

9. Richard B. Freeman, "Labour Economics," in *The New Palgrave Dictionary of Economics,* 2nd ed., ed. Steven N. Durlauf and Lawrence E. Blume (Basingstoke, UK: Palgrave Macmillan, 2008).

10. Thomas Philippon and Ariell Reshef, "Wages and Human Capital in the U.S. Financial Industry: 1909–2006," NBER Working Paper No. 14644, January 2009.

11. Michael K. Lettau, "Compensation in Part-Time Jobs Versus Full-Time Jobs: What If the Job Is the Same?" Bureau of Labor Statistics (BLS) Working Paper 260, December 1994.

12. John Siegfried and Wendy Stock, "The Labor Market for New Ph.D. Economists in 2002," *American Economic Review* 94 (May 2004) 94: 272–285.

13. CEOs of Goldman Sachs, JPMorgan Chase, Morgan Stanley, Citigroup, Wells Fargo, and Bank of America, respectively. "CEO Pay and the 99%," AFL-CIO.

14. Philippon and Reshef, "Wages and Human Capital."

15. Milton Freedman called the AMA the strongest trade union in the country. The AMA is for doctors what OPEC is to the gasoline market. Mark J. Perry, "The Medical Cartel: Why Are MD Salaries So High?" *Wall Street Pit,* June 24, 2009.

16. Anemona Hartocollis, "Medical Schools in Region Fight Caribbean Flow," *The New York Times,* December 22, 2010.

17. World Health Organization, *World Health Statistics 2010* (Geneva: WHO Press, 2010); Organization for Economic Cooperation and Development (OECD), *OECD Health Data 2012—Frequently Requested Data.*

18. Furthermore, other countries have been able to cap costs because they have adopted a more efficient system. It is much more economical to have a single not-for-profit entity organizing the medical care system than navigating through the confusing array of offerings of a free-market for-profit system. The former is much less expensive because the administrative costs are much less and costs are kept down by the bargaining power of government so that medical care does not become a business and no profits are generated.

19. Lisa Waananen, Seth Feaster, and Alan McLean, "200 Slices of Wealth," *The New York Times,* June 16, 2012.

20. John M. Keynes, *The End of Laissez-faire* (London: Hogarth Press 1926).

21. The salaries can be found at www.aflcio.org/corporatewatch/paywatch/ceou/database.cfm.

22. Gretchen Morgenson, "Lending Magnate Settles Fraud Case," *The New York Times,* October 15, 2010.

23. The causation can also run in the other direction: wages can affect productivity insofar as higher wages increase the motivation of workers to greater effort, reduce monitoring costs, and induce them to shirk less. Carl Shapiro and Joseph E. Stiglitz, "Equilibrium Unemployment as a Worker Discipline Device," *American Economic Review* 74 (1984) 3: 433–444.

24. Joan Robinson and John Eatwell, *Introduction to Modern Economics* (London: McGraw-Hill, 1974); Joan Robinson, *Economics of Imperfect Competition,* 2nd ed. (London: Macmillan, 1969).

25. Piero Sraffa, *Production of Commodities by Means of Commodities: Prelude to a Critique of Economic Theory* (Cambridge, UK: Cambridge University Press).

26. Morten L. Bech and Tara Rice, "Profits and Balance Sheet Developments at U.S. Commercial Banks in 2008," Federal Reserve Bulletin, June 2009.

27. U.S. Department of Commerce, Bureau of Economic Analysis, *Fixed Assets Accounts Tables: Table 12. Chain-Type Quantity Indexes for Net Stock of Government Fixed Assets,* last revised August 15, 2012. In 2007 it had $323 billion profit.

28. U.S. Department of Commerce, Bureau of Economic Analysis, *National Income and Product Accounts Tables: Table 7.16. Relation of Corporate Profits, Taxes, and Dividends in the National Income and Product Accounts to Corresponding Measures as Published by the Internal Revenue Service,* last revised August 2, 2012.

29. Edward N. Wolff, "Recent Trends in Household Wealth in the United States: Rising Debt and the Middle-Class Squeeze—an Update to 2007," Levy Economics Institute of Bard College Working Paper No. 589, March 2010.

30. Joseph Stiglitz, *The Price of Inequality: How Today's Divided Society Endangers Our Future* (New York: W.W. Norton, 2012).

31. Ibid.

32. "Alan Greenspan on Income Inequality," YouTube video, 5:42, posted by "johnklin," September 28, 2007, at 2:36.

33. "The Great U.S. Wealth Gap Could Cause a Social Conflict: Zbigniew Brzezinski—Fast Forward," Reuters TV video, 4:12, July 18, 2012.

34. Joan Robinson, *An Essay on Marxian Economics* (London: Macmillan, 1960), 67.

35. James Galbraith, *The Predator State: How Conservatives Abandoned the Free Market and Why Liberals Should Too* (New York: The Free Press, 2009).

36. Malcolm Gladwell, *Outliers: The Story of Success* (New York: Little, Brown, 2008).

37. Mark Zuckerberg's history is similar. He basically expropriated the idea for Facebook from fellow students.

38. Wikipedia contributors, "Warren Buffet," *Wikipedia: The Free Encyclopedia.*

39. "Berkshire's Corporate Performance vs. the S&P 500," Berkshire Hathaway, Inc., February 21, 2003.

40. Sarah Anderson, John Cavanagh, Chuck Collins, Sam Pizzigati, and Mike Lapham, *Executive Excess 2008* (Washington, DC: Institute for Policy Studies and United for a Fair Economy, 2008); G. William Domhoff, "Wealth, Income, and Power," at the site Who Rules America? available at www2.ucsc.edu/whorulesamerica/power/wealth.html.

41. Similarly, the average executive earns $6.3 million in the United States compared to $3.8 million in Germany, $2.2 million in the Netherlands, and $2.4 million in Australia. Franz Christian Ebert, Raymond Torres, and Konstantinos Papadakis, "Executive Compensation: Trends and Policy Issues," International Institute for Labour Studies, Geneva, Discussion Paper No. 190, 2008, 6.

42. A Conversation on the State of the Economy with Paul Krugman and Joseph E. Stiglitz, October 23, 2012.

43. "That money was taken, directly, from company shareholders. But the loss, viewed on a larger scale, is a loss to the community of people who believe in the capitalist free-market system. Because extortions of that size tell us, really, that the market system is not working—in respect of executive remuneration. What is going on is phony. It is shoddy, it is contemptible, and it is philosophically blasphemous." William F. Buckley, Jr. "Capitalism's Boil," *National Review Online,* April 20, 2005, as cited in John Alexander Burton and Christian E. Weller, "Supersize This: How CEO Pay Took Off While America's Middle Class Struggled," Center for American Progress, May 2005.

44. Ebert, Torres, and Papadakis, "Executive Compensation," 13–14.

45. Warren Buffett, "2002 Annual Report," 17.

46. Ronald Dworkin, *Sovereign Virtue: The Theory and Practice of Equality* (Cambridge, MA: Harvard University Press, 2000).

47. John Roemer, *Equality of Opportunity* (Cambridge, MA: Harvard University Press, 2000).

48. Ivan Boesky said in his commencement address at the University of California, Berkeley: "I think greed is healthy. You can be greedy and still feel good about yourself." Later he was imprisoned for two years for insider trading and fined $100 million. Wikipedia contributors, "Ivan Boesky," *Wikipedia: The Free Encyclopedia.*

49. There were also 45,000 ultra-high-worth individuals with wealth in excess of $50 million. Credit Suisse, "Global Wealth Report 2013"; CBS, "Census: U.S. Poverty Rate Spikes, Nearly 50 Million Americans Affected," November 15, 2012.

8

THE CASE FOR REGULATION OF MARKETS

There are many aspects of markets that are generally hidden from students in introductory textbooks. These deviations from ideal markets are so-called imperfections. I referred to these earlier as the "Achilles heels" of markets. We discuss a few of these in this chapter including "opportunistic behavior" and the problems associated with the fact that most people do not work for themselves but for others. This is the "principal-agent" problem that introduces imperfections into the smooth running of firms because workers (agents) are costly to supervise and because they are not always incentivized properly to exert optimal effort or to use best judgment to advance the firm's cause. Many CEOs and mortgage brokers took advantage of such opportunities during the run up to the financial crisis to enrich themselves at the detriment of the corporation and the economy.

PRINCIPAL AND AGENT

Shareholders are the owners of the corporation, the principals. Managers and workers are their agents who are supposed to work on behalf of the firm. However, this is incompatible with the usual assumption that people are selfish. If we presume that people are selfish, then why do we suppose that once they enter the firm, they will willingly work for the firm's benefit and not their own? The two assumptions are by no means aligned. Thus, the "principal–agent" problem refers to the fact that the workers and managers of a firm want to maximize their own well-being rather than that of the firm. Although there are many incentives that attempt to bring the interest of the agents and that of the principals in line, it is not at all easy to accomplish, as the writing and monitoring of such contingent contracts are both costly and extremely cumbersome.

Much research has been done on contract theory, with the basic conclusion that profit maximization is essentially unattainable under such circumstances. As in consumption, the principals can satisfice, that is, search for a satisfactory solution to the problem. Contracts and performance incentives are unable to dissuade managers from maximizing their own utility (salaries), even if it is to the detriment of their firms, as was demonstrated during the Great Meltdown of 2008. Dick Fuld, for instance, walked away after bankrupting Lehman Brothers with the astronomical sum of $450 million.[1] However, his shareowners walked away with nothing. Maurice Greenberg retired from AIG with a ridiculous $4.3 billion.[2] Stanley O'Neal brought Merrill Lynch to the brink of bankruptcy but received a golden parachute compensation package of $161 million. James Cayne, CEO of Bear Stearns, was named one of the "Worst American CEOs of All Time," but retained $61 million just as the firm was falling on hard times.[3] The list of modern-day robber barons and their chicanery could be extended ad infinitum. It is not as though these captains of finance were the brightest in the room. Rather, they had the character to elbow their way into the corner office. For instance, Dick Fuld was said to be arrogant, showed a lot of "misguided bravado," and a "pathetic display of macho arrogance."[4]

Another blatant example of the principal–agent conflict of interest manifested itself during the run-up to the financial crisis of 2008. Greenspan disregarded completely the principal–agent problem and thought that the financial firms could be trusted to look out for their long-run interests. After all, these were all sophisticated people. This proved to be utterly false, because firms are not entities run by individuals with the interest of the shareholders in mind. Instead, they are made up of employees who are looking out for their own short-term bonuses and generally care little about the firm's long-run viability. So the blackboard conceptualization of the modern firm makes little sense without incorporating the principal–agent problem and the inherent conflict of interest. Furthermore, competition had a ruinous effect. Those money managers who did not generate short-term profits soon lost customers in an environment in which others were making large paper profits and taking on excessive risk. The profits were well known while the risks were intangible and therefore hidden.

MORAL HAZARD

The principal–agent problem is subsumed under the umbrella of the larger concept of "moral hazard." People consider their own utility without regard to how their actions affect others. In other words, their decisions might well harm others but they do not have to bear responsibility for the consequences of those actions. This occurs in cases when there is a conflict between short-term gains at the expense of long-term losses, if the losses are hidden or uncertain, when the responsibility is diffused in a group, if monitoring is expensive or incomplete, and in case of imperfect information. The challenge within a firm at every level is to supervise the subordinates without excessive cost and to ensure the timely flow of information up the chain of command. The agents (the CEO or lower-level managers) often cannot be held responsible for their actions. The world is too complex to be able to write perfect contracts with every eventuality specified since many aspects of the future are unpredictable. It would be too costly even to contemplate such a contract.

In such a complex system, it is challenging to overcome the fundamental conflict between the manager's utility and that of the shareholders. Such an economy will have too many frictions and will not be efficient.[5] In general, there will be lots of wasted resources. For example, the legendary John Thain, CEO of Merrill Lynch, spent $1.2 million renovating his offices (and a reception area) just a few months before the firm had to be bailed out at taxpayers' expense. He also had the common sense to pay $4 billion in bonuses days before the U.S. government forced a shotgun marriage between Merrill Lynch and Bank of America. Of course, the $4 billion was not his money, and it made no difference to him at all. He was not penalized for his bad judgment.[6] AIG spent some $86,000 on partridge hunting while the government was pumping $186 billion into the company to keep it afloat.

Moral hazard is similar in this regard to a negative externality insofar as costs are imposed on third parties without their acquiescence. This is hardly a new problem. Adam Smith was already well aware of it: "The directors of such companies, . . . being the managers . . . of other peoples' money than of their own, it cannot well be expected, that they should watch over it with the same anxious vigilance with which the partners in a private copartnery frequently watch over their own. . . . Negligence and profusion, therefore, must always prevail more or less, in the management of the affairs of such a company."[7]

OPPORTUNISTIC BEHAVIOR

Opportunistic behavior denotes the problem whereby free markets open up a myriad of possibilities for people to take advantage of counterparties in an immoral, unprincipled, cunning, crafty, dishonest, or deceptive manner or with guile.[8] Much of opportunism stems from information asymmetries. People might also take advantage of ambiguous or inadequate laws or their absence, thereby enabling them to profit in ways unforeseen by lawmakers and usually by disregarding moral norms. The growth of the shadow banking system in the last three decades and the use of derivatives is a good example of this kind of a development. Opportunistic behavior also occurs when people take advantage of incomplete contracts, asymmetric information, incomplete knowledge, gullibility, inferior mental ability of counterparties, or cognitive biases.

The inherent propensity of many people to disregard the social contract and to overreach or deceive in an unscrupulous fashion implies straightaway that markets ought not to be free of regulation: we need to have constraints on people's actions such that they deter people from opportunistically taking advantage of others, for instance, by selling contaminated drugs or eggs. (There were no less than 3,000 deaths from food poisoning in 2009 in the United States.[9]) In other words, free markets would not exist for long without adequate laws and regulation.

In the past, the belief in an afterlife and faith in an all-knowing God limited opportunistic behavior much more than today. One did not expect to benefit in the long run from greedily profiting at the expense of someone else. The decline in such a belief system and the concomitant increase in opportunistic behavior necessitated the increase in government regulation. I suspect that a generation ago, old-fashioned bankers would have been much less willing to sign up people for mortgages that they themselves knew the customer was not able to repay. However, there was plenty of opportunistic behavior in the run-up to the Great Meltdown. Paul Krugman puts it this way: "there was a widely spread housing bubble. . . . This bubble was inflated by irresponsible lending, made possible both by bank deregulation and the failure to extend regulation to 'shadow banks,' which weren't covered by traditional regulation but nonetheless engaged in banking activities and created bank-type risks."[10]

The propensity for opportunistic behavior is determined to a large extent by the business culture.[11] An economy in which the culture of fraud is widespread experiences higher costs of monitoring contracts. The contemporary world has seen an epidemic of fraud in which executives are being jailed and companies are fined for fraud practically daily. In 2012 GlaxoSmithKline was fined $3 billion,[12] a Citibank executive received an eight-year sentence for embezzling $22 million,[13] and 70 people were convicted of fraud since the meltdown,[14] including hedge-fund billionaire Raj Rajaratnam, sentenced to eleven years in prison for insider trading. Rajat Gupta was also found guilty of insider trading, and Barclay's has been fined $450 million for rigging interest rates. Peter Madoff received 10 years (not to mention his brother, Bernie),[15] and Allen Stanford was sentenced to a 110-year term in a $7 billion Ponzi scheme. Dennis Kozlowski, former CEO of Tyco International, is serving an 8-to-25-year sentence. Jeff Skilling, former president of Enron, is serving a 24-year sentence; Bernard Ebbers of WorldCom, a 25-year sentence. And these are only the people who got caught—the tip of the iceberg. There were 1 million fraud complaints in 2010.[16] The FBI made 241 convictions in 2011 for corporate fraud.

In short, the corporate world is replete with corruption and opportunistic behavior. Household names such as Enron, Arthur Andersen, WorldCom, or Adelphia Communications have disappeared in the wake of fraud, embezzlement, insider trading, or obstruction of justice.[17] A recent estimate puts the number of firms with ongoing fraud at about 12 percent of major publicly traded corporations. A survey of MBA students with an average of two years' work experience asked if

Figure 8.1 **The Optimum Level of Freedom in an Economy**

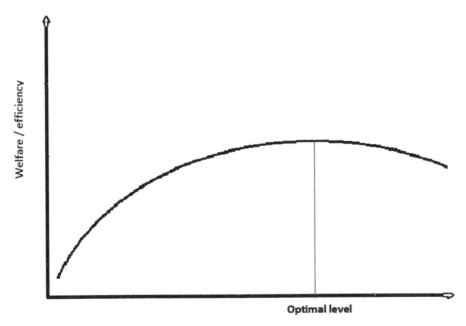

the students had been asked to do something illegal; 15 percent answered in the affirmative.[18] One cannot help but infer from this evidence that capitalism will have a hard time propagating itself in perpetuity with an elite that does not believe in norms that in earlier generations built trust and lowered the enforcement costs of contracts.

The Internet provides opportunities for innovative forms of fraud, such as identity theft, a crime with 250,000 reported victims in 2010. The IRS has found that 940,000 people submitted fake tax returns for 2010 in order to receive refunds. These identity thieves would have received $6.5 billion in fake refunds if they were not caught. But the IRS missed an additional 1.5 million fake returns with fraudulent refunds worth more than $5.2 billion. "The IRS is doing what they can to prevent this, but this is like a tsunami of fraud."[19] Fraud increases transaction costs insofar as it destroys trust and cooperation, and induces people to take extra precautions in business in order to safeguard against losses. Fear of carrying cash is a major inducement for people to pay with credit cards, costing consumers billions.

Because of opportunistic behavior, there is an optimum level of freedom in the marketplace, a level beyond which the expenses associated with opportunistic behavior outweigh the benefits of lack of regulation (Figure 8.1). Welfare and efficiency increase as freedom increases until the "optimal level"; thereafter, however, freedom decreases, because there is excessive opportunistic behavior and the damage it does outweighs the benefits of increased freedom. Daron Acemoglu suggests that economists have been complacent about opportunism: "The capitalist economy lives in an institutional-less vacuum where markets miraculously monitor opportunistic behavior."[20] This is an enormous problem in the real economy because the temptation of extra profits is high so that deceptive practices are rampant. With the decline in the belief in the Ten Commandments the intrinsic value of truth has declined.

REGULATION IN THE PUBLIC INTEREST

Although there are frequent nostalgic references to "free markets" as a theoretical construct, in reality the concept is obsolete in the age of globalization. Free markets are passé in the 21st century: they cannot exist for long because of the increased possibility of opportunistic behavior and the increased importance of other imperfections. Government regulation has to increase exponentially with the complexity of markets; otherwise these would become chaotic or even implode.

A proper framework provided by regulation is essential to any modern economy because of the many imperfections that exist in markets. Regulation can be in the form of counteracting the "Achilles heel" of markets, such as imperfect competition, opportunistic behavior, instability, consumer protection, protection of children, protection of the rights of future generations, ensuring the safety of products, or providing a safety net for people in dire need, redressing power imbalances, limiting pollution and other externalities, and creating limits and standards (such as minimum gasoline engine performance standards).

Deregulation often poses considerable risks to the stability of markets, as we witnessed in the financial crisis of 2008. Similarly, the deregulation of the electricity market in the 1990s led to the Enron lobbying and bribery scandal. Regulation is needed in order to stop abuses, for example, manipulation of students by for-profit colleges.[21]

Even a simple exchange such as purchasing gasoline needs oversight by a governmental agency in order to make sure that the pumps measure the flow of gasoline properly and that it does not contain toxic additives such as lead. The use of leaded gasoline carries a fine of $10,000. The government has to regulate even the size of print on ingredient labels so that consumers are informed of what they are buying. Firms would not do that on their own because it is not in their best interest to do so. On the contrary, the empirical evidence indicates that it is in the interest of corporations to confuse consumers.

For instance, banks were unwilling to follow accepted legal procedures for the foreclosures of homes. State agencies had to step in in order to stop the illegal practice of robo-signing legal documents.[22] Bank of America broke into a home illegally wanting to take possession.[23] How long would the securities market exist without the Securities and Exchange Commission (SEC) or the banks without the Federal Deposit Insurance Corporation (FDIC) and the Federal Reserve? It is doubtful that they would be stable for long, because fraud would destabilize the system. To be sure: fraud persists in the current environment: we have all heard of Bernie Madoff, and such schemes to defraud investors are widespread.[24] Nonetheless, without governmental oversight the financial markets and banking system would soon implode.

Negligence is not a benign matter; an unregulated market can be very dangerous.[25] Practically every market has safety issues that need oversight in order to prevent disaster—from bus companies to blood supplies.[26] Legal remedies seldom work in such cases because the cost of reaching, say, Chinese companies is prohibitive and because it is easy for "unscrupulous" businessmen to disappear.[27]

Consider the Dalkon Shield, an ill-conceived intrauterine contraceptive device (IUD) that was not properly tested before it was marketed.[28] Instead of being an effective contraceptive, the "shield" caused serious injury to women and 300,000 lawsuits were filed against the company. It is just one dangerous example in which the seller's claim was not scrutinized by government prior to marketing, resulting in serious damages. There are thousands of other examples, mostly having to do with safety issues and imperfect information.[29] When we buy hamburger meat, we do not know and do not have the capability of finding out how many bacteria, such as *E. coli,* are embedded in the package. So we urgently need government to inspect the meat factories. In spite of legislation in this regard, manufacturers still try to save money and sell ground beef that is not safe to eat. Tens of thousands of people are sickened every year in the United States alone and some even die from such poisoning.[30] Salmonella poisoning is another example: 500 million contaminated eggs were recalled in August of 2010.[31]

Hence, we need government regulation, oversight, and enforcement in order for markets to function safely and morally. Markets were not designed to do so by themselves in such a complex world. The invisible hand is inefficient in a global marketplace. Moreover, we need government to help dampen the volatility of the business cycle and also to provide a safety net that improves our peace of mind. All societies expect governments to provide some services in case of emergencies like Hurricane Katrina or the BP oil spill in the Gulf of Mexico. In some cultures, governments are also expected to look out for future generations, making sure that the economy will be sustained. Governments are also among the most important providers of education, ensuring that the next generation has the sufficient amount of human capital necessary for the complex economic system. Governments can also help us to obtain a higher quality of life, reduce inequality and uncertainty, dampen volatility, protect the environment, ensure sustainable development, provide public goods, ensure the stability of markets, protect us from the concentration of power, and make certain that future generations have enough resources for a decent life.

Economists often use the metaphor of people voting with their dollars for what is to be produced, claiming this is a "democratic" process. Of all the misleading mainstream notions, this is one of the least logical, because dollars are not equally distributed; some people are born with the privilege of having a lot more of such "votes" than others, so the process cannot possibly be democratic.[32] That is another argument for taking some decisions out of the realm of markets and into the political realm. For given the current distribution of income, markets are not democratic at all in the sense of dollar votes. In the market, the rich have more votes than the poor, hence their wants dominate. This is less so in politics—at least theoretically. That is an important reason why we should never relinquish the right of political institutions to oversee the workings of the market, especially if the poor tend to be alienated and are discouraged from voting.

REGULATORY CAPTURE

However, regulation in the public interest is far from straightforward, because lobbies spend a lot of money and effort in order to influence government officials and agencies to serve their own interests. As a consequence, the common interest suffers as lobbies extract benefits for their members at the expense of the whole.[33] Moreover, firms and wealthy individuals generally invest heavily in lobbying Congress and influencing other governmental agencies while ordinary citizens each have only a tiny stake in the matter as individuals despite their far greater numbers.[34] This unbalanced incentive structure makes it possible for the wealthy to gain the upper hand and to persuade the regulators to tilt the playing field in their favor (Figure 8.2). This is called regulatory capture and it has taken on immense proportions.

The business community can provide yet another kind of incentive to regulators who cooperate—high-paying jobs in the future after they leave government service.[35] The public interest loses out as government agencies become subordinated to corporate interests, such as in the case of the financial bailout.[36]

There is yet another pathway to influencing the regulators, namely by "intellectual capture," also referred to as "ideological, cognitive, or cultural capture." "'Intellectual capture' means that essentially

Figure 8.2   **Corporate Interests Invest Heavily in Order to Tilt the Playing Field in Their Direction**

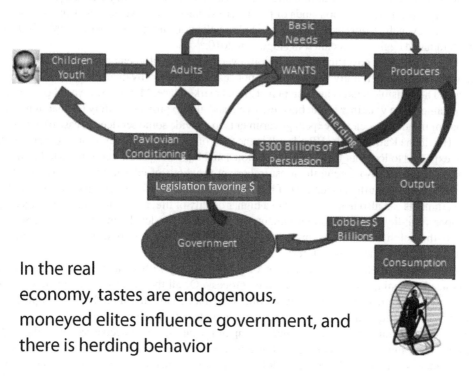

In the real economy, tastes are endogenous, moneyed elites influence government, and there is herding behavior

the financial industry has convinced us . . . [that] what's good for Wall Street is good for America. And they've somehow convinced us that we shouldn't ask about what's right or what works or what's good for America. We should ask what's productive, what's efficient, what helps grow the economy. It is this 'intellectual capture' that prevents a reform movement from taking hold."[37]

According to Simon Johnson, "The intellectual capture of Washington by Wall Street . . . is now complete."[38] Timothy Geithner's cozy relationship with the financial oligarchs is a good example. He wined and dined with them at posh restaurants, had breakfast, played tennis, and rubbed elbows at receptions on a regular basis.[39] He had a "continuing series of close contacts—breakfast, lunch, dinner, coffee, charity board meetings, etc.—with a set of very rich, very powerful, very impressive people who all believed in the importance of Wall Street, and the importance of lighter regulation of Wall Street, and the importance of making sure that Tim Geithner believed in it too. It's doubtful that there was anything close to a countervailing influence from people who thought that Wall Street was taking excessive risks and needed to be reined in."[40] He did not meet any representatives of Main Street, the unemployed, evicted, or homeless. No wonder that Geithner was completely captured: "he has internalized a worldview in which Wall Street is the central pillar of the American economy . . . [and] the importance of those banks justifies virtually any measures to protect them . . . and anyone who doesn't understand these principles . . . just doesn't understand the way the world really works. . . ." Thus, "as long as the powerful people in Washington, . . . [continue to believe in this worldview] Wall Street's power and ability to make money will be secure. That is the importance of cultural capital."[41]

MORAL CONSTRAINTS

The free market does not function well without moral constraint, because specifying laws is insufficient to maintain orderly and nonviolent exchange. One also needs to specify contracts, and without considerable trust and norms it becomes too costly to enforce them. After the Second World War, the business community was well served by the Ten Commandments, which kept greed and opportunistic behavior from running rampant. Businessmen were afraid to meet their maker with a bad conscience. That inanimate constraint has evaporated and trust has diminished, with the consequence of increasing business costs and companies all too often attempting to defraud customers. Of course, some are caught and prosecuted, but that is an insufficient deterrent for most corporations from taking advantage of loopholes without a binding moral constraint. Examples abound: Verizon wireless overcharged customers;[42] foreclosures were carried out illegally; banks break rules without scruples.[43] The Libor rigging scandal is just one example of the epidemic of opportunistic behavior: Barclays was fined $450 million, United Bank of Switzerland was fined $1.2 billion, and the Royal Bank of Scotland was fined $610 million for manipulating the Libor interest rate.[44] The British bank Standard Chartered paid a $340 million fine for money laundering.[45] ING also paid laundering fines of $619 million and Barclays paid $298 million in 2010.[46] "GlaxoSmithKline, the British drug giant, agreed to pay $750 million to settle criminal and civil complaints that the company for years knowingly sold contaminated baby ointment and an ineffective antidepressant."[47] Referring to one of the mortgages sold by his bank, Angelo Mozilo wrote in an April 17, 2006, email: "In all my years in the business, I have never seen a more toxic product."[48] Yet that did not deter him from marketing and profiting from it. His net worth is in the $600 million range.[49] The list could continue ad infinitum. The real damage caused by these wrongdoers is unfathomable.

PROPERTY RIGHTS

Property rights are the strictly legal and socially sanctioned powers to do with a good as one will without infringing on the rights of others. The definition of rights changes over time.[50] Such rights are the basis of the free-enterprise system. Although corporations are not natural persons, they are organizations that are legally recognized as having the right to own property.

MARKET FAILURES

Market failure exists if markets do not achieve Pareto optimality. Inefficient allocation can be due to the absence of markets (in human capital), common property (air), imperfect information, collusion, transaction costs, legal structure, imperfect property rights (ocean), pollution, or noncompetitive behavior (deception). Insofar as most markets are competitive but imperfectly so, it is fair to say that most markets are, in fact, inefficient.[51] Once we accept this common-sense inference, we can work on devising institutions to improve market outcomes and move them closer to the social optimum. That is the task in the century ahead. Consider the California electricity crisis of 2000 and 2001, in which energy wholesalers were able to "game the market" to create artificial electricity shortages and blackouts at a cost of some $40 billion.[52] We have to learn from our mistakes. Enron was one of the firms that reaped huge speculative profits from manipulating the market. Standard & Poor's and Moody's found it easy to collude with Lehman Brothers to fix the ratings of their bonds.[53] The Arthur Andersen accounting firm also did not find it difficult to rationalize the fixing of books at Enron in order to hide its liabilities and deceive the investors.

OPEC is an important oil cartel in existence since the early 1960s and successfully colluding to fix the price of oil above competitive levels. But even at the local level there is considerable tacit collusion that prevents price competition. Consider real estate agents. There are millions of them, yet practically all of them charge the same fee of exactly 6 percent. It is difficult to find an exception such as someone willing to sell one's house for 5.9 percent.[54] Such an unofficial cartel is not supposed to exist theoretically, but it does. The reason for this discrepancy is that theory does not take into consideration the sociological factors associated with competition. By lowering their commission, individual realtors would be ostracized by their peers. The social pressure is such that the members of the profession conform to an unwritten rule not to compete with price but with quality. It is collusion using social norms as the enforcement mechanism. There are more ways to collude than is mentioned in textbooks.

Price discrimination is another market imperfection. While it might increase welfare in some cases, for instance, granting discounts to youth on airplane travel, most of the time it is a nuisance as it is used to extract more money from consumers and increase corporate profits. Generally speaking, price discrimination penalizes those at the lower end of the income distribution because it is designed in such a way as to be more expensive for those who have less knowledge about the good or service in question, who cannot afford to seek additional information, or who have a harder time understanding the implications of signing a particular contract. It takes considerable effort to elude the surcharges of business strategies intended to ensnare the customer. Price discrimination often exploits disadvantaged minority groups who might possess less social capital and therefore might have to pay a higher price to obtain the necessary information to make an informed decision.

The phone company that offers the customer a lower price after she declines to accept their initial offer is an example of price discrimination. There is a lot of price discrimination with cell phone contracts. Companies deliberately make it so complicated that it takes half a genius to comprehend and compare the various plans. Companies also try to outsmart customers by using so-called "decoys," higher-priced products they are not really trying to sell. The strategy behind the higher-priced decoy is to make the lower-priced version appear more appealing in comparison to it.[55] The people designing such programs and contracts have a lot more information on average than the typical consumer, and they specialize in that kind of activity and are therefore able to outsmart customers. In other words, companies take advantage of their comparative advantage in order to structure offers in such a way as to get the better of a bargain and thereby increase their profits. Price discrimination should be regulated in order to ensure that it is moral and serves the public service.

Moreover, almost all market structures (except a negligible number of perfectly competitive ones) create inefficiencies. Hence, most of the economy, consisting of oligopolies and monopolies, produces waste since perfectly competitive firms are a negligible share of the economy. We could and should set ourselves the goal of squeezing these inefficiencies out of our economic system. For instance, oligopolies should also be included in antitrust legislation in order to improve the efficiency of the economy. There are thousands of ways to improve the efficiency of the economy.

Speculation with other people's money poses systemic risks, particularly when new products are concerned. Asset price bubbles often occur with new products whose value is challenging to ascertain and people have not had sufficient experience with them. Examples in this category are the recent Dot.Com bubble and Greenspan's bubble in collateralized debt obligations, credit default swaps, and mortgage-backed securities. Investors did not have sufficient experience with these financial instruments to gauge their risk properties or their systemic effects accurately. Hence, both the private and social costs of risk were underpriced. Investors were also unable to internalize the negative externalities. The extent to which such speculation poses systemic risks by too-big-to-fail institutions is for the regulatory authorities to ascertain and control. If these authorities are sleeping on the job as they did during the run-up to the Meltdown of 2008, then speculation can get out of hand and create spillover effects into the other sectors of the economy. The continual praise of the benefits of speculation by some textbooks is distasteful after the Meltdown of 2008.

EXPLOITATION

The concept of exploitation does not exist in conventional economics. I define it as follows: one party exploits another if the exchange takes place under conditions of asymmetric information or asymmetric cognitive endowment and one party knowingly deceives the other in order to profit from the exchange. The person who takes advantage of a counterparty in such an unfair manner can be said to be exploiting the weaknesses of the other. Such relationships form the basis of predatory capitalism. It is like playing poker with a stacked deck and without scruples.

Such exchanges were rampant during the run-up to the crisis of 2008. Predatory lending involved "balloon payments with unrealistic repayment terms," "excessive fees not justified by the costs of services provided and the credit and interest rate risks involved," "abusive collection practices," "excessive interest rates," "fraud," "lending without regard to ability to repay," and "equity stripping."[56] Ameriquest Mortgage, the largest subprime mortgage lender, was accused of having broken the law, "deceiving borrowers about the terms of their loans, forging documents, falsifying appraisals and fabricating borrowers' income to qualify them for loans they couldn't afford."[57] It was fined just $325 million.

TRANSACTION COSTS

Transaction costs are important hindrances to efficiency because in most cases we first have to search in order to discover what the alternatives are. Searching is hindered by the fact that we have limited time in which to do so and often we do not even know what alternatives are available. In such cases, intuitive judgment and experience are important, as we have to make important decisions along the way without all the necessary information available to us and even before we know what our choices will be in the future.

Transaction costs receive scant attention although they hamper trade and exchange and therefore put a damper on welfare and pose an impediment to attaining efficiency. There are search, information, policing, and enforcement costs: "The parties to a contract have to find each other, they have to communicate and to exchange information. The goods must be described, inspected, weighed and measured. Contracts are drawn up, lawyers may be consulted, title is transferred and records have to be kept. In some cases, compliance needs to be enforced through legal action and breach of contract may lead to litigation."[58] Furthermore, search costs can lead to monopoly prices.[59] Thus, transaction costs use up resources but do not increase welfare.

One problem with transaction costs is that they most hurt those who can least afford it. Searching for information is a time-consuming, hence costly, operation that businesses, from health insurance companies to car dealerships, all impose when it is in their interest to do so.[60] The price of automobiles is seldom advertised, for example, making it more difficult to comparison shop. Health insurance companies make their contracts so complicated that searching will be so time-consuming that consumers give up and buy the product before they are done. One does not know how costly it would be to acquire further information. Only in the process of search does one begin to ascertain incrementally what costs are involved.[61] These imposed costs make it much harder for consumers to reach an efficient level of consumption and for the markets to be efficient.

TIME AND SPACE

The importance of time and space are not fully appreciated in mainstream thinking. This is a serious conceptual shortcoming, because both variables are essential to understanding why markets are generally inefficient. Space imposes significant transaction costs and also makes the acquiring of information more difficult and uncertain. The recent development of the new economic geography, which emphasizes the clustering and regional disparities in economic activity, has not been integrated into Econ 101.[62]

Time has six important and unique features that distinguish it from every other resource endowment: (a) it is the only resource distributed perfectly democratically throughout the life course, (b) it is the only resource that is an essential element in every economic action or decision, (c) one cannot substitute for time in the sense that, for example, labor can be substituted for capital, (d) you cannot borrow or lend time as you can money, (e) one cannot accumulate time, and finally, (f) it moves only in one direction, that is, it cannot be reversed. These unique attributes pose insurmountable obstacles to the smooth and efficient functioning of markets: they lead to inefficiencies, to regrets, and to path dependence.

Path dependence, or sequential decisions, today are influenced not only by the objective conditions today but also by the irreversible decisions that were made yesterday without knowing what today would be like. This implies that our investment or consumption decisions today may not be efficient on account of the constraints imposed by earlier decisions. The implementation of new technologies, the creation of institutions, or the adoption of new social norms is generally not a single event. Rather, each involves a series of developments that evolve in space and time. The problem is that both consumers and producers face an uncertain future as neither possesses perfect foresight and hence neither knows how technologies (or other features of the economy) will develop over time. They therefore base their choices on current knowledge, and these initial choices may lock them into a developmental path such that in the future the optimal technology or the optimal institution is no longer attainable. Hence, free markets, even with perfect competition, may not lead to optimum outcomes if the sequence of decisions occurs over time without perfect foresight.

In addition to uncertainty about the future and the lack of perfect foresight, first-mover advantage can pose obstacles to attaining the optimal outcome. Learning by doing might lower the production costs of those who produced a product first to such an extent that a latecomer can never catch up. In this case, a firm might be a low-cost producer for no other reason than having the luck of being the first to have produced a good. Network externalities have similar effects. The technology that might have been optimal but was not yet known at the beginning of the process may no longer be attainable. This is particularly true in case of increasing returns to scale, which means that as the quantity produced increases, average cost decreases.[63] Most firms working with modern technologies do experience decreasing costs as the scale of operation increases. This means that first-mover advantage can lock in a particular technology that was perhaps not as efficient as an alternative technology that was discovered later. A small random event such as IBM ordering an operating system from Microsoft can provide such initial advantages that even better technologies will be priced out of the market. Consequently, competition by no means guarantees that the best technology will emerge as the winner in the competition if consumers and producers do not possess perfect foresight, if increasing returns are in effect, or if there are network externalities. Hence, an inferior outcome, that is, a socially inefficient equilibrium, is not only possible but more than likely as the economy evolves in the absence of perfect foresight.[64]

PATH DEPENDENCE

The orthodox hype is that free competition guarantees that the best technologies will be the winners and therefore an optimum outcome is assured. Inferior technologies are supposed to become unprofitable and lose out in a market economy. However, this theory overlooks the complex, uncertain, and sequential nature of technological change in real time in the presence of imperfect information and in the absence of perfect foresight. Technological progress is an evolutionary process; the future offshoots and implications of the initial technology are not yet evident at the time when preliminary but crucial decisions have to be made. Time only moves in one direction and most processes are irreversible. Once investments are made in highways, railroads, or a dam, it is costly and difficult to change them. The conventional wisdom would be correct if investors had perfect foresight into the infinite future and if all technologies relevant to a decision were known. The usual assumption is that firms decide to invest at time T and expect a payoff in the future, say at time T + 2 two years later (Figure 8.3). In the example shown in the figure, there are four possible technologies from which to choose, with payoffs as indicated. Under such a circumstance, the optimal choice is a "no brainer": firms will choose technology A, the one with the greatest payoff. Most economic problems are structured in this simple way.

Figure 8.3 **Investment Decision with Perfect Foresight Two Periods Ahead Is Easy**

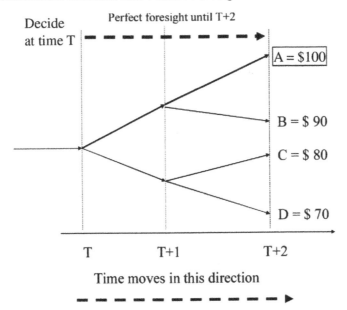

However, the outcome is different if at time T, when the initial decision is made, the technologies that will exist at T + 2 are not yet known. Suppose only the two options at T + 1 are known at time T and one has perfect foresight only until T + 1 (Figure 8.4). In other words, firms make an investment decision without knowing the technological offshoots of technologies E and F. In this case, the optimal choice is F. The difference between the perfect foresight model and the path-dependent (sequential choice) process becomes evident at time T + 1, because at T + 1 the two technologies E and F have offshoots A, B, C, and D, which were not known at time T. What happens now? Having chosen F, the firm is unable to adopt technologies A and B and is thus "locked"

Figure 8.4   **Investment Decision with Perfect Foresight One Period Ahead Is Also Easy**

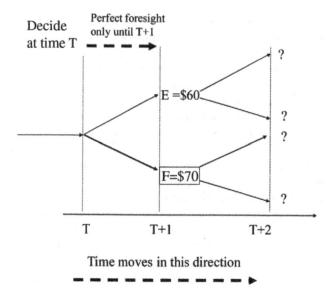

Time moves in this direction

into a choice between C and D. In this case, the rational choice becomes C insofar as the globally optimum technology A can no longer be attained (Figure 8.5). In short, in spite of the fact that one chose the optimum in each period, with only one-period-ahead foresight one is locked into an inferior technology, C.[65] This is quite different from the neoclassical assumptions that optimizing rational investors will achieve an optimum outcome. In the path-dependent framework, allocations might well be Pareto inferior even with a free market, that is, the equilibrium reached might well be inefficient. For instance, arguably the Windows operating system is not the best in the world. It won the competition because of chance and an early-mover advantage.

Network externalities also imply that the early adoption of a technology can provide sufficient benefits even if it is inferior, so that it can win the competition with a latecomer that is higher cost because of the small number of adopters. The reason for this is that as people adopt the early technology, its production costs decline and the first-mover advantage persists and is a barrier to entry to other technologies that come on the market later even if they were superior.

To be sure, there might be cases in which the decision to choose F is reversible and the firm could switch to E at time T + 2 even if it involves transaction costs. But the switching is worthwhile only if it costs less than $20, the value of the difference between using technology C and A. Furthermore, vested interests might be able to prevent the switch to the social optimum at E, regardless of the switching costs.

This model is applicable beyond technological change to many other kinds of consecutive choices, including institutional change or investment in education. Suppose 30 years ago a high school graduate decided not to go to college because good jobs were available without a college degree. Thirty years later she might find out that the decision was suboptimal because the evolution of technologies devalued a high school diploma. In other words, there is no guarantee that people will be able to make optimal investment decisions in a sequential-choice framework without perfect foresight.

Standardization is a similarly costly path-dependent process. An example is the gauge of track used by railroads. It was difficult for the market by itself to create a standard without

Figure 8.5   **With Sequential Decision, Optimum Technology "A" Is No Longer Feasible**

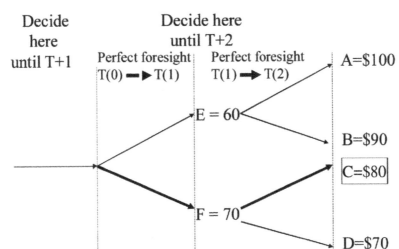

Time moves in this direction only

government help. In the United States, about one-quarter of railroads had standard gauges in the middle of the nineteenth century and the share rose slowly to reach 90 percent by the century's end.[66] Such processes are inefficient, because they impose additional transaction costs on the industry.

Investment decisions are complex and involve exploring alternatives. Once those are identified, choices require considerable planning over an extended period of time. In other words, the economic problem resembles a puzzle more than the simple choices usually depicted in textbooks. In order to solve such problems, we need considerable intuitive judgment, perseverance, will power, caution, and introspection in order to see if we are getting closer to our goals. We need to update our information set and be flexible enough to change course if we find that we are not on the right path. And the market has difficulty executing long-range plans. That is why we are still relying on foreign oil four decades after the formation of OPEC, although common sense would have dictated that we should develop renewable energy instead of buying cheap Chinese consumption goods. But the markets are focused on immediate gratification. They do not have the patience to build infrastructure that might pay handsome dividends for subsequent generations.

Learning to plan sequentially is an important part of succeeding in the economy. Choosing a job, for instance, starts many years earlier in high school when one chooses courses that one will need later in life. One has to work appropriately so that the grades suffice for the level of aspirations. The choice between becoming a doctor or a plumber is not made on the spot. Its realization takes years. Investment strategies such as buying a house require planning years in advance for a down payment. The strategic planning and perseverance needed to reach these goals must be learned and practiced over an extended period of time. Such decisions are much more complex than a one-period optimization problem. The poor are trapped in a culture of poverty partly because they do not have the means to learn these skills early in life.

NONEXISTENT MARKETS

Missing markets pose a truly existential challenge to our welfare and that of future generations. No one owns the atmosphere and consequently pollution has become our very biggest global threat. How much of the ecosystem should be preserved? How quickly we should use the available resources and how much we should leave for subsequent generations are crucial questions, but future generations are unable to influence these decisions even though they will be affected by them. As a consequence of this missing market, there is no mechanism to solve this problem. These are by no means negligible issues in an age in which global warming poses an ominous threat to our very future,[67] when the sustainability of economic growth itself is being questioned,[68] and when Americans have been transferring an increasing amount of national debt onto the shoulders of generations yet unborn.[69] These future generations cannot implore us to reduce our living standards in order not to increase the national debt at their expense.[70]

Ecological problems can lead to tensions of tectonic-force proportions. Two hundred fifty years after the beginning of the Industrial Revolution, economic growth has brought us to a crucial juncture and it is not at all clear that we are going to be able to solve the challenges imposed upon us as an unintended consequence of economic development.[71] The absence of these essential markets implies that only through political pressure and moral suasion can we counter myopic market impulses.[72] The free market is incapable of solving the ecological problem and incapable of caring for the welfare of generations yet unborn.

There are now efforts underway to create markets to trade pollutants. Pollution is a negative externality whereby the action of an individual imposes costs on others without their consent. Whenever the cost of pollution is not incorporated into the price system, markets are inefficient. An environmental externality such as global warming is an important example. Those who pay for the pollution are not compensated sufficiently for their burden. Markets, by themselves, produce too much pollution and too little basic research.[73]

LIMITS AND STANDARDS

Setting limits and standards by decentralized markets is extremely difficult. The inability of markets to set limits gives us too many stores, most of which are practically empty most of the time. The underutilization of so many resources is inefficient. Moreover, the common wisdom is that the market provides us with plenty of choices and that can only improve our lives. However, psychologist Barry Schwartz documents that too much of a good thing can turn into a negative—that, for example, having 275 salad dressings on the shelf is excessive choice and actually detracts from our ability to make wise choices and thus decreases welfare.[74] He suggests that having "more is less," as the conventional thinking does not take into consideration the confusion created by too much choice and the time and effort needed to learn about the products offered. The market does not find adequate limits. Moreover, when we have too many choices we can become paralyzed and have difficulty deciding what we want, and when we finally do choose we are less happy because we keep on questioning whether we have made the right choice. In short, we become confused as the abundance in choice makes it difficult for the time-strapped consumer. Excessive choice therefore detracts from our ability to choose efficiently.

CHAPTER SUMMARY

In order for markets to function well, they need a proper framework that only government regulation can provide. Otherwise, there are too many imperfections in markets such as pollution, moral hazard, accumulation of power, and opportunistic behavior that prevent markets from being efficient. The characteristics of oligopolies are that they choose the price at which they sell their products and earn profits as opposed to price taking firms in competitive equilibrium. That also means that markets in the 21st century are as a rule inefficient. Efficient markets are the exception. In addition, markets are highly volatile as the Meltdown of 2008 amply demonstrated.

QUESTIONS FOR DISCUSSION

1. What do you think could be done in order to raise ethical standards in the marketplace?
2. Do you know of anyone who acted opportunistically in order to advance his own cause at others' expense?
3. Are there some markets that should be more tightly regulated?
4. Have you ever bought an unsafe product?
5. Do you think that predatory lending should have been prohibited?
6. Do you think that there is too much freedom in the financial markets?
7. Do we need government meat inspectors, or could the meat industry regulate itself?
8. Are markets good at providing safe products? Why or why not? Give examples.
9. Markets are democratic as you vote with your dollars instead of the ballot box. Discuss.
10. Do you think that lobbying is part of the democratic process, or outside of it?
11. Do you think that corporations should be allowed to contribute to political campaigns?
12. Do you think that Wall Street has too much influence in Washington?
13. Have you ever been outsmarted by a company?
14. Have you ever paid more for a product than you should have?
15. Do you think that corporations can devise contracts so as to exploit the weaknesses of some people?
16. Has the cost of searching ever made it difficult for you to buy the product best suited for you?
17. Do you know anyone without health insurance?
18. Have you regretted purchasing a product?
19. Have you ever found that your choices were limited by decisions you made at an earlier period without full knowledge of their hidden consequences?
20. Did you ever make hasty choices because of the lack of time?
21. Can you give an example of path dependence?
22. Do you think it would be useful to adopt an energy policy that would free us from our dependence on foreign oil supplies?
23. Do you think the government should invest heavily into solar energy?
24. Are markets patient, or do they emphasize immediate gratification?
25. Did you ever have to make sequential choices in the presence of uncertainty?
26. Do you think that global warming will be a threat in your lifetime?
27. Should we preserve the ecosystem (endangered species) for your grandchildren?
28. Do you think trading pollutants is a good idea?
29. Are you sometimes overwhelmed by the amount of choices available to you?

NOTES

1. Wikipedia contributors, "Richard S. Fuld, Jr.," *Wikipedia: The Free Encyclopedia.*
2. Mary Williams Walsh, "Insurance Giant A.I.G. Takes Ex-Chief to Court," *The New York Times,* June 14, 2009.

3. "Portfolio's Worst American CEOs of All Time," CNBC.

4. William D. Cohan, "Lehman E-Mails Show Arrogance Led to the Fall," *Bloomberg View*, May 6, 2012.

5. Richard J. Arnott and Joseph E. Stiglitz, "Labor Turnover, Wage Structures, and Moral Hazard: The Inefficiency of Competitive Markets," *Journal of Labor Economics* 3 (1985): 434–462.

6. His current salary is still in the $6 million per year range though he did repay the million dollars he spent renovating the office he soon had to vacate.

7. Adam Smith, "Of the Expenses of the Sovereign or Commonwealth," Book V, Chapter I, Section 107 in *An Inquiry into the Nature and Causes of the Wealth of Nations*, ed. Edwin Cannan (London: Methuen & Co., 1904), available online at Library of Economics and Liberty.

8. Wikipedia contributors, "Opportunism," *Wikipedia: The Free Encyclopedia.*

9. There were also 48 million cases of food poisoning in 2010 last year. William Neuman, "New Estimates of Food Poisoning Cases," *The New York Times*, December 15, 2010.

10. Paul Krugman, "Wall Street Whitewash," *The New York Times*, December 16, 2010.

11. Because the possibility of fraud with credit cards is high, I had to fax my driver's license and facsimile of my credit card to the business where I had ordered something, which imposed additional costs on me.

12. The company discovered that its diabetes drug Avandia posed risks to the heart. "But instead of publishing the results, the company spent the next 11 years trying to cover them up . . ." Gardiner Harris, "Diabetes Drug Maker Hid Test Data, Files Indicate," *The New York Times*, July 13, 2010; Peter Landers and Jeanne Whalen, "Glaxo to Plead Guilty, Pay $3 Billion to U.S. to Resolve Fraud Allegations," *The Wall Street Journal*, July 2, 2012.

13. "Gary Foster, Ex-Citigroup Exec, Headed to the Slammer," *Huffington Post*, June 29, 2012.

14. Michael Rothfeld, "In Gupta Sentencing, a Judgment Call," *The Wall Street Journal*, October 10, 2012.

15. "Raj Rajaratnam—Galleon Group Founder Convicted in Insider Trading Case," *The New York Times*, December 1, 2011.

16. U.S. Department of Commerce, U.S. Census Bureau, *The 2012 Statistical Abstract. 337: Fraud and Identity Theft—Consumer Complaints by State: 2010.*

17. Wikipedia contributors, "List of Corporate Collapses and Scandals," *Wikipedia: The Free Encyclopedia.*

18. Alexander Dyck, Adair Morse, and Luigi Zingales, "How Pervasive Is Corporate Fraud?" available at www.haas.berkeley.edu/groups/finance/DyckMorseZingales20130306.pdf.

19. Lizette Alvarez, "With Personal Data in Hand, Thieves File Early and Often," *The New York Times*, May 26, 2012.

20. Daron Acemoglu, "The Crisis of 2008: Structural Lessons For and From Economics," January 11, 2009, available at http://economics.mit.edu/files/3722.

21. Editorial, "Let the Students Profit," *The New York Times*, September 11, 2010.

22. And they squeezed $26 billion fines from the banks. Nelson D. Schwartz and Shaila Dewan, "States Negotiate $36 Billion Agreement for Homeowners," *The New York Times*, February 8, 2012.

23. Andrew Martin, "In a Sign of Foreclosure Flaws, Suits Claim Break-Ins by Banks," *The New York Times*, December 21, 2010.

24. Trevor Cook's swindle amounted to "only" $160 million but sufficed to buy him a mansion for $2.8 million. That is what he needed to lead a happy life.

25. Even the weight of fashion models is regulated in Israel, Milan, and Madrid, after models Ana Carolina Reston and Luisel Ramos died in 2006 after going overboard in weight loss in order to succeed in their careers. Eric Wilson, "Health Guidelines Suggested for Models," *The New York Times*, January 6, 2007.

26. Contaminated supplies of Heparin, an anticoagulant, were exported from China, killing 81 people. Gardiner Harris, "U.S. Identifies Tainted Heparin in 11 Countries," *The New York Times*, April 22, 2008.

27. Years of litigation followed problems with Chinese drywall. Andrew Martin, "Drywall Flaws: Owners Gain Limited Relief," *New York Times*, September 17, 2010. Patrick McGeehan, "Federal Officials Shut Down 26 Bus Operators," *The New York Times*, May 31, 2012.

28. The U.S. Food and Drug Administration did not begin to require testing and approval of IUDs until 1976.

29. Fifteen died and more than 200 were hospitalized in a meningitis outbreak due to drug maker negligence involving tainted doses of steroids. Reuters, "Another Death Reported in Meningitis Outbreak," *The New York Times*, October 13, 2012.

30. Diarrhea is not the only result. A person in 2009 had convulsions and eventually became paralyzed from consuming *E. coli*–tainted ground beef. Michael Moss, "The Burger That Shattered Her Life," *The New York Times,* October 3, 2009. Gardiner Harris, "E. Coli Kills 2 and Sickens Many; Focus Is on Beef," *The New York Times,* November 2, 2009.

31. FDA commissioner Margaret Hamburg said that "there is no question that these farms that are involved in the recall were not operating with the standards of practice that we consider responsible." In July, the FDA started requiring large farms to improve refrigeration and do more disease testing, steps it said would reduce *salmonella* infections by more than half. Erik Eckholm, "Egg Industry Faces New Scrutiny After Outbreak," *The New York Times,* August 23, 2010. Britain and New Zealand, with a more effective oversight, had an overall low prevalence rate for salmonella. David McSwane, "Prevention Before Recalls," *The New York Times,* August 24, 2010.

32. Tibor Scitovsky, "On the Principle of Consumers' Sovereignty," *American Economic Review* 52 (1962) 2: 262–268.

33. Mancur Olson, *The Rise and Decline of Nations: Economic Growth, Stagflation, and Social Rigidities* (New Haven, CT: Yale University Press, 1982).

34. Mancur Olson, *The Logic of Collective Action: Public Goods and the Theory of Groups* (Cambridge, MA: Harvard University Press, 1971); Olson, *The Rise and Decline of Nations.*

35. One of the thousands of examples is Wendy L. Gramm, who granted Enron an exemption from regulation in trading of energy derivatives while she headed the Commodity Futures Trading Commission. After she left the commission she was appointed to Enron's board of directors and received between $1 and $2 million in compensation. Her husband was also well treated by Enron. Wikipedia contributors, "Wendy Lee Gramm," *Wikipedia: The Free Encyclopedia*; Bob Herbert, "Enron and the Gramms," *The New York Times,* January 17, 2002.

36. Neil Barofsky, *Bailout: An Inside Account of How Washington Abandoned Main Street While Rescuing Wall Street* (New York: The Free Press, 2012).

37. David Corn and Kevin Drum, interview with Bill Moyers, PBS, January 8, 2010.

38. Simon Johnson, "Protect Consumers, Raise Capital, and Jam the Revolving Wall St–Washington Door," *Baseline Scenario,* September 20, 2009.

39. "Geithner's Calendar at the New York Fed," *The New York Times,* April 26, 2009.

40. Jo Becker and Gretchen Morgenson, "Geithner, Member and Overseer of Finance Club," *The New York Times,* April 26, 2009.

41. James Kwak, "Pierre Bourdieu, Tim Geithner, and Cultural Capital," *Baseline Scenario,* April 27, 2009.

42. Editorial, "Verizon Wireless Says Oops," *The New York Times,* October 5, 2010.

43. David Streitfeld and Gretchen Morgenson, "Foreclosure Furor Rises; Many Call for a Freeze," *The New York Times,* October 5, 2010.

44. Simon Johnson, "The Market Has Spoken—and It Is Rigged," *Baseline Scenario,* July 12, 2012.

45. Jessica Silver-Greenberg, "British Bank in $340 Million Settlement for Laundering," *The New York Times,* August 14, 2012.

46. Ibid.

47. "[T]he latest in a growing number of whistle-blower lawsuits that drug makers have settled with multimillion dollar fines." Gardiner Harris and Duff Wilson, "Glaxo to Pay $750 Million for Sale of Bad Products," *The New York Times,* October 26, 2010.

48. Gretchen Morgenson, "How Countrywide Covered the Cracks," *The New York Times,* October 16, 2010.

49. Wikipedia contributors, "Angelo Mozilo," *Wikipedia: The Free Encyclopedia.* Condé Nast Portfolio ranked Mozilo second on their list of "Worst American CEOs of All Time."

50. Property in human beings is no longer permitted, for example. One is also not permitted to transfer the ownership in one's own labor by selling oneself into temporary servitude, which was allowed in the eighteenth century (indentures). The government also reserves itself the right to force the sale of property for public purpose via a concept known as "eminent domain."

51. "People of the same trade seldom meet together, even for merriment and diversion, but the conversation ends in a conspiracy against the public, or in some contrivance to raise prices." Adam Smith, "Of Wages and Profit in the Different Employments of Labour and Stock," Book I, Chapter X, Section 82 in *An Inquiry into the Nature and Causes of the Wealth of Nations.*

52. Wikipedia contributors, "California Electricity Crisis," *Wikipedia: The Free Encyclopedia.*

53. Gretchen Morgenson, "Raters Ignored Proof of Unsafe Loans, Panel Is Told," *The New York Times,* September 26, 2010.

54. I must have asked at least half a dozen realtors when I was about to buy a house and they were all adamant about not competing with price, but all claimed to be the best in town in terms of some ambiguous dimension of quality. They were insulted that I dared to question their professionalism by asking about price. In short, their collusion is tacit, but is nonetheless real and was kept in place under the guise of professionalism even during the recession of 2008–2009.

55. Alexis Madrigal, "Apple's Brilliant Decoy Pricing Game," *Atlantic,* October 5, 2010.

56. FDIC, Office of Inspector General, "Challenges and FDIC Efforts Related to Predatory Lending," Report No. 06-11, June 2006.

57. Mike Hudson and E. Scott Reckard, "Workers Say Lender Ran 'Boiler Rooms,'" *Los Angeles Times,* February 4, 2005.

58. Jürg Niehans, "Transaction Costs," in *The New Palgrave Dictionary of Economics,* 1st ed., ed. John Eatwell, Murray Milgate, and Peter Newman (Basingstoke, UK: Palgrave Macmillan, 1987).

59. Joseph Stiglitz, "Information and the Change in the Paradigm in Economics," *American Economic Review* 92 (2002) 3: 460–501, here p. 477.

60. Sharon Begley, "Looking for a Good Doctor? Good Luck," Reuters, September 27, 2012.

61. Oliver Williamson, *Markets and Hierarchies: Analysis and Antitrust Implications* (New York: The Free Press, 1975).

62. Anthony J. Venables, "New Economic Geography," in *The New Palgrave Dictionary of Economics,* 2nd ed., ed. Steven N. Durlauf and Lawrence E. Blume (Basingstoke, UK: Palgrave Macmillan, 2008).

63. W. Brian Arthur, *Increasing Returns and Path Dependence in the Economy* (Ann Arbor: University of Michigan Press, 1994).

64. Paul A. David, "Clio and the Economics of QWERTY," *American Economic Review* 75 (1985) 2: 332–337.

65. Brian Arthur. "Competing Technologies, Increasing Returns, and Lock-In by Historical Events," *Economic Journal* 99 (1989): 116–131; David, "Clio and the Economics of QWERTY."

66. Douglas Puffert, "Path Dependence in Spatial Networks: The Standardization of Railway Track Gauge," *Explorations in Economic History* 39 (2002): 282–314.

67. Wikipedia contributors, "Global Warming," *Wikipedia: The Free Encyclopedia.*

68. Herman Daly, "Economics in a Full World," *Scientific American* 293 (2005) 3: 100–107.

69. Laurence J. Kotlikoff, *Generational Accounting: Knowing Who Pays, and When, for What We Spend* (New York: The Free Press, 1992).

70. Ibid.

71. Emilio F. Moran, *People and Nature. An Introduction to Human Ecological Relations* (Oxford, UK: Blackwell, 2006); Herman Daly, *Steady-State Economics: The Economics of Biophysical Equilibrium and Moral Growth* (New York: W.H. Freeman, 1978).

72. Diane Coyle, *The Economics of Enough: How to Run the Economy as if the Future Matters* (Princeton, NJ: Princeton University Press, 2011).

73. Joseph E. Stiglitz, *Making Globalization Work* (New York: W.W. Norton, 2006).

74. "[W]e assume that more choice means better options and greater satisfaction. But beware of excessive choice: choice overload can make you question the decisions you make before you even make them, it can set you up for unrealistically high expectations, and it can make you blame yourself for any and all failures. In the long run, this can lead to decision-making paralysis. And in a culture that tells us that there is no excuse for falling short of perfection when your options are limitless, too much choice can lead to clinical depression." Barry Schwartz, *The Paradox of Choice: Why More Is Less* (New York: Ecco, 2003). Schwartz also has a number of great lectures on video in the Internet: "Barry Schwartz: The Paradox of Choice," YouTube video, 20:23, posted by "TEDtalksDirector," January 16, 2007; "The Paradox of Choice—Why More Is Less," YouTube video, 1:04:08, posted by "GoogleTalksArchive," April 27, 2006.

9

MICROECONOMIC APPLICATIONS ON AND OFF THE BLACKBOARD

In this chapter we apply some of the ideas delineated in the previous chapters to analyze typical issues in real-world economics. The difference between the standard textbook analysis of these problems and the analyses elucidated below is that the former applies the perfectly competitive model to their solution, whereas we consider such models irrelevant in today's economy and therefore use models characterized by imperfect competition. The conclusions differ accordingly.

MINIMUM WAGE

The minimum wage generally has a bad reputation among mainstream economists. They argue that it leads to unemployment among low-wage workers and is therefore inefficient: fewer people are hired than would be the case if wages were determined freely by market forces. In a perfectly competitive market in which there is no profit, this assertion would indeed be correct. However, that model is inappropriate for today's economy, dominated as it is by oligopolistic firms that do make profits. In such a market, the increase in wages comes out of profits and does not lead to unemployment. No wonder there is no empirical evidence that the minimum wage causes unemployment.[1] The federal minimum wage peaked at about $10 in the late 1960s (in 2009 dollars) but is now merely $7.25, a decline of some 27 percent. This is so low that it is not even binding, especially in larger cities, and many states and municipalities set the minimum wage above the federal level.[2]

Imperfect competition is central to the analysis of the implications of the minimum wage because of the existence of market power by firms who hire at or below the minimum wage at the local level. For instance, many teenagers, poor people, and those looking for part-time work do not have regular transportation available to commute far outside of their neighborhoods. They generally search for work near home. That means that local businesses hiring those workers have a captive market and exert market power in setting wages. This is called a monopsony. It is like a monopoly except the market power is not used in setting prices for goods but in setting wages when one is buying labor. Monopsonists can offer wages below the market rate, because they know that the neighborhood workers cannot afford to look for work outside of their immediate vicinity.

In such a labor market a minimum wage does not necessarily decrease employment but can even increase it. The reason is that a monopsonist takes advantage of the lack of competition in the local labor market and is able to dictate a low wage. He hires fewer workers than a competitive firm would, because he would have to raise the wages of all workers (including those he already employs) if he were to hire additional workers.[3] The increased wages bill would exceed the increased output of the additional worker.[4] Thus, a minimum wage above the monopsonistic wage would induce the firm to hire more workers because the extra revenue produced by the additional workers exceeds their wage.

There is another problem with the mainstream view: it assumes that the firms in question do not earn profits in competitive equilibrium. But that condition does not hold with oligopolies, that is to say, with all of the corporations that hire most of the 4.4 million people who work at or below the minimum wage. McDonald's certainly competes with other fast-food chains but still makes a hefty profit, because it enjoys a quasi-monopoly position locally. This implies that it did not have to raise the price of its hamburgers at all when the minimum wage was raised by 70 cents in July of 2009 to $7.25. It could absorb such a tiny increase in wages into profits (perhaps 2 cents per hamburger) (Figure 9.1). It did not need to increase the price of hamburgers, and the demand for its products was not affected by the increase in the minimum wage. Nor would it decrease its labor force (Figure 9.1). Besides, Burger King would have also increased its wages and consequently McDonald's would not be at a disadvantage vis-à-vis its competitors. So a more realistic model implies that the minimum wage need not lead to unemployment but to a redistribution of income from profits to workers. In other words, a model with imperfect competition provides more insight into the working of today's low-wage sector than the perfectly competitive model does.

Even at the minimum wage the working poor live a miserable life of bare subsistence.[5] As of 2010, full-time annual income at minimum wage was about $15,000, which is at the poverty level for a household with one adult and one child.[6] In addition, there are exemptions to the minimum-wage laws. In 2010 there were 1.8 million people who worked for the minimum wage while 2.5 million others were employed for less than the minimum wage, many of them receiving tips, which hopefully made up the difference.[7]

In addition to raising some households above utter destitution, the minimum wage has some other positive effects: (a) in the long run it might induce some firms to substitute capital for labor, which would lead to capital deepening and increased productivity; (b) if there are fewer job opportunities for teenagers, it should induce them to stay in school longer;[8] (c) an increase in minimum wage might be an incentive for workers to expend more effort and to decrease shirking on the job insofar as the job becomes more valuable; (d) the minimum wage is used in the labor market as a benchmark to which other wages are pegged. An increase in the minimum wage will therefore lead to a rise in the wages of other workers as well, thereby affecting the distribution of income.

PRICE CONTROLS

Price controls are similarly harmful in the mainstream's view. Mainstream economists argue that such controls create shortages and or lower the quality of products concerned. To be sure, price controls are superfluous and can have negative consequences if certain conditions are met in perfectly competitive markets, such as the reasonable distribution of income and no overriding ethical considerations such as with food and medicine. However, as these conditions do not always hold, one has to consider the implications of price controls beyond the basic model. Indeed, there are circumstances in which price controls are warranted. For example, during World War II they were a necessary pre-condition to channeling the productive forces of the economy toward the common aim of winning the war.[9] They were appropriate for that aim and for successfully controlling inflation. Decentralized markets do not have the ability to do that by themselves. In other words, *context matters*. That is one reason why we need to keep a watchful eye on markets and maintain democratic control over them.

The delivery of basic needs to all is a legitimate social and political concern and a function that the market by itself cannot always accomplish. For example, it does not seem fair that the rich

Figure 9.1 **Profits of a Quasi-Monopolist Without Fixed Costs**

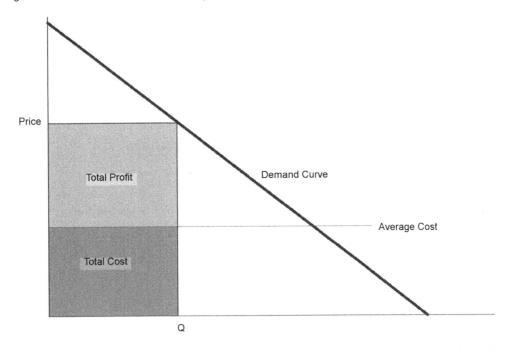

are more advantaged at obtaining gasoline during an oil embargo, such as the one of 1973. The increase in the price of basic necessities, such as food or gasoline, affects the welfare of the poor much more than that of the rich. Hence, the concern of politicians to redress these imbalances and to modify unacceptable aspects of market outcomes is legitimate, indeed. The uneven distribution of basic goods can be socially destabilizing. In the case of shortage of gasoline, using the queuing mechanism to do the rationing seems fairer in an emergency, insofar as we all have the same amount of time available to us, whereas money is unevenly distributed. Competition for gasoline would then be on a more level playing field. Although the wealthy would be aggravated at having to queue for gasoline, the working poor would be aggravated as well if they were unable to get to work at Walmart because they could not afford to buy gasoline (of course, the super-rich could still send their servants to stand in the queue). Hence, waste, inefficiency, and aggravation would arise with the market solution as well. The distribution of aggravation would differ. In case of a shortage in supply, it is undesirable to let the market allocate a product that fulfills basic needs. This is precisely the case with health care.[10]

Price ceilings can also induce monopolists and oligopolists to lower their price, increase output, and produce closer to the socially optimum output, thereby increasing social welfare (Figure 9.2).

UNIONS

Unions usually get short shrift in Econ 101. Basic economics texts invariably depict labor unions as an unwarranted intervention in markets by special interests to raise the wages of their members above the market rate and therefore cause inefficiency and unemployment.[11] However, such logic obtains only in perfectly competitive markets, yet unions seldom existed in such markets. Rather, they have been most active in sectors that are dominated by oligopolies and are therefore earning

Figure 9.2   **Price Ceiling in Case of a Monopolist Without Fixed Costs**

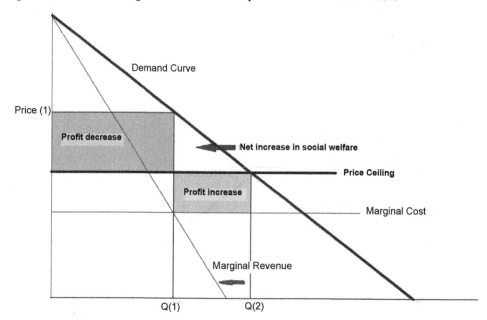

substantial profits. They have also been successful in the public sector—where wages are determined administratively and not through the monetary value of output—and in an environment in which there is endemic unemployment.

A firm with just a handful of competitors such as Apple and McDonald's is an oligopolist. The profits of such a firm are illustrated in Figure 9.3. The demand for its product is such that it can be produced by seven workers. Because the firm has market power, it is producing fewer goods than a perfectly competitive firm would in order to be able to charge a higher price for them. Workers receive a wage of $8 per hour even though their marginal product ($12) is greater than their wage. In such cases, the role of a union is to extract a bit of the excess profit, the difference between $8 and $12, and increase wages to, say, $9. Note that for this oligopolist, the number of workers would remain at seven, because this number depends on the quantity of goods that the oligopolist sells at the price it sets. Thus, the increase in the wage to $9 would not affect the level of employment at all; it would only decrease the profits earned by the firm. That is not such a bad outcome. The union is merely defending a more equitable distribution of income and supporting a more living wage to the workers. Thus, the aim of the unions has been to obtain a share of the profits for the employees.

There is no evidence at all that unions cause unemployment. Note that the decline of unions over the last couple of generations did not bring about a diminution in the unemployment rate; rather, it redistributed power and profits to the corporate world. As discussed in Chapter 7, the decline in union bargaining power is the most plausible explanation for (a) the divergence in productivity and wages after 1980 (Figure 7.1); (b) the stagnation in median income of men since about 1973 (Figure 7.2); and (c) the decline in median household income since 1998.

There is evidence that unions were able to bargain so that the growth in wages kept up with the rate of increase in workers' productivity in the 1950s and 1960s. When union power was at its peak, wages did actually keep pace with productivity growth: both increased at an annual rate

Figure 9.3 **Profits of an Oligopolist Employing Seven Workers**

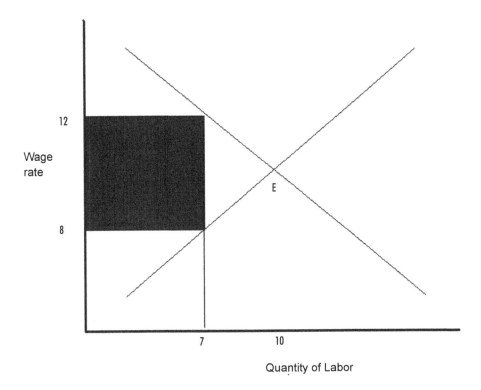

Quantity of Labor

of 3.2 percent. However, with the decline in union power, wages lagged way behind productivity growth after 1980. Why? Previously, unions had economic advisers on their payroll who were knowledgeable enough to ascertain the increases in productivity, information that union leaders translated into bargaining power, a countervailing power sufficient to keep wages and productivity in line. However, with the demise of the unions, individual workers did not have that information available to them, and they lost the power to bargain for wage increases with the threat of unemployment looming large. Workers became powerless without the backing of organized labor.

The steep rise in inequality began in the early 1980s with the acceleration of globalization, which hammered the U.S. industrial sector and was accompanied by the demise of the unions. Beginning with the presidency of Ronald Reagan—and his notable suppression of the air traffic controller's union—the government adopted a rather antagonistic attitude toward unions and embraced the ideology of deregulation, which enabled the corporations to gain the upper hand. This changed the balance of power in the labor market in favor of corporations, which had the wealth and held the reins of power. Corporations were mobile and could move their capital around the world instantaneously, while labor did not have the same capability. That put capital at a distinct advantage, and unions were no longer able to provide countervailing support to workers.

Well-paying jobs for high school graduates declined and are in short supply today: "low-wage, temporary jobs have become so widespread that they threaten to become the norm."[12] This is not supposed to happen in a democratic economy. It could only happen because a substantial number of poor people were unable to recognize their own self-interest and voted for people who were clandestine advocates of the interests of the wealthy. They directed the attention of the voters to other issues using states' rights, pro-life, pro-freedom, antigovernment, and antitax rhetoric while lowering the taxes of the rich by a lot more than they lowered those of the poor, destroying the unions that protected the wages of the working class, and opening the country to imports, which closed factories. So government policy was tilted heavily in favor of the rich and super-rich and against the lower and lower-middle class, but the issues were framed in such a way that the poor failed to recognize the hidden aspects of the policy.[13]

Over time, wealth begat wealth and power begat power, both economic and political, so that economic inequality begat political inequality. Lawmakers can safely disregard the general will in most cases and cater to the preferences of the affluent.[14] We may well have reached a tipping point beyond which this tendency cannot be reversed for generations, if at all.[15] Thus, most of the wealth created by the economy is accruing to an increasingly smaller share of the population (Figures 7.8 and 7.9). The top 5 percent of income earners increased their share of total income from 17 to 22 percent, whereas the bottom 40 percent of income earners decreased their income share from 15 percent to 12 percent.

Consider Apple Inc.'s wage structure. Its CEO, Tim Cook, has a net worth of some $400 million. He received a salary of $900,000 in 2011 and a walloping $500 million worth of stock bonus distributed over a ten-year period. That would make his annual earnings in the $51 million range. Several vice presidents of the company received salaries of $700,000 with stock bonuses of around $30 million—again over a ten-year period.[16] Apple has been earning a profit on the order of $6 billion to $8 billion year in and year out. Contrast this to the wages of Jordan Golson, a salesman for Apple, who sold $750,000 worth of products in a three-month period and makes $11.25 per hour, gets no incentive pay, and receives no bonuses or stock options.[17] We are unable to determine if Cook's or Golson's salary comes close to their marginal product, and I seriously doubt that Apple could either. Both are guesses that come out of the history of wages at Apple and similar companies, but common sense tells me that neither wage is plausibly close to the value of their marginal product For one thing, output is a joint product: Apple could not exist without Golson or Cook. Golson's salary is low because the unemployment rate keeps a ceiling on his wages, while Cook's salary is protected from competition, although many would be willing to do the job as well for much less. When it was time to fill Cook's job, it was not advertised. There was no search for a competitive bid. Moreover, neither salary is fair. Golson's salary was just 0.7 percent of the value of the merchandise he sold. If there were a union at Apple, it might have been able to increase Golson's salary to, say, that paid by Tiffany's for their salespeople: $15.60 an hour. That would increase Golson's wage to just 1 percent of his sales, not an inordinate amount by any means and not enough to catapult him into the middle class, but 40 percent more than the subsistence wage he is now getting.

Suppose the union were able to increase each salesperson's salary by $4.35, and let's suppose furthermore that the 30,000 sales force works 2,000 hours per annum. That would mean an additional expense for Apple of a mere $300 million, reducing profits from $6 billion to $5.7 billion—that is, by 5 percent—surely not an inordinate amount. Conclusion: without the help of a union, the sales force is arguably kept at a living standard of the working poor. Not a very reasonable outcome, by which I mean—after John Rawls—that were I to design the system behind a veil of ignorance, I would certainly not design one with a divergence of incomes ranging from $11.25 to $25,000 per hour.

One should not be surprised that without the countervailing power of unions to offset the power of corporations, the share of national income going to labor has been declining. Labor's share of output was 65 percent between 1947 and 1983. However, it declined thereafter to reach 58 percent in 2010, to the advantage of profits.[18] The correlation with the decline in union power cannot be merely coincidental. Note that labor's share has been declining even though it includes the billions earned by CEOs: their income and bonuses are counted as wages just as those of a salesclerk. Thus, the concept of labor is not used in that statistic in the classical sense of blue-collar workers, but includes a lot of rents captured by top management.

Furthermore, it is noteworthy that the per capita income of men has been stagnating throughout the last quarter of the twentieth century, just as labor union membership was declining.[19] If labor unions had depressed the wages of the rest of the labor force, as argued by the mainstream, one would expect that average salaries of the nonunionized would increase with the decline in labor unions. Of course, nothing could be further from the truth—only women's wages have been increasing, on account of improvements in their education. Yet even women's wages have been stagnating since 1998. I infer that incomes have been stagnating because the weak labor unions meant that workers had to fend for themselves in a labor market in which endemic unemployment was constantly putting a downward pressure on wages, which in turn enabled management to obtain a bigger share of profits. Union membership was about 21 million when Ronald Reagan took office but is 12.4 million today—a mere 8 percent of the labor force—and continually under pressure.[20] Without unions, the American Dream is no longer within reach of an increasing share of the population.

The reason unions are crucial is the asymmetric power relationship between labor and management.[21] There are two sources of the lack of power among workers without substantial education: (a) endemic unemployment means that they are in constant competition to keep their jobs and therefore have no voice to try to increase their wages; (b) workers lack the savings to live on during a period of unemployment and must have a constant source of income to survive.[22] In contrast, management has sufficient savings and sufficient power to control its own destiny. Moreover, capital does not have basic needs and as a consequence can stay idle for a long time without diminishing in value. This uneven relationship with respect to the timing of income means that management has the upper hand in negotiations. Unions used to provide the essential countervailing power. Thus, they were an integral part of the success of the mid-century American middle class. It was possible then for those with a high school education to earn a decent living. These opportunities are mostly gone today. By not considering power relationships, conventional economics comes to the wrong conclusion with regard to the usefulness of unions for ordinary workers.

DISCRIMINATION

Discrimination is ultimately benign according to the mainstream view, as it is self-correcting through competition. The neoclassical assumption is that those who are discriminated against are willing to work for less and will be hired by firms that are not discriminating and who thus will be able to offer their product at a lower price, thereby driving the discriminating firms out of the market.[23] One might begin by asking if it is fair that those who are discriminated against should work for less. Note, furthermore, that in this "Alice in Wonderland" economy there is no unemployment, no imperfect competition, no imperfect information, and above all, no peer pressure (such as the Ku Klux Klan) to maintain a united front against the group who is being discriminated against, such as the African American community, which experienced centuries of not-so-benign discrimination.

The reason is that the social pressure to enforce the norm of discrimination is so strong that there may not be any nondiscriminating firms in the first place to compete with discriminating firms. Certainly there were no bus companies that competed with the ones that made blacks sit in the back of the bus in Montgomery. Moreover, the above scenario assumes that productivity is easily ascertained and that the non-discriminating firm can withstand the strong peer pressure to accept the norm of the society. Suppose members of the discriminated group are willing to work for a lower wage than is commensurate with their true productivity. But if there is uncertainty with regard to productivity, which is generally the case, then nondiscriminating firms might well assume that group members are willing to accept the lower wage only because of their lower productivity and it would not be attractive for them to hire the discriminated worker at a lower wage, even without peer pressure. In fact, that competition was incapable of eliminating discrimination is part of the historical record. Rather than markets, it was social movements and political action that finally abolished it.

Joseph McNeil, Franklin McCain, Ezell Blair, Jr., and David Richmond were not served coffee at the Woolworth's lunch counter in downtown Greensboro, NC, because of the color of their skin. It is very strange that free markets would be structured in such a way that one's ability to buy a coffee sitting down depended on their skin color. It took the Civil Rights Act of 1964 for them and others of their color to buy coffee in the shop of their choice in a supposedly free market.[24] These rights were not obtained through competition from nondiscriminating entrepreneurs who wanted to profit from the discrimination of others.

REDISTRIBUTION

Poverty can be either an absolute or a relative physical and psychological deprivation. It is absolute if a household is unable to meet its basic needs and its members' survival is at stake. Disregarding such a possibility would be unethical.[25] In addition, one can feel disadvantaged relative to the consumption of a reference group even if one's basic needs are met. In either case, the social order can be threatened by deprivation, as many societies have found out in the past. In addition, the distribution of benefits produced by the economy can be skewed in favor of a group out of proportion to its contribution to social welfare and thus become unjust.[26]

A policy of redistribution might be supported out of a feeling of moral obligation, a sense of justice, empathy for the plight of the disadvantaged, or because of concern for social upheaval. The feeling of discomfort among third parties created by the suffering of the poor in a land of wealth is a negative externality. So the urge to ameliorate inequality can also come from a desire to overcome a negative externality. The goal is not to strive for perfect equality but to create a fairer distribution that is less skewed and that ensures that at least basic needs—including health and education—are met for all of the population, especially for children, who are not accountable for the circumstances into which they were born. It makes little sense to allow 45 percent of single mothers to be poor[27] while the top 50 hedge fund managers have a combined income of $29,000 million, or about $600 million each.[28] Such astronomical salaries are in reality rents, that is to say, not deserved. These individuals would have done their job at a fraction of that salary.

Rawls also argued that the current distribution of income is unjust, because "no one deserves his place in the distribution of talents, nor his starting place in society." Rewarding talent, in other words, is rewarding our random genetic configuration or the luck of having been born into a well-endowed family. He continued, "In the light of what principle can free and equal moral persons permit their relations to be affected by social fortune and the natural lottery?"[29] By "natural lottery" he means that we did not earn or deserve our initial endowment in life that is going to be so important throughout the life course. These include the social status of the family into which we were born as well as our genetic predispositions. It was a matter of luck that we were born with a particular genetic code into a particular family. The substantial advantages or disadvantages those provide were not earned through our own effort, hence are not deserved, and there is no reason to be rewarded for them. The initial endowments were not just; rather, they were distributed randomly. Nonetheless, these talents, wealth, privileges obtained at birth, or the lack thereof play an immense role in one's economic prospects.[30] We do not deserve to be born into a rich or into a poor family, or to be smarter or better looking than average, or to be of a certain skin color or ethnicity. We have not done anything at all for these attributes and therefore our reward is an economic rent; we should not be rewarded for what is simply a random allocation. The assignment of property rights in these attributes is arbitrary. Hence, the privileges of the moneyed elite are not all that different from those of the aristocracy of the feudal age. Neither class deserved its riches, as both were based more on birth than on merit. There is no good reason why one newborn should have advantages unavailable to another just because of the happenstance of birth. In short, the extensive economic inequality has no moral basis, as people's "life prospects are significantly affected by their family and class origins," that is, through no action of their own.

In a similar vein, Malcolm Gladwell notes that "the biggest misconception about success is that we do it solely on our smarts, ambition, hustle and hard work."[31] There are many variables involved in one's success that are external; our achievements depend also on the social environment. Gladwell notes that success "is grounded in a web of advantages and inheritances, some deserved, some not, some earned, some just plain lucky."

Because of the decreasing marginal utility of income, the total utility of the society could be increased greatly if we were to redistribute income from the wealthy to the poor (Figure 9.4). However, the argument against redistribution is that we are unable to compare utility levels across individuals. While it is true that some may adore the flavor of fresh oranges just as others might well find it distasteful, it is safe to assume that people differ in their basic needs but infinitesimally. The pangs of hunger for one cannot possibly be that much different from those of most others. A broken bone for one is much like that of anyone else. Yet we back away from such assumptions, even though we have no problem assuming that a single agent can represent everyone when we

Figure 9.4   **Redistribution Increases Total Utility and Social Welfare**

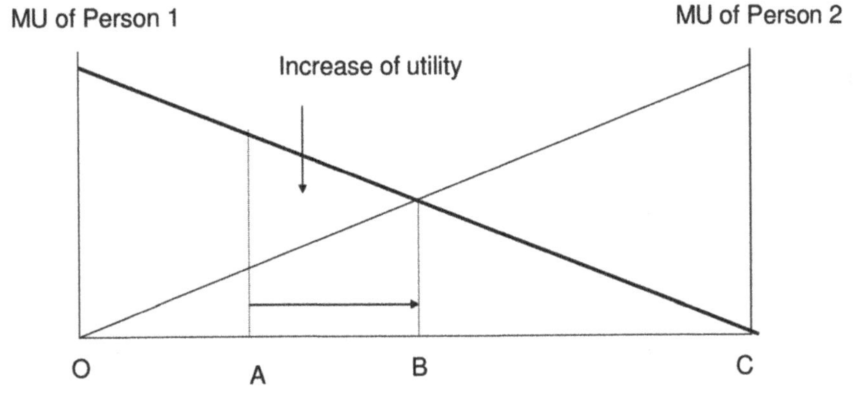

Total income = OC; initial income of poor is OA and of rich AC
After redistribution each have OB=BC.

Marginal utility of two identical individuals with unequal income.
Total utility would increase with redistribution. Reduction of income of rich from
A to B and increase of poor would increase total utility by the triangle

do macroeconomics, an assumption that implies a homogeneous society. The habit of using these two sets of assumptions is inconsistent.

Conventional economists argue that income redistribution through taxation generates inefficiencies. This supposed efficiency-equity tradeoff works by reducing the incentive for high-productivity workers to work more, thereby decreasing total income. However, this inference is based on inappropriately oversimplified assumptions. It assumes without empirical evidence that people actually work less if the tax rate increases for all. In other words, they assert that if someone's after-tax salary is $1,000 per hour she will work less than if she were to earn $1,200 per hour. However, Warren Buffett—the investor guru—thinks otherwise,[32] and there is no actual evidence supporting such a claim.[33] Would the 403 American billionaires work less if their tax rate were doubled?[34] Would Beyoncé sing fewer songs? I doubt it. I suspect that the only effect it would have is to reduce the intensity of conspicuous consumption and the negative externalities it causes.

Furthermore, efficiency does not have to be reduced at all through taxation. The government is not wasting the money. Rather, it invests a lot of it on education, infrastructure, health care, and basic research, all of which are crucial for economic growth. It is precisely for this reason that the Western European and Northern European economies have actually done quite well in spite of redistribution. Thus, there is substantial evidence—disregarded by conventional models—that social spending actually fosters, rather than inhibits, economic development.[35] The reason is that additional incomes are not crucial in creating incentives among the super-rich as conventionally assumed, while they are, in fact, indispensable in providing social services and safety nets, universal education, and health care, and thus increase productivity among lower-income groups. Hungry children attending inferior schools and growing up in dysfunctional families and neighborhoods have far less likelihood of becoming productive members of the community than their more privileged counterparts. Thus, I think that the inefficiencies associated with redistribution are illusory.

There are direct positive effects of a safety net on average welfare. It provides security, so we feel better knowing that if unexpected disaster strikes we have something to fall back on. Moreover, people who have no other source of income are more likely to commit crimes. Countries with a tighter safety net are much less prone to random acts of violence. So people are freer to leave their homes at night. They are less anxious about the safety of their children and experience far fewer break-ins, car thefts, murders, and personal assaults. So all in all they live with less stress and can therefore enjoy a better quality of life. In other words, a higher level of taxation at the upper end of the income scale leads to a more balanced society, which, in turn, leads to a higher average welfare.

LIVING STANDARDS

The standard of living is usually not discussed in mainstream textbooks although it is one of the more important concepts in economics. Instead, the emphasis is placed on individual utility, income, and, at the aggregate level, on gross national product (GNP). Yet the standard treatment discusses neither the distribution of income nor the problem of aggregating income or utility. If utility levels are not comparable across individuals as is claimed, then adding individual incomes is not an accurate measure of aggregate living standards at all. How should one judge the U.S. case, for instance, in which GNP has been growing but the real wages of the bottom 20 percent of the population have not increased since 1969 and the median wage is lower now than it was in 1999 (Figure 9.5).[36] Consider also that the $5 per day paid to workers by the Ford Motor Company in 1914 would be worth about $115 per day today (or $14 per hour). Among the 75 million members of the U.S. labor force today who are working for an hourly wage, only 40 percent earn

Figure 9.5   **Median Household Income in 2009 Dollars by Ethnicity**

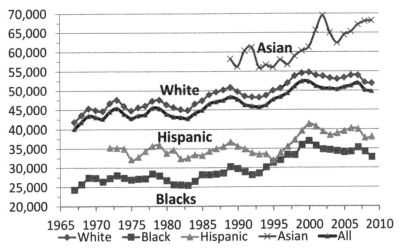

Source: www.census.gov/compendia/statab (accessed July 24, 2012)

Figure 9.6   **Distribution of Earnings of Wage Workers in the United States**

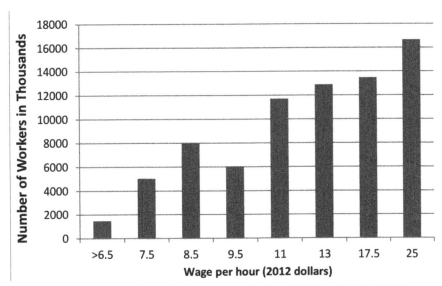

Source: Data kindly provided through private communication with Mary Bowler, U.S. Bureau of Labor, based on the Current Population Survey

more than the Ford workers earned in 1914, adjusted for inflation. Suddenly, the rise in living standards becomes less certain.

Insofar as utility is not measurable, it cannot be aggregated, and therefore we use income or GNP as an aggregate proxy measure of living standards instead, as they are denominated in dollars and can be aggregated. However, if utility is not comparable across individuals, these measures are also not comparable across individuals and ought not to be aggregated. An additional dollar to

Donald Trump means absolutely nothing, but to the homeless lady on my street corner it means enough for her to bless me as I give it to her. In other words, the mainstream treatment of utility is incoherent, because at times we are not allowed to compare individual utility across individuals but some pages later we nonetheless aggregate it by implicitly adding it, using income as the measure of utility. We could not aggregate income as a measure of living standards unless people's individual utilities were comparable.

Given these limitations, we place far too much emphasis on such monetary measures. They have other shortcomings as well: they are limited to market activity and disregard many factors that are important to welfare and the quality of life, such as the damage to the environment due to pollution. They do not consider the hours of labor input, or the psychic costs of the uncertainty that permeates the market economy. Many risks borne by individuals in the realm of their education, employment, health insurance, and retirement induce a feeling of insecurity that is responsible for many of the stresses that prevent us from leading care-free lives.[37] The reality of the business cycle, in other words, is not a benign attribute of the economy. It is a threat that imposes actual psychic and monetary costs that are not subtracted from GNP. The implication is that we should pay much more attention to data that reflect welfare directly, such as child poverty, school achievement scores and graduation rates, longevity, morbidity, health including mental health, gun violence and other crime statistics, as well as subjective evaluations of welfare. Money measures are not as useful an indicator of well-being as we have been led to believe.

Relative deprivation is another major issue to consider. The mainstream asserts unequivocally that the level of income is important in generating utility, yet that is contradicted by the evidence that our feeling of well-being has been declining or stagnating even as per capita income has increased substantially since World War II. The alternative view—that utility is not generated by the absolute level of income but by our place in the social pecking order—appears to be more accurate. If it were the absolute income that mattered, we would certainly be much more satisfied with our lives than we actually are. Although we are richer than our grandparents, we are by no means happier and most likely even less content. We are envious of others who obtain a greater share of the pie than we do and more anxious about the future than prior generations. The average full-time worker is still working forty hours a week in spite of higher incomes in order to maintain her place in the social pecking order.[38] One would think that with incomes increasing one would enjoy more leisure insofar as leisure is a normal good. The main reason why this is not the case is that we need to work harder in order to "keep up with the Joneses" in the competition for status.[39]

We might also consider that we are judging developments by looking backward. This is hardly an impartial perspective as we are accustomed to our environment and have become used to current culture, levels of material comfort, competition, anxiety, and stress. However, there is another way of considering developments, namely looking forward: What would people living in, say, 1900 think of our world today? Would they be dazzled by our material comfort, longer life expectancy, and technological advances, or would they be confused, or perhaps even repulsed, by the concomitant social, cultural, and spiritual changes? I think that the judgment of a hypothetical person considering our quality of life from the vantage point of 1900 is much more likely to be negative, for I doubt that people living in 1900 would want to change places with us in spite of our riches. While we have adapted to our harried, stressful, disorderly, anxiety-ridden lifestyles, mass shootings, and our dysfunctional families and neighborhoods, these would likely scare them if they could not know in advance where they ended up in our society.[40] They would probably feel very uncomfortable living in our civilization and consider the concomitant price of material comforts too costly in terms of their own ethical values.

Hence, we are not able to assert unambiguously that progress has been made in all dimensions of human existence since technological advancement has been gained at a social cost that needs to be part of the calculation if we are to have an unbiased view of economic development. One cannot assert that the standard of living has risen unless there is an unambiguous way to judge that it has done so. This, however, is impossible. All we could argue is that from our perspective it has risen on average, but for a large segment of the population, income has been declining for some time. In fact, 90 percent of all employees in the "Food Preparation and Serving Related" occupation and 70 percent of all workers in the "Healthcare Support" sector earn less in real terms than Ford workers did in 1914.[41] In other words, for the lower classes as well as for the lower middle class the standard of living, measured in monetary units, has not increased at all in these 100 years. Thus, we should not be considering only average incomes. Their distribution also matters, and it matters a whole lot, as for many the American Dream has slipped well out of reach.[42]

One study found that "when the real wages of the majority of the U.S. workforce declined in the 1970s, 1980s and the first half of the 1990s, household labor supply increased. Consequently, real family income in the bottom eighty percent of the income distribution rose. Wage-earning households were not only struggling to maintain their acquired standard of living as real wages were declining, but they were also . . . trying to raise their standard of living. It was precisely when household labor supply hit a ceiling in the second half of the 1990s, that household debt exploded. Surging household debt from the late 1990s until 2007—driven primarily by home mortgage debt—suggests that the culturally powerful 'American Dream' motivated wage-earning households to seek and expect a continuously rising standard of living via home ownership even in the face of topped out work hours and historically low real wages."[43] Peter Whybrow describes the situation of American families this way: "working longer hours, sleeping less, cutting back on vacations, neglecting our families and . . . taking on debt—massive amounts of debt. Before 1985 American consumers saved on average about 9 percent of their disposable income but by 2005 the comparable savings rate was zero as mortgage, credit card and other consumer debt rose to 127 percent of disposable income."[44]

In sum, competition for status means that we are unable to allocate our time wisely between work and leisure.[45] The reason is that we expect additional income to improve our lives and elect to work instead of choosing leisure. But income is rivalrous: that is to say, if our position in society remains constant, additional income does not produce as much welfare as we anticipated. So we choose to work more, but our additional income also has negative externalities because it forces other people to feel worse as they are unable to keep up with our level of consumption. As any negative externality, this externality should be taxed also so that we impose smaller burdens on others. As a consequence, increased tax on labor income can improve the quality of life as we would enjoy more leisure, and others would have to work less in order to keep up with our level of consumption. The race for status is futile as it is a zero-sum endeavor.

The inference is that the economic system as now construed does not easily lead to satisfactory lives for most of the population. Rather, it is more likely to lead to a futile effort to keep up with the social norm. Businesses devote incredible sums to persuade us that the things we have are no longer the best or in style. As a consequence, they sow the seeds of discomfort within us at the same time as they provide new products. While this implies growth in GNP, the growth is overstated as it does not subtract from GNP the diminution of the value of goods already in one's possession. Schumpeterian creative destruction pertains not only to technologies but also to consumption goods. This never-ending process does not lead to contentment; instead, consumption becomes a vicious circle of fulfilling newly induced desires, which we did not have initially, which we had not wanted, and which are created by business interests through outside stimuli. In other words, one is not allowed to remain satisfied. Businesses are intent on getting us out of our equilibrium by creating a feeling of dissatisfaction in us and that becomes a vicious, insatiable circle: the more we have the more we want.

HAPPINESS AND GROWTH

We tend to make the mistake of automatically equating economic growth with improvements in living standards. However, polls and surveys contradict this perspective.[46] In spite of all the growth in our lifetime, satisfaction eludes us because growth comes at a high social and psychological cost that is not part of our initial calculation. Repeated surveys have actually found that life satisfaction (or happiness) has not increased at all since 1946, which is as far back as records have been kept.[47] This result has been popularized extensively since Richard Easterlin's seminal essay of 1974, which thereafter spawned a large literature.[48]

The research based on surveys designed to estimate subjective life satisfaction suggests unambiguously that the effect of increases in income on life satisfaction is minimal in the long run as long as two conditions are met: (a) income is above the amount required for basic needs; and (b) average income increases as well. However, increases in income do affect life satisfaction markedly for individuals living at or below subsistence, and also if one's income increases relative to the social norm or relative to that of a reference group. Yet if our income increases absolutely but average income rises as well, so that our relative income does not increase, then we do not experience a gain in our subjective well-being. That is why average life satisfaction is not greater today than it was 60 years ago. However, if our social status improves, we do feel better. That is why richer people in a society are happier on average than poorer ones. Their income is higher relative to the average. If the model propagated by the mainstream were true, however, and absolute income led to utility, we would have to be much happier today than people in the past, because we are immensely wealthier and should therefore have higher utility levels. We find instead that once basic needs are met, further income is not the key determinant of happiness (Table 9.1). The United States is sixteenth in the world ranking of life satisfaction, which is not too bad from the point of view of the 200 or so countries in the world, except that on the basis of average U.S. income you would expect it to rank higher: only Norway has a higher per capita income than the United States on that list. The Scandinavian welfare state seems to be the best model to provide for a thriving society that supports its members who are in need.

Consequently, it should be clear that absolute income is not the most important determinant of life satisfaction over time unless one is hungry and thirsty: however, relative income does matter a lot. For instance, the "World Happiness Report, 2012" suggests that, "the world's economic superpower, the United States, has achieved striking economic and technological progress over the past half century without gains in the self-reported happiness of the citizenry. Instead, uncertainties and anxieties are high, social and economic inequalities have widened considerably, social trust is in decline, and confidence in government is at an all-time low. Perhaps for these reasons, life satisfaction has remained nearly constant during decades of rising Gross National Product (GNP) per capita."[49] According to Peter Whybrow, "It is the paradox of modernity that as choice and material prosperity increase . . . personal satisfaction decline[s]. . . . And yet it is the rare American who manages to step back from the hedonic treadmill long enough to savor his or her good fortune."[50]

We must accentuate that the quality of life is a multidimensional concept that should not be measured with money alone.[51] How satisfied people are with their lives depends on factors such as the amount of effort required to obtain income, working conditions, how much income fluctuates

Table 9.1

Percentage of People Thriving in 2011

Denmark	82	Israel	62
Finland	75	Australia	62
Norway	69	Canada	62
Netherlands	68	Austria	57
Sweden	68	Brazil	58
Venezuela	64	Panama	58
New Zealand	63	USA	57
Costa Rica	63	Belgium	56
Switzerland	62	UK	54

Source: Gallup Global Wellbeing: The Behavioral Economics of GDP Growth (Washington, DC: Gallup Inc., 2010)

over time, how much stress and uncertainty are associated with it, the safety nets available in case of need, as well as how the national income is distributed.[52] And these are just those features of life directly related to the economy; there is an array of social aspects as well that are indirectly related to the economy, such as health, leisure, security and relationships such as peer network, family life, love, and friendship that affect life satisfaction in meaningful ways. So let's be clear: by itself, average income is a misleading measure of well-being and we should not assume that further economic growth will lead to an improvement in our lives if it has not done so up to now. We need to acknowledge and stress that there is much more to life than what money can buy. No wonder that large increases in income have been accompanied by stagnant life satisfaction.

For instance, a job with a higher salary but requiring greater commuting time may well lead to frustration eventually. Conventional analysts might argue that if this were the case, the person would not accept such a job. However, such an argument overlooks the fact that one's attention may be anchored on the salary gain and discount excessively the opaque future stresses. In other words, the salary gain is immediately obvious while the sacrifices of the daily commute, such as missing one's child's Little League game, are not so clear. Hence, the temptation to choose the greater salary (at the expense of intangible future losses) is great and quality of life might well suffer in the long run.[53]

Moreover, the life satisfaction of women relative to that of men has actually been declining in the United States since the 1970s, in spite of the women's liberation movement and in spite of the fact that women's incomes have risen greatly relative to those of men.[54] If absolute income were so important in their utility function, why are today's women not happier than prior generations? Why are people living in Latin America as satisfied with their lives as those in Germany or France or the United States, although their per capita income is one-quarter of ours? In other words, something must be wrong with equating income with living standards, a habit that is deeply anchored in conventional economics.[55] Joseph Stiglitz refers to this fallacy as GNP fetishism.[56]

Our tastes and desires are manipulated by the prevailing culture, influenced by those who have the power to do so. For instance, Christopher Lasch recognized a generation ago that we are developing a collective narcissistic personality disorder "closely linked to self-centeredness."[57] (A narcissist is one who is "excessively preoccupied with issues of personal adequacy, power, prestige and vanity."[58]) Lasch asserted that "the culture of competitive individualism . . . in its decadence has carried the logic of individualism to the extreme of a war of all against all, the pursuit of happiness to the dead end of a narcissistic preoccupation with the self."[59]

We are unable to lead the good life because corporations keep on redefining and repackaging the good life so that it continues to elude us. Corporations cannot profit if we are satisfied with what we have. Hence, the only way to develop a better quality of life is to limit the power of corporations.[60]

Understanding that people are often more sensitive to changes than to absolute levels suggests that we ought to incorporate into utility analysis such factors as habitual levels of consumption. Instead of utility at time t depending solely on present consumption, $c(t)$, we should acknowledge that it also depends on a "reference level," $r(t)$, which, in turn, depends on such factors as past consumption c $(t-1)$, or expectations of future consumption E_t $[c$ $(t+1)]$, or the consumption of peer groups, or of the average level of consumption in the society.[61] Our mind adapts to past consumption levels.[62] Hence, instead of a utility function of the form $u_t(c_t)$, utility should be written in a more general form, $u_t(r_t, c_t)$. This theory illuminates why people went into debt as they tried to keep up with the consumption of the wealthy, whose incomes were actually increasing even as their own income was stagnating or decreasing. So behavior that is not easily understood by conventional theory can be explained if one considers a utility function with a reference level.

In sum, it is important to realize that growth is not the answer to our problems. Growth has not led to improvements in our life satisfaction in the past. Thus, growth should not be our focus, but creating a more equitable distribution of income and building a caring society on the Scandinavian model should be our goal so that an increasing number of our fellow citizens will feel that they are thriving—that they are satisfied with their lives and need not worry where their next paycheck is coming from. The number of people thriving in Denmark is 44 percent higher than the number in the United States (Table 9.1). In order to catch up with the Scandinavian societies we need to realize that additional material goods advocated by Madison Avenue have rapidly diminishing returns. Rather, we need to feel good about ourselves and about our place in society, which we can only achieve if we are healthy (physically and mentally), have financial security with dignity, and nourishing personal relationships.

POVERTY

According to Amartya Sen, poverty is deprivation that makes one incapable of leading "a minimally acceptable life." Our ability to survive depends not only on income but also on entitlements to such programs as food stamps, medical services, or access to food during famines. Poverty is capability deprivation as a consequence of a lack of entitlement to resources or advantages.[63] Starvation occurs when entitlement to food falls below the minimum level for survival.

People in poverty are the losers in the competition for jobs and income. The chances are that poverty has been in their family for several generations and that they grew up in dysfunctional families and neighborhoods where schools were inferior and poverty and crime were endemic.[64] The persistence of poverty in the United States is greater than in European countries. About 42 percent of sons of low-income fathers remained poor in the United States whereas in Denmark only 25 percent did. At the same time, only 8 percent of low-income fathers struck it rich in the United States, while in Denmark 14 percent did.[65] So the idea of exceptional social mobility in the United States is a thing of the past. The information technology (IT) revolution caused people who were not well educated to become redundant and therefore excluded from the labor market. Hence, those who are unable to obtain a decent education lack the means to escape from poverty.

Poverty varies considerably over time and across countries. With around 15 percent, the United States has the highest poverty rate among industrialized countries. Among single mothers the discrepancy is even higher: their poverty rate is 45 percent in the United States compared to 4

Figure 9.7   **Poverty Rate (%) Among Children by Ethnicity**

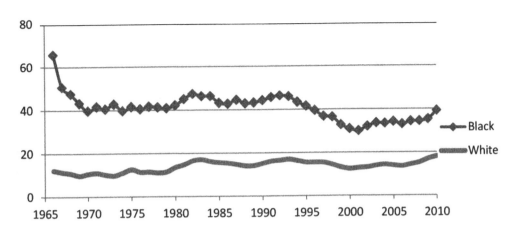

Source: U.S. Department of Commerce, U.S. Census Bureau, Historical People. www.census.gov/hhes/ www/poverty/data/historical/people.html (accessed October 2, 2012)

percent in Sweden, 5 percent in Finland, 13 percent in France, and 20 percent in the Netherlands.[66] Furthermore, in 2011, 46 million people were counted as living in poverty in the United States—up from 30 million in 2006, prior to the meltdown, an astounding increase of 50 percent.[67]

The recession also induced "a large expansion in the share of households with zero or negative net worth from 19 percent to 24 percent."[68] In other words, one-quarter of households own nothing but debt.[69] At the same time, 22 percent of all children in the United States are poor, the highest rate among industrialized countries, but among black children the poverty rate is a disquieting 38 percent (Figure 9.7). Among white children the rate is higher than at any time since statistics begin in the mid-1960s.[70]

INDEBTEDNESS AND THE OBESITY EPIDEMIC

The spread of indebtedness and the spread of obesity are highly correlated in their timing. They have both reached epidemic proportions during the last generation.[71] About two-thirds of the U.S. population is either overweight or obese, that is to say, has an unhealthy body weight.[72] This is a precarious development for the future of our health but is also another clear sign that we—as a society—have lost our ability to take care of ourselves. This is a similar development to our concomitant stupendous increase in consumer debt.[73]

Consumer debt was just 10 percent of U.S. expenditures in 1950 but grew to 20 percent by 1975 and 25 percent by the 1990s.[74] Meanwhile, mortgage debt increased from 40 percent of personal disposable income to above 100 percent. Hence, total personal debt doubled from about half of personal income to about 130 percent. This is a modern form of debt peonage. In my view, the increased prevalence of indebtedness is similar to that of obesity because both reflect the accumulation of an attribute that has good short-run effects but bad long-run ones. Such a prevalent perverse effect could take place only if time-preference is tilted heavily toward the present, that is, the negative future effects are discounted greatly or disregarded entirely. These trends imply that the willpower of the population has weakened and that instant gratification dominates.[75]

Arguably, we did not become like that on our own. Commercial interests spent trillions of dollars to convince us to consume immediately as the sales won't last and to adopt a careless attitude toward the future. What made matters worse, of course, is that government favored business over the public interest so there was insufficient countervailing power to offset this psychological offensive, implying that consumer protection was limited or mostly nonexistent.[76] Under the influence of the food industry, we ate more often outside of the home and when eating at home, we relied far too often on unhealthy prepared foods, often eating them while watching television, which meant that we were not careful about how much we were eating.[77] For instance, there were no advertisements beseeching us to be circumspect, to think of the future, to eat healthy meals at home, to take care of our children's meals, to save and not to borrow, and to be wary of adjustable-rate mortgages.[78] Public education in home economics was all but nonexistent. The prevalence of obesity and of indebtedness should make us aware of the urgent need for consumer protection in order to defend the individual from powerful business interests. Laissez faire and caveat emptor do not always provide for the common good. As Stiglitz suggests: "the invisible hand is often invisible because it is often not there."[79]

CHAPTER SUMMARY

In this chapter we provided examples of the ways in which the application of conventional economic reasoning to real-world problems provides incorrect policy insights. In a perfectly competitive market, in which the labor market is in equilibrium, unions are superfluous, even counterproductive. However, that does not hold in an economy dominated by oligopolistic firms and in which unemployment is an endemic feature of the labor market. In such a market it is useful to consider John Kenneth Galbraith's concept of the countervailing power provided by unions. Once we include the concept of power to set wages and prices, in other words, to abandon the price-taking model, we can understand better why there has been a considerable wedge between increases in productivity and increases in wages over the course of the last three decades. With imperfect competition and with the threat of unemployment, unions no longer cause an increase in unemployment but protect the salaries of workers at the expense of profits. The minimum wage in such a model does not cause unemployment but raises the living standards of the laboring poor.

In addition, we ought to keep in mind that economic policy has ethical facets as well. Without the proper cultural and moral values, markets will not arrive at acceptable prices or an acceptable distribution of income. Basic needs should supersede conspicuous consumption in our value structure, and providing excellent schooling for all children should be a top priority. After all, children are unable to fend for themselves and markets will not provide for them; they have nothing to offer markets except an IOU. There is no rational reason for the steep quality gradient in schools in the country. So a redistributive state with the wisdom to care for the long-term well-being of its members, as well as those yet unborn, is an absolute must for a decent society.

QUESTIONS FOR DISCUSSION

1. Do you think that minimum wage should have kept up with inflation?
2. Have you ever worked for minimum wage?
3. Do you think gas stations should be allowed to raise the price of gasoline during an oil embargo?
4. How should scarce drinking water be rationed during a hurricane?
5. Do you think unions empower workers to obtain a living wage?

6. Why don't CEOs need unions?

7. With so many poor people not voting, it is little wonder that their interests are not represented in government. Discuss.

8. Do you think there should be equal pay for equal work for women? For African Americans?

9. Do you think that part-time workers should receive the same wage per hour as full-time workers doing the same work?

10. Would a basketball player play fewer games if his tax rate were higher? Would he change occupations?

11. How much utility does $1,000 give you?

12. Are you better off than your father or mother was at your age? Would they want to change places with you?

NOTES

1. John Schmitt, "Why Does the Minimum Wage Have No Discernible Effect on Employment?" Center for Economic and Policy Research, February 2013.

2. The minimum wage in San Francisco was $10.55 an hour in 2013.

3. Assuming an upward-sloping supply curve, and assuming that all workers receive the same wage.

4. Example: Suppose the monopsonistic wage is $1.00 per hour and the firm employs 10 workers at this wage. Suppose, furthermore, that in order to increase the number of employees to 11 the firm would have to increase the wage to $1.10 per hour. That would mean that the additional worker would cost $1.10 plus $1.00 = (10*0.10), or $2.10 in total, because the firm would have to raise the wages of all those who are already employed in the firm by $0.10 per hour if discrimination is not possible. If the last worker only produces $2.00 in value then it would not be in the firm's interest to hire the eleventh worker. However, if the firm had to pay a minimum of $1.10 per hour anyway, then it would be in its interest to hire the eleventh worker because she costs only $1.10, which is less than the $2.00 the eleventh worker produces, so the firm would earn a profit of $0.90 on her labor.

5. In the words of Franklin Roosevelt, "Liberty requires opportunity to make a living—a living decent according to the standard of the time, a living which gives man not only enough to live by, but something to live for." Franklin D. Roosevelt, "Speech before the 1936 Democratic National Convention" (Philadelphia, PA, June 27, 1936).

6. U.S. Department of Commerce, United States Census Bureau, "Poverty Thresholds 2009."

7. U.S. Department of Labor, Bureau of Labor Statistics, "Labor Force Statistics from the Current Population Survey: Characteristics of Minimum Wage Workers: 2010," last modified March 9, 2011.

8. Richard Sutch, "The Unexpected Long-Run Impact of the Minimum Wage: An Educational Cascade," NBER Working Paper No. 16355, September 2010.

9. Hugh Rockoff, *Drastic Measures: A History of Wage and Price Controls in the United States* (Cambridge, UK: Cambridge University Press, 2004).

10. A monopolist drug maker is charging $28,000 for a vial of medication that cost $1,650 in 2007 and costs just $300 to produce. Andrew Pollock, "Questcor Finds Profits, at $28,000 a Vial," *The New York Times,* December 29, 2012.

11. Paul Samuelson and William Nordhaus, *Economics,* 19th ed. (New York: McGraw-Hill, 2009), p. 260.

12. Erin Hatton, "The Rise of the Permanent Temp Economy," *The New York Times,* January 26, 2013.

13. Jacob Hacker and Paul Pierson, *Winner-Take-All Politics: How Washington Made the Rich Richer—and Turned Its Back on the Middle Class* (New York: Simon & Schuster, 2010).

14. Martin Gilens, *Affluence and Influence: Economic Inequality and Political Power in America* (Princeton, NJ: Princeton University Press, 2012).

15. Demos, "Stacked Deck: How the Dominance of Politics by the Affluent & Business Undermines Economic Mobility in America."

16. Simon Gerard, "Apple CEO Tim Cook Made $378 Million in 2011," Celebrity Networth, January 14, 2012.

17. David Segal, "Apple's Retail Army, Long on Loyalty But Short on Pay," *The New York Times,* June 23, 2012.

18. Susan Fleck, John Glaser, and Shawn Sprague, "The Compensation-Productivity Gap: A Visual Essay," *Monthly Labor Review* 134 (2011) 1: 57–69.

19. Richard P. McIntyre, *Are Worker Rights Human Rights?* (Ann Arbor: University of Michigan Press, 2008).

20. U.S. Department of Labor, Bureau of Labor Statistics, "Labor Force Statistics from the Current Population Survey: Access to Historical Data for the Tables of the Union Membership News Release," last modified June 21, 2007.

21. "Strong, responsible unions are essential to industrial fair play. Without them the labor bargain is wholly one-sided. The parties to the labor contract must be nearly equal in strength if justice is to be worked out, and this means that the workers must be organized and that their organizations must be recognized by employers as a condition precedent to industrial peace." Cited in Osmond Kessler Fraenkel and Clarence Martin Lewis, eds., *The Curse of Bigness: Miscellaneous Papers of Louis D. Brandeis* (Port Washington, NY: Kennikat Press, 1965), p. 43.

22. Naomi Mannino, "Survey: Nearly Half Have No Emergency Savings," Always Easy Finance, October 9, 2012.

23. "Nondiscriminating firms could enter the market, undercut the costs and prices of the discriminating firms by hiring mainly brown-eyed workers, and drive the discriminating firms out of business." Samuelson and Nordhaus, *Economics,* p. 262. Note that they assert that they "could" enter the market, but of course that does not mean that they, in fact, will and ameliorate the injustice.

24. Wikipedia contributors, "Greensboro Sit-Ins," *Wikipedia: The Free Encyclopedia.*

25. Famines are special cases analyzed in detail in the Amartya Sen classic *Poverty and Famines: An Essay on Entitlement and Deprivation* (Oxford: Oxford University Press, 1981).

26. "The top 5 percent in income earners—those households earning $210,000 or more—account for about one-third of consumer outlays." Motoko Rich, "Wealthy Reduce Buying in a Blow to the Recovery," *The New York Times,* July 16, 2010.

27. Karen Christopher, "Welfare State Regimes and Mothers' Poverty," *Social Politics* 9 (2002): 60–86.

28. Jenny Anderson, "Wall Street Winners Get Billion-Dollar Paydays," *The New York Times,* April 16, 2008.

29. By "social fortune" he means the family in which one is born, and by the "natural lottery" he means the accident of being born with certain talents. John Rawls, "Some Reasons for the Maximin Criterion," *American Economic Review* 64 (1974) 2: 141–146.

30. John Rawls, *A Theory of Justice* (Cambridge, MA: Harvard University Press, 1971).

31. Malcolm Gladwell, *Outliers: The Story of Success* (New York: Little, Brown, 2008).

32. Warren Buffett, "Stop Coddling the Super-Rich," *The New York Times,* August 14, 2011.

33. "Empirical evidence . . . suggests that the damage of taxes on work effort is limited. . . . Most studies find that taxes have only a small impact on labor effort for middle-income and high-income workers." Samuelson and Nordhaus, *Economics,* 19th ed., p. 333.

34. Together their wealth adds up to $1.3 trillion. "In Pictures: Richest 25 American Billionaires," *Forbes,* October 3, 2010.

35. Peter Lindert, *Growing Public,* vol. 1, *Social Spending and Economic Growth Since the Eighteenth Century* (Cambridge, UK: Cambridge University Press, 2004).

36. Wikipedia contributors, "Household Income in the United States," *Wikipedia: The Free Encyclopedia;* Erik Eckholm, "Recession Raises Poverty Rate to a 15-Year High," *The New York Times,* September 16, 2010. See also James Kenneth Galbraith, *Created Unequal: The Crisis in American Pay* (Chicago: University of Chicago Press, 2000).

37. In the extreme, frustration can lead to killing rampages, which have increased over time. Christine Haughney and Nate Schweber, "A Bumpy Life Ends in a Fatal Rampage," *The New York Times,* August 30, 2010.

38. U.S. Department of Labor, Bureau of Labor Statistics, "Current Employment Statistics-CES (National): Technical Notes to Establishment Survey Data," last modified May 8, 2012.

39. Robert H. Frank, *Luxury Fever: Why Money Fails to Satisfy in an Era of Excess* (New York: The Free Press, 1999).

40. The insecurity of markets induces anxiety about one's status.

41. Bureau of Labor Statistics, "Occupational Employment Statistics."

42. Barbara Ehrenreich, *Bait and Switch: The (Futile) Pursuit of the American Dream* (New York: Metropolitan Books, 2005).

43. Zachary A. Saltis, "The Economic Consequences of Declining Real Wages in the United States, 1970–2010," unpublished PhD dissertation, University of Manitoba (2011).

44. Peter C. Whybrow, "Dangerously Addictive: Why We Are Biologically Ill-Suited to the Riches of Modern America," *The Chronicle of Higher Education,* March 13, 2009.

45. Juliet B. Schor, *The Overworked American: The Unexpected Decline of Leisure* (New York: Basic Books, 1993).

46. Frank, *Luxury Fever*; Bruno Frey and Alois Stutzer, *Happiness and Economics* (Princeton, NJ: Princeton University Press, 2002); Michael Marmot, *The Status Syndrome: How Social Standing Affects Our Health and Longevity* (London: Bloomsbury Press, 2004); Richard Layard, *Happiness: Lessons from a New Science* (New York: Penguin Press, 2005).

47. Robert H. Frank, "How Not to Buy Happiness," *Dædalus* 133 (2004) 2: 69–79.

48. Richard Easterlin, "Does Economic Growth Improve the Human Lot?" in *Nations and Households in Economic Growth: Essays in Honor of Moses Abramovitz,* ed. Paul David and Melvin Reder (New York: Academic Press, 1974); Tibor Scitovsky argued similarly in *The Joyless Economy: An Inquiry into Human Satisfaction and Consumer Dissatisfaction* (Oxford: Oxford University Press, 1976). See also Bruno S. Frey and Alois Stutzer, "What Can Economists Learn from Happiness Research?" *Journal of Economic Literature,* 40 (2002) 2: 402–435.

49. John Helliwell, Richard Layard, and Jeffrey Sachs, "World Happiness Report, 2012," p. 3.

50. Whybrow, "Dangerously Addictive."

51. Charles Jones and Peter Klenow, "Beyond GDP? Welfare Across Countries and Time," NBER Working Paper No. 16352, September 2010; "Robert F. Kennedy Challenges Gross Domestic Product," YouTube video, posted by "colinatpyramid," September 11, 2008.

52. An excellent introduction to the difficulties and challenges of modern life can be found in Elizabeth Warren, "The Coming Collapse of the Middle Class: Higher Risks, Lower Rewards, and a Shrinking Safety Net," YouTube video, posted by "UCtelevision," January 31, 2008. Elizabeth Warren, "The Vanishing Middle Class," in *Ending Poverty in America: How to Restore the American Dream,* ed. John Edwards, Marion Crain, and Arne L. Kalleberg (New York: The New Press, 2007).

53. "[P]eople are happier when they spend money on experiences instead of material objects, when they relish what they plan to buy long before they buy it, and when they stop trying to outdo the Joneses." Stephanie Rosenbloom, "But Will It Make You Happy?" *The New York Times,* August 7, 2010.

54. Betsey Stevenson and Justin Wolfers, "The Paradox of Declining Female Happiness," *American Economic Journal: Economic Policy* 1 (2009) 2: 190–225.

55. Rosenbloom, "But Will It Make You Happy"; Amartya Sen, "Mortality as an Indicator of Economic Success and Failure," *Economic Journal* 108 (1998) 446: 1–25.

56. I am not alone: see Joseph Stiglitz, "GDP Fetishism," *Project Syndicate,* September 7, 2009, available at www.project-syndicate.org/commentary/gdp-fetishism.

57. Christopher Lasch, *The Culture of Narcissism: American Life in an Age of Diminishing Expectations* (New York: W.W. Norton, 1979), p. xv.

58. Wikipedia contributors, " Narcissistic Personality Disorder," *Wikipedia: The Free Encyclopedia.*

59. Lasch, *Culture of Narcissism*, p. xv.

60. Julie Ray, "High Wellbeing Eludes the Masses in Most Countries Worldwide," *Gallup,* April 19, 2011.

61. Or past expectation of current consumption $E_{t-1}[c(t)]$.

62. This is also called habituation.

63. Amartya Sen, "The Possibility of Social Choice," *American Economic Review* 89 (1999): 178–215, at pp. 194–195.

64. Barbara Ehrenreich, *Nickel and Dimed: On (Not) Getting By in America* (New York: Metropolitan Books, 2001).

65. Markus Jäntti, Bernt Bratsberg, Knut Røed, Oddbjørn Raaum, Robin Naylor, Eva Österbacka, Anders Björklund, and Tor Eriksson, "American Exceptionalism in a New Light: A Comparison of Intergenerational Earnings Mobility in the Nordic Countries, the United Kingdom and the United States," IZA Discussion Paper No. 1938, January 2006, p. 33.

66. Christopher, "Welfare State Regimes."

67. U.S. Department of Commerce, United States Census Bureau, Table 3, People in Poverty by Selected Characteristics: 2010 and 2011.

68. Edward N. Wolff, "Recent Trends in Household Wealth in the United States: Rising Debt and the Middle-Class Squeeze—an Update to 2007," Levy Economics Institute of Bard College Working Paper No. 589, March 2010.

69. In 2010, 6.8 million people (5 percent of the labor force) had to work two jobs in order to make ends meet. U.S. Department of Labor, Bureau of Labor Statistics, Data Retrieval: Labor Force Statistics (CPS), Table A-16.

70. Among Hispanic children it is 32 percent. Suzanne Macartney, "Child Poverty in the United States 2009 and 2010: Selected Race Groups and Hispanic Origin," *American Community Survey Briefs*, U.S. Census Bureau, November 2011.

71. Eric Schlosser, *Fast Food Nation: The Dark Side of the All-American Meal* (New York: Harper Perennial, 2002).

72. John Komlos and Marek Brabec, "The Trend of BMI Values of US Adults by Deciles, Birth Cohorts 1882–1986 Stratified by Gender and Ethnicity," *Economics and Human Biology* 9 (2011) 3: 234–250.

73. Juliet B. Schor, *The Overspent American: Why We Want What We Don't Need* (New York: Harper Perennial, 1999).

74. "Consumer Spending," Muhlenkamp & Company, Inc.

75. "Brain systems of immediate reward were a vital survival adaptation millennia ago, when finding a fruit tree was a rare delight and dinner had a habit of running away or flying out of reach. But living now in relative abundance, when the whole world is a shopping mall and our appetites are no longer constrained by limited resources, our craving for reward—be that for money, the fat and sugar of fast food, or for the novel gadgetry of modern technology—has become a liability and a hunger that has no bounds. Our nature has no built-in braking system. More is never enough." Whybrow, "Dangerously Addictive."

76. Gary Ruskin and Juliet Schor, "The Junk Food Nation," *The Nation,* August 29, 2005.

77. "The per-capita number of fast-food restaurants doubled between 1972 and 1997," and the calories available for consumption increased by some 20 percent in the late 1980s and 1990s. Shin-Yi Chou, Inas Rashad, and Michael Grossman, "Fast-Food Restaurant Advertising on Television and Its Influence on Childhood Obesity," *Journal of Law and Economics* 51 (2008): 599–618, at p. 568.

78. The share of total food expenditures spent on eating outside of the home increased from 24 percent in 1950 to 45 percent in 1995. Avner Offer, *The Challenge of Affluence: Self-Control and Well-Being in the USA and Britain Since 1950* (Oxford: Oxford University Press, 2001).

79. Joseph Stiglitz, "Doctor of Honoris Causa Ceremony Speech," University of the Basque Country, Bilbao, Spain, May 23, 2006 (accessed May 7, 2012). See also his Nobel Prize lecture: Joseph Stiglitz, "Information and the Change in the Paradigm in Economics," Stockholm University, Aula Magna, December 8, 2001. Joseph Stiglitz, *Making Globalization Work* (New York: W.W. Norton, 2006); Joseph Stiglitz, *The Roaring Nineties* (New York: W.W. Norton, 2003).

PART IV

REAL-WORLD MACROECONOMICS

10

WHAT IS MACROECONOMICS?

In the prior chapters we analyzed microeconomic issues—economics considered from the bottom up, from the point of view of individual consumers and producers. We now turn to the opposite end of the telescope and explore a bird's-eye view of the economy that considers aggregate aspects of economic activity such as gross national product (GNP), or the stock of money. Instead of analyzing individual demand in a market or the output of a firm, we now consider economy-wide aggregates such as total demand in all the individual markets combined or total output of an economy. So our perspective is now broader than in earlier chapters.

KEYNES THE SAVIOR

John Maynard Keynes is the father of modern macroeconomics. The revolution he sparked in the 1930s saved the intellectual foundations of capitalism from the competing ideologies of fascism and Marxism by turning squarely against his neoclassical forerunners. His genius was to be revolutionary in thought while maintaining the basic structure of democratic capitalism, that is, he upheld two basic pillars of the established order: private property and the free market with its price system. His basic insight was that with massive persistent unemployment in the industrialized world in the 1930s, it was obvious that the free market was not self-regulating and it would be ludicrous to continue to rely on wishful thinking for the economy to be self-correcting, as the classical economists unrelentingly maintained. There were too many impediments preventing the simple feedback mechanisms—which were supposed to reinstate equilibrium—from eliminating the "general glut."

The obstacles to the establishment of a new macroeconomic equilibrium included long-term contracts such as mortgages and leases, which bound individuals and firms to a series of payments in nominal terms. They were unable to void such commitments, and as prices declined the real value of these payments ballooned. Deflation—a decline in the general price level—meant that debt became a bigger burden to households and a drag on the economy as people in debt had less purchasing power for durable goods, exacerbating the downturn. The diminution in aggregate demand meant that prices would decline further, thereby establishing a vicious circle that extinguished the momentum of economic growth.

In addition, Keynes fundamentally rejected the view that the participants in the market were rational utility maximizers. Rather, both investors and consumers were subject to herding behavior, so-called "animal spirits"; that is to say, they were prone to psychological swings of optimism and pessimism. In addition, they were copying what others were doing, so these mood swings took on widespread proportions.[1] Keynes thought that it was, therefore, fallacious to depict aggregate demand as a stable function of prices. Rather, effective demand was far from stable, as the Great Recession

177

Figure 10.1 **U.S. Consumer Confidence Index, 1996 = 100**

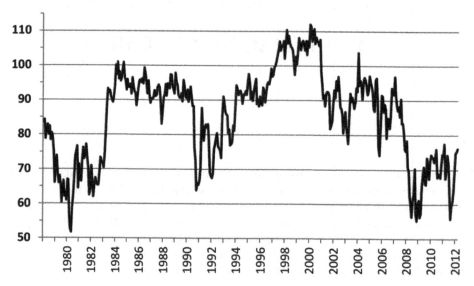

Source: Thomson Reuters, University of Michigan, "Surveys of Consumers," www.sca.isr.umich.edu/ (accessed October 21, 2012)

has just amply demonstrated. Consumer confidence and expectations could fluctuate with considerable volatility and have been near historical lows since the recession began (Figure 10.1).[2]

To be sure, the demand for necessities (such as coffee) does not fluctuate due to animal spirits, but the demand for business investments and big-ticket items such as furniture, automobiles, and houses does (Figure 10.2). For instance, the demand for automobiles declined from 4.5 million units to 1.1 million units in 1932, but even in "normal" times demand can be quite volatile: from 7.9 million units in 1955 to 4.5 million units in 1958 (Figure 10.3).

Expectations also played a role in aggregate demand: as long as prices were likely to decrease, consumers would not buy expensive items but would wait instead for prices to stop falling. Moreover, wages were inflexible downward for psychological reasons. Workers were accustomed to their nominal income and declining wages were resisted vehemently and often enough violently. After all, many contracts including rents and mortgages were denominated in nominal terms and a decline in nominal wages would have meant that they would be unable to meet those commitments. Yet, constant nominal wages and a decline in the price level meant that real wages—at least of those employed—actually increased at a time when they should have been declining, thereby contributing to ominous levels of unemployment. In short, the economic system was not as flexible as neoclassical economists assumed and a new equilibrium would not be easily attained at a lower level of prices. Thus, aggregate demand could remain indefinitely below full-employment level. Furthermore, these problems would not remain confined to the economic realm. People are more than statistics, and the hungry and destitute threatened the stability of the system and might even overturn it as in Russia, Germany, and Italy. In other words, unemployment endangered political stability: the social order would unravel faster than the economic system would repair itself.[3] Politics and economics were intertwined.

Keynes was among the few perspicacious enough to realize that such a situation threatened the very foundations of democracy and would change it in unrecognizable ways unless some

Figure 10.2   **Index of Expenditures on Some Items During the Great Depression**

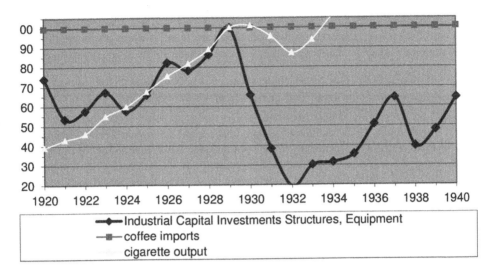

Figure 10.3   **Automobile Production in the United States, 1900–1970**

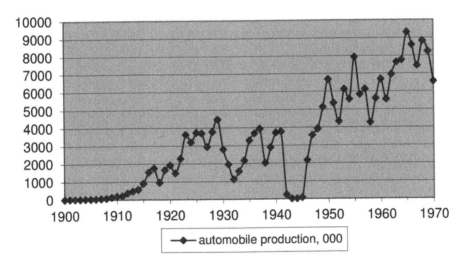

dramatic democratic reforms were introduced into the economic realm. His solution was amazingly straightforward: instead of relying on wishful thinking and letting the market flounder until perhaps it would find a new equilibrium, all one had to do was to increase government expenditures and a new equilibrium would be established in short order. When the private sector fails to spend enough and a wide gap exists between actual and potential output, the public sector should make up the difference through deficit spending. Public spending—particularly on much-needed infrastructure—would have a magnified impact through the multiplier: the initial beneficiaries of the government purchases would also spend their income and, in turn, would increase the income of others. This was a simple but brilliant and novel insight: the multiplicative effects were crucial in breaking out of the downward spiral of unemployment and deflation, thereby reestablishing a new full-employment equilibrium. It was also bold for abandoning the classical framework and not relying on the private sector to realign through price and wage adjustments. The system was so out of kilter that, left to themselves, markets were unable to find a new equilibrium or at least not quickly enough to matter to the lives of most people suffering in the throes of the Great Depression.

Thus, with the help of what later became known as fiscal policy, the markets could adjust to new full-employment equilibrium. It would be established not through flexible prices and wages but through the increase in effective demand through public spending (combined with the salutary effect of the multiplier). The economic system created by this new activist government would be a more humane form of capitalism, which—unlike Marxism—retained private property rights as well as the social pecking order but would crucially alleviate the scourge of unemployment and the misery and political instability associated with it. These basic but brilliant insights made Keynes one of the greatest economists of all time.

Another major Keynesian innovation was the concept of the liquidity trap. Monetary policy affects aggregate output mainly through the interest rate, which in turn directly affects investment decisions. However, the interest rate cannot be lowered below zero, so at that point monetary policy becomes ineffective. The discontinuity at zero rate of interest is crucial insofar as only fiscal policy can impact aggregate demand in that situation. This was precisely the predicament in the Depression of the 1930s; it manifested itself again after a very long hiatus during Japan's "lost decade" of the 1990s and again during the Great Recession of 2008. Monetary policy has been ineffective, although Fed chairman Ben Bernanke increased the monetary base by a factor of four: to no avail. Bernanke's leaning against the Keynesian liquidity trap was mere wishful thinking—like pushing on a string.

To be sure, one of the main functions of central banks is to be the lender of last resort at a time of panic by providing liquidity to solvent banks. But most of the banks supported by the Fed were insolvent. They were bailed out because they were deemed too big to fail, meaning their failure would have too many repercussions in the economy. Lehman Brothers was the only bank that was allowed to go bankrupt. The rest of the big banks were essentially insolvent and would have had to declare bankruptcy had the government not injected trillions of dollars into the financial system. Ben Bernanke is running an experiment with the economy, because he is propping up a fragile system with an unprecedented amount of money creation. It remains an open question if the stability of the system can be maintained under such circumstances in the long run. The prospects are uncertain. In any event, it should be obvious that Schumpeter's model of creative destruction was not allowed to run its course. That implies that inefficient firms were maintained artificially and saved from bankruptcy. The Paulson-Bernanke-Geithner bailout will in all likelihood yet come back to haunt us.

NEOCLASSICAL SYNTHESIS

After World War II, Keynesian economics became dominant through the neoclassical synthesis popularized by Paul Samuelson. The synthesis was the basis of mainstream economics between circa 1950 and 1980 and arbitrarily combined the Keynesian macroeconomic framework with neoclassical microeconomic concepts by assuming the existence of *Homo economicus* at the microeconomic level but not at the aggregate macroeconomic level. In this framework, individuals are themselves rational (and maximize utility) but at the aggregate level markets do not adjust as smoothly as in the neoclassical model.[4] For instance, the price of labor is not as flexible as prices in the product market.

As a consequence, there can be involuntary unemployment in the Keynesian model: wages fail to adjust within the relevant time frame as they would in the standard demand and supply model.

One of the key ideas of Keynesian macroeconomics was the "Phillips curve," which postulated that there was a tradeoff between unemployment and inflation.[5] When inflation increased unemployment would decrease and when inflation decreased unemployment would increase. According to this theory, as prices rose, the real wages of workers fell but they were willing to continue to work for the same nominal wage because they focused on the nominal amounts and were oblivious to the price index. This "money illusion" benefited firms, because they were receiving higher prices for their products but their wages bill remained unchanged. Thus, their profits increased, inducing them to hire more workers. Wages in the form of money payments in the present were thought to have a larger weight in workers' decisions than a price index based on thousands of products that has not yet been calculated. However, it should have been clear that this could only work in the short run and—as Milton Friedman famously and correctly argued—money illusion could not go on forever, especially in unionized sectors. Sooner or later, workers would realize that their real wages were eroding and therefore would demand higher nominal wages, thereby erasing firms' profits. Inflation cannot create jobs permanently by itself.

This is exactly what happened in the 1970s when an extended period of inflation was accompanied by unemployment and a period of "stagflation." This was seen as a major conundrum for Keynesian principles, so Keynesian policies fell out of favor and the dominance of neoclassical macroeconomics began.

THE MONETARIST COUNTERREVOLUTION

There were five elements in Keynes's theory that were utter anathema to neoclassical economists and provoked a monetarist backlash beginning in the 1970s, with Milton Friedman leading the charge. The key objections were that (a) Keynes's theory was not conceived (from the bottom up) on classical microfoundations, that is, it was not based on standard models of rational utility-maximizing agents and profit-maximizing firms; (b) it prescribed too large a role for government, thereby limiting individual freedom; (c) it suggested that the amount of money mattered to aggregate output whereas the classical school contended that money played a passive role by determining only the price level but not real output; (d) it assumed that people were not always rational, that consumption could be influenced by their optimistic or pessimistic moods; and (e) it was not a perfectly competitive equilibrium model: markets existed which included wages that did not adjust sufficiently to demand conditions.

While the Keynesians were analyzing aggregate economic behavior starting with economy-wide variables such as total output, unemployment rate, and aggregate demand, Keynes's detractors were intent on beginning the analysis by aggregating these variables from the bottom up. The latter group—the real-business-cycle school—begins their inquiry by specifying standard microeconomic foundations of aggregate behavior. In order to accomplish that, they use rational utility-maximizing rules of individual behavior that are summed up in order to obtain the desired aggregate variables and thereby explain macroeconomic phenomena. This implies also that they assume that everyone in the society can be represented by a single person—an odd assumption to make for those who assert in other sections of their text that utility functions cannot be compared because everyone is different. In any event, as far as macroeconomics is concerned everyone is supposed to be the same.

For several decades before the Meltdown of 2008, mainstream macroeconomics has been dominated by this school. However, the school has shown the utter emptiness of its theories by having absolutely nothing relevant to say about the current lingering crisis. Its proponents neither warned us of the coming of the crisis nor are they now able to prescribe remedies on how to extricate ourselves from it, because such crises are not supposed to occur in their framework.

According to their models, the economy and all of its component markets are always and everywhere in perfect equilibrium except if technological change surprises people. Otherwise, aggregate demand equals aggregate supply and prices act to bring the two into line. There is no unemployment by definition—or more accurately, no "involuntary" unemployment—just random changes in some real variables such as technology that at times perturb the simple system. According to their logic, some can choose not to work because they prefer to watch television than flip hamburgers at McDonald's, but that is their choice.

This is just an indication that macroeconomics has been dominated by radicals determined to conceptualize the aggregate economy from the point of view of a stereotype, an ideal abstraction called the "representative agent." They are convinced that methodological individualism is the right way to analyze the macroeconomy and contend that the representative agent—a *Homo economicus*—is the essential unit of analysis rather than higher-level units such as society as a whole.[6]

However, such models defy common sense. Every person is unique, and no one can possibly represent the 308 million people in the U.S. economy.[7] There is no discussion of how an average person is to be conceived among them. It is just assumed that she/he exists. One wonders in vain what the gender, age, ethnicity, personality, social class, occupation, education, provenance, wealth, and IQ of that representative agent is. The adherents of the real-business-cycle models refuse to contemplate the complexity and heterogeneous nature of the modern economy. Instead, they assert with excessive self-confidence that "economists and the agents they are modeling should be placed on an equal footing: the agents in the model should be able to forecast and profit-maximize and utility-maximize as well as the economist . . . who constructed the model."[8] In other words, the high school dropout with an IQ of 85 from a dysfunctional neighborhood can forecast as well as the academic economist with an IQ of 130 working on a high-speed computer. It takes a lot of hubris to build an axiomatic framework around such propositions.

Another major shortcoming of these models is that they do not allow for interaction effects among people, which, according to Keynesians, are the key to understanding macroeconomics. Anyone who has been in a crowd or observed group behavior must know well that we act differently alone than when we are in a group. So such models exclude, for instance, the "animal spirits," the contagious and dominant feeling of optimism or pessimism that governs so many of our investment and consumption decisions.[9] The analysis of macroeconomic phenomena that operates as though society were merely a collection of identical individuals is known as the "fallacy of composition," or the "aggregation problem." What is true for the part is not necessarily true of the whole. Even if all individuals were rational, one should not infer that their collective behavior in the society is also rational. Hence, approaching macroeconomics from the point of view of the individual is a nonstarter. The analogy from physics is that classical mechanics applies to the world as long as the domain is restricted to large objects and these do not approach the speed of light. However, at the subatomic level, where particles approach the speed of light, those laws no longer hold. There is a regime change so that new laws take effect. Similarly, in economics, we ought not to assume that the society is merely an aggregation of its constituent parts because we would be overlooking important effects of interaction, which matters a lot.

A MACROECONOMIC POLICY VOID

As a consequence of the above ideological schism, macroeconomics is in intellectual disarray. It has been for some time, but the Meltdown of 2008 accentuated the divide among competing schools of thought and demonstrated vividly that neither side has the effective policy instruments to allay the deep anxiety in the population.

The utter inadequacy of these theories is illustrated vividly by the news conference held at Princeton University to honor Christopher Sims and Thomas Sargent who had just received the 2011 Nobel Prize for their work on macroeconomics.[10] A reporter asked them their "opinion about what the government has done so far in the United States to support the economy. If you think it has been appropriate. How can we actually support the economy, create jobs? You know . . . those questions everybody [is] asking themselves." Their response, after a prolonged nervous laughter during which the two scholars looked at each other seemingly amused, indicated all too clearly that the real-business-cycle school was clueless about the application of economic policy off the blackboard. Sims finally hesitantly opined, "I think part of the point of this prize and the area that we work in is that answers to questions like that require careful thinking, a lot of data analysis, and that the answers are not likely to be simple. So that asking Tom and me for answers off the top of our heads to these questions is umn . . . You shouldn't expect much uh from us [Laughter]."[11] To which Sargent boldly added: 'I don't have much to add to that . . . may be . . . I was hoping you'd ask me about Europe [Laughter]."

Great fun! Four years into the most severe economic crisis in 80 years, two Nobel Prize–winning macroeconomists had not yet had enough time to think about solutions to the problems confronting the nation and were utterly unable to respond cogently and coherently "from the top of their heads." They had nothing substantial to say. They were lost outside of the classroom. Instead, the best they could do is to trivialize a crucial and very serious question. I think that is indicative of the confused state of macroeconomics at the beginning of the twenty-first century at a time when Europe and the United States are contending with burgeoning government debt, very high levels of unemployment (Figure 10.4), and a volatile economy for which neither side of the economic debate has convincingly constructive antidotes.[12] While Keynesian policies made a brief comeback during the early phases of the 2008 crisis, they turned out to be politically unsustainable and fell out of favor yet again. The real-business-cycle school is silent. What is left is Ben Bernanke's printing press and a lot of wishful thinking; what Paul Krugman often calls voodoo economics.[13]

The deep crisis of macroeconomics is mirrored in the helplessness of elected officials. Only a handful of countries with a more prudent leadership are able to weather the storm without excessive problems. Government debt as a percentage of gross domestic product (GDP) is small in Australia (11 percent), Switzerland (20 percent), Norway (26 percent), New Zealand (31 percent), South Korea (32 percent), Sweden (34 percent), and Canada (36 percent).[14] In contrast, the U.S. federal debt has risen to 75 percent of GDP, the highest level since the end of World War II, and the prognosis is unpleasant.[15] It is most likely that we have entered a Japanese-style "lost decade" at a high level of average income.

So we need to think about new macroeconomic perspectives. The German or Swiss model of capitalism might well be a good place to start thinking about a new form of Keynesianism for our time, as their economies are characterized by the virtues of discipline, thrift, and precision, with a sprinkling of the old-fashioned Protestant ethic.[16] Unemployment there is just 5 percent. Instant gratification, greed, debt, and 1930s-style Keynesianism will not be able to provide the socioeconomic and political stability that we hope for.

CHAPTER SUMMARY

Keynesian macroeconomics was born as an antidote to the misery of the Great Depression. Its prescription was straightforward: if aggregate demand is insufficient to provide work for all because

Figure 10.4 **Unemployment Rate, 2011**

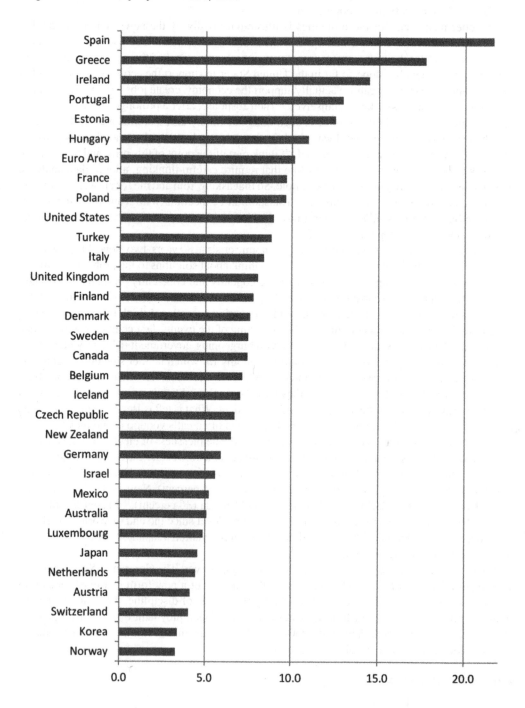

private consumption is low and investment is too low then the only institution that remains to save the day is the government. The government can borrow and spend and thereby increase aggregate demand and put people back to work. But this policy instrument was abhorred by those who feared governments in their subconscious because of their fear of Nazism and Fascism and Communism and Socialism. The rational side of their mind preferred unfettered Capitalism because they were insensitive to evidence contradicting their intuition: they were unwilling to admit that the free labor market is incapable of providing jobs for everyone so that unemployment becomes chronic. In addition, they were not capable of seeing examples of governments in Denmark and Norway, and Sweden and The Netherlands, and Finland and Switzerland which were not based on totalitarian principles yet created institutions that guided the markets in order to provide higher quality of life to their citizens. In sum, macroeconomics is basically in intellectual disarray; it is incoherent with too many competing schools of thought and does not provide effective guidance as a policy tool.[17] As a consequence, we are trapped by our ideologies and unconscious biases unable to solve the considerable challenges posed by the Great Recession.

QUESTIONS FOR DISCUSSION

1. What was Keynes's contribution to economics?
2. Did Keynes believe that people were rational?
3. What was his solution to the Great Depression?
4. Why does deflation pose difficulties for the economy?
5. Who is threatened most by deflation?
6. What is the implication of Keynes's notion of "animal spirits"?
7. What is the role of expectations in the formation of aggregate demand?
8. What is the multiplier and the liquidity trap and how do they work?
9. What is the neo-classical synthesis?
10. What is the Phillips curve and what explains it?
11. What are the assumptions of the real-business-cycle school of macroeconomics?
12. Which school of macroeconomics has better policy recommendations in your opinion?
13. If you were a politician, do you think you would advocate Keynesian countercyclical fiscal policy?

NOTES

1. In Keynes's own words, "Even apart from the instability due to speculation, there is the instability due to the characteristic of human nature that a large proportion of our . . . activities depend on spontaneous optimism . . . Most, probably, . . . our decisions to do something . . . [are] the result of animal spirits—a spontaneous urge to action rather than inaction. . . ." John Maynard Keynes, *The General Theory of Employment, Interest and Money* (London: Macmillan, 1936), 161–162.

2. Just ask Richard Wagoner, CEO of General Motors at the time when the government had to bail it out before it went bankrupt.

3. There are two murders per day in places of work in the United States. "[V]iolent workers today are triggered by losing their jobs. . . ." Dan Fastenberg, "Workplace Violence: Is the Recession Inspiring Worker Rage?" AOL Jobs, August 3, 2012. Reuters, "Workplace Shooting Leaves 5 Dead in Minnesota," AOL Jobs, September 28, 2012.

4. Bruce C. Greenwald and Joseph Stiglitz, "Externalities in Economies with Imperfect Information and Incomplete Markets," *Quarterly Journal of Economics* 101 (1986): 229–264.

5. Irving Fisher, "A Statistical Relation Between Unemployment and Price Changes," *International Labour Review* 13 (1926) 6: 785–792; reprinted in the *Journal of Political Economy* 81 (1973) 2: 496–502.

6. George Akerlof, "Behavioral Macroeconomics and Macroeconomic Behavior," *American Economic Review* 92 (2002) 3: 411–433.

7. Christopher Carroll writes, "Larry Summers's remark (quoted by Robert Waldmann) that the day when economists first started to think that asset prices should be explained by the characteristics of a representative agent's utility function was not a particularly good day for economic science." Christopher D. Carroll, "Punter of Last Resort," VoxEu, March 13, 2009.

8. Thomas J. Sargent, *Bounded Rationality in Macroeconomics* (Oxford: Oxford University Press, 2010), 21.

9. George A. Akerlof and Robert J. Shiller, *Animal Spirits: How Human Psychology Drives the Economy, and Why It Matters for Global Capitalism* (Princeton, NJ: Princeton University Press, 2009).

10. "Princeton News Conference with Nobel Prize in Economics Winners," YouTube video, 53:25, posted by "princetonuniversity," October 10, 2011.

11. To which he added the commonplace observation: "My own view is that what we ought to do is the kind of thing that Chairman Ben Bernanke urged the U.S. government to do: make good long-run plans for resolving our budget difficulties without imposing severe fiscal stringency in the short run and accommodating monetary policy is a good idea. But these are not very original ideas." Ibid.

12. Unemployment among 16-to-24-year-olds in the United States is 16 percent, in the UK it is 20 percent, and in the EU (outside of Germany) it is 31 percent. Floyd Norris, "Recovery in Germany Is Faster than Elsewhere" *The New York Times,* May 10, 2013.

13. Paul Krugman, "Ludicrous and Cruel," *The New York Times,* April 7, 2011.

14. Organization for Economic Cooperation and Development (OECD), "OECD Statistical Extracts."

15. Congressional Budget Office, "An Update to the Budget and Economic Outlook: Fiscal Years 2012 to 2022," August 22, 2012.

16. Only 7.4 percent of transactions in Germany are paid by credit cards and two-thirds of Germans don't even have a credit card. Tom Fairless, "Germans Warm to Credit Cards—Slowly," *The Wall Street Journal,* October 17, 2012.

17. Steven Keen, *Debunking Economics: The Naked Emperor Dethroned* (Revised Edition, London: Zed Books, 2011).

11

MACROECONOMIC AGGREGATES AND VARIABLES

In this chapter we introduce and discuss some of the variables that are important in analyzing and understanding the macroeconomy. These include most importantly the labor market, which has such a big impact on our lives. We suggest that the way the labor market is constructed is essentially unfair insofar as the available work is distributed so unevenly with some people working seventy hours per week while others have no work at all.

GROSS NATIONAL PRODUCT

GNP is the total amount of goods and services produced in the economy. While in some ways it is a useful indicator of productivity, if, for instance, we compare GNP of developing countries to those of the developed part of the world, the excessive focus on it in the developed part of the world is extremely misleading. There are many reasons why GNP is a misleading gauge of welfare and productivity but the most important reason is that GNP is measured inaccurately. Many problems, such as pollution, are counted as increasing GNP. For instance, we do not charge for carbon dioxide emissions into the atmosphere. A correct accounting of GNP would deduct from it the value of environmental degradation. The fact that we do not charge for CO_2 emissions means that products that pollute the atmosphere are mispriced and from that follows that all products are mispriced and consequently GNP is miscalculated.

There are many other factors that lead to errors. Consider health care, which was 17 percent of U.S. GNP in 2012. The U.S. system is extremely inefficient compared to Western Europe, because its administration is so much more convoluted and imposes substantial transaction costs on the population. So immense amounts are wasted but they nonetheless appear as a final product in the GNP accounts. Consider in this regard also that pre-term births cost 10 times more than full-term infants; they added $26 billion to U.S. GNP in 2010 and have increased by one-third since 1980. Yet, it is absurd that phenomena associated with harm and the lack of precautionary measures makes it appear as though output and welfare are actually greater than before.[1] Officially the Gulf oil spill increased GNP rather than diminished it. Such negative externalities imply that GNP is a welfare measure of dubious value.

Yet the emphasis on GNP growth is a central tenet of our culture even though we have been growing for years without creating sufficient jobs to put people to work. The factors affecting the jobless recovery will be discussed later; suffice it to say here that it means that GNP growth should not be our focus.

In addition, average growth rates hide a very important aspect of the rise in inequality. The benefits of GNP growth have accrued mostly to the top 1 percent of U.S. households, whose

Table 11.1

Growth in Income of U.S. Households by Quintiles Between 1979 and 2004

Group	Increase	
	(%)	2004 Dollars
0–20%	6	800
20–40%	17	4,700
40–60%	21	8,500
60–80%	29	15,300
80–100%	69	63,100
Top 1%	176	553,800

Source: Aviva Aron-Dine and Arloc Sherman, "New CBO Data Show Income Inequality Continues to Widen," Center on Budget and Policy Priorities, January 23, 2007

incomes increased by more than $500,000 during the quarter-century ending in 2004 (Table 11.1). In contrast, the income of the bottom 20 percent of households increased by merely $800. In short, in spite of all the hype about economic growth, the great majority of the U.S. population has not benefited at all from growth since the 1970s.[2] In other words, average growth rates are a misleading measure of welfare of the median person. An additional aspect to consider is that conspicuous consumption brings about negative externalities through envy. This means that as the income of the 1 percent increases by 176 percent, it is folly to think that the happiness of those whose income is stagnant will remain unchanged. On the contrary, relative deprivation means that the happiness of the bottom 20 percent of the population will likely decline.

UNEMPLOYMENT AND UNDEREMPLOYMENT

Unemployment and underemployment of labor and of capital are inefficient, insofar as the economy does not produce as much as it could, given its available resources (Figure 11.1). Idle resources imply that the economy is inside its production possibilities frontier, thereby violating the optimality condition of production. In 2012, about 22 percent of the capital stock was idle (Figure 11.2). The official unemployment rate has been high for five years and is now around 7 percent, implying that the economy is wasting a lot of human resources (Table 11.2). What is even worse is that there is no end in sight: full employment seems out of our reach.

Another indication of the tight job market is that only 58 percent of the population of adults has a job (population/employment ratio), having declined by 5 percent in the course of the Great Recession.[3] In addition, the long-term unemployed—those out of work for more than half a year—has exceeded 40 percent since 2010. In October 2012 some 5 million people were unemployed for longer than half a year and half of the unemployed were out of work for longer than five months.[4] It is not easy to keep one's head above water that way.

Thus, the underemployment rate—13.8 percent at the end of 2012—is actually a better measure of idle resources in the economy, insofar as it also counts those people who are working part time but would prefer to work full time as well as those who are discouraged from looking for employment after sending out dozens or even hundreds of resumes. Thus, the official unemployment rate is conceived so as to put the best possible spin on the size of the problem of idle resources, that is, of waste and inefficiency in the economy. The underemployment rate provides a much better insight into the real pain in the economy. That metric includes about 8.3 million people who work

Figure 11.1   **Inefficient Use of Labor** (%)

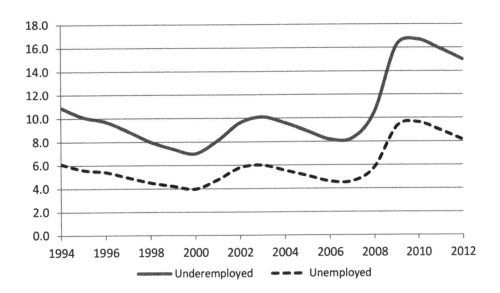

Figure 11.2   **Industrial Capital Utilization** (%)

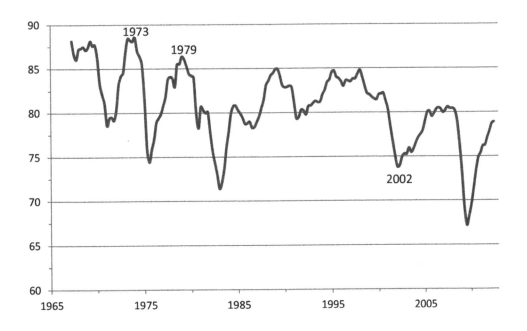

Table 11.2

The U.S. Labor Force, October 2012

	Millions	
Civilian adult population	244.0	
Civilian labor force	155.6	
Employed	143.4	
Full-time		115.2
Part-time		28.2
Unemployed	12.3	
Long-term		5.0
Discouraged workers		0.8
Part-time involuntary		8.3
Underemployed	9.1	
Un- & Underemployed	21.4	

	Percentage of Labor Force	
Unemployed	7.9	
Blacks		14.3
Teenagers		23.7
Black teenagers		40.3
Un- & Underemployed	13.8	

Source: Bureau of Labor Statistics, "The Employment Situation—October 2012"

part time because they were unable to find full-time work. Although they are considered employed, they are, in fact, *underemployed*, working around 20 hours a week.[5] The number of these hidden unemployed has doubled since the onset of the Great Recession (Figure 11.3). The rest of the 19.9 million part-time workers prefer not to work full time because they go to school or have another obligation, such as taking care of their children.

There are also about 800,000 people who are discouraged from looking for work; they have dropped out of the labor force altogether because the prospect of being successful no longer appears plausible to them. Thus, not classifying them as being unemployed is deceptive. Therefore, the official unemployment rate is actually a lower bound of the real unemployment rate and the real suffering caused by the shortage of jobs: the number of people in distress is actually closer to about 21 million. This number still does not include a substantial number of the working poor: those who are employed but barely make ends meet. It also does not include the dependents of the underemployed.

Another problem with the restructuring of the labor market after the meltdown—in addition to the lack of jobs—is the utter shortage of well-paying jobs. The jobs that are available are predominantly low-paying ones, those paying less than $10 an hour, while newly created middle-class jobs, paying at least $19 per hour, are few and far between.[6]

Yet those who do have full-time jobs work an average of 40 hours per week and close to half of them work more. In stark contrast to the unemployed, there are millions who are working overtime or hold two jobs. Among male managers and professionals, average hours of work in the 1980s and 1990s increased from 44.0 to 45.1 hours per week, and the share working more than 49 hours a week increased from 31 percent to 38 percent, implying that they are almost certainly living harried lives.[7] Furthermore, the time worked by dual-earning families has increased by 10 hours within a generation at the end of the twentieth century from 81 to 91 hours per week.[8] And Americans work 400 hours more per annum than most of their Western European counterparts,

Figure 11.3 **The Number of Part-Time Workers Unable to Work Full Time**

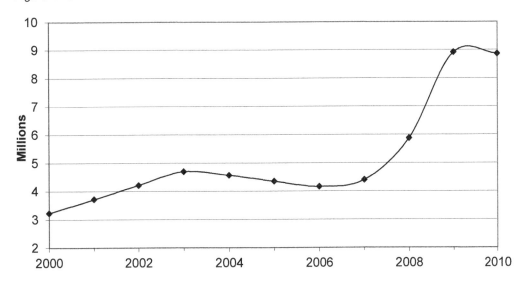

even though Americans' income is higher and one would think that they would be able to afford to work less.[9] Thus, it is somewhat ironic that at a time of endemic and extensive underemployment, a large number of U.S. workers are truly overworked.[10]

It appears, therefore, that the available amount of work—like wealth and income—is also unevenly distributed.[11] The problem lies in the organization of the labor market: fluctuations in the demand for workers bring about adjustments in which workers are dismissed, causing their labor time to fall suddenly from 40 hours to zero. We might call this institution a binary labor market: one either has a job or one does not. Would anyone in his right mind design a rigid system with such extremes—with working times ranging from 0 to 70 hours per week—if he were to design the framework for a market from scratch, "behind a veil of ignorance" not knowing if he would end up among the ranks of the overworked or those of the unemployed? Risk-averse people would be too apprehensive about ending up among the group that loses their job periodically. It would be much more equitable and reasonable to have the adjustment occur in the number of hours worked so that instead of laying off workers, the available work would be divided among the labor force. A work-sharing program would be a much more flexible and equitable shock absorber of a decline in the demand for labor.[12] We could thereby eliminate the very concept of unemployment.[13]

In the spring of 2012, for example, the average full-time employee worked 41.9 hours per week and the average part-time employee 20.6 hours. The total number of hours worked by full-time workers (114.5 million people) and those part-time workers who wanted to work full time (7.9 million people) totaled some 5 billion per week.[14] Dividing the 5 billion hours of available work by 135.9 million (the number of people who work or who would like to work full time), one finds that the full-employment average number of hours worked per week is about 36.5.[15] Thus, instead of accepting unemployment, one could reduce the number of hours worked for everyone by roughly an hour a day. Admittedly, the earnings of those previously employed might be reduced as well, but the government could offset part of their losses through a subsidy (instead of unemployment payments and financed partly by corporate taxes), and everyone would have more leisure time to enjoy. Such a system would increase the quality of life because it would reduce the psychological burden of unemployment, increase leisure time, and reduce envy by reducing conspicuous consumption. In addition, it would be a much fairer method of distributing the pain of a recession than the prevailing "either-or" binary system. If one were designing a labor market from scratch, one would surely design one similar to the one sketched above, because it lowers the uncertainty associated with being unemployed and because it shares the pain rather than concentrating it.

Profit-sharing wages have also been proposed as a way of alleviating (or at least diminishing) unemployment.[16] Wages would increase in good times and decrease in bad times, so that workers would not have to be fired, keeping the share of total wages in revenue unchanged.[17] Furthermore, governments could also be the employer of last resort at a time of recession. In sum, one could introduce different shock absorbers into the system instead of the crude binary one we have now. It would be much more reasonable to distribute the burden of cyclical economic downturns more equitably than concentrating it among 14 percent of the workforce. Apparently, the market is not a good institution to distribute income, wealth, or work fairly or uniformly.

A fairer distribution of work would be important not only for financial reasons but also because unemployment has adverse side effects. It has a destabilizing effect on society both politically and socially. In short, the unemployed produce negative externalities such as an increase in criminality or an increase in stress and anxiety about losing one's job. Of course, Europeans have not forgotten that the Nazis would never have come to power if unemployment had not reached one-quarter of the labor force.

Work is also important from a psychological perspective: the unemployed are excluded from the labor market and therefore feel degraded and unwanted. The unemployed do not consider themselves useful members of society and lose self-esteem. Their skills depreciate during an extended spell of unemployment so that they become unemployable. In other words, unemployment increases the misery in a society. The underemployed are twice as likely to be sad or depressed than the employed and 50 percent more likely to be angry.[18] They were also more likely to be struggling financially (54 percent) in contrast to 38 percent of the employed.

THE NATURAL RATE OF UNEMPLOYMENT

Economists consider the natural rate of unemployment the minimum level of unemployment attainable without inflation, given the structure and institutional aspects of the labor market. These structural characteristics include the cost of searching for a job or the time needed to find a match between suppliers and demanders of labor. Theoretically, a lower rate of unemployment would be possible temporarily, but only at a cost of an accelerating rate of inflation, and in the long run unemployment would return to its "natural" level at a higher inflation rate. In short, according to common wisdom, due to frictions and imperfections in the marketplace, it would be futile to try to use monetary or fiscal policy to force the unemployment rate below the natural rate. It would only lead to inflation. The natural rate of unemployment is the noninflationary equilibrium rate in the labor market, according to the mainstream view. That is why some economists (such as Ben Bernanke) misleadingly but emphatically refer to a 5 percent level of unemployment as "full employment."

In reality, the natural rate of unemployment is a disingenuous concept; it merely rationalizes the inability of the labor market to provide a sufficient number of jobs for all workers. It does not allow for the possibility that the imperfections can be reduced or removed altogether by creating new institutions or new policies; furthermore the concept makes it appear as though some level of unemployment is inevitable—a natural phenomenon inherent to the economic system as though the institutions of the labor market were made in heaven. Thus, the concept makes it appear as though the natural rate of unemployment is an acceptable equilibrium value and must be tolerated since nothing can be done about it. It is just the way the economy works and it is necessary to put up with it.

It is clear that unemployment cannot be eliminated entirely or even lowered permanently using current standard policy instruments. However, our goal should be to create new labor-market institutions that will be effective in eliminating unemployment completely. In the age of the information technology (IT) revolution it ought to be possible to match vacancies to willing workers instantaneously, thereby eliminating frictional unemployment. The government could subsidize the cost of relocation and retraining. Moreover, if the above-mentioned work-sharing and profit-sharing strategies are adopted along with the government's taking on the task of being the employer of last resort, we would be able to eliminate unemployment in its entirety. It is not true that we have to accept 5 percent unemployment as natural. After all, the UN's Universal Declaration of Human Rights states that, "Everyone has the right to work . . . and to protection against unemployment."[19] There is no reason why that right should not be implemented.

ECONOMIC GROWTH

Economic growth has been an important goal of macroeconomic policy and is in the constant focus of public and media attention. Insofar as growth has been more or less continuous in the West for nearly a quarter of a millennium, that is, since the Industrial Revolution, with the conspicuous exception of the Great Depression, it is practically assumed that it will continue indefinitely as an inherent aspect of capitalist development. We've gotten used to it without appreciating sufficiently the wealth it has made available to us.

However, indefinite growth and development is not dictated by an actual economic law. Whether an economy will continue to grow is contingent upon how the factors that determine growth evolve. Besides capital, land, labor, resources, institutions, and the educational level of the labor force, the productive capacity of an economy is determined by technological change, which, in turn, is determined by the creativity, culture, entrepreneurship, and willingness to bear the risk of innovation. The government plays an essential role in that process insofar as it provides most of the infrastructure of the economy, much of the education of the labor force, and is dominant in providing basic research, a public good—as it did with the Internet. Innovation and new knowledge creation is important insofar as it has many positive externalities (spillovers) so that many benefit who did not have to bear the cost of producing that knowledge.

However, we have been putting too much emphasis on growth without acknowledging—as discussed in the previous chapters—that it has not brought us the kind of Nirvana that we thought it would. In fact, it has not raised our sense of well-being at all. We need to question seriously how much additional growth we need in the developed part of the world and how to squeeze as much happiness as possible out of the current state of wealth. Instead of stressing growth for its own sake, we need to start putting much more emphasis on sustainability, minimizing our environmental footprint, improving the quality of life, and creating socially inclusive growth.

This is especially the case since growth and unemployment have been decoupled by technological change and globalization. We are still advocating growth with the illusion that it will eliminate unemployment. The fact that it has not done so until now is a clear indication that it will not do so in the future either. Growth is no longer related directly to unemployment, because the economy has been segmented into a skill-intensive high-tech growth sector to which the majority of the low-skilled unemployed have no access due to their lack of qualifications. In addition, we have been so successful at creating advanced technologies that we no longer need workers to produce as in the past. Instead, we have robots to produce for us. That is one reason we have experienced a jobless recovery after the Meltdown of 2008. That makes it all the more important to distribute the available work more equitably than is currently the case.

CHAPTER SUMMARY

GNP is a misleading indicator of the living standard of a population insofar as it is measured so inaccurately. If the damage done by pollution would be subtracted from GNP, growth rates would be at least one percent below official estimates. The official unemployment rate is also misleading because it does not count discouraged workers, those who have given up looking for work because finding work seems so hopeless. There are also millions of people who are working part time only because they could not find full-time work. In addition, there are people who dropped out entirely from the labor market by registering for social security disability payments. Hence, the official unemployment rate is a misleading indicator of the true pain experienced in the labor market because of the shortage of work. The endemic underemployment implies that the economy is producing well below capacity and is therefore extremely inefficient.

The shortage of jobs is exacerbated by some people working excessive amounts of hours, leaving less work for others. As is income and wealth, the available amount of work is also distributed unevenly and unfairly. A more equitable distribution of work would be obtained if the adjustment in the labor market to the periodic downturns in aggregate demand would be accomplished by lowering the number of hours worked rather than dismissing workers and reducing their hours worked to zero. The shock absorber in the labor market would not be the unemployment rolls but the reduction in the number of hours worked. Moreover, we have become addicted to economic growth that no longer provides us additional satisfaction. At the level of development of the wealthy industrialized countries we should be more concerned about increasing life satisfaction by creating a more inclusive and just society.

QUESTIONS FOR DISCUSSION

1. Why is GNP a misleading measure of welfare of the people living and working in an economy?
2. What do you think happened to the well-being of the population whose income put them in the bottom 20 percent of the distribution?
3. Do you think that the damages caused by pollution should be subtracted from GNP?
4. Will growing the economy solve our problems?
5. Are we addicted to growth?
6. What is most important: economic growth, the environment, or the quality of life?
7. Should we leave the environment as good as we found it for future generations?
8. Should the benefits of economic growth be shared widely?
9. Do you think everyone has a right to a job?
10. Would you say that the official unemployment rate is a good estimate of the idle human resources in the economy?
11. Do you think that we should strive for full employment? Do you think it is attainable?
12. Do you think the economy is efficient, given the immense number of underemployed people?

13. Do you think that work sharing instead of laying people off is a good idea?

14. Do you think that discouraged workers should be counted as unemployed?

15. Do you think that it is unfair that the available work is distributed so unevenly?

16. Would you say that the "binary" labor market is efficient or just?

17. How would you organize the labor market if you were to create it from scratch behind a "veil of ignorance"?

18. Would you be willing to participate voluntarily in a work-sharing program as an insurance against unemployment?

19. Do you think that the right to a job should be guaranteed in the Bill of Rights?

20. How could we induce people to be more content with what they have?

21. How important is the government to economic growth?

22. Do you think that environmental protection is as important as economic growth or more important?

23. Do you think we are addicted to growth and will never be content?

24. Do you think sustainable growth is a worthy goal?

25. Do you think it is great that we have robots working for us in the few remaining factories?

NOTES

1. Christopher P. Howson, Mary V. Kinney, and Joy E. Lawn, eds., *Born Too Soon: The Global Action Report on Preterm Birth* (Geneva: World Health Organization, 2012). Pre-term births in North America are about 70 percent higher than in Europe. Stacy Beck, Daniel Wojdyla, Lale Say, Ana Pilar Betran, Mario Merialdi, Jennifer Harris Requejo, Craig Rubens, Ramkumar Meno, and Paul F.A. Van Look, "The Worldwide Incidence of Preterm Birth: A Systematic Review of Maternal Mortality and Morbidity," *Bulletin of the World Health Organization* 88 (2010) 1: 31–38.

2. This pattern obtained even though more people were working in 2004 than in 1979. In 1979, 64 percent of the population was working, while in 2004, 66 percent of the population was working. U.S. Department of Labor, Bureau of Labor Statistics, "Labor Force Statistics from the Current Population Survey," Series ID: LNS11300000.

3. U.S. Department of Labor, Bureau of Labor Statistics, "Labor Force Statistics from the Current Population Survey."

4. U.S. Department of Labor, Bureau of Labor Statistics, "Table A-12. Unemployed Persons by Duration of Unemployment."

5. U.S. Department of Labor, Bureau of Labor Statistics, "Table 20. Persons at Work 1 to 34 hours in All and in Nonagricultural Industries by Reason for Working Less than 35 hours and Usual Full- or Part-Time Status."

6. Jeff Madrick, "Our Crisis of Bad Jobs," *The New York Review of Books,* October 2, 2012.

7. U.S. Department of Labor, Bureau of Labor Statistics, "Are Managers and Professionals Really Working More?" *Issues in Labor Statistics,* May 12, 2000.

8. Sloan Network, "Questions and Answers About Overwork: A Sloan Work and Family Research Network Fact Sheet" (Chestnut Hill, MA: Boston College, 2008).

9. Organization for Economic Cooperation and Development (OECD), "OECD Statistical Extracts."

10. Juliet Schor, *The Overworked American: The Unexpected Decline of Leisure* (New York: Basic Books, 1993).

11. John Maynard Keynes, *The General Theory of Employment, Interest and Money* (London: Macmillan, 1936), Chapter 24, 372.

12. Dean Baker, *Work Sharing: The Quick Route Back to Full Employment* (Washington, DC: Center for Economic and Policy Research, June 2011).

13. Some tentative steps in this direction were already taken in the 2012 "Job Creation Act." Such a program works in Germany where total employment did not decrease at all during the meltdown. Paul Krugman, "Kurzarbeit," *The New York Times,* September 2, 2010.

14. There are an additional 0.5 billion hours worked per week by part-time workers who do not want to

work full time and multiple job holders combined. I am not counting them in this counterfactual exercise, as they would not have to be provided a full-time job.

15. Full employment = full-time workers + unemployed + part time who want to work full time + discouraged workers.

16. Cooperatives are more likely to adjust pay to fluctuations in demand rather than the number employed. Ben Craig and John Pencavel, "The Behavior of Worker Cooperatives: The Plywood Companies of the Pacific Northwest," *American Economic Review* 82 (1992) 5: 1083–1105.

17. Martin Weitzman, *The Share Economy* (Cambridge, MA: Harvard University Press, 1984).

18. Jenny Marlar, "The Emotional Cost of Underemployment," *Gallup,* March 9, 2010; Anna Manchin, "Depression Hits Jobless in UK, U.S. More than in Germany," *Gallup,* November 21, 2012.

19. United Nations, "The Universal Declaration of Human Rights."

12

ASPECTS OF MACROECONOMIC PERFORMANCE

We shall examine the role of government in the economy and argue that government is essential because it provides public goods and information that the private sector has little incentive to supply. The government's role in the economy is further entrenched by its using fiscal and monetary policy to influence aggregate demand and thus reduce the volatility of the business cycle.

THE ROLE OF GOVERNMENT

Government is frequently depicted as inimical to efficiency: indeed, it is often painted practically as a cancer on the economy. However, it is not the enemy of the people's finances or of their well-being. Government is a vital and essential part of the economy. The economy could not function without an effective government, and government expenditure is an important part of the economy. In the United States it is about 24 percent of GDP and in many European developed countries it is as high as 40 to 50 percent.[1] The government not only spends, and transfers money to the needy, it also invests. In 2010, state, local, and federal governments invested some $510 billion; that is 22 percent of all investments.

The government is we, and in a democratic polity the people, not the markets, have the ultimate legitimate power. The government has many legitimate functions that cannot be relegated to markets: consumer protection, national defense, provision for future generations, regulation of economic activity, protection of the environment, smoothing of the business cycle, providing laws, enforcing contracts, providing money to the economy, and being the lender of last resort. It has the responsibility to maintain domestic order, to maintain democratic institutions by preventing the accumulation of economic power, and to protect its citizens from those market forces that are morally unacceptable to them, such as racial or gender discrimination.

In general, governments should protect their citizens from harm in order to improve social welfare. An example is the graphic warning on cigarette packs about the damaging effects of smoking. Another example is providing default options on application forms that "nudge" the individual to voluntarily make the socially desirable choice, such as save for retirement or donate an organ. Thus, there are numerous significant justifications for government regulation of private markets, including reducing harm caused by addiction.

Subsidizing savings (as in Germany) is welfare enhancing since many people are myopic about their needs in retirement, and because many people's self-control has been weakened by the universal buying hype. Such self-control is a prerequisite of saving. Self-control problems also justify mandated upper limits on interest rate charged on credit cards. The goal of government policy should be to enhance the quality of life of those who need help in making decisions without imposing excessively on those who do not need such help.

THE IMPRACTICALITY OF KEYNESIAN FISCAL POLICY

Keynesian fiscal policy is the "steering wheel" of the economy.[2] However, it is crucial to realize that the steering should be against the wind and not with it. That is to say, according to Keynes, fiscal policy should be countercyclical: expansionary in downturns but contracting in upswings as the boom gathers momentum. In such a way, government budget would be balanced over the business cycle and government expenditures would not be at the expense of private spending. At a time when there is slack in the economy, that is, when resources are idle, government spending does not crowd out private investments.

In other words, Keynes did not want government debt to accumulate. The government should borrow and spend during recessions, and when the recession has subsided, the government should pay back the borrowed funds by increasing taxes and/or by cutting back government expenditures. Unfortunately, the Keynesian prescription of countercyclical fiscal policy to smooth out the business cycle (and "fine tune" the economy) turned out to be impractical in practice. The reason is that in a democracy, elected politicians would lose popularity and especially campaign contributions from the business elite with policies aimed at cooling down the economy. Hence, they found it too difficult to decrease spending in good times and risk alienating their constituents and financial supporters. It would not make sense to the electorate. Deficit spending or cutting taxes during a recession was easy, but limiting aggregate demand at the peak of the business cycle was unfeasible in many countries. Switzerland is perhaps the only country that enacted a balanced-budget law in the spirit of Keynesian countercyclical policy, so that deficits would not accumulate.[3]

An additional reason for the difficulty of cooling the economy was that vocal and powerful coalitions formed in order to protect vested interests and prevent the government from either increasing taxes or cutting back on expenditures. In other words, the Keynesian prescription to smooth out the capitalist business cycle was brilliant in theory but turned out to be impractical in the long run in most countries. Politicians and their advisers lacked both the vision and the fortitude to take away the punch bowl just when the party was reaching fever pitch.

This was also partly why Friedrich Hayek and Milton Friedman were critical of Keynesian macroeconomics from the very beginning. Another problem was that many mistook Keynesian theory as a prescription for economic growth. That it was not; it was really not meant to serve that purpose. Keynes knew well that deficits could not accumulate indefinitely. His aim was to bring the economy out of the glut of the Depression, shorten the breadlines, and thereby alleviate the worst shortcomings of capitalism. In other words, his focus was entirely on the real ongoing Depression. To be sure, his prescription would make the economy grow out of its doldrums, but long-run growth would come subsequently from the usual sources: innovation, education, technical change, and capital accumulation. That was not his main concern, however. He was not analyzing long-run growth and development. His focus was on the here and now as reflected in his famous saying, "in the long run, we are all dead."

MONETARY POLICY

Monetary policy is one of the important pathways by which the government influences the economy. The Federal Reserve (or a central bank) affects aggregate economic activity by setting the discount rate—the interest rate it charges on loans to member banks—by creating money (putting money into circulation), by purchasing financial assets such as government bonds, by setting reserve requirements of banks, or by buying foreign currency. The monetary school holds that the quantity of money in circulation is directly proportional to nominal GNP. However, this is a mistake for either M1 (currency + demand deposits) or for M2 (M1 + time deposits) (Figures 12.1 and 12.2). One of the reasons is that in the short run, people can purchase goods and services on credit cards and are therefore not at all constrained by the money stock. Moreover, how much money individuals and banks hold in their accounts or in reserve depends on the uncertainties in the economy: how likely it is that they will lose their jobs, for instance. Thus, the velocity of M1—the rate at which money changes hands in a year—was 10 during the Meltdown of 2008; this meant that a dollar changed hands 10 times a year. However, the velocity declined to 7.5 in 2011, implying

Figure 12.1 **The Velocity of Circulation of M1**

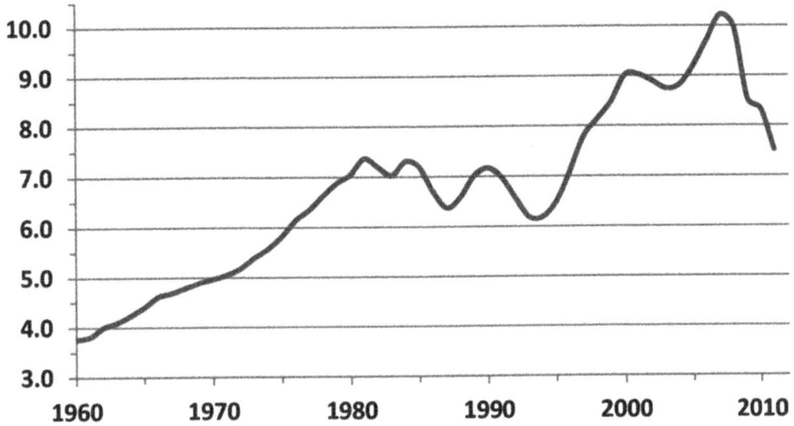

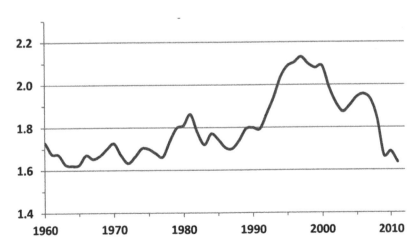

Sources: Board of the Federal Reserve System, FRB H6: Data Download Program www.federalreserve. gov/datadownload/choose.aspx?rel=H.6; U.S. Department of Commerce, Bureau of Economic Analysis, National Economic Accounts, www.bea.gov/national/index.htm (accessed January 13, 2013)

Figure 12.2 **The Velocity of Circulation of M2**

that Bernanke's insistence on pumping money into the economy did not affect the real economy to any meaningful extent. Instead, it merely lowered the velocity of circulation. Both M1 and M2 declined by about 25 percent between 2007 and 2011. In addition, it will be extremely difficult for Bernanke to devise a strategy to get back to the normal business of not subsidizing the financial sector with a zero interest rate.[4] How the Fed will ever get back to normal interest rates of 4 or 5 percent without causing a crash in the stock market is an open question.

The Federal Reserve directly controls the monetary base, that is, the actual cash it puts into circulation along with the reserves of banks. By buying Treasury securities (known as open-market operations), it puts more money into circulation, while if it sells securities, it is decreasing the quantity of money in circulation. In addition, the Federal Reserve can influence the money supply indirectly by setting reserve requirements: the lower they are, the more money banks can lend.

However, the private banks also influence the money supply by setting the stringency with which they lend money. Thus, much of the money creation is done by the financial system, although the Federal Reserve plays an important role both directly and indirectly. Generally, the lower the interest rate it charges member banks on short-term loans, the less it costs banks to borrow from the Federal Reserve, and as a consequence they can lend more money. But of course, firms and consumers have to be willing to borrow. If they are overextended and have too much debt relative to income, as in 2008, and are trying to deleverage, or lower their debt burden, then lowering the interest rate is not effective.

In addition, when the nominal interest rate reaches zero, as is the case now—the situation known as the liquidity trap—the Federal Reserve loses its ability to influence monetary policy for all intents and purposes, regardless of how hard it tries, because it cannot lower the nominal interest rate below the zero limit. In order to overcome this limitation and further try to stimulate the economy through monetary polity the Fed introduced a new program called "quantitative easing" in 2008 after the demise of Lehman Brothers, a large investment bank. Through this expansionary monetary policy the Fed pumped trillions of dollars into the economy by purchasing long-term assets including bonds of commercial firms and mortgage-backed securities hoping that this would induce banks to invest more aggressively in the economy. However, the program of injecting money into the economy through quantitative easing led primarily to an inflation of asset prices rather than to investments in the real economy, as banks invested in the stock market. However, investment in the real economy continued to appear less attractive because of the weakness in aggregated demand.

Another consideration is that usually when the interest rate decreases, foreign investors will take their money out of the United States and put it in the currency of another country with a higher interest rate. That has not happened recently, because the rest of the world economy is also in turmoil and the dollar is a reserve currency and still considered the safest currency. Hence, the dollar's value cannot be devalued vis-à-vis foreign currencies despite the fact that the Federal Reserve has pumped about $3 trillion into the economy between 2008 and 2013. Foreigners have been willing to invest into dollar-denominated bonds even though the real interest rate (nominal interest rate minus the rate of inflation) is effectively negative in the United States. Treasury securities of the U.S. government are considered a safe haven, so that investors are willing to bear the cost of holding such investments because they are concerned about other governments defaulting on their debt.

Generally, the more banks lend, the more money will be in circulation through the deposits they create. However, during the current financial crisis there is a lot of deleveraging, which means that banks are not lending as readily as they did before; instead, they accumulate capital in order to make up for the losses they suffered through the erosion of the value of their portfolios. This is just one of the reasons so many economists are baffled by the Great Meltdown. They are not used to thinking of deleveraging in the context of macroeconomics.

CROWDING OUT

Neoclassical economists believe that public spending crowds out private spending and is therefore both counterproductive and inefficient. However, this obviously does not hold when unemployment is endemic and is also not the case when the government invests in public goods that spur economic growth in the long run, such as the Eisenhower Interstate Highway System, which is generally agreed to have had such a positive effect.[5] Investment in education, public health, basic research, and renewable energy has similar multiplier effects and is a complement to, if not a prerequisite of, long-term economic development. In short, government does not only "spend." It also invests. In fact, about a quarter of total U.S. investments are made by government (local, state, and federal).

INFLATION

Inflation is harmful for the people in the economy because it devalues savings and therefore is an invisible tax. By reducing the incentive to save, it lowers the savings rate and therefore makes less money available to invest. It is also an inconvenience insofar as it makes it difficult to keep track of all the changes in relative prices in the economy, because not all prices change at the same rate.

Deflation is the opposite of inflation. It is also bad for the economy, as it puts a damper on production. Producers are engaged in long-range contracts with workers and suppliers, and if their product price is falling, they expect a decline in their profits as well and therefore they reduce production. In addition, deflation increases the real value of debt such as mortgages, which are denominated in nominal terms, thus increasing the probability of default. Even if the debtor does not default, mortgage payments will make up a greater share of income, leaving less money to be spent on everything else, thereby reducing aggregate demand. Thus, inflation and deflation are both nuisances to avoid, and their control is one of the two missions of the Federal Reserve System; the other is to reduce unemployment.

NOMINAL VS. REAL WAGES

The importance of nominal versus real wages is a contentious issue between the two main schools of thought. In the models of the real-business-cycle school, real wages matter to employment, whereas in the Keynesian's view, nominal wages are most important since employers set wages in nominal terms and the course of the price level in subsequent periods is fuzzy at best as far as workers are concerned. This is a question of asymmetric information. In the main, firms are concerned with the price of their product and the prices of their inputs and can afford specialists to do the necessary calculations, whereas workers need to anticipate the movement in hundreds of prices in order to ascertain the inflation rate, and therefore their real wages, by themselves. This is beyond their capability, especially since prices are changing at different rates. That is one of the reasons unions are essential to maintaining the real wages of workers: they are in a much better position to overcome this formidable information problem and track the rates of inflation and productivity growth.

In addition, nominal wages are not downwardly flexible because of psychological effects such as fairness and the endowment effect. Workers are unwilling to give up a nominal wage that they have already achieved and feel they deserve. This is behind the social unrest and confrontations with the police related to the euro crisis in Spain and Greece. Workers think it is unfair that they are the ones who have to sacrifice at a time when the bankers, who are responsible for the crisis in the first place, are indulging themselves with conspicuous consumption.

SAVINGS

Savings are an important aspect of economic development and provide an important cushion for unexpected expenditures for individuals, firms, and governments. Yet the importance of savings has not been adequately acknowledged. The reason is that it is not in the interest of corporations to have people save. On the contrary, it is in their interest if people do not save, because then they will spend more, thereby increasing the demand for the corporations' products. No wonder there are no advertisements pointing out the benefits of saving that might induce people to be more cautious in spending money.

But such an imbalance in savings also implies that there is excessive borrowing, with increasing fragility of the financial system. The increase in indebtedness played a substantial role in the run-up to the crisis of 2008. The other aspect of the indebtedness was that the rate of saving was declining since the mid-1980s. By 2008 it approached zero, and then rebounded slightly after the meltdown (Figure 12.3). Ideologically committed economists argue that the decline in the savings rate was caused by the introduction of Social Security in 1935 and Medicare in 1965, which provided some financial security for people in retirement. However, the trend in savings does not support such a contention since the saving rate was increasing throughout the post–World War II period until circa 1982, well after the enactment of these social safety nets. The rate began to decline steeply only in 1985.[6]

Is it a coincidence that this was exactly the moment when inequality began to increase markedly and when wages began to lag behind the increases of productivity? I should think not. With income inequality increasing, and real wages lagging well behind increases in productivity, it appears most plausible that the middle class did not want to fall behind the consumption norm set by top earners. The only way they could keep up with the consumption patterns of the elite was by dipping into their savings, although by then most families had two earners instead of one, as was the case just a decade or two earlier, and by going into debt. Moreover, this was the first generation to reach adulthood having been bombarded by TV advertisements that hyped the wonders of consumption, while no one advocated the importance of saving. That also reinforced the development of an instant gratification culture.

No wonder that American families save so little; they are struggling: half have no savings at all and an amazing two-thirds live paycheck to paycheck without any backstop whatsoever.[7] Yet dual-earner couples with children work 10 hours a week more than they did 25 years ago.[8] Thus, Madison Avenue has won: instant gratification became the dominant cultural characteristic of the American way of life. However, the lack of domestic savings increases the amount of risk borne both by individuals and by society; there is a social cost when people have less of a cushion to withstand shocks to their budgets. With an increase in the debt burden, economic life becomes more volatile.

Saving received bad publicity from policymakers and the media because of the paradox of thrift. In the standard Keynesian short-run models, an increase in savings implies that consumer spend less, thereby lowering GNP and economic growth in the short run. Thus, politicians are wary of an increase in the rate of saving as it reduces consumption and therefore reduces aggregate demand in the short run, threatening to create unemployment and also putting a damper

Figure 12.3 **Personal Savings as a Percentage of Personal Income**

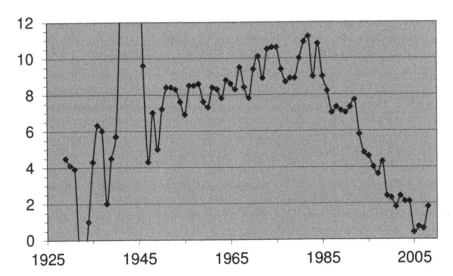

Source: U.S. Department of Commerce, U.S. Census Bureau, Statistical United States: 2010. 657-Relation of GDP, GNP, Net National Product, National Income, Personal Income, Disposable Personal Income, and Personal Saving: 1990 to 2008, www.census.gov/compendia/statab/2010/tables/10s0657.pdf

on growth and revenue. Of course, this assumes that an increase in savings will not lead to an increase in investments, which may or may not be the case, depending on the availability of credit from abroad.

Under normal conditions, increased savings would reduce interest rates, make more credit available for investment, and boost growth in the long run. Investment in a closed economy is possible only to the extent that there are savings to be invested. Under such circumstances, then, saving is an important determinant of long-run economic growth. This is the case in most developing economies. However, in today's financial environment, with immense amounts of savings floating around in China and Japan looking for investments, these surplus funds are made available to the U.S. economy at a negative real rate of return, thereby rendering domestic savings by Americans redundant. Yet this also means that in the medium term the return on these investments will accrue to an increasing extent to foreigners, putting a damper on the growth in income of future generations of Americans. As a result, their living standards will be negatively affected by the lack of current savings, and the American Dream will be that much more difficult to attain for most people.

TAXES

American popular culture is not only inimical to saving, it has also been adamantly and aggressively against paying taxes ever since the birth of the nation. This feeling is probably stronger than in any other country. Textbooks feed on this stereotype and reinforce it by suggesting that "taxation subtracts from incomes, reduces private spending, and affects private saving. In addition it affects investment and potential output."[9] However, this is an extremely biased perspective, because it does not mention that governments and taxes are instituted in the first place in order to improve the welfare of the population.

Hobbes, Locke, and Rousseau all argued that governments are established in order to avoid the chaos in the state of nature. They are essential to the welfare of the population. Without taxes there can be no government, and without government life would be inferior to the one we obtain once we enter into a social contract. Thus, without taxes life would be chaotic, and the introduction of taxation is actually Pareto optimal. All members of society benefit from it.

To be sure, once taxation is instituted, there are at least four substantial problems to solve, which has not been an easy task, as Louis XVI could attest: (1) How much government service to provide is a bone of contention. (2) Free riding becomes an attractive alternative, with people devoting resources to justify and defend their ability to enjoy the benefits of government services without actually paying their fair share. (3) Due to taxpayer resistance, it becomes attractive to pay for government services by borrowing against the earnings of generations yet unborn. Since future generations are unable to advocate for themselves, there is a tendency for government indebtedness to rise. There is no valid economic argument to counter such a tendency; one has to resort to a moral argument such as: to transfer the burden onto future generations is not fair but as they are unable to defend themselves, such arguments do not have much force. (4) The distribution of tax payments is a contentious issue. As long as income is egalitarian, it is not a problem: taxpayments can also be egalitarian. But once income distribution becomes differentiated, tax payments will have to be skewed. In such a case, taxes should be distributed in such a way that the utility of after-tax income is equal for all households. As a consequence of the declining marginal utility of income, this means that the wealthy should pay much more tax than the poor. Because of the contentious nature of these four issues, however, the determination of how the burdens and benefits of government taxation should be distributed has become ideologically insurmountable.

Yet we should acknowledge that the government does not only spend money. The citizenry obtains essential goods and services in return, and very frequently the government is able to obtain those services at a lower cost—because of economies of scale—than if individuals were to pay for those services themselves. Taxes are not consumed by government, and only a tiny fraction of total revenue is spent on maintaining the institutions of government. Taxes pay for vital services of policemen, firefighters, teachers, and judges. They support health and unemployment insurance, pay for pensions of the retired, and care for the disabled. They provide food for the needy, without which the social order would be difficult—even impossible—to maintain, and support those who have been excluded from the labor market. Taxes also used to pay for investments in infrastructure such as harbors, roads, airports, bridges, satellites, dams, and basic research, without which the economy would be dysfunctional.

It was the government that paid for the basic research leading to the Internet, that developed rocket science—making satellite communication possible—and funded the biotechnology that is revolutionizing medicine. We tend to take for granted these contributions of taxes to the economy. There are 2.2 billion users of the Internet worldwide today. So taxes do not only subtract from income, they also add an immense amount of economic value that is not so visible but that nonetheless has major scientific and commercial implications, laying the foundations of economic growth in the long run. Today's technological revolution would be utterly impossible without having received substantial government support. In other words, taxes also grow the economy in substantial ways. To overlook these very important contributions by government to innovation and economic growth is utterly biased and misleading.

The second richest man in America agreed in 2010: billionaire Warren Buffett—who earned some $63 million—suggests outright that he knows no one who makes investment decisions on the basis of the tax rate:[10] "I think that people at the high end, people like myself, should be paying a lot more in taxes. We have it better than we've ever had it," he said in an interview. When the interviewer pointed to critics' claims that the very wealthy need tax cuts to spur business and capitalism, Buffett replied, "The rich are always going to say that, you know, 'Just give us more money, and we'll go out and spend more, and then it will all trickle down to the rest of you.' But that has not worked the last 10 years, and I hope the American public is catching on."[11]

The contention that the low tax rate of the top income earners induces economic growth, thereby benefiting the rest of the population, is also known as trickle-down economics or supply-side economics. Paul Krugman calls it "old voodoo economics—the belief, refuted by study after study, that tax cuts pay for themselves."[12] It is not based on either economic theory or empirical evidence. Instead, it is based on purely magical thinking. What matters for investment decisions— as students of Econ 101 should know—is the incentive of potential profits to be earned and the degree of uncertainty associated with earning those profits. In the real world, the tax rate plays a minor role in that decision. In fact, about 130 millionaires signed a petition asking Congress to raise the tax rate.[13]

The economist Arthur Laffer has argued that lowering tax rates actually increases revenue. But the evidence does not support his contention.[14] The tax rate could be as high as 70 percent without having a negative effect on either revenues or output. In addition, the consumption tax-revenue curve does not have a peak at all.[15] That means that the tax on consumption could be increased without having a negative effect on total revenues collected. Moreover, the economy grew just fine when the top tax rates were several multiples of the current levels. In short, there is no relationship between top tax rates and economic growth: "the reduction in the top tax rates have had little association with saving, investment, or productivity growth. However, the top tax rate reductions appear to be associated with the increasing concentration of income at the top of the income distribution. The share of income accruing to the top 0.1 percent of U.S. families in-creased from 4.2 percent in 1945 to 12.3 percent by 2007 before falling to 9.2 percent due to the 2007–2009 recession"[16] (Table 12.1). The reason for the lack of relationship between the top tax rates and economic performance is that labor services are supplied inelastically and investments are related more closely to profit opportunities than to tax rates. Furthermore, higher tax rates on millionaires lower the pursuit of rent seeking and thereby improve efficiency.[17]

Krugman suggested that in 2007 the top 0.1 percent of taxpayers (that is about 150,000 people who earned more than $2 million a year) "had a combined income of more than a trillion dollars. . . . It wouldn't be hard to devise taxes that would raise a significant amount of revenue from those super-high-income individuals."[18] Moreover, the top 12 percent of American taxpayers, some 17.4 million households, earned an income of $3.8 trillion in 2009.[19] The government could have collected an additional half a trillion dollars from this privileged group without pinching their conspicuous consumption habits excessively. Furthermore, corporate profits after taxes were about $1.5 trillion; one could easily raise a matching sum from this source.[20] This would have

Table 12.1

There Is No Relationship Between Economic Growth and the Top Tax Rates

	Top Marginal Tax Rate	Top Capital Gains Tax Rate	GDP / Per Capita Growth Rate
1950s	90%	25%	2.40%
Today	35%	15%	1.00%

Source: Thomas L. Hungerford, "Taxes and the Economy: An Economic Analysis of the Top Tax Rates Since 1945," Congressional Research Service, September 14, 2012, 7-5700

erased almost the entire budget deficit; the rest could have been erased with a transactions tax on financial services, taxing Internet usage, and lowering military expenditures. While politically this is unfeasible, the point is that we could raise sufficient revenue to balance the budget without a substantial impact on the quality of life of the population.

However, balancing the budget does not fit well into the spirit of the times. For ideological reasons, President Ronald Reagan decreased the top tax rate markedly and inaugurated a long period of federal budget deficits the main goal of which was to "starve the beast," that is to say, to minimize the size of government by choking off government revenues in the hope that government expenditures would follow suit. That policy was both flawed and unethical. It was flawed because it failed to consider the reality that vested interests (such as the military-industrial complex) would strongly resist lowering expenditures, and the outcome of the political process would be to take the easiest road, which led to deficit financing. The "starve-the-beast" policy was also unethical because it transferred the burden of financing the government onto future generations.

The accumulation of deficits was reversed briefly by Bill Clinton's short-lived budget surpluses but resumed under the George W. Bush administration's irresponsible tax cuts, which brought about a long series of deficits. Government deficit in 2009–2011 was at an unsustainable level of about $1.3 to $1.5 trillion, or 12 percent of national income. Hence, about 40 percent of federal expenditures were financed by borrowing, mostly from abroad.[21] In addition, military expenditures increased substantially and reached $646 billion in 2011; that was about half of the deficit and a quarter of all revenues.[22] At the same time, the effective corporate tax rate was halved from about 40 percent in the 1950s to less than 20 percent today at the beginning of the twenty-first century. Corporate income taxes were a mere 1.2 percent of GNP in 2011 and merely 16 percent of individual income taxes.

Lower taxes introduce inefficiencies that are associated with higher crime rates: many firms, including the McDonald's near my house, hire private police in order to maintain safety in the evening. This is an extra expenditure that is superfluous in systems with higher public expenditures and a concomitant lower crime rate. Insofar as the crime rate is affected by the educational level of the population and hence the school system, the "starve-the-beast" strategy—which deprives schools of adequate funding—leads to a myriad of tiny and hidden inefficiencies in the economy that add up to a substantial amount at the aggregate level. Higher taxes mean less income redistribution through robberies and break-ins (and lower insurance costs); since taxes counterbalance inequality and lower the crime rate, they thereby foster social capital formation, social cohesion, trust, and cooperation, all of which lower transaction costs and lead to a higher quality of life. The net burden of crime in the United States is estimated to exceed a massive one trillion dollars and this does not count $600 million that was transferred from firms and individuals to criminals through illegal activity.[23] This is a net burden of some $4,000 per capita. If this is not inefficient, nothing is.

There are many laissez-faire capitalist economies in Western and Northern Europe in which inheritance is taxed at a much higher rate than in the United States, with the consequence being that the distribution of income is much more equal. The skewed income distribution in the United States gives rise to various forms of conspicuous consumption. For example, the daughters of Formula 1 manager Bernie Ecclestone (Petra, age 23, and Tamara, age 27) bought two houses for $150 million;[24] elsewhere, needy college students try desperately to pay off their bills by selling sex to retired millionaires.[25] Such discrepancies produce a society with a lower quality of life: there is more envy, more peer pressure to keep up with the Joneses, more anxiety about the future, and more angst about unemployment, about becoming sick, or about being robbed. People are more relaxed and less stressed and harried in an egalitarian environment.

High-tax-rate countries generally rank at or near the top of surveys pertaining to the quality of life whereas the United States is usually at the low end of industrialized countries. Sweden and the Netherlands had an unemployment rate in September 2010 of 7.8 percent and 4.4 percent, respectively, compared to the United States' 9.6 percent.[26] They also had 100 percent health insurance coverage, which enabled their citizens to live one to two years longer than do people in the United States. They also spend half of what Americans do on health care, and live safer with less crime, fewer depressed people,[27] and a relative child poverty rate of 5 to 7 percent compared to the United States' 22 percent.[28] Moreover, the cost of college education in those countries is borne by the society at large so that graduates leave the university with zero debt, in contrast to the $23,300 debt accumulated by 37 million U.S. graduates for a total outstanding debt of almost $1 trillion.[29]

Thus, by fostering equality in disposable income, taxes increase efficiency by improving educational quality. Suddenly higher taxes do not seem so bad after all. In the words of James Kwak, we "need a narrative about the role of government in our political and economic life" which holds that "taxes are a means of raising funds for necessary collective endeavors, that regulation can just as easily promote as stifle freedom (such as the freedom to avoid toxic drugs and unsafe food), and that government can, as the Founders recognized, promote the general welfare."[30] Maybe higher taxes in Europe are not such a bad idea as they are made out to be, as people live longer and more satisfactory and less harried lives. They work less and have longer vacations; they are subject to less uncertainty and less criminal activity; they have fewer slums and poor schools and eliminate the need for such high levels of indebtedness among the young.

CAUSE AND EFFECT: FISCAL POLICY AT THE BEGINNING OF THE OBAMA ADMINISTRATION

What was the effect on the economy of Obama's stimulus package of February 2009? Analyzing and answering such a question is challenging and consequently controversial, because it is not enough to know the actual performance of the economy in 2009; rather it requires answering a counterfactual question: What would have happened had the policy not been adopted? What actually happened in 2009 is insufficient to understand the impact of the policy, because there were other forces at work. The aim of answering the question is to isolate those other forces from the effects of the policy measure. The problem is that how such a stimulus works its way through the economy is also controversial.

Note that the unemployment rate had been increasing at a rate of 0.5 percent per month during the three months prior to the bill's adoption. This meant that at the peak of the Great Recession, the number of unemployed was increasing at a rate of nearly 800,000 people per month. After the adoption of the stimulus, the rate of increase of the unemployed was much less—220,000 per month. Although that was a substantial decline (to one-fourth of its pre-stimulus level), it is still not convincing evidence that the decline was caused by the stimulus, because those who are ideologically antagonistic to Keynesian policies argued that the rate of increase in the number of unemployed was bound to decline in any event. They argued it could not possibly continue indefinitely at the 800,000 per month level. The increase in the number of employed during November and December of 2009 also failed to convince the skeptics, although the number employed continued to increase during the following years. These facts are not contested even if some might argue that we should also consider the *under*employment rate.

Yet these numbers do not help us to ascertain the effect of the stimulus. After all, what happened after the stimulus was not necessarily caused by the stimulus. So we need prior theories on how the economy works and how various variables in the economy interact, and thus we frame the problem in terms of the counterfactual question—what would have happened in the absence of the stimulus. That is, the true effect of the nearly $800 billion worth of tax reductions and government expenditures specified in the act cannot be assessed in a definitive way because the way in which we approach that problem and the assumptions we make in order to solve it depend in large part on our a priori ideological belief system. Thus, liberal economists—not surprisingly—lined up in favor of the stimulus program, while conservative ones argued vociferously against it.

A headcount was not taken, but the Congressional Budget Office—which is an independent agency—estimated (using Keynesian principles) that GDP in 2009 was at least 1.4 percent above what it would have been in the absence of the stimulus, and perhaps as much as 3.8 percent above it.[31] Moody's Analytics, an independent forecasting firm, estimated that the stimulus saved about 2.5 million jobs.[32] Nonetheless, the conservatives are unwilling to concede these numbers. Economics is not like a natural science. Preconceived ideologies play a major role in the way we perceive the economic universe and rational arguments cannot overcome those intuitive notions.

CHAPTER SUMMARY

Former president Ronald Reagan was ill-informed when he contended that "government is the problem." Milton Friedman was similarly mistaken in railing against government in his influential television program "Free to Choose," which had substantial influence on popular culture. Actually, the government is an essential partner in the economy. There is no way around it. The market is incapable of providing adequate oversight to avoid all the pitfalls of free markets, such as imperfect information, opportunistic behavior, and power imbalances. The government alone can provide public goods essential to the efficient functioning of markets, and it alone provides basic research in science and technology that promotes economic growth. It alone can provide countervailing power to offset the hegemony of big business.

Hence, regulation ought not be seen as a burden to business but as a prerequisite to the smooth functioning of markets. Of course, it can be overdone, like anything else, but it is clear that in the run-up to the economic crisis of 2008, deregulation was the slogan and regulators were in office who did not take their responsibilities seriously. The ensuing crisis caused permanent damage to the global economy.

Ever since the influence of Keynesian ideas, governments have used fiscal and monetary policy in order to smooth out aggregate demand over the business cycle. Unfortunately such policies turned out to be too difficult for many governments to execute, because they required the cooling down of the economy at the peaks of business cycles, which was unpopular among the business elite and therefore was politically untenable. Thus, Keynesian policies led to endemic government deficits in many countries and an accumulation of public debt that, after the financial crisis, forced many to reduce government expenditures just at a time when they should have been increasing them. This became an internal contradiction to the way Keynesianism was actually practiced and an immense challenge to economic policy. We often forget that government spending often involves investments crucial for the efficient functioning of the economy.

Saving is important for investment and it also provides a cushion for hard times. Unfortunately, the culture has turned against saving. Yet its importance has been overlooked because so much cash has been available for investors in the global economy that the significance of domestic savings has been underestimated. On the contrary, Madison Avenue emphasized a culture of instant gratification from which its impatient clients could profit. Tomorrow would be too late; it is better for consumers to spend their money today. There is no profit to be had from people saving for a rainy day. That led to excessive debt burden that unfortunately contributed to the instability of the economy during the run-up to the financial crisis of 2008.

QUESTIONS FOR DISCUSSION

1. How efficient would the economy be without government?
2. Imagine the economy today without the Internet.
3. Has your family benefited from government expenditures?
4. Why is both inflation and deflation bad for the economy?
5. Was the Federal Reserve's Quantitative Easing program successful?
6. Why have foreigners continued to buy U.S. government securities in spite of the low returns?
7. What are some differences between Keynesians and their opponents, the real-business-cycle school of macroeconomists?
8. Do you think workers are interested mostly in their nominal or real income?
9. How do unions serve their members?
10. Do you think that subsiding savings would be desirable?
11. Do you think that "keeping up with the Joneses" was mainly responsible for the increase in indebtedness of the U.S. consumer?
12. Has anyone suggested that you save for a rainy day?
13. Have you seen any advertisements urging you to save? Why or why not?
14. Discuss: saving is not important anymore as so much money is available for us in China and Japan. They can do our saving for us.
15. How much debt/savings do you or your family have?
16. Can you think of advertisements that encourage instant gratification?
17. How could one incentivize Americans to save more and spend less?
18. Are taxes bad for the economy?
19. Do you agree with Warren Buffett that millionaires should pay higher taxes?
20. Name some important items you use that were subsidized by taxes.
21. Do you think it is fair that a few people are able to capture a large portion of the income generated by the economy?
22. Do you think that millionaires are job creators?
23. Do you think that "starving the beast" is an unethical goal?
24. Do you think that we should adopt a balanced budget amendment?
25. Do you think that lowering taxes increases the quality of life?

NOTES

1. Congressional Budget Office, "Historical Budget Data—January 2012 Baseline."

2. Abba Lerner dubbed it as such.

3. The budget does not have to be balanced each year but over the business cycle. Wikipedia contributors, "Balanced Budget Amendment," *Wikipedia: The Free Encyclopedia.*

4. Wikipedia contributors, "James G. Rickards," *Wikipedia: The Free Encyclopedia.*

5. Built at a cost of some $425 billion (2006 dollars), the system is 47,000 miles long. Wikipedia contributors, "Interstate Highway System," *Wikipedia: The Free Encyclopedia.*

6. U.S. Department of Commerce, U.S. Census Bureau, *The 2012 Statistical Abstract. Income, Expenditures, Poverty, & Wealth.*

7. Jim Forsyth, "More than Two-Thirds in U.S. Live Paycheck to Paycheck: Survey," Reuters, September 19, 2012. Harry Bradford, "Nearly Half of Americans Have Less than $500 in Savings: Survey," *Huffington Post,* October 23, 2012.

8. James T. Bond, Cindy Thompson, Ellen Galinsky, and David Prottas, *The 2002 National Study of the Changing Workforce: Executive Summary* (New York: Families and Work Institute, 2002).

9. Paul Samuelson and William Nordhaus, *Economics,* 19th ed. (New York: McGraw-Hill/Irwin, 2009), 376.

10. Laura Saunders and Siobhan Hughes, "Buffett Builds His Tax-the-Rich Case," *The Wall Street Journal,* October 13, 2011.

11. Why is Warren Buffet, who is the second-richest person in the United States, paying a lower marginal tax rate than his workers? "Buffett isn't the only billionaire who has argued for higher taxes. Both Microsoft co-founder Bill Gates and his father, Bill Gates, Sr., recently came out in support of a Washington state measure to 'create a 5 percent tax rate on annual income exceeding $200,000 for individuals and $400,000 for couples, and a 9 percent tax rate on income that tops $500,000 for individuals and $1 million for couples.'" Amanda Terkel, "Warren Buffet: I 'Should Be Paying A Lot More in Taxes,'" *Huffington Post,* November 21, 2010. "Executives Who Support Tax Increases to Fix the Deficit," *The Wall Street Journal,* October 25, 2012. Ryan Grim and Sabrina Siddiqui, "Top Two Percent to GOP: Tax Us," *Huffington Post,* December 5, 2012.

12. Paul Krugman, "The New Voodoo," *The New York Times,* December 30, 2010.

13. Among them is the well-known economist Nouriel Roubini. "Patriotic Millionaires for Fiscal Strength."

14. Don Fullerton, "Laffer Curve," in *The New Palgrave Dictionary of Economics,* 2nd ed., ed. Steven N. Durlauf and Lawrence E. Blume (Basingstoke, UK: Palgrave Macmillan, 2008), p. 839.

15. Mathias Trabandt and Harald Uhlig, "The Laffer Curve Revisited," *Journal of Monetary Economics* 58 (2011) 4: 305–327, p. 314.

16. Thomas L. Hungerford, "Taxes and the Economy: An Economic Analysis of the Top Tax Rates Since 1945," Congressional Research Service, CRS Report for Congress, 7-5700, September 14, 2012.

17. "A Conversation on the State of the Economy with Paul Krugman and Joseph E. Stiglitz," Institute for New Economic Thinking (INET), October 23, 2012.

18. Paul Krugman, "Things to Tax," *The New York Times,* November 27, 2011.

19. U.S. Internal Revenue Service, Individual Statistical Tables by Size of Adjusted Gross Income.

20. U.S. Department of Commerce, Bureau of Economic Analysis, *National Income and Product Accounts.*

21. Congressional Budget Office, "Historical Budget Data—January 2012 Baseline."

22. Ibid. Very strange to keep such a large military at a time when the avowed enemy is about 500 al-Qaeda fighters and perhaps 30,000 Taliban. Greg, "Intel Officials Estimate Al Qaeda Numbers Fewer than 500 Operatives," Defensetech.com, July 1, 2010. Gareth Porter, "U.S. Military Low-Balling Size of Taliban Forces? Deferring to Petraeus, NIE Failed to Register Taliban Growth," Common Dreams, February 14, 2011.

23. The transfers are not net losses to the economy in the same way as the guards at McDonald's are. David A. Anderson, "The Aggregate Burden of Crime," *Journal of Law and Economics* 42 (1999) 2: 611–642.

24. One is a 57,000-square-foot home. "Sisters Spend $150 Million for Two Houses," *The Wall Street Journal Live* video, May 17, 2012.

25. Amanda M. Fairbanks, "Seeking Arrangements: College Students Using 'Sugar Daddies' to Pay Off Loan Debt," *Huffington Post,* April 30, 2012.

26. Organization for Economic Cooperation and Development (OECD), Stat Extracts.

27. Anna Manchin, "Depression Hits Jobless in UK, U.S. More than in Germany," *Gallup,* November 21, 2012.

28. UNICEF Innocenti Research Centre, *Child Poverty in Perspective: An Overview of Child Well-Being in Rich Countries* (Italy: The United Nations Children's Fund, 2007), Report Card 7.

29. Some 14.4 percent of borrowers have past-due balances. Meta Brown, Andrew Haughwout, Donghoon Lee, Maricar Mabutas, and Wilbert van der Klaauw, "Grading Student Loans," Federal Reserve Bank of New York, March 5, 2012.

30. James Kwak, "The Government Does Have Something to Do with It," *Baseline Scenario,* October 6, 2010.

31. Congressional Budget Office, "Estimated Macroeconomic Impacts of HR 1 as Passed by the House and by the Senate."

32. David Leonhardt, "Economic Scene: Judging Stimulus by Job Data Reveals Success," *The New York Times,* February 16, 2010.

13

OPEN ECONOMY MACROECONOMICS

International trade is an important aspect of the economy. We will analyze its impact on the economy especially in the presence of unemployment and in case of persistent trade deficits.

INTERNATIONAL TRADE

No other theorem is as firmly engrained in the mainstream's firmament as the theorem of comparative advantage. It is one of the unquestioned pillars of free-market ideology. It holds that all countries benefit from trade if they specialize in the production and export of those goods in which they have a comparative advantage.

However, this theorem is misleading.[1] There are many reasons for this: (1) The theorem as usually discussed is actually about barter and not trade in the modern sense of using money as a unit of account. Once money is introduced, trade becomes complicated by the possibility of trade deficits and exchange-rate volatility or manipulation. In turn, trade deficits can create unemployment if the exchange rate does not respond or is not allowed to respond appropriately to bring trade into balance. (2) The theorem does not consider the possibility of unemployment. It assumes that those who lose their jobs as a consequence of trade will find employment instantaneously in another sector. However, if that assumption does not hold and trade does cause unemployment, benefits may not accrue at all and instead there might be losses. (3) It is well known that only some people benefit from trade while others lose. The decline in the relative price of labor-intensive goods, for instance, will depress the wages of labor. However, the ethical nature of the redistribution is overlooked. The question is framed in terms of the increases in total welfare, and the fact that trade is not Pareto optimal is disregarded; this is inconsistent: some welfare-enhancing policies are prohibited because they are not Pareto optimal, while other policies are advocated although they are not Pareto optimal. (4) The theorem is derived for two countries trading two goods being produced by two factors. However, the theorem no longer holds with many countries and many goods and many factors. (5) The theorem assumes that goods traded are produced under competitive conditions and does not take into consideration that most traded goods today are produced by oligopolistic firms. (6) Free trade is not a prescription for economic growth.

The theorem pertains only to welfare in the static sense under very special circumstances and not at all to economic development. No underdeveloped country—not Germany, or the United States in the nineteenth century, nor Japan, Korea, or China more recently—was able to catch up with developed countries without protecting its economy from competition of the more advanced countries.[2] In short, the theorem is applicable only in very narrow circumstances. Yet it is applied as though it were a universal law, applicable without restraint in the real world where these assumptions do not hold.

TARIFFS AND WELFARE

According to the theory of comparative advantage, tariffs detract from welfare. Samuelson and Nordhaus offer a typically simple example of the consequences of a tariff as follows: suppose that the initial price of clothing is $4 per unit and domestic output is 100 units and consumption is 300 units, so that 200 units are imported (Figure 13.1). After a $2.00 per unit tariff is introduced, the domestic price increases to $6 and domestic production increases to 150 units and consumption declines to 250 units so that imports fall to 100 units. They conclude that "the overall social impact [of the tariff] is . . . a gain to producers of $250, a gain to the government of $200, and a loss to consumers of $550. The net social cost (counting each of these dollars equally) is therefore $100."[3]

These amounts are calculated as follows: the area A equals the gain to producers (2 * 100) + 0.5(2 * 50) = 250, but it is at the expense of consumers. Hence, this is not a loss but a transfer from consumers to producers. The first term (2 * 100) is the increase in price times the amount produced initially, while the second term 0.5(2 * 50) is the area of the triangle, which is the increase in the amount produced (50) times the tariff (2) divided by two. The area C is government revenue, which they pass back to the consumers so it is not a loss either. The areas B and D are each 0.5(2 * 50) so they add up to 100. That is what is considered to be lost to the economy. The area B is the value of labor and other factors of production that had to be paid a premium wage in order to induce them to produce clothing instead of something else, and the area D is the loss in utility for consuming less clothing than before.

However, there are many hidden assumptions and problems in this standard model. For instance, in the microeconomics section of the standard textbook, mainstream economists argue that the utility of one individual ought not be compared to that of another. Yet in the macroeconomics section they stealthily do just that. They compare the income gained by producers to that lost by consumers. But incomes are not the relevant unit of comparison unless they are converted into utility, since a dollar produces a different amount of utility for one person than for another. Here economists find it obvious to "count each dollar equally," as asserted above inconspicuously by Samuelson and Nordhaus. Hence, there is a flagrant inconsistency between the microeconomic and macroeconomic sections of the standard textbooks that is not likely to be caught by students. One would have to consider how much utility is being produced by these different dollars, but that cannot be done rigorously. One must use common sense and argue that because of the diminishing utility of income, a dollar for a person living from unemployment benefits has greater utility than for a millionaire who might not even know how much money he has.

The assumption of full employment in this model is also completely hidden from the students. It is not even stated explicitly. This is odd, considering that unemployment is an endemic component of the economic system. However, if there is unemployment then area B would not be a loss at all but a gain of $50 to workers who now have a job. In addition, area E would also be a gain, because these wages now accrue to workers who were previously idle so they do not have to be induced away from other sectors of the economy at all. That would be a gain of 4 * 50 = 200 that is transferred from foreign workers to domestic workers. Hence, the total gain to domestic workers is $250 and the presence of unemployment turns the whole calculation on its head: it converts an alleged social loss of $100 to an actual gain of $250 – 100 = $150.[4] The increase of $150 in the domestic economy will also have multiplier effects in the presence of unemployment, so the actual gain is greater.[5]

Another issue left unmentioned in conventional analysis is that the losses are spread among

Figure 13.1   **The Effect of Tariffs on Domestic Production and Consumption**

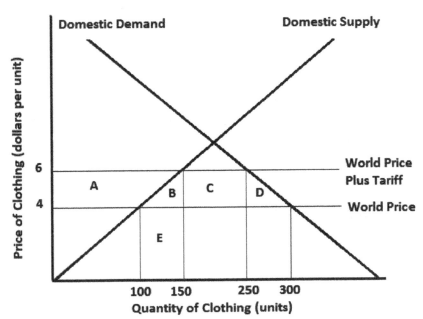

many consumers but the gains are concentrated among a few workers. So if the $100 loss were divided among, say, 10,000 consumers, then the $0.01 loss per person would have a trivial impact on those consumers' utility level. They may not even notice it. In contrast, if the gain to workers of $250 were divided among, say, 5 workers, then the gain per worker of $50 may well mean a substantial improvement to their livelihood and a substantial increase in their level of utility. In other words, the social losses are divided among the many while the gains accrue to a few, implying that, measured in terms of utility, the calculus is even more in favor of the tariff. In sum, unemployment is a crucial issue to consider in economic policy. The general rule should be that tariffs should be lowered and old industries phased out at a rate such that the displaced workers can be absorbed by expanding industries, or that the unemployed are actually fully compensated for their losses by the gainers, making the policy Pareto optimal.

The aficionados of free trade also disregard the issue of Pareto optimality that is emphasized in the microeconomic section of their textbooks. Suppose we begin the analysis with the $2 tariffs in place. The mainstream would argue that the elimination of the tariff is welfare enhancing by the $100 discussed above. However, this hides the inconvenient fact that the elimination of the tariff is not Pareto optimal because there are losers, namely the domestic producers and workers. The argument is often made that such policies should be enacted nonetheless since the gainers gain more than the losers lose and the latter could be compensated. Yet, that is little consolation for the losers, and in the microeconomic section it is argued that there is no moral justification for enacting a policy that benefits some at the expense of others. The Pareto efficiency principle is invoked vociferously, for instance, in the discussion of redistribution: we are not allowed to redistribute income because that would hurt someone and would therefore contradict the principle. Yet in the case of tariffs, such redistribution causes us no such ethical problems. This is a major inconsistency between micro- and macroeconomics.

The theorem merely assumes that workers who lose their jobs because of the elimination of tariff protection can find a job somewhere else in the economy. That might have been true in the 1950s when jobs were plentiful, but is no longer so. How are workers with a high school education displaced from low-skilled occupations supposed to find jobs in the IT sector? The best they can do is to trade their lower-middle-class income for Walmart wages and join the ranks of the working poor on food stamps.[6] There were 2.3 million people in 2009 who were unemployed for longer than a year.[7] Shouldn't the loss of their wages be subtracted from the gains from trade? Is it moral at all to embark on a policy that hurts some people? In short, the simplification of the standard trade analysis overlooks the main social, political, and ethical problems of coping with the effects of factory shutdowns as a consequence of trade liberalization. Humanistic economics would prescribe not only that "America as a whole" benefit, but that no one in America be hurt as a consequence of international trade. That is to say, the losers should be fully compensated by the winners. Then trade would be Pareto optimal.

TRADE AND GROWTH

Free trade is not a prescription for growth of less developed economies. Even if international trade would increase welfare, and would not cause unemployment, and if losers were fully compensated by the gainers, there is nothing in the theorem of comparative advantage that predicts the growth of the economy. As a matter of fact, no country was able to catch up to the most advanced country of the time by practicing free trade, not even England. It gained competitive advantage over the Dutch in the seventeenth century not through free trade but by the mercantilist protection provided by its Navigation Acts, which prohibited the use of foreign ships for trade between the mother country and its colonies, which earned it a lot of profits. In other words, developing countries cannot catch up unless they protect some parts of their economy from the products of the technologically most advanced countries. These sectors could otherwise not stand up to foreign competition and the inflow of foreign goods would create unemployment and social turmoil.

China has been following exactly such a protectionist policy astutely and successfully for the last four decades, with extraordinary growth rates. Germany and the United States did as well in the nineteenth century, and the Asian tigers did the same after World War II. In other words, free trade is hardly a formula for economic growth unless one is at the technological frontier, and even then one has to consider the extent to which free trade causes resources to become unemployed. Without substantial protection, the Asian tigers would not have been able to compete with the technologically advanced nations and their growth would have been stifled.

INFANT INDUSTRIES

Infant industries can be fostered through protection. For example, suppose computers have just been invented in country A and a firm can produce them for $100 dollars in year 0. As it starts manufacturing them it accumulates knowledge about how to build them better and cheaper—called learning by doing—and by year 1 can build them for $95. Now firms in country B see the opportunity but do not have the specific knowledge on the best practices, so they would have to start the process from the beginning as a higher-cost producer at $100. In other words, they are only going to be able to produce computers if the government gives them a $5 subsidy or levies a tariff of $5 on computers. First-mover advantage means that follower countries have to play catch-up and free trade does not work to their advantage in that case. A current example is the penetration of the Chinese wind turbine manufacturers into the U.S. market, to the detriment of the fledgling home industry.[8]

Figure 13.2   **U.S. Trade Deficit in Goods and Services**

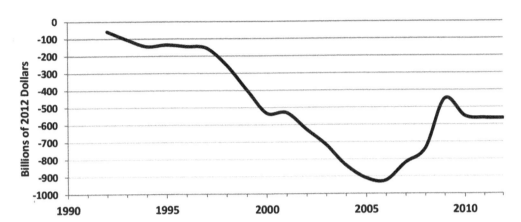

Sources: Price Data: U.S. Department of Labor, Bureau of Labor Statistics, "Top Picks" http://data.bls.
gov/cgi-bin/surveymost?bls; U.S. Department of Commerce, U.S. Census Bureau, "Foreign Trade Historical
Series," www.census.gov/foreign-trade/statistics/historical/

UNBALANCED TRADE

In the real world with money, trade in goods and services does not automatically lead to equilibrium
between exports and imports: the U.S. trade deficits have been enormous for at least a generation.
In 2011, the trade deficit was $560 billion (Figure 13.2). This means that the United States is send-
ing more than half a trillion dollars abroad instead of spending it domestically. The trade deficit
is a job destroyer of major proportions: since the country imports products it otherwise would
have produced, jobs are exported abroad and millions of U.S. workers are put on the unemployment rolls.[9] During the last two decades, the trade deficit amounted to a $10 trillion stimulus to
the rest of the world's economy, which drained an immense amount of purchasing power out of
the U.S. economy (Figure 13.3).[10] No wonder the Chinese economy has been booming with such
a stimulus. It is quite doubtful that the benefits of lower-priced imported goods outweigh these
immense costs.

   According to economic theory, the market should resolve this problem on its own by devaluing
the dollar. But it has not done so because the dollar is a reserve currency; that means that foreign
governments, individuals, and firms want to own dollar-denominated assets in order to trade among
themselves or hold as an investment. This means that the United States is unable to devalue its
currency and thereby eliminate its current account deficit. This imbalance has led to a massive
export of IOUs on which interest has to be paid in the future.[11] While this buoys up current living
standards, it does so at the expense of generations yet unborn.

IMPORT CERTIFICATES

Warren Buffett, the famous investor, urged us years ago to "halt this trading of assets for consum-
ables" by using import certificates.[12] He suggested an ingenious way to fix the problem without
picking on any other single nation, and also without raising tariffs on any single good. He warned,

Figure 13.3 **U.S. Cumulative Trade Deficit**

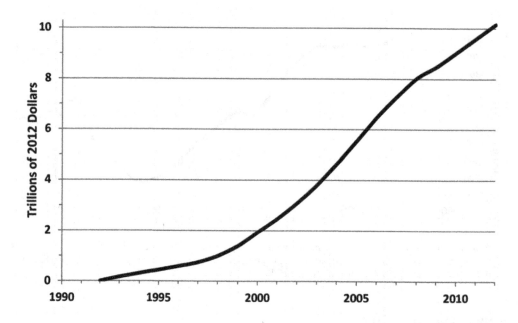

"The U.S. trade deficit is a bigger threat to the domestic economy than either the federal budget deficit or consumer debt and could lead to political turmoil. . . . Right now, the rest of the world owns $3 trillion more of us than we own of them." Note that since he wrote those lines the amount of indebtedness has risen to $5 trillion, and most of this amount—$4.5 trillion—was U.S. Treasury securities, that is, claims on U.S. citizens of about $15,000 per capita. Japan alone was in possession of financial securities worth $1.8 trillion, while China held a nearly equal amount of $1.6 trillion. The interest on them probably will have to be paid in perpetuity. This large stash of savings also enables Chinese companies to buy up U.S. businesses: in 2012 they paid $118 million for Complete Genomics, a California DNA sequencing company.[13] This means that we are exchanging the ownership rights to firms for Chinese consumer goods and obviously the profits from such firms will no longer accrue to U.S. citizens.

Buffett's suggestion was that the U.S. government issue import certificates to all exporters in amounts equal to the value of the exported goods. In turn, the exporters could sell these certificates to importers. By establishing a market for import certificates, firms (United States and foreign) would have powerful incentives to bring the trade deficit into balance. All foreign firms sending goods to the United States would have to buy the certificates in the appropriate amounts from U.S. exporters. Overall, the market for certificates would lead to balanced trade.[14]

Importantly, the trading partners of the United States would not have the means to retaliate. The price of U.S. exports would decline by the amount of the value of the certificates, giving firms an extra incentive to find markets abroad. Implicitly, that would be a sort of export subsidy paid by importers. U.S. companies would find it much easier to export their products, and thereby could afford to hire the unemployed. At least 2 million U.S. jobs would be created, which would also generate new government tax revenues and ease the budget deficit. Admittedly, the price of imports might increase, but likely not by much. We might have to pay a dollar more for a shirt or $100 more for a BMW. The gains would be concentrated among the unemployed, who really need a break, while the inconveniences would be diffused throughout the rest of the population and would be so small that it would be hardly noticed.[15]

In 2011, U.S. imports were $2.66 trillion, or 27 percent higher than the $2.10 trillion worth of exports. If we phased in the balanced trade policy, we might initially grant, say, $1.20 worth of import certificates for every $1.00 worth of exports. That would reduce the deficit by only 6.6 percent of the value of exports, or $140 billion. Still, it would eliminate one-quarter of the trade deficit, creating a half-million jobs—in effect a stimulus bill that would not cost the government a penny. This would not be bad for starters, and we could build from there, eventually eliminating all the deficits within four years with a big boost to the economy.

NEW TRADE THEORY

The old trade theory of David Ricardo and its modifications were refuted by Paul Krugman, although most textbooks disregard this inconvenient truth, even if he received the Nobel Prize for it. The motivation for the refutation of the old theory was that it was contradicted by modern trade patterns between nations. Instead of trading Portuguese wine for British textiles based on factor endowments, as in Ricardo's example, today most advanced industrialized countries trade basically the same products among themselves: Volkswagen cars are sold in France while Citroen cars are sold in Germany. The motivation in such trade is not comparative advantage but the existence of economies of scale, perceived quality of the product, branding, patent rights, diversity in consumption, or a certain amount of randomness. If the two cars are close substitutes, meaning that if it makes little difference which car one drives, then the choice between them is at random, implying that both cars will find markets in both countries. In addition, these goods are produced not in perfectly competitive markets as supposed by Ricardo, but by oligopolists or by competing monopolists. The essence of VW cars is that it is a monopoly of Volkswagen A.G. and these rights are legally protected and enforced by the state and its coercive agencies. No one else is allowed to produce cars with the VW logo on them. So the perfectly competitive model does not apply to its products. This implies that there are profits to consider that are not part of the old trade theory but are crucial, for they are the source of taxes, future innovation, and growth.

Furthermore, there are economies of scale in production and first-mover advantages to consider. Once these brands are established, they become monopolies and the profits they generate are not easily competed away. Thus, Belgium has no particular comparative advantage in producing Godiva chocolates, but once they are produced there—through historical happenstance—they can establish a quality reputation that serves as the source of trade. Through first-mover advantage firms gain and benefit from economies of scale and learning by doing—they can produce at a lower unit cost than firms that just entered the market—and these provide barriers to entry by competing firms, as in the infant industry example above.

In addition to first-mover advantage, the size of the domestic market also matters. The larger the domestic market, the more a firm will produce and benefit from economies of scale. Thus, its competitive advantage of lower unit cost is not generated by factor or resource endowments but by economies of scale in production. The large domestic market in Germany for high-quality automobiles provided comparative advantages to BMW, Mercedes, Porsche, and Audi to compete in the high-quality niche of the international market.

Increasing-returns technology also changes markedly the static analysis of tariffs. With the increase in tariffs seen in Figure 13.1, the firms increased domestic production of clothing, and, according to the conventional point of view, welfare decreased. That was the end of the analysis. However, if the good is produced with increasing returns to scale, the larger domestic production could mean that costs would decline, thereby changing the calculus considerably depending on the size of the cost decline. In short, the new trade theory modifies the obvious case for Ricardian free trade, which implies that there is room for trade policy through subsidies or tariffs, as in the import-certificate example above.

There is also a role for industrial policy and government investment to help domestic firms capture economies of scale. Of course, there is reason to question the agility of government agencies to design and foster such trade-enhancing policies. Nonetheless, the theoretical case for free trade is no longer absolute; rather, it is diminished considerably depending on the context.[16] The question remains: Can we transition to a set of institutions that foster full employment, which would have to include a trade policy that is much more nimble than the current one? These issues must be put on our agenda both academically and politically if we want to create a more balanced approach to solving our economic problems.

CHAPTER SUMMARY

International trade can be an engine of growth and enhanced welfare, but it can also destroy jobs and send them to distant parts of the world. Its effects are often misunderstood because economists analyze the impact of trade in case there is full employment and disregard the possibility that such trade might cause some people to lose their jobs and become permanently unemployed. In the presence of unemployment, the presumption that trade increases welfare evaporates. In addition, endemic deficits are also ruled out by mainstream theory. Yet the United States has been experiencing a trade deficit continuously for two decades. Under such circumstances, the deficit means that the United States is becoming increasingly indebted to foreign nations and implies that future generations yet unborn will have to bear the burden of that debt. Moreover, the benefits of trade are distributed unevenly: some gain while others lose. It is not ethical to benefit some at the expense of others even if the net benefit were positive. In short, international trade is not always welfare-enhancing as generally claimed, and is not a prescription for economic development. The United States has spent some $10 trillion abroad between 1990 and 2012. This trade deficit is an immense stimulus to the global economy at the expense of domestic producers, and has destroyed millions of jobs in the United States.

QUESTIONS FOR DISCUSSION

1. What should be done about our endemic trade deficits?
2. Do you think we should protect American industries?
3. Do you know anyone who has become unemployed because of competition by foreign producers?
4. Do you think it is fair to introduce economic policies that help the economy grow but hurt some individuals?
5. Do you think that those workers who lost their jobs because of the NAFTA (that introduced free trade among Mexico, Canada, and the U.S.) agreement should have been fully compensated for their losses and guaranteed a job with as high a wage as they had prior to the change in tariffs?
6. Do you think it was a good idea to bail out GM and Chrysler?
7. What are some major challenges we face in today's globalized world?
8. Do you think that free trade is beneficial to the U.S. economy?

NOTES

1. Samuelson and Nordhaus even refer to it as being true without qualification: "Notwithstanding its limitations, the theory of comparative advantage is one of the deepest truths in all of economics. Nations that disregard comparative advantage pay a heavy price in terms of their living standards and economic growth." Paul Samuelson and William Nordhaus, *Economics,* 19th ed. (New York: McGraw-Hill/Irwin, 2009), 349.

2. Ha-Joon Chang, *Kicking Away the Ladder: Development Strategy in Historical Perspective* (London: Anthem Press, 2002); Ha-Joon Chang, *Bad Samaritans: The Myth of Free Trade and the Secret History of Capitalism* (New York: Bloomsbury Press, 2008).

3. Samuelson and Nordhaus, *Economics,* 353.

4. Another way of seeing this is to subtract the $550 loss of consumers from the total amounts gained by producers, workers, and government: $250 + 200 + $250 = 700 and 700 − 550 = 150.

5. There have been just a few observers who warned against the adverse consequences of free trade. John M. Culbertson, "The Folly of Free Trade," *Harvard Business Review* 64 (1986) 5: 122–128.

6. From the front page of the *Wall Street Journal* (February 3, 2009), the caption was "Gloomy Prospects: People Began Lining Up Saturday to Apply for Miami Firefighter Jobs." There were thousands in the crowd for the 35 openings.

7. Bureau of Labor Statistics, *Labor Force Statistics from the Current Population Survey, Characteristics of the Unemployed,* 2012, Table 30, "Unemployed Total and Full-Time Workers by Duration of Unemployment."

8. "We cannot sit idly by while China races to the forefront of clean energy production at the expense of U.S. manufacturing," said Senator Sherrod Brown, an Ohio Democrat. Tom Zeller, Jr., and Keith Bradsher, "China's Push into Wind Worries U.S. Industry," *The New York Times,* December 15, 2010.

9. Senator Byron L. Dorgan, *How Corporate Greed and Brain-Dead Politics Are Selling Out America* (New York: Thomas Dunne Books/St. Martin's Press, 2006).

10. Board of Governors of the Federal Reserve System, "Industrial Production and Capacity Utilization—G.17," last updated January 16, 2013.

11. U.S. Department of Commerce, Bureau of Economic Analysis, "U.S. International Transactions Accounts Data, Table 1, 2012."

12. Warren Buffett, "America's Growing Trade Deficit Is Selling the Nation Out from Under Us. Here's a Way to Fix the Problem—and We Need to Do It Now," *Fortune,* November 10, 2003.

13. Andrew Pollack, "U.S. Clears DNA Firm's Acquisition by Chinese," *The New York Times,* December 30, 2012.

14. Robert E. Scott, "Re-balancing U.S. Trade and Capital Accounts: An Analysis of Warren Buffett's Import Certificate Plan," EPI Working Paper No. 286, December 2009.

15. There could be variations on the policy and exemptions for strategic products such as oil. We could also have "threshold values" so small importers would be exempted. And the policy could be phased in over a number of years to give everyone time to gain experience with it.

16. Paul Krugman, "Scale Economies, Product Differentiation and the Pattern of Trade," *American Economic Review* 70 (1980) 5: 950–959. Elhanan Helpman and Paul Krugman, *Market Structure and Foreign Trade* (Cambridge, MA: MIT Press, 1989).

14

MACROECONOMIC EXTERNALITIES

In this chapter, we will discuss the pressing issues pertaining to the environment and sustainable economic growth.

ENVIRONMENT

The earth, its oceans, and its atmosphere are public goods. It would be desirable to maintain them for future generations to enjoy. Put another way, we do not have a right to destroy the environment as we are now in the process of doing. After all, we are the custodians of nature and not its owners. With fewer people having children in the developed world, this is an extremely difficult task. The reason is that while the developed world could afford to clean up the environment, with fewer people having descendants, fewer people care deeply about the plight of future generations. In addition, the incentive for any one individual to decrease the amount of pollution he or she is putting into the atmosphere is negligible. One of the insurmountable flaws of free markets is that future generations are unable to bid for resources; hence, they are unable to influence our decisions about how we treat the environment. This is an insoluble externality as we do not even know those who will be affected by our actions today. We just know in a nebulous way that we will be affecting third parties who are yet unborn.[1] It is difficult to adopt strict policies to sacrifice current consumption under such circumstances.

Markets are generally unable to limit externalities such as CO_2 pollution unless they are regulated; however, the problem is that governments are not keen on enforcing such regulation because it is seen as slowing economic growth and putting the country at a disadvantage vis-à-vis the firms of other countries. This also has implications for the military-industrial complex as slower economic growth also affects military power. Hence, the welfare of future generations loses out against these powerful immediate interests.

Efficient use of natural resources is difficult—if not impossible—to establish in the presence of externalities. However, we could at least establish an institution of the ombudsman, who would be the trustee for the interests of future generations as far as the environment is concerned and advocate sustainable development with zero subjective time preference.[2] This would be mandated with setting prices for carbon dioxide emissions, for instance, or with bidding for resources. Of course, such prices would still be rough approximations, but would at least treat the environment as an endowment and thereby introduce a modicum of intergenerational equity.[3] Furthermore, we should consider that national accounting has always been imperfect, and this mechanism would at least make the accounts more comprehensive, hence it would be an improvement.

The consequence of the power imbalance between present and future generations is that we are threatened by global warming and its effects, as evinced by superstorm Sandy—the largest

Atlantic hurricane on record.[4] We hear of environmental disasters on a regular basis such as the BP oil spill in the Gulf of Mexico in 2010, which polluted 68,000 square miles of ocean with 210 million gallons of oil. The damage was not confined to the environment: 11 people perished, and the human psychological toll was also substantial; for instance, the number of people with a clinical diagnosis of depression increased from a pre-spill level of 5.6 percent to 20.4 percent among coastal residents.[5]

It is obvious that the Industrial Revolution, which started some 250 years ago, has altered our environment to such a degree that the probability of catastrophic changes in the lives of future generations is increasing substantially.[6] We will have to learn to live with changes in ecosystems, water resources, food availability, and large-scale climate events. Coastal regions, river deltas, and small islands are likely to be inundated. Up to 30 percent of the extant species are at risk of extinction. The sea level has risen in Norfolk, Virginia, by a threatening 14.5 inches, causing tidal flooding. The expenditures needed to protect the residents will be considerable.[7] They have to bear the cost that was not caused by them. That is the reality of a negative externality and today's environmental degradation. On the global scale, estimates of annual environmental damage run as high as 11 percent of the world's GNP, and as far as global warming is concerned, the damage may well be irreversible.[8] It would be a pity to destroy this nice earth of ours for the sake of additional economic growth whose benefits are most likely to accrue to those who do not really need the additional income.

SUSTAINABILITY

Will future generations enjoy the level of living standards prevailing today? Should this concern us at all? Do we have the moral right to diminish the prospects of people yet unborn to enjoy our standard of living? How much natural resources should we leave for future generations? These are all deep philosophical questions to ponder for which there are no obvious answers. But for those who believe these are important ethical concerns, it is absolutely necessary that economics incorporate these conundrums into its theories and models not as a mere epiphenomenon but as a central concern. It is unacceptable, for example, that the standard diagram of the circular flow of macroeconomic activity often pays little or no attention to the contribution of the environment to the economy.[9] This is foolhardy, insofar as the contribution of the world's ecosystem services and natural capital to the economy is both substantial and essential.[10]

Economic development is sustainable if the present level of living standard is not obtained at the detriment of future generations. The challenge is posed not only by the current level of pollution but by the fact that people in the developing world aspire to the consumption level of the developed world and if they were to approach it, the impact on our ecological footprint would be an order of magnitude greater and threaten the earth's survival as we know it. The ecological deficit created by the United States is five times that of China; from this difference one can easily infer that as the developing world's living standard increases, the threat to sustainability will increase markedly as well. In short, our addiction to economic growth is dangerous and will continue to lead to natural resource depletion and strain our environment. We ought to care about the waste we produce (for instance, nuclear waste), but atomistic markets are unable to set proper limits on pollution in the absence of collective action.

We ignore this threat at our own peril. Yet there are no effective plans to face this inconvenient truth. Growth and greed are not the answer. Frugality with our resources, conservation, recycling, reducing waste, precaution, and renewable energy would be a more commonsensical approach.[11]

We should also be more cautious about innovations in order to ascertain their safety before their full-fledged adoption.

This is also the message of the "degrowth" movement.[12] Nicholas Georgescu-Roegen advocated a generation ago that economists should consider the binding nature of resources as expressed by the second law of thermodynamics: processes involving energy are irreversible; energy is used up in the economic process and once used cannot be regenerated.[13] Hence, growth cannot go on forever, especially since we are depleting many of our resources at an alarming rate.[14] In order to increase our frugal use of available energy we should: demilitarize, lower population growth, not waste energy, harness solar and wind energy, "cure ourselves of the morbid craving for extravagant gadgetry," "get rid of fashion," goods should be made more durable, and "we must come to realize that an important prerequisite for a good life is a substantial amount of leisure spent in an intelligent manner."[15]

To be sure, there are those optimists who believe that technological change in the future will provide sufficient remedies to cure these ills. While this possibility cannot be ruled out, to rely on yet-undiscovered innovations is far too risky. Instead, we should have fail-safe plans that will work in all eventualities. It would be unfortunate if those technologies did not materialize and we found ourselves unprepared for the consequences. In contrast to growth fetishism,[16] the goal of a humanistic economics should be to "sustainably optimize quality of life," which is a difficult task given the complexity of the ecosystem, its invaluable contribution to the economy, and the fact that the environment—from the ozone layer to the tropical rainforests—is irreplaceable. So before we throw caution to the wind we need to develop a fail-safe policy.[17] This should include a tax on carbon emissions in order to reduce greenhouse gases in the atmosphere. The social cost of carbon emission should be between $50 and $100 per ton, but it currently does not cost anything to emit CO_2 into the atmosphere. That can only lead to uneconomic growth.[18]

GREEN NATIONAL ACCOUNTING

Full-cost accounting subtracts from GDP the environmental damage and resource depletion caused in the process of production or consumption and provides a better indicator of welfare than conventional indicators. In contrast to conventional GDP accounts, green net national product makes allowances for the fact that the amount of air pollution caused by CO_2 gases causes a great deal of environmental damage and detracts from our welfare as well as that of future generations. The World Bank's World Development Indicators series discusses "green" national accounts in which resource depletion and environmental damage are estimated and subtracted from GDP. This reduces GDP growth by 1 to 2 percent per year, which would reduce the effective growth rate to zero for most developed nations.

Natural capital is the stock of resources and ecosystems found in the environment. These are not made by humans and are therefore nonreproducible by humans, although some (coral reefs, for example) reproduce themselves if left undisturbed. Green accounting advocates that the value of nonrenewable resources, such as oil, should not be included in GNP insofar as their depletion implies that we are using up a stock of resources.[19]

CHAPTER SUMMARY

The problem of the commons is one of the "Achilles heels" of markets. Unfortunately pollution is degrading the environment to such a degree that the economy as we know it is threatened by global warming and other environmental calamities. Nature is striking back with a vengeance.

Degrading the value of such public goods as the atmosphere and the ocean and depleting our natural resources is an immense problem which we seem unable to control. Collective action is urgently needed in order to adopt a more commonsensical economy which wastes less, respects the environment, relies mostly on renewable energy, and is less focused on economic growth.

QUESTIONS FOR DISCUSSION

1. Have you done something about decreasing your carbon footprint on the environment?
2. Do you consider global warming a major threat and do you think we will be able to control it?
3. What is more important: growing the economy or saving the environment?
4. Should we leave the environment as good as we found it for future generations?
5. If you were a politician, what policies would you advocate in order to save the environment?
6. Are you concerned about the welfare of future generations?
7. Do you think that a carbon tax would be useful?
8. Do you think that offshore drilling for oil is a good idea?
9. Do you think we should set a goal of sustainable development?
10. Do you think we should be more frugal with natural resources?

NOTES

1. Natural Resources Defense Council, "The Cost of Climate Change," last revised May 21, 2008.

2. Ibid.

3. James Tobin, "What Is Permanent Endowment Income?" *American Economic Review* 64 (1974) 2: 427–432.

4. It had a diameter of 1,100 miles, and it devastated the U.S. mid-Atlantic region in October 2012, causing damages of about $50 billion and killing 209 people. Hurricane Katrina in 2005 caused $81 billion in damages and killed 1,833 people.

5. Dan Witters, "Gulf Coast Residents Remain Worse Off Emotionally Post-Spill," *Gallup,* May 7, 2012.

6. Intergovernmental Panel on Climate Change, "IPCC Fourth Assessment Report: Climate Change 2007."

7. The city is now spending $1.25 million on a short stretch of the shoreline to help protect a single neighborhood. Leslie Kaufman, "Front-Line City in Virginia Tackles Rise in Sea," *The New York Times,* November 25, 2010.

8. United Nations Environment Programme (UNEP) Finance Initiative, "Universal Ownership: Why Environmental Externalities Matter to Institutional Investors," October 2010. See also blogs on the Web site TRUCOSST.

9. Herman E. Daly and Joshua Farley, *Ecological Economics: Principles and Applications* (Washington, DC: Island Press, 2004). Herman E. Daly, *Ecological Economics and Sustainable Development* (Northampton, MA: Edward Elgar, 2007).

10. By some estimates it is as high as $50 trillion a year. This is roughly the value of the world's total gross domestic product at the beginning of the twenty-first century. Paul C. Sutton, Sharolyn J. Anderson, Benjamin T. Tuttle, and Lauren Morse, "The Real Wealth of Nations: Mapping and Monetizing the Human Ecological Footprint," *Ecological Indicators* 16 (2012): 11–22.

11. Herman E. Daly, *Beyond Growth* (Boston: Beacon Press, 1997).

12. Yuval Rosenberg, "Forget GDP: The Radical Plans to Go Beyond Growth," *Fiscal Times,* April 5, 2012. This is also the message of the steady-state-economy movement. Center for the Advancement of the Steady State Economy. Research & Degrowth.

13. Nicholas Georgescu-Roegen, *The Entropy Law and the Economic Process* (Cambridge, MA: Harvard University Press, 1971).

14. Barry Commoner was another early advocate of ecological economics that included reducing pollution, increased conservation, respecting and maintaining the environment, and an energy policy that concentrated on renewable resources. Barry Commoner, *The Closing Circle: Nature, Man, and Technology* (New York: Knopf, 1971). Barry Commoner, *Making Peace with the Planet* (New York: Pantheon, 1990).

15. Nicholas Georgescu-Roegen, "Energy and Economic Myths," *Southern Economic Journal* 41 (1975) 3: 347–381.

16. A fetish is an irrational reverence or obsessive devotion—a fixation—an almost superstitious trust in something like a totem pole, in this case, the free market.

17. Thomas Princen, *The Logic of Sufficiency* (Cambridge, MA: MIT Press, 2005). Thomas Princen, "Consumption and Its Externalities: Where Economy Meets Ecology," *Global Environmental Politics* 3 (2001) 1: 11–30.

18. Martin Weitzman, "On Modeling and Interpreting the Economics of Catastrophic Climate Change," *Review of Economics and Statistics* 91 (2009) 1: 1–19.

19. The German Green Party is one of the few national political movements advocating putting some of these ideas into practice. See Bündnis90/Die Grünen Bundestagsfraktion, "We Look at the Big Picture. Review 2005–2009," 2009.

15

THE FINANCIAL SECTOR
AND THE GREAT RECESSION

In this chapter we explore the causes and consequences of what Alan Greenspan called the greatest "tsunami" since the stock market crash of 1929: the financial crisis of 2008.

BUSINESS CYCLES

Macroeconomic instability is an integral part of our economic system and has been since time immemorial. However, the financial sector is particularly vulnerable because of fractional banking and maturity mismatch. The revenue generated by assets is not timed perfectly well with the payment stream obtained from liabilities. The instability manifests itself in the cyclical nature of economic activity so that GDP, all its components, income, and employment vary considerably over time. The volatility is associated with substantial welfare losses that constantly threaten participants with the uncertainty of diminishing income streams associated with unemployment and decline in asset prices. These threats lead to the insecurity of having to cope with falling incomes and consumption.

However, business fluctuations began to have smaller amplitudes in the mid-1980s due to improved demand management and monetary policy.[1] The pre-meltdown tranquility misled economists into thinking that business cycles were no longer a substantial threat to employment and welfare.[2] Robert Lucas's overconfident presidential address to the American Economic Association in 2003 declared that the "central problem of depression-prevention has been solved, for all practical purposes."[3] Similarly, a year later Ben Bernanke declared prematurely, and with considerable hubris, the new era of the "Great Moderation," stating that business cycles had become less volatile. Both were wrong: the Great Moderation did not last long for a tsunami was on the horizon.[4]

To be sure, there were plenty of warnings, such as the bankruptcy of the important hedge fund Long-Term Capital Management in 1998. It should have given financiers and regulators some pause that the assumed sophistication of the money managers was deceptive and the Black-Scholes option-pricing formula was not always working well. Yet the claim continued to be made that quantitative finance was so advanced that regulators did not need to worry about the financial sector.

Brooksley Born alone, as chair of the Commodity Futures Trading Commission, attempted in vain to regulate derivatives as far back as 1998—even before Warren Buffett famously referred to them as "financial weapons of mass destruction." Buffett had the common sense to warn the world of their hidden dangers, but his call for caution was ignored also and soon forgotten.[5] In 2001, Steve Keen warned about the dangers of the skyrocketing debt to GNP ratio.[6] Dean Baker was the very first to recognize (in 2002) that a housing bubble was, in fact, in the making and warned of the dangers of the loss in wealth when the bubble burst.[7]

Raghuram Rajan also cautioned that the nature of financial innovation was deceiving. He spoke of perverse developments so that managers have "the incentive to take risk that is concealed from investors—since risk and return are related, the manager then looks as if he outperforms peers given the risk he takes. Typically the kinds of risks that can be concealed most easily, . . . are risks that generate severe adverse consequences with small probability, but, in return, offer generous compensation the rest of the time. These risks are known as tail risks. A second form of perverse behavior is the incentive to herd with other investment managers on investment choices because herding provides insurance that the manager will not underperform his peers. Herd behavior can move asset prices away from fundamentals."[8] This is what Charles Prince—the CEO of Citigroup—meant when he quipped in July of 2007, "as long as the music is playing, you've got to get up and dance."[9]

"In fact," Rajan continued, "the data suggest that despite a deepening of financial markets, banks may not be any safer than in the past. Moreover, the risk they now bear is a small . . . tip of an iceberg of risk they have created. . . . They [banks] also may create a greater (albeit still small) probability of a catastrophic meltdown." Furthermore, in 2006, Nouriel Roubini suggested that an "ugly" recession was in the making. Thus, there were plenty of warnings, but in an economy in which regulators were not keen on regulating, believing that the financial sector can regulate itself, no one was listening to those voices that threatened to spoil the party.

Interviews Ben Bernanke gave at the time are indicative of the mind-set that prevailed at the Fed as the housing crisis was brewing. In 2005, when asked by a reporter about a possible housing-market bubble, Bernanke conceded, "unquestionably housing prices are up *quite a bit*." Not only did he mislead the public about the extent of the price increases—they had doubled since 1998—he proceeded to rationalize them away: "I think it's important to note that fundamentals are also very strong: we've got a growing economy, jobs, incomes; we've got very low mortgage rates; we've got demographics supporting housing growth; we've got restricted supply in some places; so it's certainly understandable that prices would go up *some*. I don't know whether prices are exactly where they should be, but I think it's fair to say that what's happened is supported by the strength of the economy."[10] That is about as willfully deceptive as one could possibly be, but note that in Bernanke's ideological framework, bubbles were not supposed to happen. In fact, as Dean Baker had reported three years earlier, the housing prices were completely unrealistic and a major bubble was in the making.[11] Bernanke was wearing ideological blinders although there were ample warnings, including, prominently, that of John Cassidy in *The New Yorker*.[12]

When another reporter asked Bernanke for his worst-case scenario, he responded disingenuously, "I guess I don't buy your premise; it's a pretty unlikely possibility. We've never had a decline in house prices on a nationwide basis." (Had he not heard of the Great Depression?) "So what I think is more likely is that house prices will slow, maybe stabilize, might slow consumption spending a bit; I don't think it will drive the economy too far from its full employment path though."[13] Note that in addition to being dead wrong about the economic situation, it is also strange that Bernanke spoke of full employment at a time when there were some 7.6 million people officially unemployed and another 9 million underemployed (of which 5 million wanted a job but were discouraged in seeking one and another 4 million were working part time although they wanted to work full time).[14] Notwithstanding the damage his false prognosis did to the economy and the pain he caused many people who invested in property relying on his statements, Bernanke's appointment to the Fed was renewed in 2010.

EXPECTATIONS

Expectations pertaining to the future course of events play a major role in economic activity. They are a formidable challenge to macroeconomic theory and policy, because most of our actions today are predicated on what we expect to happen tomorrow. This is the basis of Keynes's notion of "animal spirits." Saving, investment, consumption, and production, and therefore current prices, all depend on our expectations of what prices and interest rates and business conditions will prevail in the future. Yet, when the average brain is faced with complex problems associated with uncertainty, it does rather poorly at calculating probabilities and processing information in such a way that our actions will be prudent and commensurate with actual level of uncertainty. The subprime mortgage crisis demonstrated just how much pillage can be wrought when people's expectations are way off the mark and fail utterly to price risk properly. Kahneman and Tversky proved years ago that people are naïve and biased about risk, do not understand the basic principles of probability at all, and in some cases are unreasonably eager to enter into wagers in which they could lose excessive amounts.[15] Their results have not yet entered the consciousness of policymakers.

Uncertainty has been a major problem not only for the unsophisticated borrowers who accepted variable rate mortgages but also for seasoned supposedly sophisticated investors who based their models on untested formulas for evaluating risk and on inadequate empirical observations.[16] Their data did not reach back to the Great Depression of the 1930s. In any event, Alan Greenspan and his entourage were convinced that this time the situation was different.[17] There were going to be no "black swans,"[18] meaning unexpected, extremely rare events that can cause considerable havoc in markets when they do appear. Yet the decline in housing prices throughout the United States was just such an unanticipated event, demonstrating that expectations were incorrect. Such rare events—housing prices had not declined throughout the United States since the 1930s—make the pricing of risk very difficult, even for specialists.

MINSKY'S MODEL AND THE MELTDOWN OF 2008

The Meltdown of 2008 was straight out of Hyman Minsky's playbook.[19] Beginning in the mid-1960s, Minsky stressed continuously but in vain the inherent instability of the financial system, the dangers of debt accumulation, as well as the endogenous nature of financial crises.[20] He was particularly skeptical about "financialization," which meant that the financial industry was gaining an exaggerated role in the economy at the expense of manufacturing.[21] Indeed, the financial industry accounted for just 4 percent of GDP in 1980 but its importance doubled by the early twenty-first century to 8 percent.[22] At the time of the meltdown, 40 percent of all profits in the United States were made in finance rather than in trade or in commodity production.

Debt played a crucial role in Minsky's model of the business cycle, whereas in conventional macroeconomics the financial sector is often omitted completely and hence concepts such as leverage, debt, and default are dismissed as epiphenomenon. However, his framework includes loan contracts, which commit firms to pay a stream of money out of their expected future profits. The question naturally arises about the extent to which those future profits were correctly anticipated and what happens if those expectations are not realized.[23] In Minsky's incredibly powerful and prescient words: "the greater the weight of speculative and Ponzi finance, the greater the likelihood that the economy is a deviation amplifying system. The first theorem of the financial instability hypothesis is that the economy has financing regimes under which it is stable and financing regimes under which it is unstable. The second theorem of the financial instability hypothesis is that over periods of prolonged prosperity, the economy transits from financial relations that make for a stable system to financial relations that make for an unstable system." After a bubble bursts asset prices will decline and the net worth of firms "will quickly evaporate. Consequently, units with cash flow shortfalls will be forced to try to make position by selling out position. This is likely to lead to a collapse of asset values." Systemic risk implies that one bankruptcy brings about the bankruptcy of other firms so that a snowball effect develops and the whole economy spins out of control. This is the exact scenario of the Meltdown of 2008.

Thus, the price level determines the profit of firms and indirectly the ability to pay back the debt. A fall in prices inflates the real value of debt and leads to difficulties of repayment and to bankruptcies both business and personal. In addition, these developments depress personal consumption and business investments. Without a debt economy, a fall in prices would lead to increased consumption and hence to a decline in unemployment. However, if a fall in prices increases the real value of debt, it will have exactly the opposite effect and decrease consumption and increase unemployment—contrary to conventional analysis. Instability arises also because "market processes do not assure that effective demand always will be sufficient to yield profit flows large enough to enable bankers and businessmen to fulfill their commitments on debts."[24] In other words, in the real world profit expectations can be far off the mark. The upshot is that instability is inherent in free markets with debt, because the feedback mechanism amplifies the instability and makes it self-sustaining rather than bringing the economy back toward equilibrium.

In Minsky's framework, stability uncannily breeds instability. The reason is that long periods of stability enable entrepreneurs to learn how to circumvent the constraints of regulation by innovating and creating new business models outside of the purview of regulators. Furthermore, and reinforcing this development, the stability at the same time deceives regulators into complacency, leaving room for money managers to undermine the very institutions that were responsible for the stability in the first place. They thereby obtain opportunities to engage in risky behavior. This is precisely what happened during the decades prior to the Great Meltdown. The shadow banking system blossomed, outsmarting the regulations that were enacted after the Great Depression, and regulators were in no mood to regulate it in any case. They became complacent. Things were running smoothly, and naysayers—such as Brooksley Born—were mercilessly silenced and gotten out of the way.

Minsky also emphasized that "euphoric" booms were the main cause of financial instability.[25] Euphoric lending meant that both lenders and borrowers made systematic errors in judgment about the loans they contracted by undervaluing the probability of default. Expectations were biased. This framework—derived from the historical record rather than from a priori theorizing about idealized markets—did not fit well into the popular rational agent models.

Consequently, Minsky's ideas were completely ignored by mainstream economists and policymakers.[26] Yet his model predicted exactly what happened. The regulations that were enacted in the wake of the Great Depression served the economy well and promoted a half-century of economic growth with what Paul Krugman dubbed "boring banking." For example, the Glass-Steagall Act of 1933 prohibited commercial banks from investing in the stock market, so banks could not speculate with other people's money. This made sense, as bank deposits were backed by the government so it would have been imprudent to allow banks to assume excessive risk by speculating with deposits backed by a third party.

However, the financial sector evolved and, exactly as Minsky predicted, did so in such a way as to emasculate the regulations. The "shadow banking system" that came into being was not regulated by the same rules as the commercial banks which accepted retail deposits from the public. In addition, the financial institutions of the shadow system did not have access to Federal Reserve lending. In fact, these investment banks were hardly regulated at all, so they could create new financial products. However, these innovations were not designed to improve the productivity of the real economy, that is, to increase the efficiency of investments (and thereby to increase GNP); instead, they were designed for rent seeking (obtaining a bigger share of profits). Furthermore, these new financial instruments created many unforeseen problems, because they injected an immense amount of imperfect information and systemic risk into the macroeconomic system, all of which eluded the purview of the sophisticated economists at the Federal Reserve.

Another major problem was that the investors buying these new financial instruments had absolutely no experience pricing the risks associated with them: historical evidence of their volatility during a bubble, downturn, or panic was nonexistent. Therefore, during the euphoric years of easy money, the risks were woefully mispriced. The overall financial architecture was not designed to easily accommodate such innovations. The extraordinary profits were deceptive since they were immediate and obvious, whereas the costs in terms of the excessive risks were intangible, opaque, and uncertain. It was practically impossible to remain a prudent banker under such conditions. Moreover, the investment banks were highly leveraged and had to roll over their debt continually in order to remain in business. When it became apparent that they had made systematic errors in pricing the risks associated with their investments, the flow of credit was interrupted and they were all threatened with bankruptcy. So it was a very risky business model with many hidden dangerous trigger points based on negative externalities.

There was an abundance of speculative borrowers, investment banks in the shadow banking system such as Bear Stearns and Lehman Brothers. Speculation was not confined to the investment banks. One of the largest speculators was the insurance company AIG, which wrote innovative insurance contracts called credit default swaps. There was also an abundance of consumers in search of lucrative investments who assumed excessive risks, thereby falling prey to predatory lending in the housing market. In sum, risk was ubiquitous and ill understood.

Fundamentally, the shadow banking system bypassed the institutional safeguards put in place in the 1930s by using new financial instruments to increase profits but at the same time inadvertently increasing the amount of risky assets in the system. Instead of diversifying risk, as it was supposed to do, the financial system amplified it by an order of magnitude. A good example of such risky innovation is the credit default swap, which is basically an insurance policy on a financial instrument such as a bond. Suppose Goldman Sachs buys a bond from Lehman Brothers, say, and then insures it against default with AIG. AIG receives monthly payments from Goldman Sachs for the insurance, which is good business for AIG in the short run, because it is all profit. The problem is, however, that when Lehman Brothers went bankrupt AIG did not have the money to honor all of its credit default swap contracts. The swaps were not regulated so that AIG was not compelled to have sufficient capital to cover the contracts. The swaps were not called insurance so that they would not come under regulations pertaining to insurance contracts and did not have to be backed by mandatory reserves that insurance companies are required to have by law on regular insurance contracts. It was a clever way to get around regulation.

Hence, the emergence of the shadow banking system, the explosive growth of subprime mortgages, and their impact on the macroeconomy fit perfectly into Minsky's model of financial instability. As the hard times of the Great Depression faded from memory, financial stability was taken for granted and assumed to be the new normal. In the meanwhile, the institutions created by FDR to safeguard against bank runs became outmoded as they were not modernized to keep up with new business practices. So the shadow banking system could creatively circumvent the existing regulations. In addition, many of the Great Depression–era regulations that were the guarantors of "boring" banking were slowly dismantled. Deemed archaic and superfluous, the Glass-Steagall Act itself was repealed in 1999. According to dogma current at the time, the financial markets could regulate themselves and did not require strict oversight. In short, the institutions that were put in place during the Great Depression were being gradually eroded for decades by overconfident regulators, ideological politicians, and financiers. Anyone who dared to bring up the possibility of creating new institutions to keep up with the evolution in the financial sector was literally vilified.[27]

A financial market is inherently unstable without a lender of last resort even in the best of times, because banks' assets are long-term while their liabilities are short-term. This maturity mismatch makes banks susceptible to runs, as the case of Lehman Brothers so vividly demonstrated. But in September of 2008, an explosive mix of developments created a financial tsunami. The apparent stability of the prior half-century, combined with animal spirits craving for euphoric profits, low interest rates, plenty of money chasing assets, and lax regulation, induced investors to buy risky assets whose complexity was ill understood and also to increase leverage well beyond prudent limits until excessive debt accumulated that could be rolled over but not repaid if anything went contrary to expectations. Thus, precisely as Minsky had predicted, a robust economy morphed endogenously into a fragile one as markets were unable to set safe limits to speculation. Hence, the financial system experienced an "unsustainable speculative euphoria."[28] Instability bred fragility, which mutated into a bubble and when the bubble burst a crisis of debt deflation began. That is a skeleton version of Minsky's model of the business cycle, the "financial instability hypothesis."[29]

There was an ideological background to the crisis as well. Milton Friedman and Ronald Reagan initiated an ideological revolution that was basically antigovernment and promoted the erroneous and dogmatic belief that "free" markets were self-regulating. The economic profession provided succor to the free marketeers by arguing that regulation was essentially growth-inhibiting and superfluous.[30] This ideology turned the spirit of the times in favor of deregulation. After all, if the people in charge of the economy such as Alan Greenspan do not believe in regulation, the chances are that the analysts in the financial sector will find ways to get around regulations.

The Great Meltdown had all the ingredients that make markets dysfunctional: (a) it had plenty of asymmetric information, as the buyers of mortgage-backed securities were not well informed about the subprime mortgages that were included in the bonds; (b) it had plenty of opportunistic behavior, as banks took advantage of information on riskiness of assets that they did not properly disclose; (c) expectations were misaligned; (d) incentives were incorrect; and (e) regulators were not keen on regulating.[31]

DELEVERAGING

Mainstream models pay insufficient attention to credit markets. In post-meltdown economics, monetary policy has to consider more closely the conditions under which consumers and firms are able to borrow. Greenspan's easy-money policy led not only to the double-bubbles of the turn of the twenty-first century,[32] but also to people using their housing wealth as an ATM, which in turn fueled consumption well beyond sustainable levels.

Excessive leverage was another reason for the instability of the financial system. During the run-up to the meltdown, investment banks were leveraged in excess of 30:1. This means that their own capital made up a tiny fraction (3 percent) of their working capital. To make matters worse, they used creative accounting to hide their risky assets from investors. If the value of their assets declined by just a few percentage points, their capital would evaporate and they would become bankrupt. This is an extremely risky business model and one prone to bank runs. This was the case with Bear Stearns and Lehman Brothers, as they relied on investors lending them millions of dollars every day. However, as their balance sheets deteriorated, that is to say, the value of their assets plummeted, investors were increasingly less willing to lend them the money they needed for their day-to-day operations. Only with government support was the system ultimately saved.

The amount of debt declines during an episode of deleveraging. Deleveraging follows on the heels of a financial crisis. So after the subprime housing bubble burst in 2008, those individuals who were deeply indebted, as well as most large financial institutions, needed to reverse the process of leveraging by paying down their debt in order to bring their balance sheets in order. Almost all of the cash needed by the banks to deleverage was provided by the government. Deleveraging amplified the recession, because it meant that instead of lending, the banks were using the government subsidies to improve their portfolios. The outcome was a credit crunch and slower economic growth that will continue for some time.

THE BAILOUT AND THE GREAT RECESSION

By the fall of 2008, all five big investment banks were history: Lehman Brothers was bankrupt, Bear Stearns was taken over by JPMorgan Chase with $29 billion worth of financial assistance from the Federal Reserve, the Federal Reserve also blackmailed Bank of America to take over Merrill Lynch in a "shotgun wedding," while Goldman Sachs and Morgan Stanley sought the safety of the federal government by acquiring traditional bank charters and remained solvent with the help of billions of dollars from the taxpayers.[33]

Mainstream macroeconomists did not teach the dangers inherent in the financial system. Minsky's name was banned from textbooks, which taught mainly the outlines of boring banking in which the financial system served as the stuffy middleman routinely channeling savings to investors. So when the bubble in asset values did burst, Bernanke was surprised by the fragility of the system. He, Secretary of the Treasury Hank Paulson, Alan Greenspan, and others at the Fed overlooked the elephant in the room, the obvious interlinkages, which meant that the failure of one firm would bring about a loss of asset values of many other firms, causing panic, classic bank runs, and a cascade of bankruptcies. That is the nature of systemic risk, a form of negative externality. It was nothing new. It has been part of the historical record at least since the South Sea Bubble of 1720.

The Great Recession followed the bursting of the subprime mortgage bubble with a substantial decline in income, an increase in un- and underemployment, a spectacular rise in foreclosures, and pain and suffering of the U.S. population. For instance, the investment in residential housing was cut by half between 2006 and 2009, which put a $400 billion hole in aggregate demand. Net investment in tangible assets (which includes housing) declined by even more, dropping by 78 percent of its original value, or by $614 billion.[34]

Arch-conservative Paulson was very quick to abandon the laissez-faire principles he advocated as CEO of Goldman Sachs and invoked the power of the state when it came to serving his and his friends' interests by bailing out Wall Street. To paraphrase Joseph Stiglitz, capitalism remained the economic system for Main Street, while socialism was reserved for Wall Street.[35] By bailing out Wall Street, Paulson and Bernanke created an unsustainable financial sector that many economists such as Simon Johnson, Nouriel Roubini, and Nassim Taleb believe will lead to a "doom loop" and recurring financial instability.[36]

By purchasing trillions of dollars' worth of toxic assets, an interventionist Fed resuscitated Wall Street to be sure, but at the same time introduced so much moral hazard into the system and maintained too-big-to-fail banks so that any of the giant banks can blackmail the taxpayer again for further funds at any time in the future. By doing so the Fed basically destroyed the logic of "creative destruction," which Schumpeter deemed to be the essence of progress under capitalism. It has socialized losses and privatized gains and left bonuses in place, all with the greatest redistribution of wealth from the poor and the middle class to the wealthy in the history of the world. It is questionable that such a system can be maintained in the long run with as much moral hazard as exists today. However, with endemic un- and underemployment[37] and millions of people thrown out of their homes annually, the Fed and the Treasury failed miserably in their stated goal of bailing out Main Street.

Another major factor overlooked by many is that the economy was fundamentally on an unsustainable path prior to the Great Meltdown. It had immense trade imbalances and immense budget deficits. These weighed heavily on future growth and living standards. In addition, the economy went from one bubble to another, that is, from the dot.com bubble to the housing bubble, as a consequence of Greenspan's easy money policies. In other words, the housing bubble burst at a time when both monetary and fiscal policy were counterproductive. As if that were not enough, inequality increased, with people attempting to keep up with the Joneses by going into debt at an accelerating pace. Hence, the economic growth of the previous decade was a mirage underwritten by funds from the Chinese politburo. The idea propagated by the members of the Obama administration that we can "grow the economy" by humongous across-the-board tax cuts and normal Keynesian policies rings hollow in light of the tremendous imbalances and structural problems of the economy prior to the crisis. By not instituting fundamental structural reforms that would have redressed the above fundamental and persistent imbalances, by neglecting to invest in education and in infrastructure that were needed for long-run economic growth, and by failing to support "green industries" sufficiently to bring about energy independence, the administration and Congress condemned the economy to linger.

All in all, the handling of the crisis was inimical to the long-run health of the economy. Gallup reported at the end of 2010 that Americans were in a "sour mood" as only 17 percent of the population was satisfied with the way things were going.[38] Most dissatisfaction was with the economy (30 percent) and with unemployment (24 percent). So the economic policy was not propitious. In contrast, satisfaction level was at 60 percent at the beginning of George W. Bush's presidency. In an engaging article, Jeffrey Sachs concluded that the crisis was a culmination of an extended period of misplaced macroeconomic policies: "The crash of 2008 exposed deep failures at the core of macroeconomic policymaking . . . in the United States. . . . The American purveyors of the ancient régime hope that a few superficial fixes will get us back on our way. This is not to be. Sustained and widespread future prosperity will require basic reforms in global macroeconomic governance and in macroeconomic science . . . [requiring] new ways of thinking. Yet business as usual could prove calamitous. . . ."[39]

In contrast to Sachs's suggestion, the policies forged by Obama's economic team of Summers, Geithner, and Bernanke retained an aura of old economic thinking: (a) choose the path of least resistance by propping up the banking system at any cost, as quickly as possible, and leave it unscathed so it can start lending again; and (b) at the same time, prescribe some conventional Keynesian pump priming straight out of Econ 101 to "get the economy growing again." While the Fed did learn *some* of the lessons of 1929, it was unable to modify them sufficiently to accommodate today's challenges. In the end, Bernanke chose to fight today's battles with yesterday's strategies. True to his promise to Milton Friedman, he effortlessly printed more than two trillion dollars, creating an asset bubble in the process—but who was counting?[40] Moreover, the interest rate was right (you cannot do better than zero), so the banks were not only resuscitated but brought back to full power thanks to the unlimited supply of cheap money from Uncle Sam. Consequently, the financial kingpins could continue to draw their zillion-dollar bonuses—some $80 billion in all since the meltdown—while the rest of us ended up paying for their toxic assets, the infamous "cash for trash" program.[41] And the eviction of the plebeians continued, as in earlier epochs, justified by metaphors rather than by substantive arguments.

This was a no-win strategy from the start. The Obama–Wall Street alliance radically altered the dynamics of the social contract and made sense only as long as the latter needed Uncle Sam's backing. However, once revived, the Lords of Finance did all they could to undermine efforts to regulate them. Apparently, no one in the administration had read Machiavelli with sufficient care to anticipate how one treats one's adversary once he becomes superfluous. As a result, the basic problems of too-big-to-fail banks remained unchanged, and credit remained limited.[42] Geithner ended up deferentially beseeching the Lords to support the recovery, while the president, using pitiful rhetoric, preached "that the nation's lenders, supported by taxpayers in the crisis, need to 'fulfill their responsibility' by lending to small businesses still struggling to get credit."

Krugman's ironic appeal for the return of "boring banking" went unheeded.[43] So the mega banks remained in the hands of, in effect, compulsive gamblers, who were as unrepentant as ever but were not keen on jump-starting the recovery. Credit default swaps were much more exciting . . . but they could go sour: so recently JPMorgan's mountain of chips shrank by six billion dollars' worth.

The fiscal stimulus also had an Achilles heel. As Nobel laureate Krugman has repeatedly pointed out, the stimulus was small relative to the "well over 2 trillion hole in the economy,"[44] was spread over two years, and half of it was made up of lame tax breaks, which accrued mostly to the rich, who were not going to spend it in the United States so there was not going to be a significant multiplier effect. Often a little medicine—such as half a dose of antibiotics—can be worse than no medicine at all. It just makes the bacteria more resistant and is therefore counterproductive. The stimulus's chief accomplishment was to discredit Keynesianism for a very long time to come. Moreover, to Everyman, $787 billion sounded like real money down the drain as little visible good came of it and the counterfactual arguments rang hollow. The general disillusionment led to the formation of the pseudo-populist Tea Party faction, proving that bad economics and bad politics are two sides of one counterfeit coin.

In sum, the economic policy was not only based on incorrect assumptions, but was erroneously conceived, badly timed, inadequately coordinated, poorly designed, politically ineffective, and strategically naïve. Finding themselves face to face with such a feeble foe, the Republicans embarked on a recalcitrance that added insult to injury. Furthermore, the majority of the population considered the policy unjust, since it obviously further skewed the distribution of economic benefits toward the society's upper echelons.[45] Thus, it further eroded the social contract, that is to say, the very foundations of capitalism: Everyman did not imagine that the federal government would have the nerve to favor the one percent with such brazen disregard of the rest.

To its credit, the triumvirate's strategy did stop the economy's free fall, but at the cost of any chance of genuine reform and the prospects of a solid recovery. Although GDP has been growing, as Geithner, Bernanke, and Summers have all conceitedly stressed, population grew as well so on a per capita basis GDP is still below its peak level of 2007 (Q4) in 2012 (Figure 15.1).[46] No wonder the so-called recovery feels much more like a lingering depression, or what Krugman dubbed a "sour economy."[47]

The trickle-down bailouts failed miserably even though they averted a depression in the short run. They created an economic system that has been put on a road similar to that of Japan's lost decade. Moreover, they supported the conspicuous income of the financial elite to the tune of trillions of dollars while at the same time throwing pittances at—or at worst, neglecting—the millions of people who were suffering at the low end of the totem pole.

Figure 15.1 **U.S. GDP per Capita**

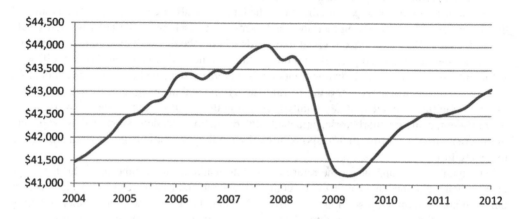

The common wisdom is that we absolutely needed to transfer the trillions to the bankers in order to avoid "falling off the cliff" in common parlance, and if we had done nothing the suffering would be even greater now. In Timothy Geithner's words: "If we had not put out the fire that was AIG, it would have spread. . . . Look at the impact not just on the savings of Americans, which fell by over 10 trillion dollars, but on the thousands of businesses that had to close, and the millions of workers who were laid off."[48] Metaphors were not in short supply, but common sense was.[49] The Paulson-Geithner-Bernanke-Summers[50] crew seems to have forgotten that doing nothing was not the only alternative to bailing out AIG and Wall Street. We could have bailed out the banks but not the bankers and attached enough strings to the bailout package so that the taxpayers would have owned the upside as well, not only the downside. We could have easily bailed out Main Street, for instance, by first nationalizing the banks.

Leaving it up to the bankers to "help the American people" was naïve. Even conservative Republicans such as Lindsey Graham and Alan Greenspan were not opposed to a different strategy: nationalization of the giant bankrupt banks. Greenspan actually said, "it may be necessary to temporarily nationalize some banks in order to facilitate a swift and orderly restructuring."[51] Stiglitz also advocated the idea,[52] as did Roubini: "you take banks over, you clean them up, and you sell them in rapid order to the private sector—it's clear that it's temporary. . . . The idea that government will fork out trillions of dollars to try to rescue financial institutions, and throw more money after bad dollars, is not appealing because then the fiscal cost is much larger. So rather than being seen as something Bolshevik, nationalization is seen as pragmatic. . . . The proposal is more market-friendly than the alternative of zombie banks."[53]

Nationalization would have had immense advantages: there would have been no more too-big-to-fail banks, hence no more systemic risk; no bailouts, hence no moral hazard and no "Tea Party"; no more foreclosures, hence no more toxic assets; and, most importantly, President Obama could have directed the banks by executive order to lend again, to restructure the underwater mortgages, and to end homeowner-eviction policies the likes of which have not been seen in recent memory. Then the taxpayers could have scrapped the executive bonuses and we could have put people in charge who would have bailed out Main Street. Instead of providing loans to the banks at a zero interest rate, the nationalized banks could have refinanced troubled mortgages at a nominal interest rate.[54] Mortgaged-backed obligations would not have been toxic anymore. There would have been only a few foreclosures, and all the problems associated with them would have been mitigated.

Everyman would have benefited from zero interest rate financing instead of the banks. The recession would have been much milder and less prolonged. If, let us say, the government would have purchased 6 million mortgages at $250,000 each, the total bailout would have amounted to merely $1.5 trillion, much less than half of the current level of bailouts, with far greater beneficial effects for Everyman on Main Street as well as on the economy at large. I think that would have been the first step toward humanely overcoming the challenges of the crisis.[55]

This strategy would have meant that effective regulation of the financial sector, including the resurrection of the Glass-Steagall Act, could have become reality. Much of the profits of the financial sector, a not inconsiderable sum of half a trillion dollars annually, would have accrued to—guess who?—Uncle Sam, and not to the likes of Jamie Dimon and Lloyd Blankfein. Add a substantial tax on financial transactions and the "starving beast" would have been no more. Instead of becoming subservient to the banks, Everyman would have tried on the shoes of the Lords of Finance and would have found the fit very comfortable, indeed.

The result would have been that Obama would have been hailed by the masses not only as a knight in shining armor of capitalism with a human face, but as willing and able to wield his lance. The Democrats would have avoided the thrashing of 2010, and malaise and the quandary in which we find ourselves in 2012 would have been nothing but a bad dream.

Bernanke was aware that such a scenario was indeed feasible. An internal memo concluded that helping homeowners would be a viable option: "The costs of the plan are moderate, and the benefits should help not only the participating homeowners but also the housing industry, the financial markets, and the economy more broadly."[56] But he found it more convenient to transfer the trillions to the same financiers whose greed had gotten the nation into this quagmire in the first place. Five years after the crisis, it does seem like bailing out Main Street would have been much better both politically and economically than bailing out Wall Street. After all, as of this writing we are still locked into a high level of endemic un(der)employment and dangerous political deadlock.

In sum, in order to implement the fundamental structural reforms that were urgently required, the country needed a leader with unflinching self-confidence backed up by a creative team of experts, not one burdened by a heavy load of past mistakes. Instead, we had a president who, when bankers or Republicans called his bluff, was all too ready and willing to blink. The deep structural imbalances of the U.S. economy could not be mended as a gentlemanly sport. The economy is path dependent: its institutions, as well as the momentum of the social, cultural, and political processes in which it is embedded, cannot be transformed easily. With the strategy and policies outlined above, we could have transitioned from turbo-capitalism to a more humanistic form of capitalism, but only if a leader combining the tensile strength of Lincoln with the cunning conviction and self-confidence of FDR or LBJ had been occupying the Oval Office. Instead, President Obama chose valiantly to protect the bankers from the pitchforks.[57]

This was hardly accidental: the president and his administration personify the prevailing culture of impatience. The conservative sociologist Daniel Bell argued more than a generation ago that capitalism creates a culture based on instant gratification, which slowly undermines the Protestant work ethic that was fundamental to its success in the first place. In 1976, he foresaw precociously that there was a "problem of managing a complex polity when the values of the society stress unrestrained appetite. The contradictions I see in contemporary capitalism derive . . . from the influence of the hedonism which has become the prevailing value in our society."[58] A society characterized by impatience will find it difficult to make long-range plans, which would be so sorely needed to overcome America's macroeconomic malaise in the twenty-first century.

CHAPTER SUMMARY

The financial crisis of 2008 was a momentous event in the history of mankind. Stiglitz compared it to the fall of the Berlin Wall.[59] It came about because Alan Greenspan, Ben Bernanke, and others in positions of power foolishly disregarded the warnings voiced during the run-up to the crisis by a large number of economists such as Dean Baker, Paul Krugman, Hyman Minski, Raghuram Rajan, Nouriel Roubini, and Robert Shiller to name just a few. In other words, it is not true that no one saw the threats accumulating. The people in positions of authority were simply unwilling to listen and keep an open mind.

The Great Recession that followed the Meltdown of 2008 will have as much significance in the evolution of the world economy as the Great Depression did in the 1930s. The Great Depression essentially ended classical capitalism in which the government had played a negligible role in economic activity. Similarly, the Great Meltdown ended the "American Dream." After 1929, markets were known *not* to be self-correcting and needed continued government supervision and support with fiscal and monetary policy. We are now at the cusp of a new era with the ascendancy and dynamism of China, India, and other emerging markets such as Brazil. The hegemony of the U.S. economy is a thing of the past. What remains is a bifurcated economy in which half of the population is doing quite well, one percent of the population is doing extremely well, while the rest is struggling to make ends meet. Creative ideas are lacking for how to convert this unbalanced economy into one that is inclusive and can provide a decent living for all. The purpose of these pages is to light a fire in the minds of students so that they can imagine a capitalism with a human face, so that the next crisis to come will not be wasted and we will have some progressive ideas to confront the challenges ahead.

QUESTIONS FOR DISCUSSION

1. Why do you suppose Alan Greenspan did not heed the warnings voiced during the run-up to the financial crisis?
2. Why is the financial sector so volatile?
3. Why do you suppose the ideas of Hyman Minsky were banned from mainstream economics?
4. Do you think that the financial sector should be allowed to have such a large weight in the economy?
5. Do you think that "too-big-to-fail" banks should be broken up like AT&T in 1982 and Standard Oil in 1911?
6. Why does the accumulation of debt lead to economic instability?
7. Explain why stability bred instability in the financial sector.
8. What is boring banking? Would you advocate bringing back boring banking?
9. Did financial innovations have a positive impact on the real economy?
10. What was the shadow banking system?
11. What kind of insurance is a credit default swap?
12. Do you think it was a major mistake to repeal the Glass-Steagall Act?
13. Do you think we should have bailed out Goldman Sachs, JPMorgan Chase, Citigroup, Morgan Stanley, and Bank of America?
14. Do you think that Dick Fuld should be allowed to keep the $450 million he earned while bankrupting Lehman Brothers?
15. Do you think that Main Street should have been bailed out also?

16. Discuss Stiglitz's quip that Capitalism is for Main Street, Socialism is for Wall Street.

17. Why do you think that Main Street was not bailed out?

18. Do you think that Obama's stimulus package was effective?

19. What are the major challenges faced in today's globalized world?

20. Do you think that the "American Dream" will be within your reach in your lifetime or that of your children and grandchildren?

21. Do you think that Ben Bernanke consciously misled the public during the run-up to the financial crisis or do you think that he did so in order to advance his career?

22. Do you think that the financial sector has become too powerful?

23. What is your opinion of President Obama's economic team?

24. What is your opinion of President Obama's handling of the financial crisis?

NOTES

1. The standard deviation of real GDP growth in the United States declined from 2.7 percent between 1960 and 1983 to just 1.6 percent thereafter. James Stock and Mark Watson, "Has the Business Cycle Changed and Why?" in *NBER Macroeconomic Annual 2002,* vol. 17, ed. Mark Gertler and Kenneth Rogoff (Cambridge, MA: MIT Press, 2003), 159–230.

2. Anya Schiffrin, *Bad News: How America's Business Press Missed the Story of the Century* (New York: The New Press, 2011).

3. Robert E. Lucas, Jr. "Macroeconomic Priorities," *American Economic Review* 93 (2003) 1: 1–14.

4. Ben Bernanke, "The Great Moderation," speech at the meetings of the Eastern Economic Association (Washington, DC, February 20, 2004).

5. PBS, *Frontline,* "The Warning," October 20, 2009. Warren Buffett, "Berkshire Hathaway Inc. 2002 Annual Report."

6. Steve Keen, *Debunking Economics: The Naked Emperor of the Social Sciences* (London: Pluto Press and Zed Books, 2001).

7. Dean Baker, "The Run-up in Home Prices: A Bubble," *Challenge* 45 (2002) 6: 93–119.

8. Raghuram Rajan, "Has Financial Development Made the World Riskier?" NBER Working Paper No. 11728, November 2005.

9. According to legendary investor George Soros's comments in the 2010 movie "Inside Job," the music had stopped playing by the time Prince made those remarks, but that misjudgment did not stop Prince from walking away with a $38 million bonus severance pay in November of that year. This is just one example of the irresponsible way major investors were being rewarded for making cavalier decisions.

10. "Ben Bernanke Was Wrong," YouTube video, posted by "Marcus C. Macellus," July 22, 2009.

11. "[T]he collapse of the housing bubble will lead to a loss of between $1.3 trillion and $2.6 trillion of housing wealth." Baker, "Run-up in Home Prices."

12. John Cassidy, "Blowing Bubbles," *The New Yorker,* July 12, 2004.

13. "Ben Bernanke Was Wrong."

14. Bureau of Labor Statistics, *Labor Force Statistics from the Current Population Survey. Characteristics of the Unemployed,* Tables 1, 20, and 35. Available at ftp://ftp.bls.gov/pub/special.requests/lf/aa2005/pdf/cpsaat1.pdf, ftp://ftp.bls.gov/pub/special.requests/lf/aa2005/pdf/cpsaat20.pdf, and ftp://ftp.bls.gov/pub/special.requests/lf/aa2005/pdf/cpsaat35.pdf, respectively.

15. Daniel Kahneman, "Maps of Bounded Rationality: Psychology for Behavioral Economics," *American Economic Review* 93 (2003) 5: 1449–1475.

16. Nassim Taleb, *Fooled by Randomness: The Hidden Role of Chance in Life and in the Markets* (New York: Random House, 2001).

17. Carmen M. Reinhart and Kenneth S. Rogoff, *This Time Is Different: Eight Centuries of Financial Folly* (Princeton, NJ: Princeton University Press, 2009).

18. Nassim Taleb, *The Black Swan: The Impact of the Highly Improbable* (New York: Random House, 2007).

19. Steve Keen, "Finance and Economic Breakdown: Modeling Minsky's Financial Instability Hypothesis," *Journal of Post Keynesian Economics* 17 (1995) 4: 607–635.

20. See also Charles P. Kindleberger, *Manias, Panics, and Crashes: A History of Financial Crisis,* 1st

ed. (New York: Basic Books, 1978). Hyman Minsky, "The Financial Instability Hypothesis: Capitalistic Processes and the Behavior of the Economy," in *Financial Crises: Theory, History, and Policy*, ed. Charles P. Kindleberger and Jean-Paul Laffargue (Cambridge, UK: Cambridge University Press, 1982), 12–29.

21. It was a new form of capitalism in his view, a "money manager capitalism," in which financial leverage became paramount. Instead of working with one's own capital, one borrowed extensively and invested the borrowed sums at a higher rate of return.

22. Thomas Philippon, "The Evolution of the US Financial Industry from 1869 to 2007: Theory and Evidence," unpublished working paper (2008).

23. Hyman Minsky, "The Financial Instability Hypothesis," The Jerome Levy Economics Institute of Bard College, Working Paper No. 74, May 1992.

24. Hyman Minsky, *Stabilizing an Unstable Economy* (New York: McGraw-Hill, 1986), 26.

25. Hyman Minsky, "Financial Instability Revisited: The Economics of Disaster," unpublished manuscript (1966).

26. Ben Bernanke does make a fleeting reference to Minsky, but in a dismissive way: "Hyman Minsky (1977) and Charles Kindleberger (1978) have . . . argued for the inherent instability of the financial system, but in doing so have had to depart from the assumption of rational economic behavior." "Nonmonetary Effects of the Financial Crisis in the Propagation of the Great Depression," *American Economic Review* (1983), 3:257–276, at p. 258. Bernanke added in a footnote to the above statement: "I do not deny the possible importance of irrationality in economic life; however, it seems that the best research strategy is to push the rationality postulate as far as it will go." I do not know on what basis he determined what the best strategy is. It just "seemed" to him that the best strategy was to disregard Minsky.

27. Brooksley Born tried to regulate derivatives but was overwhelmed by the "free marketeers" led by Alan Greenspan, Larry Summers, and Robert Rubin. See PBS, *Frontline*, "The Warning."

28. L. Randall Wray, "Minsky Crisis," in *The New Palgrave Dictionary of Economics*, online ed., ed. Steven N. Durlauf and Lawrence E. Blume (2011), available at www.dictionaryofeconomics.com/dictionary. Paul McCulley, "The Shadow Banking System and Hyman Minsky's Economic Journey," PIMCO, May 2009.

29. Minsky, *Stabilizing an Unstable Economy*.

30. Wikipedia contributors, "Inside Job (film)," *Wikipedia: The Free Encyclopedia*.

31. Goldman Sachs was fined $550 million for questionable dealings with mortgage backed securities.

32. The dot.com and housing bubbles.

33. The literature on the crisis is now very extensive; see, for example, Simon Johnson and James Kwak, *13 Bankers: The Wall Street Takeover and the Next Financial Meltdown* (New York: Pantheon, 2010); Robert Shiller, *The Subprime Solution: How Today's Global Financial Crisis Happened, and What to Do About It* (Princeton, NJ: Princeton University Press, 2008); Carmen M. Reinhart and Kenneth Rogoff, *This Time Is Different: Eight Centuries of Financial Folly* (Princeton, NJ: Princeton University Press, 2009); Paul Krugman, *The Return of Depression Economics and the Crisis of 2008* (New York: W.W. Norton, 2009).

34. Board of Governors of the Federal Reserve System, "Flow of Funds Accounts of the United States. Flows and Outstandings Fourth Quarter 2010."

35. Joseph Stiglitz, *Freefall: America, Free Markets, and the Sinking of the World Economy* (New York: W.W. Norton, 2010).

36. Peter Boone and Simon Johnson, "The Doomsday Cycle," *CentrPiece* (Winter 2009/10): 2–6.

37. In 2009 there were about 22 million people underemployed out of a labor force of 140 million. See ftp://ftp.bls.gov/pub/special.requests/lf/aat8.txt.

38. Jeffrey M. Jones, "In U.S., Satisfaction Dips to 17 Percent at Year's End," *Gallup*, December 20, 2010.

39. Jeffrey Sachs, "Rethinking Macroeconomics," *Capitalism and Society* 4 (2009) 3: 1–9. Bill McGuire, "Fed Loaned Banks Trillions in Bailout, Bloomberg Reports," *ABC News*, November 28, 2011.

40. McGuire, "Fed Loaned Banks Trillions in Bailout."

41. Paul Krugman, "Financial Policy Despair," *The New York Times*, March 22, 2009.

42. Simon Johnson says that the promise not to bail out any more banks is not credible. Simon Johnson, "Could Goldman Sachs Fail?" *Baseline Scenario*, April 14, 2011.

43. Paul Krugman, "Making Banking Boring," *The New York Times*, April 9, 2009.

44. "Paul Krugman: Stimulus Too Small, Second Package Likely (VIDEO)," *Huffington Post*, posted March 20, 2009, available at www.huffingtonpost.com/2009/02/17/paul-krugman-stimulus-too_n_167721.html.

45. John Rawls, *A Theory of Justice* (Cambridge, MA: Harvard University Press, 1971).

46. U.S. Department of Commerce, United States Census Bureau, 2010 "Population Estimates. National Intercensal Estimates (2000–2010)"; U.S. Department of Commerce, Bureau of Economic Analysis, "National Economic Accounts 2011."

47. Paul Krugman, *End This Depression Now!* (New York: W.W. Norton, 2012).

48. Timothy Geithner, "Secretary Geithner's Testimony on AIG," *RealClearPolitics,* January 27, 2010.

49. "When the neighbors' house is burning, you do not ask any questions about who is to blame," was another metaphor frequently repeated.

50. Laurence Summers, sometime academic, had helped repeal the Glass-Steagall Act (which had been essential to the stability of the financial sector for six decades), had railed against regulating derivatives such as credit default swaps, and had cold-bloodedly snookered Brooksley Born. Summers was rewarded generously by the Lords of Finance for letting them bully the rest of us: Goldman Sachs deemed a single speech of his a bargain at $135,000; no wonder he was able to amass a net worth of circa $25 million. Philip Rucker and Joe Stephens, "White House Economics Aide Summers Discloses Income," *Washington Post,* April 4, 2009.

51. Tunku Varadaraja, "'Nationalize' the Banks: Dr. Doom Says a Takeover and Resale Is the Market-Friendly Solution," *The Wall Street Journal,* February 21, 2009.

52. "Stiglitz: Temporary Nationalization Necessary to Save Troubled Banks," YouTube video, posted by "ColumbiaBusiness," February 19, 2009.

53. Varadaraja, "'Nationalize' the Banks."

54. "Stiglitz Says U.S. Is Paying for Failure to Nationalize Banks," *Bloomberg News,* November 1, 2009.

55. Another person who advocated a bailout of the financial system from the bottom up. His bailouts would have provided subsidies to homeowners. Allen H. Barton, "Letter: Another Take on 'Why Paulson is Wrong,'" *The Economists' Voice,* 5 (2008) 5: Article 9.

56. Chris Foote, Jeff Fuhrer, Eileen Mauskopf, and Paul Willen, "A Proposal to Help Distressed Homeowners: A Government Payment-Sharing Plan," Federal Reserve Bank of Boston, Public Policy Brief No. 09–1, last revised July 9, 2009; Allen H. Barton, "Letter."

57. Lindsey Ellerson, "Obama to Bankers: I'm Standing 'Between You and the Pitchforks,'" *ABC News,* April 3, 2009.

58. Daniel Bell, *The Cultural Contradictions of Capitalism* (New York: Basic Books, 1976).

59. Joseph Stiglitz, "Market Fundamentalism Is Dead," YouTube video, at 4:14, posted by "ForaTV," November 10, 2008.

CONCLUSION

Economics Beyond the Basics

"We may have democracy,
or we may have wealth concentrated in the hands of a few,
but we can't have both."

—Associate Justice of the Supreme Court Louis Brandeis[1]

While mainstream textbooks sing hymns to the invisible hand, this volume takes principles beyond the basics by emphasizing aspects of real existing markets that deviate markedly from theoretical ones. Without well-designed institutions and incentive structures, real markets tend to be inefficient and unstable, and to accumulate and magnify inequities. Without adequate oversight and structure imposed upon them, real markets are dangerous in that they provide disappointing results and can even become chaotic. The idea that markets can emerge through spontaneous order is, of course, sheer nonsense. In reality, markets begin to function once the guns have quieted down and the institutions that govern market participants have been decided. Imperialism in Africa, revolutions in the Arab world, destruction and deportation of native Indians to reservations, restructuring of the labor market in the United States through the Civil War, bloody strikes in the 1930s, the establishment of the EU after millions of people died fighting each other over the possession of land—the list is endless. Free markets have never existed for long, and cannot possibly exist, because opportunistic behavior coupled with the existence of military or police or financial power makes plunder irresistible in the absence of government-imposed institutional structure. Over time, people learned that markets cannot function without structure.

This is especially clear in today's global economy, in which the level of complexity poses a major challenge to our ability to navigate through the economic system. This implies, in turn, that there are too many possibilities for unstable situations to develop and for the Achilles heel of markets to prevent acceptable outcomes. This includes the formidable challenges of imperfect information, opportunistic behavior, heterogeneous cognitive ability, externalities, safety, nonexistent markets, transaction costs, uncertainty, sustainability, oligopolies, monopolies, protection of children, power imbalances, nonrationality, and the unequal distribution of wealth. These are exactly the topics that introductory textbooks are generally silent about. For the most part, the mainstream textbooks fail to mention the important breakthroughs of such Nobel Prize–winning economists as Herbert Simon (satisficing), Amartya Sen (welfare economics), George Akerlof (asymmetric information), Michael Spence (signaling), Joseph Stiglitz (imperfect information),

Daniel Kahneman (bounded rationality), Paul Krugman (new trade theory), and Oliver Williamson (transaction costs).

It is simply false that these topics cannot be studied in Econ 101 because of their complexity or because of the lack of time. Indeed, they are crucial at the very beginning of economic studies because otherwise one gains a biased view of the way markets work and distribute the fruits of their products. This volume supplements standard texts by going beyond the basics. It is to the standard texts what engineering is to theoretical physics. In theoretical physics, models are proposed without gravity and without friction, but in engineering, one had better take account of these two attributes of the physical world. Otherwise one is not going to design automobiles that actually work. Thus, this book advocates real-world economics beyond the basic theoretical models—an engineer's approach to economics. This requires that economics become more of an experimental science, that is to say, more of an inductive, rather than deductive, discipline.

In order to teach the principles of economics appropriately, we need to integrate more empirical evidence into our coursework and to acknowledge at the very outset that it is impossible to expunge ideology and value judgments from our framework. One reason is that the perspective from which we perceive economic interactions inevitably depends on our prior values, imbedded in our culture and worldview. The only way to be more rigorous and less ideological is to improve the empirical basis of the discipline. Another reason is that economics is inextricably intertwined with political and moral philosophy as well as sociology, which introduces another dimension of ideological disposition to the discipline.

Economists tend to make many value judgments: it is obvious that we value efficiency and it needs no explanation that we want the economy to grow. These are supposedly universal values. However, one might just acknowledge that others consider justice, sustainability, and a fair distribution of the rewards of economic activity to be more important than efficiency and growth. Mainstream economists believe in a tradeoff between equity and efficiency, whereas others do not see the world in those terms and believe that equity is much more significant than efficiency, or even that equity is in itself efficient.

It is necessary that future principles of economics courses acknowledge openly the endogeneity of our tastes, culture, and the utility function, as well as the importance of the Freudian unconscious and Pavlovian conditioning in our decision-making processes. Only once we gain that important insight can we begin to defend ourselves and especially shield children—at least to some extent—from the undue influence of the corporate world. If our moral values are not right, prices cannot be right. Furthermore, Econ 101 needs to expunge its emphasis on perfectly competitive markets, which are irrelevant for all practical purposes in today's too-big-to-fail (or to-jail) corporate world. Rather, our courses should focus much more on oligopolistic and monopolistic market structures in their analysis of applied issues.

Such future ideal courses will have to stress that the dominant market structures of today are inefficient. Competition by itself does not bring about efficient markets in the presence of imperfections mentioned above. Oligopolistic and monopolistic firms, that is to say, about 95 percent of the economy, are inefficient. They do not produce the right quantities at the right prices. And of course endemic unemployment is also inefficient, because a lot of productive energies are idle, thus wasting human resources. Endemic underemployment is costing us some half a trillion dollars a year.[2]

Hence, market failure is the norm. That which the mainstream considers an exception is actually the rule. The default model we use to analyze economic policy should be based on oligopolistic markets with imperfect information with consumers using rule of thumb and satisficing to make decisions with interdependent and endogenous utility functions in which status seeking plays a considerable role and in which wants are contrived and manipulated by Madison Avenue. That market is far from efficient, far from democratic, and very far from the description students receive in Econ 101.

The mantra of the free market led to the destruction of unions and with that a large segment of the lower-middle class. Thus, mega corporations were left with undue influence on the public interest, with sufficient money to bribe politicians to represent their interests instead of those of the public. The result is in plain view: large and growing inequality, no energy policy, global warming, endemic unemployment and threatening levels of underemployment—in short, a growing proletarianization of the workforce with an inordinate number of working poor, an army of people on food stamps, private and public indebtedness, inadequate schools, high rates of incarceration, dissatisfaction with the political system, a large number of people on drugs, and intractable economic and political problems. Economists are partly to blame, as argued in the film *The Inside Job,* because they advocated and disseminated the intellectual foundation of the view that regulation was superfluous, that markets left to themselves were efficient, and that the CEOs in charge were sophisticated, knew what they were doing, and hence deserved their bonuses. To be sure, those with power and influence benefited from this worldview enormously. Mainstream celebrity economists earned millions, some with their popular textbooks, others by serving on corporate boards or giving lectures at corporations for astronomical sums.

Laissez-faire ideology as a dominant paradigm is not neutral. It helps enormously the powerful, well-educated, well-born, privileged, talented, beautiful, intelligent, those who live in the right school district, those with inherited wealth or with friends and connections in high places. However, for those who were born with nothing valuable to offer to the labor market, for those who lack those endowments that lead to opportunities or who "chose" their families unwisely, laissez-faire economics becomes an unforgiving, even cruel, system that traps them in the underclass and a vicious circle of poverty leading to absolute and relative deprivation, exclusion from the labor market, and all too often, incarceration. Stressing the sanctity of private property and having the right incentives to exert effort does not help those who are not exceptionally beautiful or talented, those who live in poor school districts and get little or no education, or those with no inherited privilege. In short, individual responsibility is not a useful concept for someone growing up in a slum surrounded by crime, destitution, and deprivation, or who just lost his job at an age when retraining is no longer feasible. That the number of suicides among men in their fifties increased by almost 50 percent between 1999 and 2010 is a clear indication of the desperation of people living in an uncaring economy.[3]

We must, therefore, integrate ideas of distributive justice into mainstream Econ 101 courses, particularly as it pertains to CEO compensation. We should be aware of the fact that the astronomical increase in CEO salaries was due not to market forces, but to the ability of the CEOs to isolate themselves from competition using the institutional structure of corporate governance as a means to accomplish those goals. Their salaries were granted not by their employers, the shareholders, but by intermediaries who had no incentives to measure the marginal product of the CEOs accurately.[4] We should also acknowledge that power is a crucial factor in the economy and that it is completely disregarded in mainstream treatments of the subject. Market power, economic power, and political power are all very important in designing the framework of the institutions that determine, in the end, the distribution of income, wealth, and privilege.

Standard treatments of the subject rely excessively on the dynamics of supply and demand to determine the right price of goods, suggesting that if prices are too high for an efficient outcome, there will be excess supply and that, in turn, will exert a downward pressure on prices toward equilibrium. However, today's economy is not made up of perfectly competitive firms but instead mostly made up of monopolies and oligopolies, which do not have a supply curve at all. Hence, competition among them does not eliminate profits as in the perfectly competitive model. In such market structures an efficient equilibrium is not necessarily reached. Firms have market power and use it in order to extract a larger share of the economic pie in the form of profits. Apple Inc., for instance, continues to make immense profits in spite of brutal competition. Instead of competing with price, Apple competes with new features and styling. In 2013 an iPhone could be purchased from Apple (without a contract) for $649, while in 2007 the first version cost $500. These are, of course, different models with different features, but they are both stylish smartphones. Thus, one had to pay about the same amount for both models and for the bragging rights of owning the latest technology. It is a coveted for its value as a conspicuous consumption good. Apple did not compete with price but with new applications keeping its profit margin about the same at about 40 percent of sales price. The iPhone market demonstrates that supply-and-demand dynamics among oligopolies does not correspond to the default models depicted in textbooks.

Moreover, oligopolies spend lavishly on advertising, thereby influencing our tastes, culture, and shopping habits, that is to say our lifestyle, starting in childhood. For example, Apple has spent some $650 million advertising the iPhone since its inception in 2007. In addition, high prices may create a positive feedback loop, as they did during the recent housing bubble. In that case, investors assumed that high and rising housing prices indicated that prices would continue to increase, which created false expectations and a systematic mispricing of real estate that ultimately led to the biggest bubble in world history. So the laws of supply and demand all too often fail to lead to the free-market nirvana as depicted in the generic textbook.

We also introduced the reader to the new field of behavioral economics, which promises to be the next stage of development of the field. It provides the psychological foundations of a new micro- and macroeconomics by exploring the bounds of rationality. It replaces the rational-agent utility-maximizing model with models of satisficing, heuristics, or bounded rationality and implies that our cognitive deficiencies often lead to inefficient outcomes. We frequently use approximate rules of thumb instead of logical rules to make decisions. As consumers we often seek status and follow the crowd and use relative income instead of absolute income to gauge our welfare. As investors we are often prone to over- or under-react to news. We are also prone to a large number of cognitive biases: we have difficulty understanding risk and uncertainty, we are generally not so good at planning for the future, and we are often overconfident.

The predictive power of mainstream economists is minimal. The evidence that economic theory is in a crisis and in need of a paradigm shift comes from six major contradictions of the current received wisdom:

1. The economy has not been able to lift the quality of life of most U.S. citizens in spite of the immense increases in income and wealth since World War II. Above all, emotional prosperity continues to elude us. A larger share of the population is on antidepressants and in jail than at any time in our history. A larger share of the population is living in poverty than at any time since the 1960s. Median household income has been falling for 14 years, and median income of males has been stagnant or declining for longer than a generation. The average American is now overweight and deeply in debt, unable to control either his/her finances or appetite. These are the facts. One can infer from them that there is no reason to think that future economic growth will be socially more inclusive than it has been up to now and able to satisfy the needs of most of the population.

2. This also means that income distribution matters a lot more than hitherto thought and that absolute average income is not the key determinant of the quality of life. The mantra of "making the economy grow" is both inapt and deceiving. It is crucial to recognize that all

of the fruits of economic growth were captured by the top 10 percent of the population! The top 1 percent is made up of about 1.3 million families with an average income of about $700,000. The average income of the bottom 90 percent (137 million families) is $30,000. The top 15,000 families had an average income of $27 million. Between 1982 and 2006, the earnings of the top 1 percent of the labor force increased by some 127 percent from $800,000 to $1.8 million. In contrast, the earnings of the bottom 40 percent of the labor force rose from $19,000 to $20,000, an increase of a mere 7 percent. In 1982, the top 1 percent was earning 42 times the bottom 40 percent, while by 2006 that multiple had risen to 88.[5] Median household income has increased only because there are now more two-earner households. These developments are mind boggling and do not augur well for the future of the country.

3. Most prominent mainstream economists, including Larry Summers, Ben Bernanke, and Alan Greenspan, completely misunderstood the functioning of the financial world and money market during the run-up to the subprime mortgage bubble. They failed to understand the nature and power of systemic risk. Their ad hoc reaction to the crisis injected an inordinate amount of moral hazard into the system, from which it will be extremely difficult, if not impossible, to recover.

4. Mainstream economists are at an utter loss to propose a viable policy mix to put the economy on a road to stability and recovery with dignity. That would entail at least eliminating the double burden of government budget deficit and current account deficit. As of 2011, the United States owed foreigners $12.6 trillion—almost one year's worth of GNP—on which interest will have to be paid in perpetuity.[6] This implies that the disposable income of future generations will likely diminish. To some astute observers this decline was already evident in the 1970s.[7]

5. There is a macroeconomic stalemate about how to end the current crisis and return to "normal" levels of unemployment, which themselves were well above acceptable levels; this implies that high levels of unemployment and underemployment are going to stay with us for an indefinite period. That is the inconvenient truth not only for the United States but for most of Western Europe as well.

6. The free market has backfired to such an extent that it showed its conceptual weaknesses and inconsistencies; the advanced economy that fared best in the crisis was Germany, which is much more regulated than the United States or the UK. For instance, Germany has much stronger worker protection laws than the United States.[8] Yet with an unemployment rate of 5.5 percent and growth rate (between 2007 and 2011) of 3.5 percent since the meltdown, the German economy has shown much more resilience than that of the United States, which has an unemployment rate of 8 percent and its GDP declined during the same period by 2.7 percent (Table 16.1). These data contradict the notion that the free market's healing power is superior to a market in which there is a cooperative framework among the various major stakeholders (labor, management, government). Germany does not have the freest labor market, but it has fared well among the advanced economies. This is in spite of the fact that the United States benefited greatly from the fact that the dollar is a reserve currency and that Ben Bernanke could quadruple the money supply, whereas the German economy did not have this option.

These six major developments contradict mainstream theory and accentuate the need for a paradigm switch. It is not that markets are bad, but that markets need the right set of institutions and the right culture in order to function properly, that is, in order that their participants may live carefree, dignified

Table 16.1

Growth in GDP per Capita 2007–2011

Positive Growth		Negative Growth	
Germany	3.5	Ireland	−9.4
Switzerland	1.9	Italy	−6.6
Australia	1.1	Denmark	−5.8
Sweden	1.1	Spain	−5.4
Austria	0.8	United Kingdom	−5.2
		Norway	−4.9
		Finland	−4.4
		Japan	−3.9
		Portugal	−3.0
		United States	−2.7
		France	−2.1
		Netherlands	−1.2
		Canada	−1.2
		Belgium	−1.0

Source: GDP per head, US$, constant prices. Available at http://stats.oecd.org/OECDStat_Metadata/ShowMetadata.ashx?Dataset=SNA_TABLE1&ShowOnWeb=true&Lang=en.

lives. It requires a great deal of insensitivity to evidence to continue to teach that markets are efficient after the greatest meltdown in the history of mankind. Hence, we need to reconstruct the economics discipline so that it begins with empirical evidence as its basis rather than deductive theories written on blackboards. I hope this volume can make a modest contribution toward creating a new approach to economics that will serve as a foundation for a new system of capitalism with a human face.

NOTES

1. As quoted by Raymond Lonergan in Irving Dillard, ed., *Mr. Justice Brandeis, Great American* (St. Louis, MO: Modern View Press, 1941), 42.

2. This includes part-time workers who would like to work full time as well as discouraged workers, calculated at a rate of $30,000 salary per annum. And that does not even count the forgone production of the idle capital stock, which is likely to be in the $300 billion range. So that in all we have a total economic inefficiency in the neighborhood of $0.8 trillion.

3. Tara Parker-Pope, "Suicide Rates Rise Sharply in U.S." *The New York Times,* May 2, 2013.

4. Some 42 percent of senior managers and directors said that they knew of cases in their firms within the previous year where profits were overstated. Floyd Norris, "A Troubling Survey on Global Corruption," *The New York Times,* May 17, 2013.

5. Edward N. Wolff, "Recent Trends in *Household Wealth in the United States: Rising Debt and the Middle-Class Squeeze—An Update to 2007,*" Levy Economics Institute of Bard College Working Paper No. 589, March 2010.

6. U.S. Department of the Treasury, Treasury International Capital System, Statistics 1. Securities Data. d. Holdings of Long-Term Securities. A.1. Total holdings by all foreign countries; by type, holder and issuer. Recent data, available at www.treasury.gov/resource-center/data-chart-center/tic/Pages/ticsec3.aspx.

7. Christopher Lasch, *The Culture of Narcissism: American Life in an Age of Diminishing Expectations* (New York: W.W. Norton, 1979). Daniel Bell, *The Cultural Contradictions of Capitalism* (New York: Basic Books, 1976).

8. On a scale of 0 to 6, Germany has in place worker protection of 2.1, which ranks above the OECD average, whereas that of the United States is a paltry 0.2. Danielle Venn, "Legislation, Collective Bargaining and Enforcement: Updating the OECD Employment Protection Indicators," Organization for Economic Cooperation and Development (OECD), Social Employment and Migration Working Papers, 2009.

INDEX

Note: Italic page numbers refer to tables or figures.

A

accessibility (mental), 48, 49
Acemoglu, Daron, 137
"Achilles heel" of markets, 24, 78, 138, 222,
   241
Adorno, Theodor, 91n105
adult economics, 66
adverse selection, 104
advertising
  conditioning and, 35
  consumption, 170
  impact on unconscious, 50
  life satisfaction, 165
  sex and, 57, 87n17
  television, 65, 70
  truth in, 78
African Americans
  discrimination, 159
  income of, 123, 124, *163*
  See also blacks
aggregate demand, 177, 178, 182
aggregation problem, 113, 121, 182
AIG, 103, 134, 135
Akerlof, George, 241
altruism, 74, 89n61, 90n68
AMA. *See* American Medical Association
American dream, 68, 70, 85, 125, 159, 165,
   203, 236
American Medical Association (AMA)
  doctors' salaries, 119, *120*
  shortage of doctors, 119
anchoring (psychological), 48, 50, 60n26
animal spirits, 182
Apple, Inc.
  employee Jordan Golson, 158
  iPhone, 244
  oligopolist, 156

Apple, Inc. *(continued)*
  profits of, 97
  wages at, 158
Arthur, W. Brian, 9, 103
Arthur Andersen, 136, 141
asymmetric information, 74, 77, 82
authority, obedience to, 57

B

bailout, 126, 139, 180, 231–236
Baker, Dean, 4, 225
bandwagon effect, 68
Bank of America, 95, 97, 120, 138
  forced acquisition of Merrill Lynch, 135,
   231
banking system
  fines, 141
  nationalization of, 234
  shadow, 228, 229
  See also financial sector
bankruptcy, personal, 19
Barclays Bank, 64, 136
basic needs, 33, 35–37, 65, 112, 154, 166
basic research, 148
Bear Stearns, 230
behavioral economics, 48, 55
Bell, Daniel, 70, 71, 235
Bernanke, Benjamin, 11, 12, 75, 180, 183,
   200, 225, 226, 232, 245
biases, cognitive, 47, 48, 80
blackboard economics, 7, 11
blacks
  income of, 123, *163*
  unemployment of, 190
  See also African Americans
Blankfein, Lloyd, 78, 118, 235
Boesky, Ivan, 133n48

Born, Brooksley, 4, 225, 228
bounded rationality, 44, 45
brain
  evolution, 43
  imperfect nature of, 42
  limitations of, 42
  Madison Avenue's impact, 84
  nature of, 43
British Petroleum, 139
Brooks, David, 98
Bryant, Kobe, 72, 118
Brzezinski, Zbigniew, 125
bubble
  Dot-Com, 141
  of 2008, 136, 142
Buckley, William F. Jr., 127
budget constraint, 37
Buffett, Warren, 126, 204, 210n11, 215, 225
Burke, Edmund, 16n40
Bush, President George W., 75, 206
business cycle, 164, 225

C

Cambridge capital controversy, 122
capital
  cost of, 121–122
  with a human face, 6–8
  idle, 188
  intangible, 111
  capitalism, 133n43
  contradictions in, 71
  culture, 235
cartels
  National Basketball Association (NBA),
    118
  Organization of the Petroleum Exporting
    Countries (OPEC), 101, 142
Carter, President James, 9
Cassidy, John, 55, 226
caveat emptor, 56, 62n55, 78
Cayne, James, 134
Chief Executive Officer (CEO)
  corporation, 135
  pay, 118, 120, 121, 126, 127, 130, 132n41,
    133n43, 159, 243
children
  poverty of, 19, 169
  welfare, 20

China, 203
choices, too many, 148
Citibank, 78, 82, 136, 226
Civil Rights Act of 1964, 159
Clinton, President William (Bill), 206
cognitive
  bias, 80
  capture, 87n6, 87n10, 140
  dissonance, 55
  endowment, 56
competition
  efficiency and, 73, 96
  limitations of, 82, 83
competitive advantage, 211
complex systems, 103
concentration of market share, 96
conditioning, 35, 36
Congress, lobbying and, 64
conscious thought, 42
conspicuous consumption, 57, 79, 188, 191
consumer
  confidence, 178
  protection, 42, 80
  sovereignty, 33, 66, 67
Consumer Financial Protection Bureau, 77
consumerism, 83–85
consumption
  externalities in, 67, 80
  nature of, 33
Cook, Tim, 158
corporation
  board of directors, 130
  CEOs, 135
  fraud of, 136
  governance of, 126, 127
  influence of, 70
  as legal person, 64, 95
  power of, 63–66
  principle-agent, 135
  profits of, 97, 122
  subsidies to, 64
  tricks of, 45, 73
countervailing power, 158, 170, 208
Countrywide Financial, 98, 121
creative destruction, 105, 165
crime, 19, 162, 206
crowding out, 201
culture, 34, 65, 66, 69–71, 75, 111
custom and wages, 115

D

Dalkon Shield, 137
debt, 165, 169
deficit, trade, 218
deflation, 177
deleveraging, 230
demand
 conditioning and, 34, 35
 nature of, 33, 36
 unconscious mind and, 34
 wants, 35
democracy, threats to, 64
depression, economic. *See* Great Depression
depression, mental, 19, 85, 192
deregulation of markets, 137
desires, origins of, 33, 34
Dimon, Jamie, 78, 90n83, 118, 235
discounting
 exponential and hyperbolic, 80
 of future, 169
discouraged workers, 190
discrimination, 159
disequilibrium, 102
distribution
 income, 122, 125, 244, 245
 work, 191
Duesenberry, James, 67

E

earnings, 115
Easterlin, Richard, 168
Ebbers, Bernard, 136
ecology, 148
economic growth, 165, 168
economics
 adults, 35, 65
 assumptions in, 26, 30n53, 35
 inconsistency, 212
 mainstream, 33
 models in, 11–12
 objectivity in, 75
 positive and normative, 75
 predictions in, 75
 as a social science, 26
education
 poverty and, 168
 private versus social returns to, 79
 system, 20, 23

education *(continued)*
 taxes and, 207
efficiency
 adverse selection, 104
 competition, 96
 freedom, 137
 imperfect information, 77, 78
 institutions and, 111
 market failures, 142
 path dependence, 145
 power and, 65
 production, 72
 redistribution, 73
 signaling, 79
 sociopolitical processes, 111
 taxes, 162, 205
 underemployment, 188
 unemployment, 188
 versus equity, 71
 versus sustainability, 75
 wealth distribution, 75
Eisenhower, President Dwight, farewell
  address, 63
elites, income of, 125, 233
emotion in decisions, 48
endogenous tastes, 33
endowment effect, 38
Enron, 136, 151n35
environment, 148, 220
envy, 35, 188, 191
equilibrium, 102–104
ethics, 71, 170
executive compensation, 120
 cap on, 127
 international comparison, 127, 132n41
 outrageous, 133n43, 133n49
expectations, 178
exploitation, 78, 143
externality
 consumption, 67
 environmental, 220
 financial sector, 75
 income, 188
 network, 144

F

factors of production, 110–112, 122
fairness, 27, 71

fallacy of composition, 182
fashion, 68
FDIC, 137
Federal Reserve
  bailout and, 64
  monetary policy, 198–201
feminist economics, 69
financial crisis of 2008, 3, 112, 225–236
  principle-agent problem, 135
financial sector
  income in, 118
  instability of, 228, 231
  wages in, 115, *116*
financialization, 227
firm
  defined, 95
  moral hazard, 135
  principle-agent problem, 135
first mover advantage, 144
fiscal policy, 198, 207
Ford Motor Co., wages, 165
foreclosures, 19
foresight, perfect, 144
framing effects, 48
Frank, Robert, 67
fraud convictions since 2008, 136
freedom, 9, 137
Freud, Sigmund, 34, 65
Friedman, Milton, 9, 181, 198, 208, 230, 232
Fromm, Erich, 6, 36, 84
Fuld, Dick, 56, 74, 78, 82, 134, 135
fuzzy logic, 38

G

Galbraith, John Kenneth, 21, 63, 170
Gandhi, Mahatma, 33
Gates, Bill, 72, 126, 210n11
Geithner, Timothy, 90n83, 140, 180, 232, 234
genes, 47, 56, 57, 74
Georgescu-Roegen, Nicholas, 222
Germany, 245
Gladwell, Malcolm, 126
Glass-Steagall Act, 229, 235
GlaxoSmithKline, 136
global warming, 148, 220
globalization, 122
GNP. *See* Gross National Product

Goldman Sachs, 64, 77, 82, 97, 128, 231
government
  basic research and, 204
  big business and, 170
  countercyclical policies, 198
  debt, 198
  essential for the economy, 21, 193, 197
  expenditures, 98, 179
  fiscal policy, 198
  guidance, 110
  inequality, 158
  investment, 201
  military expenditures, 206
  oversight, 208
  regulation, 137
  supervising markets, 22
  taxes, 206
  threat of, 85
  welfare, 197
Gramlich, Edward, 4, 55
Gramm, Wendy L., 151n35
Great Depression, 179, 180, 183, 193, 198, 226, 236
Great Moderation, 75, 225
Great Recession, 11, 66, 75, 105, 177, 180, 185, 188, 190, 225–236, 245
  See also Meltdown of 2008
greed, 112, 133n49
Green National Accounting, 222
Greenspan, Alan
  cognitive dissonance of, 55
  disregard of principle-agent problem, 135
  easy money policy, 230, 232
  ideology, 3, 4, 231
  income inequality, 125
  false predictions of, 27
  nationalization of banks, 234
  overlooking systemic risk, 12
  perfectly competitive model and, 74
Greenwald-Stiglitz theorem, 130
Gross National Product (GNP)
  fetishism, 167
  mismeasurement of, 187–188
  productivity, 187
  as a welfare measure, 164, 166, 187
groupthink, 88n38
growth, 165, 168, 193
  international trade and, 211, 214
Gupta, Rajat, 128, 136

H

happiness, 11, 164–168, 188
Hayek, Friedrich, 198
health
  care and adverse selection, 23
  efficiency of, 132n18
  expenditures, 24, *25*
  life expectancy, 23
  markets, 12
  productivity and, 111
  Western Europe, 23
health insurance
  market, 45, 104
  need for government intervention, 80
herding, 67
heuristics, 48
Hollywood, 85
homeless, 19
homicide in the U.S., 19
Homo economicus
  defined, 35
  macroeconomics, 180, 182
  as social moron, 42
hours worked, 68
household
  female-headed, 19
  income, 245
  labor, 190
  production, 69
housing
  prices, 103
human
  capital, 111
  dignity, 112
  rights, 36, 193
humanistic economics, 6, 9, 214
Hume, David, 74
Huxley, Aldous, 65, 85, 104

I

IBM, 95
ideology in economics, 4, 14n4, 27, 208, 226,
    243
  laissez-faire, 243
imperfect
  comptetition, 96, 217
  markets, 148

import certificates, 215
income, 115, *116*
  Asians, *163*
  distribution of, 122–129, 162, 206,
      245
  Hispanics, *163*
  inequality of, 125–127, 158, 187, 245
  men, 159
  redistribution, 160
  relative, 166
  trend, *163*
increasing returns to scale, 144, 217
indifference curve, 37, 38
Industrial Revolution, 148, 193
IndyMac, 98
inefficiency
  of crime, 206
  of underemployment, 188
inequality
  ethnicity, *123*
  income, 160, 188, 245
  large, 19, 37, 125
  redistribution, 160
  statistics, *20*, 122
  widening, 16n42, 157
inflation, 201
information
  asymmetric, 74
  imperfect, 47, 76–79
infrastructure, public goods, 110, 208
innovation, 122
Inside Job, The (film), 243
insider trading, 64
instant gratification, 70, 202, 235
instinct in consumption, 57
institutions
  capital, 110
  capitalism and, 137
  constraints, 100
  wages, 115
insurance markets, 50, 104
intellectual capture, 139, 140
intelligence
  distribution of, 56
  quotient, 42, 182
interdependent utility, 66
international trade, 211–218
interpersonal comparison, 73, 89n55
intuition in choice, 47, 48

invisible hand, 64, 77, 78, 81, 98, 130, 170
iPod, price of, 97

J

Johnson, Simon, 78, 140, 231
Joint product, 122
JPMorgan Chase, 64, 78, 97
judgment, 75
just society, 72, 126, 160, 243

K

Kahneman, Daniel
  attribute substitution, 48
  bounded rationality, 242
  cognitive errors, 113
  indifference curves and, 38
  intuition, 47
  prospect theory, 50–55
  rationality, 42
Kaldor-Hicks criterion, 89n54
Keen, Steve, 225
keep up with the Joneses, 68, 206, 232
Keynes, John Meynard, 6, 177–183, 198,
    207, 232
knowledge capital, 111
Kozlowski, Dennis, 136
Krugman, Paul, 4, 11, 136, 183, 205, 217,
    228, 233, 242
Kwak, James, 207

L

labor
  discouraged, 190
  excluded from labor market, 168
  factor of production, 112
  force, 112, 190
  full-time, 190–192
  hours worked, 164, 191
  market equilibrium, 103
  part-time, 190–192
  share of output, 158
  unemployment, 18, 100
Laffer, Arthur, 205
Lasch, Christopher, 66, 70, 71, 167
learning by doing, 144
LeBron, James, 72, 118

legal system, 111
  and distribution of profit, 122
Lehman Brothers, 78, 98, 103, 134, 141, 200,
    230
leisure, 68, 164, 191
lender of last resort, 230
Lerner, Abba, 209n2
liberty, 9
Libor scandal, 98, 141
Life expectancy, *24*
life satisfaction, 11, 164, 166
  and growth, 193
  of women, 167
limits, 148
liquidity trap, 180
living standard, 162–166
lobbying, 30n41, 30n43, 64, 85, 139
Long Term Capital Management, 225
lords of finance, 63, 118
Lucas, Robert, 225
luxury, 35, 36, 67, 68

M

macroeconomics
  in disarray, 185
  interaction effects, 182
Madison Avenue, 36, 48, 50, 65, 68, 84, 85,
    202, 208
Madoff, Bernie, 136
Main Street, 126, 232, 233
marginal
  everything, 113
  product, 114
market
  "Achilles heel" of, 24
  "curses" of, 25
  disadvantages of, 18
  failure, 141, 242
  fundamentalism, 18
  imperfections, 148, 217
  limitations of, 23
  as man-made institutions, 18, 22
  missing, 148
  moral aspects of, 26
  providing safety, 23
  regulation, 134
  trust and, 111
marketing, 36

Maslow, Abraham, 37, 66
maximizing
  difficulties with, 46, 47
  utility, 41, 42, 45
McCloskey, Deirdre, 5
McDonald's, 154, 156
Meltdown of 2008, 13, 64, 67, 77, 97, 134,
    143, 169, 181, 182, 193, 199, 202,
    225–236
Merril Lynch, 118, 134, 135
Microsoft, 97, 105
military-industrial complex, 63
Milken, Michael, 128
millionaires, 130
minimum wage, 153, 154
Minsky, Hyman, 227–230
  disparaged by Bernanke, 238n26
missing markets, 148
models in economics, 11–12, 76
monetarism, 181
monetary policy, 198–201
money
  illusion, 181
  quantitative easing, 200
  quantity of, 199
  supply, 180, 199
monopoly
  power of, 96
  profits of, 64
  unions, 156
  Windows operating system, 99
monopsonist, 153
monopsony, 153
Montgomery bus boycott, 159
moral hazard
  defined, 78
  finance, 90n83
  within firms, 135
mortgage debt, 169
Mother Theresa, 74
Mozilo, Angelo, 98, 121

N

National Basketball Association (NBA),
    118
natural resources, 112
NBA. See National Basketball Association
necessities, 35, 178

neoclassical economics
  oversights of, 65, 66
  values of, 72
neoclassical synthesis, 180
network externalities, 144–146
neuroeconomics, 44
Nordhaus, William, 73
North American Free Trade Agreement, 73
Norway and subprime securities, 77, 82

O

Obama, President Barack
  economic stimulus, 207, 208
  financial crisis, 234
  growing the economy, 232
  support of Wall Street, 233, 235
obesity, 169
Occupy Wall Street, 9
oligopolies
  efficiency, 106
  power of, 64, 96, 130
  supply curve of, 98
  unions, 156
O'Neal, Stanley, 134
OPEC. See Organization of the Petroleum
    Exporting Countries
opportunistic behavior
  defined, 136–137
  in eighteenth century, 81
  Ten Commandments and, 82, 137
  ubiquitous, 241
optimization
  in decisions, 43
  impossibility of, 44, 45
  in sequential decisions, 144
Organization of the Petroleum Exporting
    Countries (OPEC), 101, 142, 147
overweight, 169

P

paradigm shift, 8
Pareto efficient or optimal, 105, 141, 204
  international trade, 211–213
path dependence, 144, 145
Paulson, Hank, 231
Pavlov, Ivan, 34, 65
perception, 49, 50

perfect competition
  definition of, 89n58
  efficiency and, 73
  firms and, 95, 96
  power and, 63
  prices in, 101
perfect foresight, 144
Phillips curve, 181
plutocracy, 22, 64
political conflict, 178
pollution, 148, 187
poor, 170
positional goods, 67
positive feedback effect, 55
poverty
  child, 19
  defined, 168
  government definition of, 36
  working, 170
power
  bargaining, 127
  concentration of, 65, 243
  countervailing, 158
  distribution of, 64
  economic, 63
  finance, 86n4
  market, 99, 130
  oligopolies, 130
predatory lending, 50, 111, 143
predictions in economics, 11
preference reversal, 48
price
  ceiling, 155
  control, 154
  determination, 100, 101
  discrimination, 102, 104, 141, 142
  elasticity of demand, 100
  perfect competition, 101
  rationing mechanism, 101
  signals, 79, 101
  taker, 95
Prince, Charles, 226
principal-agent problem, 78, 134–135
prison population, 19
product differentiation, 96
production possibilities frontier, 99, 100
productivity
  growth in, 114
  intangible capital, 111

productivity (continued)
  wage gap, 114–118
profit, 97, 122
  maximization, 134
  unions, 156
property rights, 141, 151n50
prospect theory, 50–55
Protestant ethic, 70, 88n43
psychology, 41–58
public goods
  capital, 111, 117
  product, 104
  productivity, 118, 208
  role of government, 197, 206, 207

Q

quality of life, 162, 166, 191
quantitative easing, 200

R

Raj, Rajaratnam, 136
Rajan, Raghuram, 4, 226
Rand, Ayn, 125
rating agencies, 103, 141
rational agent
  biases, 47, 50
  model, 35, 55
  Superman, 35, 42
rational choice, 76
rationality
  biases, 47, 48
  bounded, 44, 48
  defined, 41
  evolution and, 43
  genes and, 56
  Keynes, 177
  macroeconomics, 182
  system 2 and, 47
Rawls, John, 72, 117, 126, 160
Reagan, President Ronald, 9
  increase in inequality, 157
  on government, 208, 230
  tax cuts, 206
real business cycle, 181
real-existing economy, 66, 110, 130
real-world economics, 9, 12
recession. See Great Recession

redistribution of income, 160, 162
reference dependence, 50
regulation
    of markets, 134
    in the public interest, 138, 139
regulatory capture, 139–141
relative
    deprivation, 164, 188
    income, 67, 68
rents, as part of wages, 117, 120
representative agent
    inconsistent models of, 60n28
    macroeconomics, 181
residual claimant, 122
revolving door, 139
Ricardo, David, 217
risk seeking, 50–55, 60n32
Romney, Mitt, 13
Roosevelt, Franklin D., 22, 65, 87n15,
        171n5, 229, 235
Roubini, Nouriel, 4, 231
rule-of-tumb
    decision, 45, 48, 59n14
    wage determination, 121

S

safety net, 162
salary
    determination, 115
    doctors, 119
    executives, 120, 127, 132n41
    managers, 127
    as rent, 120
Samuelson, Paul, 73, 180
Sargent, Thomas, 183
satisficing, 9, 45–47
savings, 202
savings rate, decline of, 67
scarcity, 33
Schiff, Peter, 4
Schumacher, Ernst, 5
Schumpeter, Joseph, 3, 105, 122, 165, 231
Schwartz, Barry, 148
SEC, 137
self-interest, 74, 81
Sen, Amartya, 9, 168, 241
sex drive, 57
Shiller, Robert, 4

signaling, 79, 117
Silicon Valley, 85
Simon, Herbert, 9, 44, 45, 241
Sims, Christopher, 183
Skilling, Jeff, 136
slums, 20
social
    capital, 111, 112
    norms, 67, 70
    pressure, 82
    psychology, 68
    status, 79, 164
socialization, 66
society, 68
    unequal, 128
Somalia, famine, 101
Soros, George, 237
spillover effects, 75, 104
Smith, Adam
    on altruism, 74
    on empathy, 5
    invisible hand metaphor, 81, 98
    on moral hazard, 135
space (area), 144
speculation, 143
Spence, Michael, 241
standard of living, 8, 162–166
standards, 146, 148
Stanford, Alan, 136
"starving the beast", 21, 30n35, 206
status seeking, 67, 68
Stiglitz, Joseph, 4, 9, 65, 77, 78, 125, 167,
        170, 231, 236, 241
stimulus, economic, 208
subconscious, 36, 60n25
subprime mortgage crisis
    after 2008, 104
    anchoring and, 50
    asymmetric information, 77
    caveat emptor, 56
    externalities, 75
    Mozilo, Angelo, 121
subsidies, 197
Summers, Lawrence, 18, 21, 232
Superman or Superwoman, 35, 42, 45
super-rich, 125
sustainability, 112, 221
system 1 and 2 in choice, 47, 48
systemic effects, 104, 142

T

Taleb, Nassim, 4, 231
tariffs, 212
taste
  endogenous and exogenous, 33, *34*
  formation, 66
tax
  corporate, 206
  cuts, 232
  education, 207
  efficiency, 162, 207
  luxury goods, 68
  Pareto optimality, 204
  rates, 205
  reduction, 208
  top rate of, 121
  wealthy, 13
  welfare and, 203–207
Taylor, John, 4
technical progress, 112
technological change, 104–106
  path dependence, 145
teenagers, unemployment of, 190
Ten Commandments, 141
Thain, John, 118
  office renovation, 135
thriving people, 167, 168
time
  importance of, 144
  inconsistency, 80
  path dependence, 147
  preference, 169
  sequential decisions, 144
too-big-to-fail banks, 78, 142
Tourre, Fabrice, 128
trade
  new theory, 217
  See also international trade
transaction costs
  defined, 143
  role in choice, 47
  role in price determination, 101
  social capital and, 112
  Ten Commandments, 70
trust, 111, 112
Tversky, Amos
  attribute substitution, 48
  cognitive errors, 113

Tversky, Amos *(continued)*
  intuition, 47
  prospect theory, 50–55

U

UBS, 64
ultimatum game, 27
uncertainty in decisions, 47, 50, 144
unconscious, 34, 36, 48, 50, 65, 66
underemployment
  inefficiency, 188
  Great Recession, 190, 245
  statistics, 18, 100, 188
unemployment
  desperation, 108n17
  dissatisfaction with, 232
  Great Recession, 245
  inefficiency, 188
  international comparison, *184*
  long-term, 188
  natural rate of, 192
  statistics, 18, 100, 188
  Sweden, 207
  technological, 105
  trade and, 215
union wages, 155–159
utility
  expected versus realized, 76
  interpersonal comparisons, 164
  marginal, 113
utility function
  abstraction, 44
  development of, 65
  interdependent, 66–68
  manipulation of, 65
  prospect theory and, 50
  risk averse, 50
  risk seeking, 50
utility maximization
  defined, 41
  impossibility of, 42, 67
  social norms, 69

V

value judgment, 75
Veblen, Thorstein, 67, 79
Veblen goods, 35

veil of ignorance, 72, 129, 191
velocity of circulation, 199

W

wage
  cap on, 120, 128
  celebrities, 118
  of CEOs, 118
  determination of, 113
  distribution, *163*
  education and, 115
  Ford Motor Co., 162, 165
  high school graduates, 157
  institutional structure and, 118
  low, 190
  male-female gap, 115
  McDonald's, 154
  minimum, 153
  nominal, 201
  part-time work, 115
  profit sharing, 192
  real, 201
  return on endowed attributes, 117
  rules of thumb in determining of, 121
  trend, *163*
  unions, 155
Wall Street
  bailout, 78
  cognitive capture, 140
  Lords of, 118, 233
  resurgent, 66
  threat of, 85
Walmart, 155
  fatality in, 102

Walmart *(continued)*
  profits of, 97
  stampede in, 69
  wages, 214
wants, 36
Warren, Elizabeth, 56
Washington Mutual, 98
waste
  of human capital, 73
  underemployment, 188
Waxman, Congressman Henry, 3
wealth
  inequality, 158
  power and, 63, 86n1
  redistribution of, 73
Weber, Max, 70
welfare
  advantages of, 207
  children, 20
  efficiency and, 73
  freedom and, 137
  GNP and, 164, 187–188
  state, 19
  tariffs, 212
  taxes and, 207
  trade and, 211–214
  unemployment and, 188, 226
well-being, 8, 19
Whybrow, Peter, 43, 56, 57, 82, 83, 165, 166
Williamson, Oliver, 242
Wilson, Edward O., 74
Woolworth boycott, 160
work
  ethic, 70
  hours, 190

ABOUT THE AUTHOR

John Komlos is professor emeritus of economics at the University of Munich and visiting professor at Duke University. He has also taught at Harvard University and the University of Vienna.

Born in Budapest—just as the Russian army began its assault on the city—he became a refugee twelve years later during the Hungarian revolution, and grew up in Chicago, where he received PhDs in both history and economics from the University of Chicago and where Nobel Prize–winning economic historian Robert Fogel introduced him to the field of anthropometric history in 1982. Komlos devoted most of his academic career to developing and expanding this research agenda, which culminated in his founding the field of "Economics and Human Biology" with the journal of the same name in 2003.

Defying disciplinary boundaries, Komlos is among the very few scholars to publish in major journals of five disciplines: economics, history, biology, statistics, and demography. He was the first to explain why populations of the then-developed world became shorter in stature at the onset of modern economic growth. He also discovered that after being the tallest in the world for 200 years, Americans became shorter than Western Europeans after World War II. His work has been cited in radio, television, and in most major newspapers around the globe, including *The New York Times,* as well as in *The New Yorker* magazine.